ON POWNAL TIME

One Hundred Years In A Rural Maine Town

1908 – 2008

Donna Fulton Boyles
James G. Boyles
Craig Dietrich

Sherilyn R. Dietrich
Jennifer Blackstone Kaplan
Joseph A. Raymond

Published by the Pownal Scenic and Historical Society

Dedication

The authors dedicate this book to Esther "Ettie" Johnson Latham (1854-1934).

Ettie wrote her book, *History of the Town of Pownal*, expressly for

Pownal's Centennial Celebration in 1908, and it became

the first published history of the town.

Copyright © 2008

by the Pownal Scenic and Historical Society

All rights reserved

No part of this book may be reproduced or transmitted in any form or by any means
without permission of the publisher.

First edition, first printing

ISBN 978-0-615-20144-3

Published by the Pownal Scenic and Historical Society, Pownal, Maine 04069

Printed by Penmor Lithographers, Lewiston, Maine 04241

CONTENTS

Foreword and Acknowledgments	iv
Introduction	v
About the Authors	vi
Map of Pownal	viii

PART ONE: *LIVING IN A RURAL SETTING* — 1

   1 *One Town - Three Villages* — 3
      A New Century — 3
      War and Its Aftermath — 20
      Toward a Third Century — 48
   2 *Using Our Natural Resources* — 65
      Land — 65
      Forests — 127
      Minerals — 143
   3 *Businesses Change with the Times* — 161

PART TWO: *GOVERNING IS A CHALLENGE* — 181

   4 *Enduring Form - Increasing Complexity* — 183
      At the Centennial Year 1908 — 184
      At the Sesquicentennial Year 1958 — 188
      Nearing the Bicentennial Year — 2006 — 193
      Committees Render Invaluable Service — 202
   5 *Town Services Are Essential* — 209
      Public Works — 209
      Public Safety — 222

PART THREE: *EDUCATION IS IMPORTANT* — 235

   6 *Schools and Schooling* — 237
      Doing Our Best - But It Wasn't Easy — 237
      Running Hard to Catch Up — 246
      To Be the Best — 253

PART FOUR: *MEETING SPIRITUAL AND SOCIAL NEEDS* — 265

   7 *One Town - Two Churches* — 267
   8 *Social Groups Contribute* — 287

Appendices	304
Sources	311
Index	318

Foreword and Acknowledgments

In 1998, as people in Pownal became increasingly aware that the town's bicentennial year was approaching, leaders of the Pownal Scenic and Historical Society began to think seriously about how to celebrate that landmark with a lasting memorial. The production of a new town history had been discussed for years as a companion piece to the two existing histories—*History of The Town of Pownal* by Ettie Latham published in 1908, and *Pownal: A Rural Maine History* published in 1977 by the society. Now, society president Donna Boyles led the members to concur that this would indeed be a memorial of lasting significance to all residents.

Donna convened our group of six co-authors. Agreement was soon reached that the first one hundred years of Pownal's history had been well covered, and that we should focus on its second hundred years, the period of greatest change. We decided to start in 1908 and bring the story of Pownal right up to the present moment. And most of the resources to do this were at hand in the society's archive. Begun in 1970 and managed by Donna and Sherry Dietrich, this is an extensive collection that includes not only interviews, documents, and photographs, but also Pownal-related clippings from publications collected almost daily over all these years.

Collectively, the six co-authors brought to the enterprise all of the necessary expertise: archival skills; deep knowledge of town affairs, history, records, genealogy, etc.; photographic and design skills; and publishing experience. We intended that the book be a social history, rich in photographs and other images, and that it not neglect the present as it explored the past century. It would be packed with information, both in the text and in the captions associated with images, and would not stint on information about women, their role and lineage. In particular we wanted to illuminate just how the perception of "rural" has changed over a century's time.

The authors wish to acknowledge those who have made so many generous contributions to the society's archive, which continued to expand even as the book was in process. Shared life experiences related to the war years and more recent times have helped us flesh out those portions of the narrative. Joe Raymond's ever-increasing photographic record of scenes and events since 2005 has added hundreds of pictures to the archive, and many have found their way into this book. We thank Jane Mittel, Vice President of the Pownal Scenic and Historical Society, for her help with proof reading, and for her many insightful observations and suggestions as she reviewed the book throughout its production. We also thank the Maine Historical Society, the Maine State Archives, the Maine Historical Preservation Commission, and professional photographer Christopher Ayres for permission to use photographs from their collections.

Finally, special thanks go to members of the Pownal Scenic and Historical Society who have labored for years in so many ways to provide the financial support for this publication.

The Authors

Introduction

In 1680, the land area that is now Pownal was part of the newly formed town of Ancient North Yarmouth. This town encompassed present day Yarmouth, North Yarmouth, Cumberland, Harpswell, Freeport, and Pownal, and was located in the Province of Maine of the Massachusetts Bay colony. A bit over a century later, in 1789, Freeport, which then included what is now Pownal, separated from Ancient North Yarmouth. Then in 1808, Pownal separated from Freeport and became a self-governing town, albeit still a part of Massachusetts. The details of Pownal's founding and first one hundred years are nicely covered in the two published histories mentioned in the Foreword.

In 1908, when this history begins, the Town of Pownal celebrated its centennial, looking much as it always had. Most people lived on farms, grew crops, and raised animals, either as their principal livelihood or as a sideline. Many of their houses dated from the early or mid-nineteenth century. New innovations were making their appearance, but Pownal people carried on what, by any definition, was a rural way of life: far from any city, close to the soil, and set amidst abundant open space.

One hundred years later, public roads in town, although now mostly paved, follow exactly their original routes. Many old houses, and some original barns survive, but the modern world has transformed people's lives. Farming has almost disappeared and with it the chores that once organized daily lives. Most people work out of town. Yet many in Pownal say that they cherish their rural way of life. Clearly this cannot mean the same thing as in 1908, and yet it does point to something. Is it the town's comfortable size, the still abundant open spaces, the straightforward approachable governance, the many visual reminders of an earlier era? In the chapters of this book, we will explore what developed in those one hundred years and how things have changed even while much has remained the same. As we chronicled these changes, we were constantly reminded that a town is composed of families and individuals, many of whom are quite remarkable and whose lives merit remembrance and celebration. The following pages tell the stories of some of these people, not only as they interacted with their neighbors and families, but also as they were affected by sweeping events happening beyond the town's border: two world wars, a great depression, and other "conflicts."

Part One of the book relates the story of how Pownal's three villages negotiated the past century. Chapter 1 tries to capture the flavor and detail of life in Pownal throughout this period, while Chapter 2 explores the various ways we have used our natural resources, whether land, forest, or minerals. Chapter 3 gives snapshot views of many of the businesses that have existed or still exist in town.

Part Two examines, in two chapters, governance in its many forms: elected officials, volunteer committees, public works, and public safety.

Part Three traces the history of education, from one-room schools, where some still living in town received their primary schooling, to the creation of SAD 62, and to the proposed incorporation of the latter into a new "regional school unit."

Part Four discusses how religious and social organizations have served our needs.

Finally, a word about our title. "On Pownal Time" echoes a phrase often heard in town. Over the years, Pownal residents have tended to arrive casually late at events or meetings, nodding affably to neighbors as they agree to start "on Pownal time." This is often said with a touch of pride and a note of independence. And Pownal has had its "time" for two hundred years. For now, we hope you enjoy this picture-rich history of our second century.

About the Authors

The production of this book was a truly collaborative effort among its six authors. While some did more drafting and rewriting, all were fully involved in editing and suggesting changes throughout. Everyone contributed to decisions about length, number of pictures, layout, overall format, and the myriad other issues that arose. That having been said, as noted below, each found him or herself concentrating on particular tasks as our working partnership evolved.

DONNA FULTON BOYLES

Donna is a Registered Nurse, retired from active nursing in 1995. She and her husband Jim have lived in Pownal for thirty-eight years, during which time they raised two daughters. She is a founding member (1970) of the historical society, has served as its president for a total of sixteen years, and was editor of the society's 1977 publication, *Pownal: A Rural Maine History*. She helped initiate the society's archive collection and continues today as its curator. Community service includes ten years on the town budget committee. As chair of the author group, her varied roles included: coordinating all efforts, setting work assignments and deadlines, functioning as a prime researcher, writing all image captions, and serving as the final arbiter.

JAMES G. BOYLES

Jim is Professor Emeritus at Bates College, where he taught chemistry for thirty-two years. Jim is a long-standing member of the historical society and its current treasurer. He has served on several town committees and is the current chair of two standing committees — the Mallett Hall Building and Grounds Committee and the Capital Projects Planning Committee. He has been chair of the board of directors of SAD 62, and has been the elected moderator at town meetings for the past seventeen years. Within the author group, Jim oversaw the digitizing of all pictures and graphics.

CRAIG DIETRICH

For thirty-six years Craig and his wife Sherry have lived in Pownal, where their daughter was raised and schooled. He is Professor Emeritus at the University of Southern Maine, where he taught Chinese and East Asian history for thirty years. He is the author and editor of scholarly articles and of the college textbook *People's China: A Brief History*. Since retirement in 1997, he has served on several town committees. He organized volunteer work crews for the construction of the Mallett Hall addition from 1997 until its completion. Craig created the maps for this book and formatted text and images in publishing software.

SHERILYN R. DIETRICH

Sherry is a long-standing member of the historical society and one of the authors of the society's 1977 publication, *Pownal: A Rural Maine History*. She worked as a teacher's aide in Pownal Elementary School and has given many years of service as a 4-H leader. Her civic contributions include leading roles on numerous town committees including the planning board (for twenty-nine years), the budget committee (thirty years), the bicentennial committee, the veterans memorial sub-committee, and recently the regional planning committee for school consolidation. She served as deputy to the town positions of clerk, tax collector, and treasurer. She has been the person primarily responsible for organizing and preserving town records, and is currently working with others to inventory all of Pownal's cemeteries. Sherry's principal contribution to this book has been as a researcher and genealogist.

JENNIFER BLACKSTONE KAPLAN

Born and raised in Pownal, Jen and husband Scott are raising a daughter (now seven years old) and a son (six). Directly descended from one of the town's oldest families, she continues to live in Pownal, working as a professional artist. She is in her ninth year as secretary of the historical society. Jen has served the Pownal community as vice-chair of the board of directors of SAD 62, and as a leading member of the regional planning committee for school consolidation. Within the author group, Jen assumed the role of graphics layout designer—a role very much in keeping with her artistic talents. She is also responsible for the exemplary index.

JOSEPH A. RAYMOND

Joe is a retired IT consultant. He and his wife Delores have lived in Pownal for thirty-three years where they raised three children. Joe is a long-standing member of the historical society, and has served the Pownal community on the budget committee (fifteen years), as chair of the board of appeals (five years), and on the veterans memorial sub-committee. He has served on the board of directors of SAD 62. Within the author group, Joe used his photographic skills to take hundreds of pictures of Pownal, its residents, and its organizations.

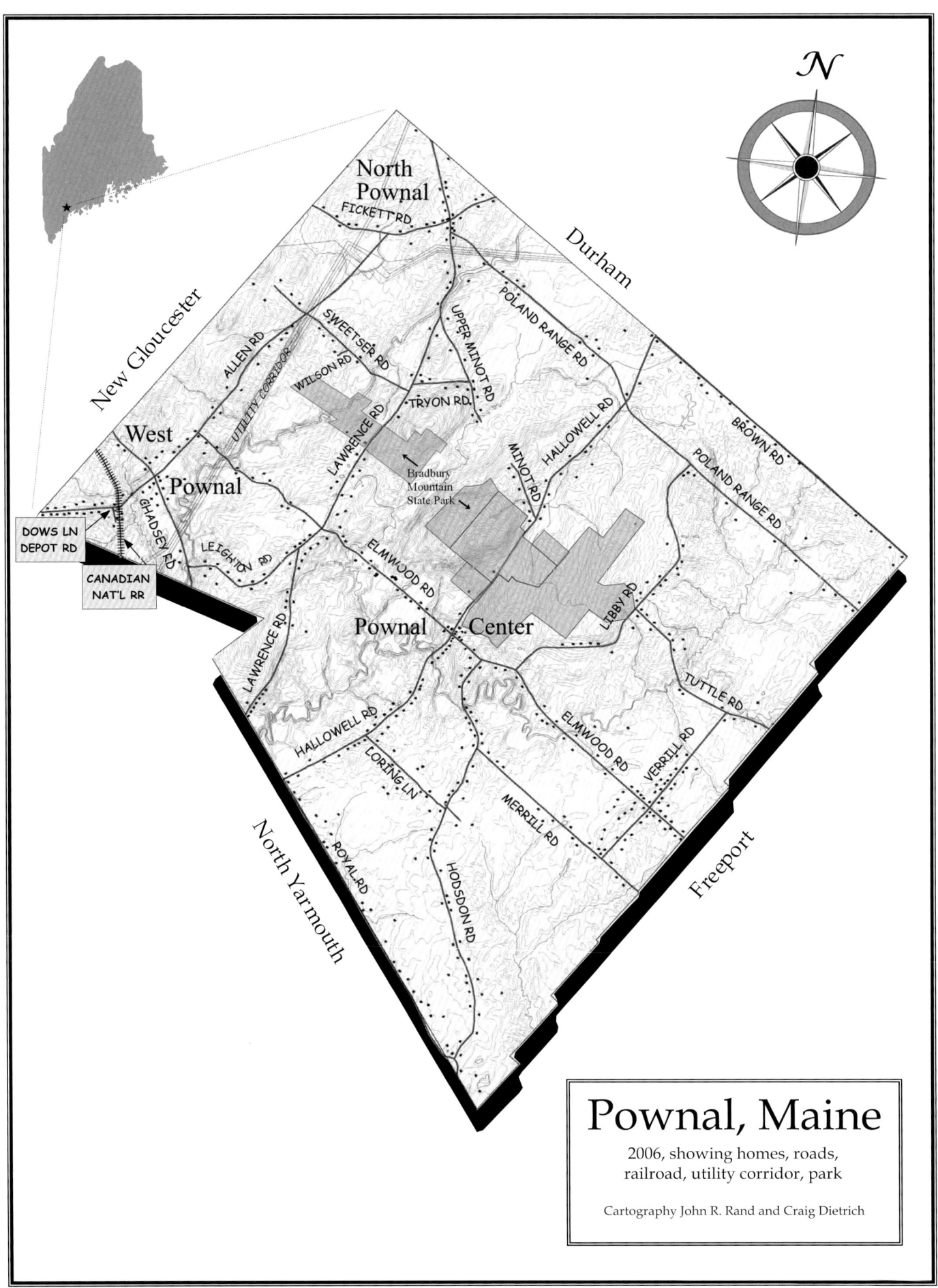

PART ONE
LIVING IN A RURAL SETTING

THEN: *Farm families worked on their homestead in town. In July of 1918 on the Upper Minot Road, Elmer and Bertha Libby, with children Ken and Mertie, work together to bring in the hay.*

NOW: *A typical weekday morning exodus in 2008. Over ninety percent of Pownal wage earners leave town on weekdays and commute to work an average of twenty-seven minutes each way.*

Chapter 1

One Town – Three Villages
A New Century

Nineteen hundred and eight was a special year in Pownal, Maine. It marked the one hundredth anniversary of the town's founding, and on September 2, a grand celebration was held. As reported in the *Daily Eastern Argus,* from early morning "carriages of all descriptions, loaded with men, women and children, came rolling [in]" bringing people from near-by towns, Portland and South Portland, and as far away as Massachusetts, New Hampshire, Vermont, and New York. All admired a large exhibition of old fashioned implements and artifacts in the Congregational Church. Athletic events lasted throughout the day. In baseball, the Pownal Centers came away two-for-three, as they nipped the Pownal 1900 team, bowed to the Cumberlands, and crushed the North Yarmouths 15 to 4. Competition was hot in the hundred-yard dash, the running and the standing broad jumps, and the high jump. The potato race, egg race, sack race, and three-legged race occasioned much amusement. Dinner was served in Mallett Hall, and afterward, twenty-one Civil War veterans posed for a photograph.

Pownal's centennial celebration was covered extensively in editions of The Daily Eastern Argus, The Lewiston Evening Journal, *and* The Boston Globe. *Pictured here (photographer unknown) is Mallett Hall as it appeared in these newspapers at that time. It was used extensively during the day's activities, particularly in serving lunch. The impressive structure was designed by Francis Fassett and Frederick Tompson in the Colonial Revival style, and was built in 1886 at a cost of $3,200. It was named for benefactor Edmund B. Mallet Jr. (For some unknown reason, the building's name later came to be spelled with two "t"s.) To the left is the (then) recently abandoned District No. 2 one-room school, soon to be pressed into service as a town storage shed.*

In the afternoon a standing-room-only crowd listened to the "literary exercises" in the Congregational Church. During the program the chorus sang "Should auld acquaintance be forgot," "My country, 'tis of thee," and "All hail the pow'r of Jesus' name!" The Rev. Daniel A. Tuttle offered a prayer of dedication, and the audience heard addresses and responses, punctuated by vocal and violin solos. Mrs. Ettie Latham took her place toward the front. It had been a time of stock taking for her, having recently completed her forty-page *History of the Town of Pownal*. She stood and read her work. It was also a time for homecoming, in person or, for Louisa Merrill Pratt, in spirit. Unable to journey back home, she had sent her poem, "Greetings from California," to be recited. Josephine H. Hodsdon obliged and read, in part:

> Thus grew our prosperous, pleasant Town,
>   Peaceful, In beauty waved its trees;
> On landscapes fine — its homes, smiled down:
>   While youth's glad shouts, rose on the breeze.

To conclude a grand day of celebration, a dance was held in the evening at Mallett Hall featuring the music of the New Gloucester Cornet Band. So began Pownal's second century.

Another homespun poet, Calvin E. Estes who in 1903 had married one of the town's "fairest maidens," also sang Pownal's praises around this time. He described:

> From the top of Bradbury's Mountain,
>   You get a magnificent view;
> Of the village, and surrounding country,
>   With the Royal River winding through.

To judge by such testimonies, Pownal folk saw their home town as a place of beauty, free from city noise and dirt. They were proud of the pioneers who had chopped out farms from forests and edged the fields with stones. They were grateful to those who had built the churches, the likes of Reverend Perez Chapin, long deceased, whom Mrs. Pratt remembered with these words:

> I see "dear Father Chapin" mount
>   The pulpit stairs, so steep, and high
> In quiet dignity,- A saint,
>   [Who] loved his people, and they vie
> In honoring him.

Collection of Maine Historic Preservation Commission

The Daily Eastern Argus *reported in its September 3, 1908 edition that Pownal's Centennial Literary Exercises were held in the First Parish Congregational Church where "every seat was taken and even standing room was at a premium." The event was also covered in editions of* The Boston Globe, *and* The Lewiston Evening Journal. *The founding of the First Parish Congregational Church was a prerequisite for the town's incorporation in 1808. The building itself, constructed in 1811, had by 1908 visually dominated Pownal Center for ninety-seven years.*

Pownal Center crossroads of Hallowell and Elmwood Roads c. 1908. Pictured here is the country store then owned by True Warren, the steeple of the First Parish Congregational Church, and poles installed for the recently arrived telephone. Elm trees line the gravel roads.

They were deeply patriotic and proud of the sons who had fought and died in the Civil War, barely forty years past, and whose graves they annually decorated with flags. They loved to see the farms and fields as they rode along Pownal's roads, or as Calvin Estes put it:

For on every side you'll see,
    Nice farms as any town can claim:
Good, and well kept buildings,
    And fields of corn and grain.

This verse paints Pownal as a simple farm town, but the reality was rather more complex. Early settlers had been drawn to the area by cheap land, abundant timber, water for sawmills, and fair proximity to the coast. They cleared forests and removed stones. However, as in most of New England, poor soils, uncertain weather, and difficult transportation severely limited commercial agriculture. Also, railroads now connected the large farms in New York, Pennsylvania, Ohio, and the midwest to the profitable eastern markets. So Pownal farmers had little choice but to adopt a mix of garden produce, fruits, grain, hay, animals, dairy, blueberries, and various home made products or services which could be sold, bartered, or used by the family. A small granite industry provided employment. Some people migrated away, causing the population to drop steadily through the nineteenth century. Those that stayed had to be resourceful and adaptable. They were ethnically and religiously uniform, modestly schooled, somewhat isolated, and independent-minded.

By 1908 many of the families whose names live on today through their descendants residing here, or as names of town roads, had long been established in Pownal. As Ettie Latham traced their origins, they included Dyer, Sawyer, Small, Sweetser, Merrill, Berry, True, Blackstone, Brown, Libby, Lawrence, Snow, Allen, Haskell, Estes, Tryon, Chapin, Mitchell, York, Hodsdon, Tuttle, Knight, Loring, and Fickett.

These families clustered in three village centers. The oldest and largest was Pownal Center, where the road toward Freeport crossed today's Route 9. The First Parish Congregational

Church was nearly one hundred years old. The original church had recently been dressed up with a handsome steeple and was about to acquire a fine bell in 1911. Across the road stood Mallett Hall, built in 1886, providing a location for government and community events. Next door sat a newly-constructed one-room school. Next to that was True Warren's general store, providing people's daily needs and postal services. There was also a blacksmith shop. Homes and farms were scattered close by along roads that still exist. A mile away down today's Hodsdon Road, Frank A. Knight Sr. and Charles H. Knight Sr. operated a sawmill on the eastern branch of the Royal River, while further along that road granite quarries were operating. Down Elmwood Road to the west of the Center, telephone central had been installed in the home of John Noyes in 1905 and moved, not long after that, to the home of Henry and Mary Sweetser, lending a certain technological sophistication.

The second oldest village was North Pownal, located where roads from Durham, New Gloucester, and Auburn converge, about four

(continued on page 8)

Looking east to Freeport on Elmwood Road with Pownal Center in the distance, c. 1908. The church can be seen in the upper left beyond cleared fields and recently installed telephone poles.

North Pownal crossroads at Lawrence and Fickett Roads, c. 1908, featuring a Ford Model "T" truck. The North Pownal General Store on the left, owned by William J. Sawyer from 1900 to 1919, sold groceries, dry goods, flour, and grain. It also functioned as a post office and perhaps a telegraph station. On the right stands the Captain Joseph Small house, then owned by Lemuel Small, currently 73 Fickett Road.

"Hand Crank Telephones Bow Out in Pownal"
(N.E. Telephone and Telegraph Company Bulletin, July, 1948)

The Pownal central office of the New England Telephone and Telegraph Company was located in the home of the Henry T. Sweetser family from shortly after 1905 to 1948. Two generations of Sweetsers ran the exchange in their front parlor, with Henry's wife Mary as agent in charge and with help from daughter Marjorie and daughter-in-law Katherine. Henry also worked for the telephone company doing "line work and monthly bill collecting in addition to running the family farm." Quoting Judy Sweetser Adcock, granddaughter, 2005.

 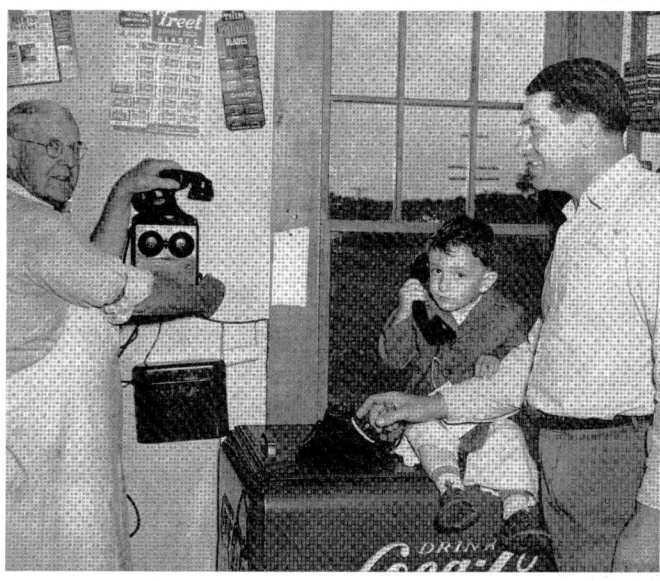

Generations of a telephone family mark the transition from hand crank telephones and central operators to dial, 1948. Left photo l. to r.: Marjorie Sweetser, her mother and retiring agent Mary Sweetser, daughter-in-law Katherine Sweetser. Right photo l. to r.: retiring payment agent A. H. Best; grandson Vernon Best, three years old; new payment agent Virgil Best.

North Pownal crossroads of Lawrence and Fickett Roads, c. 1908, looking west to New Gloucester. On the left is the Harness Shop, which has been used continuously for business since 1834. Behind it stands the home of the United Order of the Golden Cross, c. 1880-1940. An early homestead, now gone, is behind that. On the right is the North Pownal General Store owned by William Sawyer from 1900 to 1919. He sold groceries, dry goods, flour, and grain. The store also functioned as a barber shop and perhaps a telegraph station. A Ford Model "T" truck is parked next to the harness shop and a buggy sits in front of the store. The poles support telephone wires (first installed in 1905), but there are no electric power lines.

miles north of the Center on the other side of Bradbury Mountain. Similar elements of a village existed here, but North Pownal presented a slightly different atmosphere. There was no town hall, but the Golden Cross Hall (home of the United Order of the Golden Cross), a large two-storey building, provided space for meetings, bean suppers, silent movies, and frequent entertainments. The house of worship was the recently renovated Methodist Church, with its newly acquired façade and bell. Beside it, a one-room school provided for the instruction of local children, K-8. Just at the crossroads, William J. Sawyer ran a general store and barber shop, and he may also have owned the second store beside the church. Other businesses in the village center included Hathaway J. Fickett's blacksmith shop and a harness shop. About a half-mile south down today's Lawrence Road, on the middle branch of the Royal River, the sawmill that had provided the original catalyst for the settlement was still in operation. If we allow Pownal Center, with its Telephone Central, the distinction of leading technological innovation, North Pownal could be considered the town's professional center. It had always been the home of the town doctor, and ultimately, seven different physicians would live here. In 1908, Dr. S. Addison Vosmus provided care for all three villages and the outlying areas. He and his family lived on Lawrence road, across from the second store, currently 856 Lawrence Road.

The last of the three villages to emerge was West Pownal. Located on today's Dow's Lane off Allen Road, this community grew up around the Pownal station of the Grand Trunk Railroad, completed in 1854. In 1908, trains ran regularly, carrying passengers and freight, making West Pownal an export center and shipping point for milk and general farm produce. Next to the depot, Messrs. Walter Libby and Charles Dow ran a general store and the Pownal Post Office. Nearby was a boot and shoe maker, a blacksmith, a brickyard, and a grist mill. A one-room K-8 schoolhouse for the local children stood nearby. A mile to the west, just over the New Gloucester boundary, the Maine School for Feeble-Minded was just being established in 1908.

(continued on page 13)

The Oldest Tin Pedlar in America

"Tin Pedlar is coming!" That cry was often greeted with eager anticipation, particularly by the housewives and children of early rural Maine. The families in the farmhouses and homes at the turn of the century led a relatively insular existence, and most visitors were welcome. Indeed, the tin pedlar often carried news, hearsay, and stories from his travels in addition to his wares. And his stock was not confined to tin goods. He carried brooms, rolling pins, clothes pins, needles and thread, and many other small wares which the housewife needed.

Such a tin pedlar was Walter A. Small. Born in North Pownal in 1866, he earned the childhood reputation of being "talkative." His father was a doctor, and his mother, a music teacher, schooled him to proficiency on the clarinet and violin. A natural salesman, he began his house-to-house selling at fifteen with magazine subscriptions. After exploring other careers in many other places, Walter returned to Maine and the occupation he loved best—that of house-to-house salesman, a tin pedlar. He recounts that often he would entertain with his clarinet or violin in the kitchen of a farmhouse in partial payment for meals and lodging. Walter loved to barter, trade, and talk. On occasion he would return from a trip with depleted stock and little additional cash, but with a large bag of rags. In those days most women had a rag bag, and into it went every scrap of waste material. Walter and other pedlars took the contents of this bag in at least partial exchange for the wares they sold, selling the rags later for a small profit.

Walter, in 1939 at seventy-three, was described as the oldest and possibly the last tin pedlar in the country, and he was still going strong. Retiring in North Pownal at eighty, Walter described himself as "…no one of great distinction… just a pedlar." But he was distinctly and fondly remembered by many.

From Marion Knight Reed's scrapbook. Marion's mother Eva Crockett Knight is pictured here purchasing housewares from pedlar Walter Small. And, yes, Marion remembers her mother's "rag bag," a kind of savings account.

The Synergy of a Town and a Railroad

During the early 1800s, a vast inland water route between Lake Superior and the Gulf of St. Lawrence was completed. This route, utilizing the Great Lakes, rivers and canals, terminated at Montreal, Canada and established that city as the natural depot for the large amounts of Western grain bound for Europe. However, the port of Montreal was iced in six months of the year. By the 1840s, Montreal was seeking a route to an ice-free port, thus allowing the grain to move year round. Two competing railroad schemes evolved. One would link Montreal to Boston going through Burlington, Vermont. The other, one hundred miles shorter, would go through Western Maine to terminate at Portland. After much maneuvering and intrigue, involving the almost super-human efforts of Portland lawyer and businessman John Poor, the Montreal to Portland route was chosen by the Montreal Board of Trade.

Thus in 1845, the Atlantic and St. Lawrence Railroad was chartered to construct a line through the counties of Cumberland, Oxford, and Franklin toward Sherbrooke, Canada. A sister corporation, the St. Lawrence and Atlantic Railroad, was chartered to construct a line from Montreal toward Sherbrooke. In 1848 the line from Portland reached Pownal, and in 1853 regular service began between Portland and Montreal. Also in 1853, the Atlantic and St. Lawrence Railroad was leased to the Grand Trunk Railway of Canada for a period of 999 years.

The first West Pownal railroad station was built by the Grand Trunk Railway in 1854, signaling the beginning of a seventy-five-year period of prosperity for the area. In addition to passenger service and mail delivery, the rail access allowed Pownal residents to transport their grain, milk,

Pownal Grand Trunk Railroad depot, c. 1920, after renovation and modernization. The depot was sold in 1960 and moved to a business site on Route 231.

hay, and farm produce to waiting markets. Consequently, business structures developed around the depot. Eventually a granary, a general store, a post office, a boot and shoe store, and a blacksmith shop took their places in the West Pownal business district on Dow's Lane. During this period the railroad station underwent several expansions and improvements as traffic increased. The golden years for the Grand Trunk Railway were 1880 to 1920. Several long trains hauling grain and lumber passed through Pownal every day. Over one thousand railroad grain cars would be backed up in Portland waiting to be unloaded into two huge grain elevators. These elevators were located on the waterfront where seven ships of the fourteen steamship lines regularly serving Portland could be loaded simultaneously.

Site of the Pownal Grand Trunk Railroad depot and tracks in 2005. The depot was located to the left of the tracks, which are still in use today. The rails to the right were pulled in 2001.

In 1923 the Canadian National Railway acquired the Grand Trunk Railway, and by 1933 a rail line had been completed in Canada, allowing most grain and goods to be shipped through St. Johns and Halifax. With this loss in its principal freight, the railroad line between Montreal and Portland fell into decline. The number of daily runs dropped dramatically, and in 1962 the last scheduled passenger train traveled to Montreal. Finally, all passenger service was abandoned in 1967. The decline of the West Pownal business district paralleled that of the railroad. By the 1940s the area around the depot was no longer a recognizable business district, and in 1960 the much rundown station was sold for one dollar to a local individual who would haul it away.

In truth, the rise and fall of West Pownal as a recognizable business center followed closely the fortunes of the railroad passing through it. A single track still exists and is used to carry limited amounts of freight to and from western Maine. However, no trains stop here, and the many daily steam whistles of the past have been replaced by the occasional mournful three-tone diesel horn.

A Tragedy Sparks a Solution

It is late on a Friday afternoon in September, 1902, and the in-bound Montreal Express is about to pass through Pownal on its way to the Grand Trunk Railroad station in Portland. The whistle is blown and the bell rung as it approaches the unguarded road-crossing just north of the Pownal station, but the train retains its speed as it is not scheduled to stop.

Abel Bowie, his sister Rebecca, and his daughter Addie are approaching the same crossing on the Allen Road in a horse-drawn wagon, returning from a visit to Abel's brother in Durham. Their plans do not include the approaching Express, they intend to catch a later train to Portland.

Sight-lines are poor at this crossing for both the engineer and the wagon driver, and the first indication to those on the train that anything is amiss is the jolt of a collision and the shudder as air brakes are applied hard. The wagon is pulverized and three lives are snuffed out.

The deaths of these three are the worst tragedy in a long series of accidents that have occurred at this crossing, and they ignite a renewed campaign for a road underpass at this site. Pownal officials repeatedly petition the Grand Trunk Railroad for construction of an underpass, and they make many trips to Augusta to marshal support. The railroad's first response is to place an electrically activated bell at the crossing, a bell which neighboring residents claim sounds at odd times, for no apparent reason, and often remains mum when a train approaches.

Finally, in 1912, an agreement is reached whereby the town will fund and build the road approaches while the Railroad will fund and build the bridge structure. This Allen Road underpass exists today virtually unchanged from the original.

Very little good usually comes from a tragedy, but this incident provided the impetus for the construction of the underpass which has undoubtedly prevented additional mishaps.

Steam Engine No. 414 probably pulling passenger and mail cars over the Allen Road underpass sometime after 1912.

West Pownal business district, c. 1908. This village began to develop in 1854 with the arrival of the Grand Truck Railroad and depot. It prospered as an export center and shipping point for Pownal's milk and general farm produce. It included a depot, general stores, a post office, a blacksmith, a shoe and boot shop, a granary, a one-room school, and farm houses. Newly mown hay can be seen in the foreground and a pig pen can be made out on the far right of the photo.

The "prosperous pleasant town" with its "fields of corn and grain," which Mrs. Pratt and Mr. Estes praised in their poems, seems unchanging. Actually Pownal had always been adapting and would continue to do so over the next three decades. There were, of course, stabilizing forces. The rural way of life was deeply rooted. Generations had made good use of the land, timber, granite, and other resources. A core of stable families constituted much of the population. However, technological innovations were steadily transforming the way people lived.

Already in 1905 more than fifty homes had telephones. That year Mrs. Fred Marston reported that her family's new telephone saved the house from destruction by fire, because she was able to contact help quickly. By 1918 there were twenty-four cars in town, not to mention trucks and tractors. As roads began to be improved, wider vistas opened up for work and pleasure. These advances in travel and communication gradually began to diminish the insularity and separate identity of Pownal's three villages. Among other novelties, Victrola phonographs came on the market in 1906, while battery-operated radios made their appearance in the 1920s. Silent movies could be seen at the Golden Cross hall. Electrification came as well, but only gradually. At first there were a few private generators, plus one at Mallett Hall and one at the Congregational Church. Later, Androscoggin Power and Light, Cumberland County Power and Light, and Central Maine Power brought in lines. However, it was not until the 1950s that all homes enjoyed electric service.

Pownal's independence could not isolate the town from world and national events. In the decade after the town's centennial, the great event was World War I (1914-1918) which America entered in 1917. Twenty-four Pownal men were drafted, although there is no indication that any were casualties. Everyone was exhorted to buy war bonds, give to the Red Cross, sew and knit for the troops, increase farm production, and conserve food. One unintended consequence of the war was the influenza pandemic of 1918, which was spread in part by returning troops and claimed more than 500,000 victims in America. Nine Pownal residents or natives, mostly in their teens or twenties, died. Notwithstanding these global events, the community remained quite rural. In 1920, local households owned more than 250 horses and colts, 470 cows, heifers, and oxen; plus 67 pigs and 34 sheep. However, as less and less land was being cultivated, the large open fields of the previous century began to fill in with scrubby growth of alders and white pines.

After a brief but sharp postwar recession, the 1920s became a decade of prosperity and rapid social change in America. Not the least of these changes involved the status of women. The Nineteenth Amendment, ratified in 1920, gave women the vote, while bobbed hair, short skirts, and the "flapper" style alarmed traditionalists. The look of the times can be seen from the picture of Christina Blackstone in her 1928 Dodge Runabout and stylish clothes (see page 19). After teaching in Massachusetts, she married and returned to Pownal to the life of a storekeeper, teacher, and public official. But not everyone stayed or came home. In this decade Pownal's population fell to its lowest point (462 in 1930).

For those who stayed, the town remained rural, but less so than before. Townsfolk kept fewer but still considerable numbers of farm animals and some were starting to raise commercial quantities of chickens. More and more cars were bouncing over Pownal's roads. During 1919 and 1920, seventeen families purchased automobiles, bringing the town's total to 41. Over the next six years, 60 more were added to this number. Thanks to the mobility they provided, many men and women found jobs in Freeport and other nearby towns.

No discussion of the 1920s in America would be complete without mention of Prohibition. The Eighteenth Amendment and the Volstead Act went into effect in 1920. Maine already had its own Twenty-sixth Amendment of 1884, which forbade the manufacture and sale of intoxicating liquors (excluding cider), and which Democrats and "Wet Republicans" had been unable to repeal. For all the speakeasies, the bootlegging, and other repercussions nationwide, Prohibition did not seem to impact Pownal very much. In a 1976 interview, Joseph Pervier doubted that anyone in town had a still. "Probably there was a lot of fellows that they always called on [who] had a 'hen on sittin'. A lot of home brew made, probably, but I don't

West Pownal General Store and Central Town Post Office, c. 1908. This building, acquired by Francis C. Handy (1888-1952) in 1919, was located on Dow's Lane. It burned in 1933.

think that there was anybody that really went into the business the way that we had in a lot of other sections of the country..." The federal and the state amendments were repealed in 1933, and according to the recollections of Christina Blackstone, the Blackstone General Store began to sell beer some years later, probably 1944.

The stock market crash of 1929 ushered in the Great Depression of the 1930s. Many people who grew up in this period do not remember it as being distinctly different from the life they knew. As Thomas H. Vosmus Sr. (1920-2007) said in a 2006 interview, "We were happy. We saw everybody was the same. You didn't realize you were having a tough time as we were growing up. Older people realized it but we didn't." Or as Joseph Pervier (1899-1980) put it in 1976, "We were not so dependent on, well, modernity." But the depression did in fact affect Pownal. For one thing, the population trend reversed itself, reaching 574 in 1940, and although the number of households remained fairly stable, family size grew. Across Maine, city workers who lost their jobs were moving back to small towns, and this is no doubt what was happening in Pownal. The farm economy helped sustain these people. But one rural fixture, the horse-

and-buggy, was becoming a thing of the past, as the number of horses dropped sharply. Pownal too had fallen in love with the automobile.

Another result of the hard times of the 1930s was that many people could not pay their mortgages and owed back taxes. There were a number of foreclosures. As Tom Vosmus described the situation, "Well, the money just wasn't there. If you were able you could work [your taxes] off by working on the roads and things like that. When I was a kid there were houses everywhere that were just falling in. Banks had them, yes, but there was nobody that would take them. Like Bradburys' place there; eight hundred dollars would've bought the whole thing. No problem." New Deal programs also came to town. The Federal Emergency Relief Administration (1933 to 1935) and the Works Progress Administration, universally known from 1935 on as the WPA, made funds available to Maine towns. Pownal received assistance for road construction. In 1936, $1,200, forty men, seven trucks, town gravel, a town-owned tractor, and a state grader were employed for four months, and this, according to Selectman Lauren H. Tuttle Sr., "put our roads in pretty good condition." Thanks to the work on the Dyer (Freeport) Road, it became possible to travel more easily to Freeport, except during mud season. It was also at this time that federal funds supported a census of veterans in Pownal's cemeteries.

As indicated by all of the above, the people of Pownal encountered many changes, opportunities, and difficulties during the first three decades of their town's second century. But through good times and bad, they retained core values born of hard work, long hours, and uncertain rewards. Their public beliefs emphasized faith, patriotism, and individual responsibility (even as most of the country supported Roosevelt's New Deal, Pownal and Maine steadfastly voted Republican). Their private virtues emphasized neighborliness, work, adaptability, and an aversion to receiving charity. Looking back at her childhood, Priscilla DeCoster Greene wrote in 2005, "Social and moral rules were important. Talking about poverty was *out*. Instead we heard thrift, ingenuity, making do, making the most of it (whatever 'it' was), getting by. My parents must have been close to desperation at times. Nevertheless, we ate well, stayed warm, went to church, attended town meetings—actually the good life."

Picture from Postal Studio Post Card Series c. 1930. *Sitting at the foot of Bradbury Mountain at Hallowell (Route 9) and Dyer (Elmwood) Crossroads are (from left to right) the First Parish Congregational Church, the center cemetery behind a white picket fence, horse or carriage sheds, and Albert Blackstone Sr.'s General Store and gasoline pump. A period automobile is traveling on the unpaved Dyer Road. The number of glass insulators on the utility poles has increased significantly, indicating that more homes now have telephone service.*

Patriotism and War: The Home Front

Civil War veteran Horace P. Merrill (1831-1919) raises the flag on July 4, 1918. The First Parish Congregational Church is behind the photographer. In the center background the church parsonage can be seen, and the back of the general store sits on the right. Mallett Hall would be to the left, just outside the picture.

Pownal was not far into its second century when, in 1914, the First World War began. America entered the war in 1917. In 1918 Pownal celebrated the Fourth of July with optimism, as citizens gathered around their new flag pole and flag. "Never in the history of our town has a more patriotic and delightful Fourth of July been experienced by our townspeople than the one just past," said the reporter.

The organizers of the event included Select Board Chairman Charles Heywood, Mrs. Vina Vosmus, chair of the Pownal branch of the Red Cross, Miss Josephine Hodsdon, who arranged the literary program and delivered a speech (see next page), and her mother Mrs. Charles (Eliza) Hodsdon, in charge of the luncheon. The celebration featured flag ceremonies, singing of the "Star Spangled Banner" and "America," a prayer by the Rev. D. A. Tuttle, a recitation of "The Kid" by Miss Ethel H. Marshall (which was "just perfect and her bright and pleasant personality most interesting"), a patriotic address by Professor Ernest C. Marriner of Hebron Academy, and an address for the War Saving Stamp Fund given by another dignitary, Superintendent DeForest Perkins of Portland.

The participants and guests from Hebron then enjoyed a lunch on the lawn of the Noyes home, next to the church. Invited guests also included three of Pownal's remaining eight Civil War veterans: Horace P. Merrill, Albion K. P. Dresser, and James Lawrence.

In the evening the Ladies Aid society held an entertainment in the hall, which was well attended and greatly enjoyed.

"*Veterans of the Civil War, friends, and fellow townsmen –*" *began speaker Josephine Hodsdon.*

"*In times like these in which we are living every mind and heart must be stirred with patriotic emotion. There must, however, be something deeper and more lasting than mere emotion: there must be a loyal love for the flag and the country which it represents. I believe that we all know and feel such a devotion. This is proved by the fact that Pownal has given liberally for the Red Cross not once but as often as she has been called upon, that the women are sewing and knitting for the boys 'over there', that the housekeepers and homemakers are doing everything possible to conserve food, that the farmers are endeavoring to raise larger crops, that the town went 'over the top' in the third Liberty Loan, that the school children as well as 'grownups' are buying [war bonds] and today that the men, women and children of the town have made it possible to give 'Old Glory' to the breeze in this consecrated spot.*

"*This is not the first time that a flag has been raised at Pownal Centre. In July of 1865 loyal hearts performed a similar act in honor of the brave boys who fought to preserve the Union. No less than sixty-seven young men from Pownal answered the country's call in '61. Some of them were not more than sixteen years of age. It is with the deepest feelings of gratitude and respect and veneration that I salute these living veterans who proudly marched to the call of Abraham Lincoln. Veterans your work and that of your comrades in arms is appreciated more and more as the years roll by. May God protect and bless and comfort your declining years.*

"*Our boys today are just as loyal as those of former times but the population of our town is much less and consequently the number called is small, however, we are sure that the eight young men [who] have stepped out to give their all if necessary to help answer the call to war will everywhere be an honor to their town their state and their country...*" *(Excerpt from speech by Miss Josephine Hodsdson, July 4, 1918)*

Josephine Hodsdon (1872-1967) was a native of Pownal and a graduate of the Boston School of Oratory. At the time of this speech, she had been teaching English and public speaking at Hebron Academy since 1897. Colby College awarded her an honorary degree in 1915. She married Frederick C. Small in 1919, moved to Iowa, then returned to Pownal in 1932, where she lived out most of her remaining years.

"There was quite a shipping place to ship horses across… down at the Yarmouth Junction… Held the horses until they could take them into Portland and load them on the ships to ship them across [to France]. And, of course, they had to ship the food with them. The hay. Hay was quite a commodity… The bales we used to have those days weighed, well, an average of 200 pounds. I had a team of horses and I loaded a lot of hay on freight cars… The team of horses I had were rejected… They were two good horses but still they were rejected for artillery... That's what they were on mostly... " *Joseph Pervier interview, February 8, 1976.*

The picture at right shows Joseph Pervier haying in the 1920s.

Age of Transition—Horse and Buggy to Automobile

It is the summer of 1916. Claude and Villa Snow of the Lawrence Road are preparing to take a ride in their horse and buggy when...

...the Harold Randall family pays a visit in their expensive new touring automobile, possibly a Haynes. They are wearing dusters and caps to protect their clothing from the grime of the unpaved roads. Claude and Villa's daughter, Edna Snow Menchen, remembered that "Harold Randall was a partner in the Randall McAllister Company and was a neighbor of my maternal grandfather, Richard Willis Fogg, who lived in Harrison, Maine. My paternal grandfather was Jonathan Snow of the Lawrence Road, owner of Willow Farm, later Snowfields Farm."

Christina Blackstone (1905-2003) is pictured here in her 1928 Dodge Runabout, two years prior to her marriage. A graduate of Gorham Normal School, "Christy" drove this car to Massachusetts and New York State, where she taught in local schools. Her husband Albert Blackstone Sr. was the new owner of the Pownal Center General Store. Christy was well-known in town as the co-owner of the store, a substitute teacher, the town health officer, and a ballot clerk.

Merton Larrabee (1877-1941) is pictured here with his Model "T" Ford truck which he used while running his two stores in North Pownal from 1928 until his death. Villa Snow (1892-1985) remembered when interviewed in 1976 that "most of the people around here did a little farming... Mert did not farm but he would go around to area farms, pick up fresh produce, and deliver it to the farmers market in Portland... There wasn't much demand for produce here in town as everyone raised their own."

Stopping at Mert Larrabee's North Pownal General Store during the winter of 1930. The pung, with its two-horse team, has delivered firewood, and the car may be waiting to gas up at the pump. By 1928 Pownal had one hundred automobiles. There were three brands of gasoline for sale: Standard Oil, Valvoline, and Mexican Petroleum.

War and Its Aftermath

America was sliding toward war in 1940. In Pownal, those who had radios (many powered by batteries) listened to the news with growing alarm. President Roosevelt broadcast two "Fireside Chats" that year. He talked about Germany's invasion of Belgium; the evacuation at Dunkirk; the London "Blitz"; and the pact among Germany, Italy, and Japan. America, he said, had to become the arsenal of democracy. Indeed, war clouds were thickening and world events seemed to be accelerating toward some unknown climax. Nevertheless, the shooting war in Europe seemed far away, and life in Pownal moved forward at its accustomed pace. Townsfolk, with their make-do approach, had weathered the Great Depression relatively unscathed. Even the recently completed Works Progress Administration (WPA) projects creating Bradbury Mountain State Park and reconstructing certain local roads had yet to make any substantial impact on either the local economy or lifestyle.

For the time being, most Pownal citizens clung to the comfortable patterns set in previous years. A subsistence lifestyle was dominant: farming for the table, preserving foods, cutting wood (eight to ten cords per year) for fuel, hand-sewing family clothing, repairing everything. Children were expected to finish their chores before they went out to play. The growing number and popularity of cars and trucks, however, meant that staying home on the farm was no longer the only option—this in spite of the fact that few roads in Pownal were improved, and many were chewed almost to the point of being unusable during mud season. Both men and women began to "work out" (of town), and the family car quickly graduated from an indulgence to a necessity. Pownal citizens continued to be readily enticed to attend the many evening "entertainments," dances, card parties, and bean suppers held in the several town centers. The churches continued to provide their many religious activities. Women's service groups such as the Ladies Aid often headed financial support efforts. Most folk belonged to at least one of the many local organizations: the Granite Grange, the Improved Order of Redmen, Pocahontas, the 4-H Club, the newly-formed North Pownal Community Club, the Mothers Club. Community news columns in

On a summer day in 1946, photographer George French captured the then unpaved Hallowell Road looking north past newly established Bradbury Mountain State Park. Everett A. Cates, road commissioner from 1943 to 1947, maintained the town's gravel roads in very good condition.

local newspapers reported widely on family weddings, birthdays, anniversaries, graduations, and funerals. Interestingly, unlike the state trend, population in Pownal was increasing. In 1940 it had grown to 574 from its low of 462 in 1930. On balance, life was quiet and reassuringly predictable.

Then on December 7, 1941 ("the date that shall live in infamy"), America's slow slide toward war came to a dramatic climax as World War II came to us. The Japanese attack on Pearl Harbor turned the world upside down. Within days the United States had declared war on Japan, followed shortly by a declaration of war on Germany. As President Roosevelt declared in his second "Fireside Chat": "We are all in it — all the way. Every single man, woman, and child is a partner in the most tremendous undertaking in our American history." Just what this was going to mean for Pownal residents and their lifestyle was not immediately obvious. Everyone knew that change

Women Of Motor Defense Corps 1942 At Yarmouth

Members of the Women's Motor Defense Corps at Yarmouth, shown with their instructors before starting work on an automobile engine. Front row l. to r.: Theona Blackstone, Clara McLaughlin, Ruth Seabury, Marjorie Holway, Alice Morrill, June Harris. Second row l. to r.: Christy Blackstone, Leigh Mitchell, Alice Drinkwater, Florence Winslow, Susie Hodsdon, Mabelle Randall, Minnie Knapp, Helen Ross. Third row l. to r.: Celia Phillips, Virginia Turcotte, Virginia Brumm, and Elizabeth Barker, with instructors Herbert Dennison and Ernest Mason. Source: Theona Blackstone scrapbook, news source unknown.

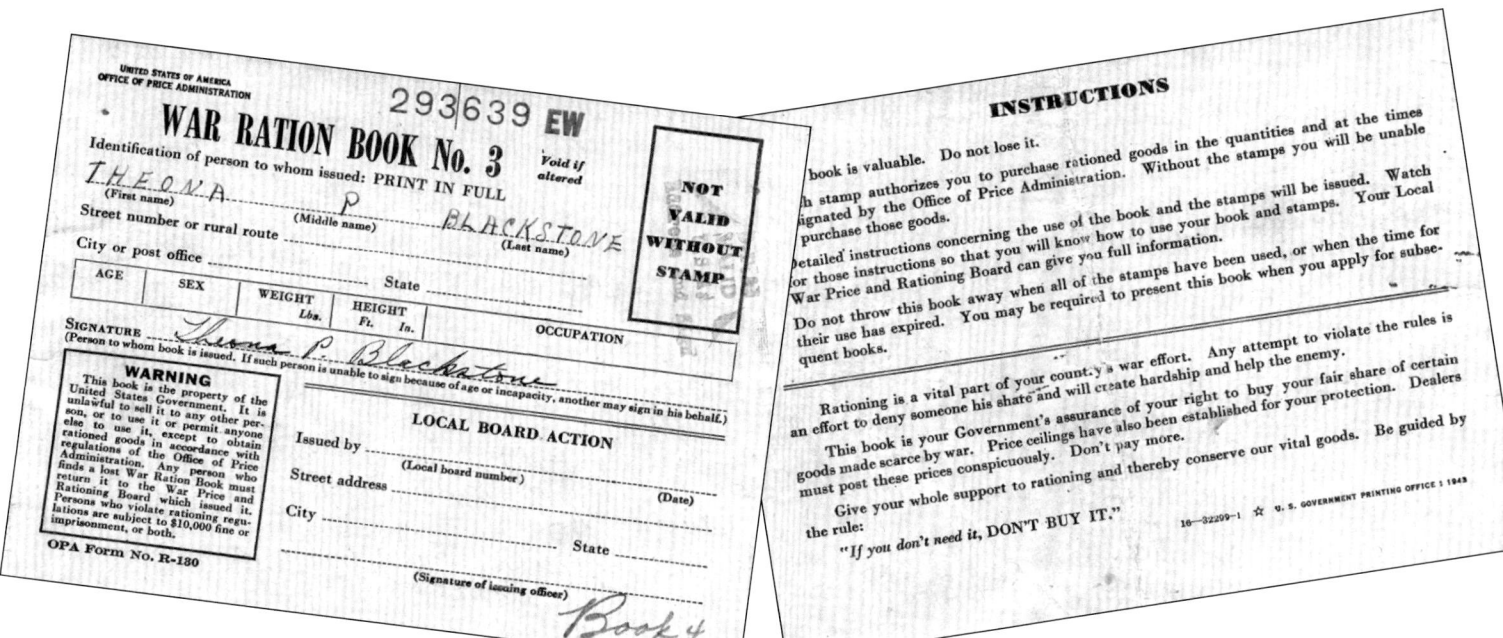

Covers of ration books issued to Theona Blackstone. Ration stamps were issued for the purchase of meats, fats, sugar, processed foods, and fuel.

was in the offing, and many suspected that life might never be quite the same again. Sacrifice and national service for all loomed ahead, with the ultimate sacrifice of life itself now a real possibility.

Support for the war effort was strong in the State of Maine, and no less so in Pownal where both men and women responded willingly to the new challenges. As Nellie Pervier recorded in her diary at the time, "All men aged twenty-one years to thirty-five years are to register." Many individuals from Pownal saw active service as part of our armed forces, and some were killed or wounded. Those who remained at home did their part. Many were employed at the New England Shipbuilding Corporation in South Portland (building Liberty Ships), at the Bath Iron Works, at the U.S. Naval Air Station in Brunswick, and at the upgrading of harbor defenses in Portland. Some in Pownal took Red Cross sponsored first aid courses; some women joined the Women of Motor Defense Corps (to learn auto repair); and many participated in building and manning an Aircraft Warning Service and Observation Post on Fickett Road (locally called the listening post). As the Office of Price Administration (OPA) began exerting its controls, almost everyone felt the price of war through the rationing of food, shoes, and petroleum products. Throughout the war's duration, everyone coped with shortages of steel, leather, and rubber. Automobile and bicycle production ceased. There were scrap drives to collect metal, paper, and animal fats, while the purchase of Liberty Bonds was encouraged as evidence of patriotism. Each family was urged to cultivate its own Victory Garden, and many also raised animals for their own consumption. Nylon was allocated to parachute and tent manufacture in 1942, creating an acute shortage of nylon stockings which women had recently fallen in love with. They had to substitute shiny, baggy rayon stockings or paint their legs and apply a faux seam in the back. According to Edna Menchen, even clothespins disappeared from the stores. It was a time of sacrifice for all. But Lois Sanders captured the deepest sacrifice when she remembered during a 2006 interview that "I was fearful for my husband in a foreign land… He was not here to support the family and the future was very uncertain."

(continued on page 32)

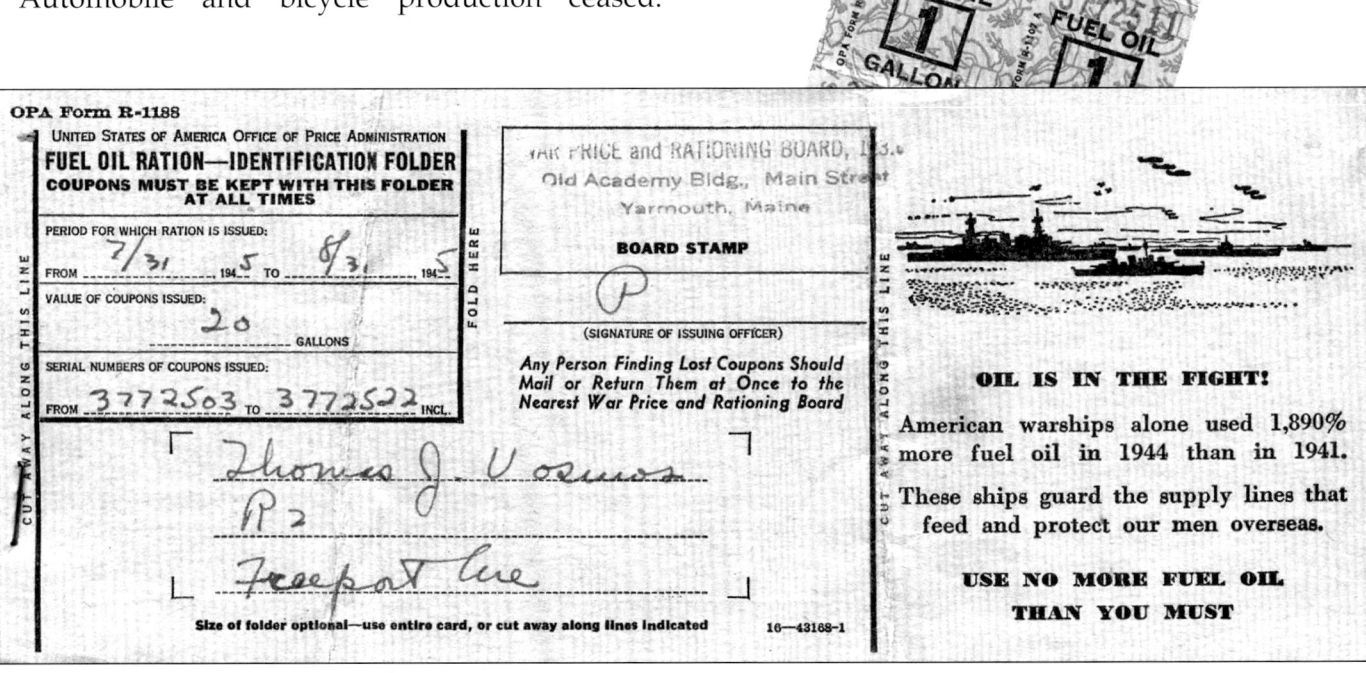

Above: Sugar ration for Chester Blackstone.

Previous page: Fuel oil ration book and fuel stamps issued to Thomas J. Vosmus. An allotment of three gallons of fuel per week was the standard, unless a person was considered an "essential worker," e.g., an employee in a war-related industry, a trucker, a doctor, or a minister.

The August 14, 1945 headline in the Portland Press Herald announced Japan's acceptance of unconditional surrender. Miniature edition from the collection of Theona Blackstone.

Civilian Defense air raid warden helmet, arm badge and V-mail letters belonging to Arthur Stackhouse of Portland, now living in Pownal. Arthur remembered: "I was thirteen years old when the war began and my father was working double shifts at the shipyard. There weren't many men around. I wanted to help in the war effort. When the siren blew, I would put on my helmet and arm badge, get my flashlight and water tank, and patrol the area around my home. If I saw lights coming from windows, I'd walk up the to the door, knock, and tell them that I could see their lights. I thought I was pretty important, but I was a little scared."

Granddaughter's Scrapbook Tells Two WW II Stories

Katie Blackstone Genovese and Theona Blackstone

Summer 1943, Riverside, CA

Chester Blackstone of Pownal Center first met Theona Penley of North Pownal at a church social. They married in December 1941, just a few weeks after the attack on Pearl Harbor. The South Portland shipyards were gearing up to produce Liberty ships, and Chester hired on as a "stage builder." The couple began to build their home just over the Pownal line in North Yarmouth. Then in the summer of 1943, Chester's draft notice arrived. In 2006 Theona remembered, "We wanted to be together. Boot camp was at Riverside California, a long train ride. I followed, worked as a civilian employee at Camp Anza until Chester was shipped out in December, 1943. I returned home to Maine to begin working at the shipyards, or as it was said, to help win the war on the home front."

In June of 1944, Chester found himself on board a Liberty Ship leaving South Hampton, England, a ship that he may well have helped build. The occasion was D-Day. The destination was Utah Beach (Normandy, France) where he served in Battery A, 407th Anti-Aircraft Artillery Unit under First Army leadership at Quinceville. During that winter, he served with General George Patton's Third Army, fighting through France and Belgium. His unit participated in the liberation of Holland. The photos and letters in his granddaughter's scrapbook carefully detail the two and one-half years Chester spent in the European Theater. It covers his happy arrival home on January 2, 1946.

Winter 1944, Belgium

Chester died in 1984; however in 2006 Theona remembered: "Everyone wanted to work at the shipyard. It was good money. At first we had classes on reading blueprints, then there would be a short internship, then we would work on an assembly line putting boat pieces together, holding chalk lines, running errands. At first I was a 'fitter,' then advanced to becoming a 'tacker.' We worked outdoors with big pieces of metal, tacking pieces of the inner bottoms together. I crawled through many an inner bottom. Liberty ships were all constructed outdoors and in the winter it was cold. We would wear slacks, overalls, and heavy boots. There was a shack with a stove where we could go to warm up, heat our sandwiches on the stove; but there was no hot coffee for us. In the winter I lived in Portland. Many would car pool. I made one dollar per hour."

After the war, Theona and Chester finished their home, raised three sons, and gave many years of public service to both Pownal and North Yarmouth.

War and the James A. Sanders Family

By the end of 1941, the amended Selective Service Act required all men between the ages of eighteen and sixty-four to register. Even so, only young single men were initially drafted, with fathers (among others) deferred. Then in late 1943 with needs burgeoning, the War Manpower Commission raised the draft-eligible age to forty-five and dropped the deferment of fathers. And in August of 1944, James Sanders (1919-2002) went to war.

Jim and Lois Sanders were the parents of two children (Roger and Connie) at the time of Jim's induction, with a third on the way. Son Dale would be born while Jim was overseas. After graduating from artillery school, Jim was sent to the European theater as a maintenance mechanic on artillery pieces. He served until war's end in France and Germany, attaining the rank of corporal.

During an interview in 2006, Lois recalled receiving V-Mail letters from Jim in response to the letters she wrote daily. Delivery was very slow and uncertain, and she never knew where her husband was since all of his letters were censored. Then in February of 1946, Jim arrived home, was reunited with his family, and saw one-year-old Dale for the first time.

Jim and Lois picked up the pieces of their lives, and by 1952 had begun building their permanent home on the Hodsdon Road. Jim, in later years, served his town as a leader in multiple ways: selectman, town meeting moderator, school board, planning board chair, and member of many committees. Both he and Lois served as active members of their church and the Granite Grange, and Lois' involvement has continued since Jim's death in 2002. She remembers the war years as ones full of uncertainty, longing, hard work, and sustaining hope, years that forged the Sanders family into one of Pownal's most respected.

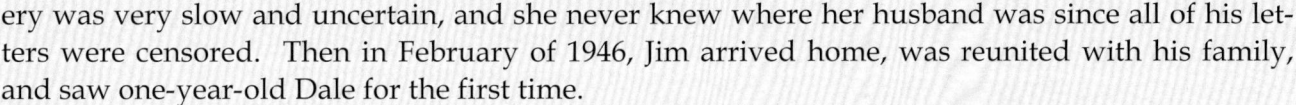

Four Sons and a Daughter Serve Their Country
Children of Carl V. Thurber (1889-1955) and Gladys C. Thurber (1899-1978)

In Memoriam

Kenneth E. Thurber (1921-1944). Kenneth's service as a member of the Maine National Guard and later in the 240th Coast Artillery paralleled that of his older brother George. He also enlisted in the army in 1943 and was admitted to Officers Candidate School. As a second lieutenant, Kenneth served with the 8th Infantry Regiment of the 4th Division and participated in the June 6, 1944 Normandy invasion. He was wounded in action and died on June 25, 1944, posthumously receiving the Purple Heart. In later years, his sacrifice was officially recognized when his family received two honor awards, one from the State of Maine signed by Governor Horace Hildreth and one from the U.S. Government signed by President Lyndon Johnson.

George L. Thurber (1919-1987). In 1939, George began his service career as a member of the Maine National Guard. From 1941 to 1943 he served in the 240th Coast Artillery in the defense of Portland harbor. He enlisted in the army in 1943 and attended Officers Candidate School. As a second lieutenant, he served in the European theater where he participated in the June 6, 1944 Normandy invasion, as a heavy weapons forward observer attached to the 16th Infantry Regiment of the 1st Division. George earned a battlefield promotion to first lieutenant. He was severely wounded in Germany on December 1, 1944 and was awarded the Purple Heart.

Arthur Thurber (1922-1993) served as a private first class in the U.S. Army Air Forces. He was stationed stateside during the war.

Gold Star Mother's flag.

The war service of Shirley Thurber (Verrill) is described on the next page.

Marvin Thurber (1925-1973) served in the U.S. Navy Seabees, Construction Battalion 111. He rose to the rank of coxswain, landed troops and equipment on Normandy beach, and later served in the Pacific Theater.

Pownal Women Answer the Call

Vina Vosmus (Litchfield) (1919-2004) graduated from the Maine General Hospital School of Nursing in 1941 and immediately entered the service as a first lieutenant in the U.S. Army Nurse Corps. During the war years, she cared for the wounded in hospitals in England.

Elsie W. Sweetser (1902-1987) studied to be a dietician at the Northfield School in Massachusetts. She joined the U.S. Army WAC Corps and managed the dietary services at Maxwell Field, Alabama, and Otis Field, Massachusetts.

Following graduation from North Yarmouth Academy in June, 1944, Shirley Thurber (Verrill) was recruited to work as a "government girl" in the Identification Division of the Federal Bureau of Investigation in Washington, D.C. At war's end, she received a Certificate of Honorable War Service signed by J. Edgar Hoover. Her extensive scrapbook chronicles her years of service and her attendance at national events such as the funeral procession of President Franklin D. Roosevelt, the inauguration of President Harry S. Truman, the parade honoring General Dwight D. Eisenhower, the V-E Day celebrations on May 8, and the V-J Day celebration of August 15, 1945.

In Memoriam

Daniel Albert Whitcher, Killed in Action, Kirkrade, Holland, and Honored There

Daniel Albert Whitcher (1924-1944)

Daniel Albert Whitcher was born in Pownal in 1924, the son of Algernon D. and Hazel Libby Whitcher. He attended Pownal Schools, graduated from Freeport High School, and was a sophomore at the University of Maine when he entered the army in 1943. His sister Josephine Whitcher Goss remembered, in 2006, that he was always eager to help others and to serve his country. Prior to America's direct involvement in World War II, Danny was a member of Boy Scout Troop 45 in Freeport, and a newspaper clipping pictures him playing a prominent part in the Freeport "Bundles For Britain Program." Ultimately, he attained the rank of Eagle Scout. He was also active in the Granite Grange of Pownal and was a leader in the Pownal 4-H program.

His obituary states that S-Sgt. Daniel A. Whitcher was a member of C Company of the 120th Infantry Regiment of the 30th Infantry "Old Hickory" Division. He was killed in action in Kerkrade, Holland on August 9, 1944, and later buried with full military honors in Elmwood Cemetery in Pownal.

In a moving tribute sixty years later, on October 2, 2004, the grateful people of Kerkrade and of Elizabeth Stift (a Catholic diocese) dedicated a plaque (in Dutch) honoring "Danny" who died heroically in the garden of the Stift during the liberation of Holland. The family was invited to attend the memorial.

William Whitcher (1929-2001)

Following Danny's death, and feeling the tremendous loss of his big brother, William Whitcher (1929-2001) at fifteen forged his parents' signatures and entered the U. S. Navy, serving from 1944 to 1946. William returned to the Pownal family farm where he and his family raised Charolais cattle and later standard bred race horses until his death in 2001.

Walter Hustus, Prisoner of War and Army Air Corps Hero

Walter Hustus, born in 1921, joined the Army Air Corps in 1943, three years after graduating from South Portland High School. During World War II, he became tail gunner on "Hell's Angel," a B-17 bomber. He and his crew flew twenty-eight successful bombing runs from December 1943 to April 1944 before their plane was shot down over Oranienburg, Germany. After hiding out in the woods for three days, Walter was taken prisoner and held for thirteen months at Camp Stalag 17-B. He was liberated by General George Patton's Army on May 3, 1945, weighing 120 pounds and sick with diarrhea.

Having recovered, he re-enlisted in the Army, and in 1947 volunteered to participate in the rescue of a B-29 crew stranded in the Arctic Circle. He participated in the Berlin Air Lift, transporting vital supplies to the people of that city. He was honorably discharged in 1951, having received six Air Force medals, the European Theatre medal, the Good Conduct medal, the Purple Heart, and the Distinguished Flying Cross. He was honored by Queen Elizabeth for his war service and received an audience with President Harry S. Truman for his part in the heroic rescue mission.

Walter Hustus (1921-1999)

When he resumed civilian life, Walter settled in Pownal where he raised cattle on his Elmwood Road farm and served as ranger at Bradbury Mountain State Park. In 1999, just prior to his death, he was named Pownal Citizen of the Year. He had been a member of the fire department for forty-five years and had served on the planning board for nine years, on the budget committee for thirty years, and on the board of appeals for three years.

POW, Camp Stalag 17-B

With his flight crew members, 1943

Following Walter's death in 1999, Barbara Hustus gave the Maine Historical Society mementos from his service experiences: photographs, medals, a prison cup and spoon, a piece of barbed wire, a chunk of dried bread, and his railroad ticket home to Maine. A transcript of his oral account of his war experiences, recorded by stepdaughter Pamela Brown, was given to the Society, which exhibited these artifacts in November 2000.

France Honors Pownal Soldier George Stone

George L. Stone Jr. (1924-). After his return to the States in 1946, George received France's "Croix de Guerre" which earlier had been awarded to him by the French military government of Metz. The citation reads (in French), "Presented for bravery in the operations for the liberation of Metz and the Mosel River in September 1944." At the time, he was not aware that he had been awarded this decoration.

George Stone served as a T/5 Corporal in the 623rd Engineers Light Equipment Company. He operated a large bulldozer. Prior to the Normandy invasion he was sent to England. In 1944 on D-Day-plus-16, he landed on Omaha Beach. Attached to the First Army, he participated in action around St. Lo, where he helped clear a convoy path through the town while under enemy fire. Later, his company was attached to the U.S. Third Army under General George Patton, serving in Germany and Austria. His unit was among those which met up with Russian troops pushing in from the east.

His other decorations include five Battle Stars B, one each for the Normandy, Northern France, Ardennes, Rhineland, and Central Europe campaigns, and the Good Conduct Medal.

George Stone's Croix de Guerre

Milton S. Stone (1926-2006), George's brother, also saw action in WW II. As a sergeant in the U.S. Marine Corps, he participated in the landing on Okinawa. Later, he re-enlisted and served in Korea.

Others Who Served *(See Appendix II for complete list)*

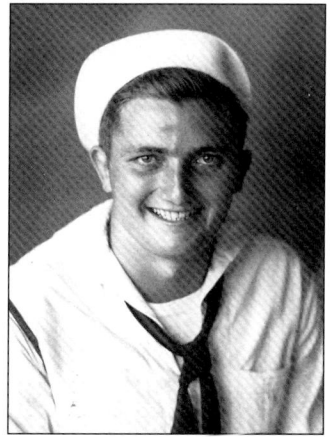  

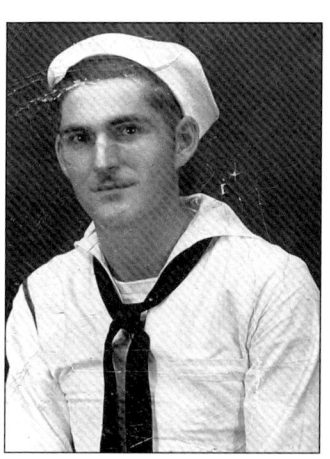  

Top: Donald Robert Litchfield (1926-1989), Coxswain, U. S. Navy. Donald served on board the USS Teton, 1944 to 1946. He saw duty in the Philippines and at Pearl Harbor, earning the WW II Victory Medal, the American Area Ribbon, and One Star on the Asiatic Pacific Area Ribbon.

Top: Edward L. Allen Sr. (1916-2005), Pfc, U. S. Army. Ed was in the U. S. Army from 1943 to 1945. His service was in the Infantry in the Philippines where he earned the Good Conduct Medal, the WW II Victory Medal and the Asiatic Pacific Area Ribbon.

Top: Donald H. Smith, Private, U. S. Army, 1942-1945, was an Anti-Aircraft Artillery crewman, seeing action in Normandy, northern France, Rhineland, and Central Europe. Awarded the EAMET Campaign Medal with five bronze stars and one Bronze Service Arrowhead, the Victory Medal, and the American Theater Medal.

Bottom: Thomas Henry Vosmus Sr. (1920-2007), Electrician Mate 3rd Class, U. S. Navy, 1943-1945. Tom served on the USS Thrush in both the American and Pacific Theaters, and was awarded the Good Conduct Medal and the WW II Victory Medal.

Bottom: Ralph Vosmus (1925-1993), U. S. Navy Seaman 1st Class, 1944-1946, served on board a repair ship in the Transportation division in Panama. He received the Good Conduct Medal and the WW II Victory Medal.

Bottom: Kenneth L. Vosmus, Pfc., U. S. Army, 1945-1946, served in the U. S. Army Infantry in Italy as a platoon leader of the Heavy Weapons section. He received the Good Conduct Medal, the WW II Victory Medal and the European Theater Medal.

This photograph by George French appeared in Down East Magazine *in 1946. Pictured in front of the general store with its gas pump are owners Albert and Christina Blackstone and son Albert Jr.*

The use of the Atomic Bomb in 1945 may have hastened the end of hostilities, but it unknowingly signaled the beginning of another war, the "Cold War" with the Soviet Union. Shooting-war worries were replaced with concerns over the sinister "Communist threat." Civilian Defense volunteers found themselves turning to confront the new threats inherent in potential atomic warfare. Still, the post-WWII years held the promise of peace and prosperity for the country. A flood of new technology brought television, jet planes, nuclear energy, plastics, expanded highways, medical advances, and more to the country, and Pownal was eager to embrace this new normalcy. By 1950, electric service was available in virtually every part of Pownal, and with this access came an easing of farm life and rural life in general. Electricity brought with it not only lights, radios, and eventually TVs, but also labor-saving appliances such as electric irons, refrigerators and washing machines. Indoor plumbing and central heating were now possible for all. This ability to readily access energy sources originating outside the town itself, coupled with the increasing ease of transportation, marks the "beginning of the end" of the relative isolation of Pownal's three villages.

Pownal could not escape the reality of its limited economic resources, however, and progress and improvements during the immediate post-WWII years, while real, were slow to appear and often not uniform throughout town. Yet the entire town was affected by the ongoing suburbanization of southern Maine, albeit not to the degree of some of its neighboring towns. Families were moving out of their crowded quarters (particularly from Portland) and looking to own a piece of land in the country. Land and houses were available in Pownal at relatively low prices even into the 1960s, and population figures reflect growth: from 574 in 1940, to 752 in 1950, to 770 in 1960, to 800 in 1970.

The post-war period was marred in the early 1950s by the Korean Conflict (1950-1953) in which more than thirty Pownal people served, and by the Vietnam War (c. 1963-1973) in which more than fifty served. And throughout the period Pownal was budgeting annually for Civilian Defense expenses to cope, ostensibly, with the Cold War.

Throughout the years 1940-1965, Pownal Center (often referred to simply as the Center) remained the population center and seat of town government, even though elected officials maintained home offices. Automobile and truck traffic noticeably increased from year to year at this busy intersection of Hallowell Road (Route 9) and Elmwood Road. Part of this trend can be attributed to the rising popularity of Bradbury Mountain State Park, and during the 1950s paving of

Crowds gather in Pownal Center to celebrate the town's sesquicentennial in 1958.

In 1946, prior to the loss of the stately elm trees planted by early settlers, George French photographed Elmwood Road looking from the Center toward the school. He captured these magnificent trees for which the road was named. The (then) Albert and Christina Blackstone homestead is pictured at the front left, with the Walter Hustus homestead in the distance. To the right behind the trees is the Fred Noyes homestead.

Hallowell Road was continued to and past the Park entrance. However, much of the increase in traffic can be traced to population growth coupled with an increasing number of church and town events. Additionally, the three one-room schools located in the Center served a portion of children from many parts of town, all of whom had to be transported to and from. These schools had been consolidated by this time, accommodating K-2 students in one building, grades three through five in another, and six through eight in another.

Albert Blackstone Sr. continued to operate his store in the Center throughout this period, as he had since 1926. However, competition had been on the scene ever since Charles Knight Sr. and Virgil Best opened a second store on Hallowell Road in 1946. In Pownal Center, people could choose where to buy their kerosene, groceries, and sundries; where to fuel their vehicles; and, after 1944, where to buy their beer. For the first time, the town had a heated (by woodstove) equipment building, when the abandoned old schoolhouse on the park side of Mallett Hall was pressed into service to house the town tractor and snowplow. Mallett Hall drew the now mobile townsfolk from all three villages to its events and "entertainments." It was renovated with a new roof, new oil-fired furnace, and new fluorescent lights in time for the town's sesquicentennial celebration. However, its unique two-story out house, added fifty years earlier for the town's Centennial Celebration, remained.

The Pownal Granite Grange won the first place award in the State of Maine Grange Community Service Project contest in 1960 for construction of the Center fire house. The town appropriated $1,000 for materials, and Granite Grange members provided the labor. Pictured here are l. to r.: Lawrence Carter, a twenty-seven-year Grange member, and Ralph Vosmus, an eighteen-year member. The Grange Master at the time was Lawrence's son, Ralph Carter.

An unidentified couple refuel their automobile with Richfield Gas at the North Pownal General Store owned by Earl Babbidge from 1947 to 1951. The carriage on the roof came from the Noyes Mitchell farm and was placed there annually for several years as a Halloween prank.

North Pownal Methodist Church, established in 1844, is pictured here during a period of revitalization in the 1940s.

One hundred and fifty years had passed since Pownal's founding when, on August 30, 1958, it celebrated its sesquicentennial. Flags and bunting snapped in the breeze as the whole town joined in the festivities. A parade, culminating in the Center, featured gaily-decorated floats, one of which contained the gold-star mothers from WWII. Speeches, events, and contests continued all day, capped by an evening dance and the crowning of Miss Pownal.

The First Parish Congregational Church would celebrate its one hundred and fifty years of existence in 1961. Difficult times had followed the death of the much-revered Reverend Daniel Tuttle in 1927. Part-time clergy occupied the pulpit, and membership declined. This trend was reversed during the 1950s and 1960s with strong leadership and overdue renovations. The roof was renewed, the building painted, and modern conveniences added. The church was rededicated on June 16, 1958, and the now-legendary bean suppers were initiated by the Ladies Aid to bolster financial support.

By 1960, the volunteer fire department (formed in 1948) had its own station in the Center, built by members of the Granite Grange with a $1,000 appropriation from the town. All was not expansion during these years however. Ironically, the Hodsdon Road sawmill, the site initially justifying the creation of the Center, succumbed to changing times and was closed. Also, the slow decline of the signature stately elm trees that lined the roads reached its ultimate end. Death, from Dutch elm disease, forced their removal and changed forever the Center's landscape.

North Pownal village experienced a slightly different evolution during these Cold War years. Traffic through these crossroads also increased, and the town budgeted to begin rebuilding and tarring portions of the Poland Range Road and the Lawrence Road, although many gravel roads remained. In spite of the many changes occurring around it, North Pownal retained much of its village character, with homes and businesses nestled together. The store on the Fickett Road, known as the North Pownal Store under a series of owners during this period, continued to provide the local community with groceries, kerosene, gasoline, beer, and sundries. In 1941 the building that had been the store on the Lawrence Road (next to the church) was purchased by a group of neighbors, who founded the North Pownal Community Club, ultimately renovating the building to serve as a social center and gathering place.

Following a period of decline, the North Pownal United Methodist Church was reactivated in April 1943. Responding to an influx of parishioners from the area, growth continued for the next twenty years. During this growth period many improvements were made to the church, including the installation of central heating and the placement of a new organ. In 1956, an active youth group was formed, as well as the Women's Service Club, a club destined to continue aiding in financial support of the church for many years.

Despite its somewhat insular atmosphere, the people of North Pownal met modern demands in much the same way as those in Pownal Center, but with fewer numbers to call on. Volunteering was an expected and welcome part of living in this rural area. When in 1948, the Pownal Volunteer Fire Department formed, efforts within North Pownal were made to provide this community with adequate fire protection. Through donations of time and money, citizens obtained a truck and rigged it with a tank and pump. A building next to the Fickett Road store was enlarged to house the new truck, and this brought with it a great sense of satisfaction and a greater sense of security.

The North Pownal school had not been included in the consolidation that had occurred with the three Pownal Center schools. Rather it continued to provide education for nine levels in one building, tending to reinforce a feeling of separation from the rest of town. The Golden Cross Hall, once a place for silent movies and other entertainments, had closed in the 1940s, as had the sawmill on Lawrence Road, a victim of declining business.

"Spring floods 1952." Floods followed a winter of heavy snow and washed out the Lawrence Road bridge.

"Stuck on the flats" on Poland Range Road, after a howling nor'easter hit Maine on February 17, 1952. The storm lasted thirty-six hours, dropped twenty-three inches of snow with fifteen-foot drifts, caused five deaths state-wide, and left towns and cities immobilized for days. Many remember the laborious task of breaking roads with the old town tractor and man-operated snow plow wings.

West Pownal was fast disappearing as a distinct village and business center. Francis C. Handy closed the store and post office due to fire in 1933. Also, for some time, there had been a general decline in shipping from the depot. For a while, the post office continued to operate here, rebuilt in the location of Handy's store. Another general store, which included a diner, was established by Fred and Jean Worden, and served this area from 1933 to 1949. Trucks and cars had made inroads in railroad services, and this, coupled with the demise of the Grand Trunk Railroad, brought an end to West Pownal as a distinct village center. When the railroad depot closed in 1960, the West Pownal business center ceased to exist. In 1968, even the post office was relocated to its present site at the intersection of the Chadsey and Allen Roads. One school, standing across the Allen Road from the present Post Office, served to educate pupils grades K-8 during these decades. It also had not been included in the consolidation experienced at the Pownal Center schools.

No matter which village they lived in, the selectmen had to address the challenges of the entire

(continued on page 40)

Back-to-Back Hurricanes Slam Maine, Cause Pownal Tragedy

George and Arlene Edwards knew that a powerful storm was in progress as they started their car for the drive to Blackstone's store to buy supplies. That drive from their home on Leighton Road and along the Elmwood Road was not particularly long, but on this day they encountered tragedy and were destined never to return.

Driving rains and winds gusting to seventy miles per hour hit Maine on September 11, 1954, as Hurricane Edna arrived just eleven days after Hurricane Carol. No other town in Maine was hit as hard as Pownal. Newspapers reported that fourteen bridges washed out in Pownal and, worst of all, that a tragedy beyond belief had happened. George (1906-1954) and Arlene Davis Edwards (1912-1954) had drowned when their automobile plunged into raging ten-foot-deep waters where the Snow Bridge on Elmwood Road had once been. At home they left a family of eleven children, seven under the age of eighteen. To make matters worse, their recently-purchased house lacked central heating and plumbing. Older brother Leroy and his wife Louise, along with their own five young children, moved in to shepherd the orphaned family.

Interviewed in 2006, Charlotte Colby, who was eight at the time, attributed the family's survival to the strength of the extended Edwards-Davis family; to local media coverage; and to a television program, "Strike It Rich," which brought national attention to their plight. Money, gifts, food, and clothing poured in. They built a new chimney and installed a furnace. In Charlotte's words, "I give my brother, Leroy (Roy to family) all the credit for keeping us together. Momma and Daddy loved us all and they loved each other so. We all graduated from high school. All have families of our own. We've done well."

Edwards family in front of Leighton Road home in 1954. Front row l. to r.: Bonnie (5), Leroy Jr. (3), Barry (2), all children of Leroy and Louise. Middle row l. to r.: Charlotte (8), Winona (11), Walter (10), Clayton (12), Betty (14). Back row l. to r.: Annie (16), holding Leroy and Louise's child Linda (1), Leroy (23), Louise holding infant Marcia, George (18), Rebecca Drew (21) with her daughter Debbie. Not pictured: Mary (19) married to John Hanlon and Carol (22) married to Norman Cook. Unpublished photograph by Life Magazine photographer Kossti Ruchomaa, used with permission of Charlotte Edwards Colby.

Cold War Era Begins

Joseph A. Raymond, Engine Man 2nd Class, Submarine Service, U. S. Navy, 1959-1965. Joe volunteered for submarine service, serving from 1959 to 1965, first on the USS Tirante, where he earned his first set of Dolphins. His next assignment was serving on the nuclear powered submarine, the USS John Marshall, a second generation ballistic missile sub, (pictured here) which patrolled the North Atlantic during the Communist threat of the Cold War era. He then earned his second set of Dolphins, the award given for outstanding service in the submarine service.

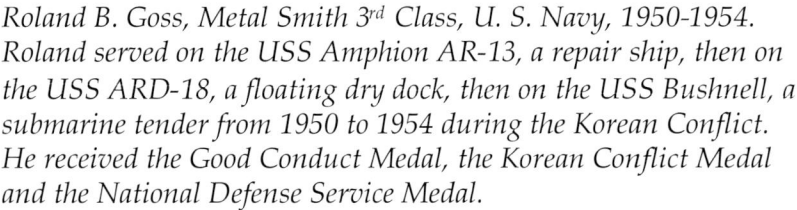

George L. Bradbury Jr. (1928-1985), Corporal, U. S. Army, 1950-1956. George served in active duty in Korea in the 7th Cavalry Infantry Regiment, APO 301, from 1950 to 1956. He earned the Combat Infantry Badge, the Korean Service Medal with one bronze star and the United Nation's Service Medal.

Arthur P. Stackhouse, Staff Sergeant, U. S. Air Force. Arthur served in the Philippines from 1950 to 1954, where he was a small-arms rifle instructor during the Korean Conflict. He received the Good Conduct Medal, the Korean Conflict Medal and the National Defense Medal.

Roland B. Goss, Metal Smith 3rd Class, U. S. Navy, 1950-1954. Roland served on the USS Amphion AR-13, a repair ship, then on the USS ARD-18, a floating dry dock, then on the USS Bushnell, a submarine tender from 1950 to 1954 during the Korean Conflict. He received the Good Conduct Medal, the Korean Conflict Medal and the National Defense Service Medal.

Ronald E. Allen, Lance Corporal, served in the U. S. Marine Corps from 1961 to 1964. He was on active duty during the Cuban Missile Crisis.

Five Sons of Benjamin Britt (1891-1957) and Nellie Wilson Britt (1892-1959) Serve Country

Robert Wilson Britt (1917-1980), Lt. Colonel U. S. Army, 1942 to 1965. Early in WW II Robert was assigned to the Pacific Theater with the 38th F. A. Battalion of the 139th Division. He flew more than 1,400 hours, 650 under battle conditions, and was much decorated.

During the Korean Conflict, Robert flew artillery-spotting planes for the 1st Cavalry Division. Over the course of his career, he received many medals and commendations, including air medals, distinguished flying crosses, battle stars, a Bravery Gold Medal, and others. He retired in 1965 and worked as a civilian program analyst with Naval Air Systems Command in Washington, D. C. Shortly before his death, he received a Superior Accomplishment Award for his contributions to the Navy Weapons Systems programs.

Roy Britt (1911-1989), Ensign U. S. Coast Guard WW II. Roy served with the Coast Guard aboard the vessel pictured here during WW II. No additional information is known.

Donald L. Britt, Staff Sergeant U. S. Marine Corps, 1949-1953. Don served in the U. S. Marine Corps, First Division in Korea. He received the Korean Service Medal with four stars, the U. N. Service Medal, National Defense Medal, Presidential Unit Citation, Korean Presidential Unit Citation, Navy Unit Citation, Marine Corps Reserve Medal and Good Conduct Medal.

Bernard Britt, Airman First Class U. S. Air Force, 1951-1955. Bernard served in the U. S. Air Force Police Unit from 1951 to 1955 stateside and in Chunchon K46, Korea. He received the Korean Conflict Medal and the Good Conduct Medal.

Harry Britt (1911-1989), U. S. Army. Harry, the oldest brother, served stateside early in WW II as an instructor, training pilots in the LINK Trainer. No picture or additional information is available.

town. They faced many of the same problems that had plagued selectmen for years, but now they felt increased pressures to change and modernize. Mandates from state and federal governments made the job more demanding each year. One of the most pressing and costly issues facing them during this period was the care of roads, with their constant maintenance requirements. The cost of equipment and upkeep continued to rise, and in 1967 the town voted to appropriate $1,000 to build an equipment building. The road commissioner was elected yearly, and thirty to fifty different local men were employed to work as crew during a year. The patching and tarring of major arteries like the Elmwood (then Dyer) Road, the Merrill Road, and the Hodsdon Road were repeatedly mentioned in town reports and debated at town meetings. As well they might be, since thirty percent of the town's budget was devoted to roads.

Nature was not always helpful. Two hurricanes, Carol and Edna, hit Maine within eleven days of one another in 1954. Winds approaching seventy-four miles per hour and drenching rains caused a total of thirteen deaths and fifteen million dollars in damage statewide. Thousands were left without power, and crop damage was severe. Pownal was hit particularly hard. President Dwight Eisenhower declared Maine a federal disaster area.

Other pressing concerns during these years involved the schools. Teachers were in short supply, maintenance costs on old buildings continued to rise, and state mandates were more explicit and harder to finance. Education costs, always high, amounted to thirty percent of the town's total budget. Consolidation with other school districts seemed desirable, and a study committee was formed to explore the possibilities. Public health programs for town citizens were continued and expanded. Immunization and health clinics, organized and funded primarily through the Mothers Club (later called the Parent Teacher Club), were held in Mallett Hall. Vaccination for diphtheria, pertussis (whooping cough), typhoid, and smallpox was encouraged. The Salk vaccine to prevent polio was newly available, as was testing for tuberculosis. Physical exams as well as dental and eye clinics provided much needed preventative health care for the children of Pownal, and were organized under the aegis of the school.

As the 1960s began, the three once relatively self-reliant village centers within Pownal had lost much of their former isolation and independence. Occupants now considered themselves more as part of a whole, the Town of Pownal. A way of living had changed forever in these three villages, as abundant transportation (coupled with improved roads), modern communications, and service networks became realities. Few called themselves farmers, and land once tilled lay fallow. Generally, the land remained in the hands of the family, but the family's livelihood depended on work outside of town.

One of the outgrowths of the continuing suburbanization during this era was a rush to build cheap or sub-standard manufactured housing. Pownal town leaders, with admirable foresight, recognized that one of the town's greatest resources was its undeveloped land and that this asset might well be in jeopardy. The unregulated growth observed in surrounding communities was noted, and planning was initiated to ad-

Clipping from Portland Sunday Telegram, *August 31, 1958, reporting Pownal's sesquicentennial celebration.*

dress the issue. Charles Whitehouse of the Maine Department of Economic Development sounded a clarion call when he spoke at the town's sesquicentennial celebration in 1958. He highlighted Pownal's strategic (and vulnerable) location in the center of a triangle defined by large cities. Given its geographical location, its undeveloped land with attractive vistas, and the presence of Bradbury Mountain State Park, he said, planning would soon be needed if the town wished to retain its local rural values. Absent this, he warned, outside influences might soon dominate Pownal's development.

The town was responsive, and by 1959 a "Building and House Trailer Code" had been adopted that regulated house and lot size, construction materials, structural design, and building placement. This code was amended in 1964, in 1965, and again in 1966. By 1963, an ordinance had been passed making it unlawful to dump, spread, or discharge viscera or refuse from poultry or fish processing onto any property within the town. Then in 1964 a planning board and a board of appeals were formed. In the late 1960s, the town's first comprehensive plan was formulated, and work was begun to craft zoning and subdivision ordinances to help guide the town's growth and development. Thus, as the 1970s approached, the stage had been set for Pownal to begin taking serious control of its future.

On a beautiful summer day in 1946, motorists could travel the well-graded gravel road, the Elmwood Road, toward Pownal Center.

Vietnam Era Veterans

Top: Jack B. St. Pierre, Staff Sergeant, U. S. Air Force, 1958-1979. In 1968 and 1969, he served with the Twelfth Air Commando Squadron on UC123s, spraying Agent Orange over the DMZ and Ho Chi Minh Trail. From 1972 to 1974 he was at the U. S. Embassy in Iran. He served in the Philippines, Taiwan, India, Pakistan and Turkey. He flew 287 Combat missions, earning eight Air Medals and three Distinguished Flying Crosses. He was honorably discharged with rank of Master Sgt. after 22 years of service.

Bottom: George Mason, Specialist 5, U. S. Army, 1964-1967. He was stationed at Ft. Rucker, Alabama and in Germany receiving Expert Marksmanship and Good Conduct medals.

Top: Christopher J. White, AWCS, served on active duty, U. S. Navy, 1965-1969, as Anti-Submarine Warfare crew member on P-3 Orion aircraft. He served in the Navy Reserves, 1969-1993. He was honorably discharged, with the rank of Senior Chief, after twenty-eight years of service.

Bottom: Michael Menchen, SP4-"A" Batry, 7th BN 11th Arty, U. S. Army, 1964-1966 (and Army Reserve until 1970). He served in Hawaii and in Vietnam as Chief Computer Operator and Intelligence Specialist. He received the following medals: Marksman Rifle M-14, National Defense Service, Vietnam Service, Vietnam Campaign and Good Conduct.

Top: Craig A. Vosmus, Seaman E5, Navy Seabees, 1968-1972, where he was in a construction-maintenance battalion. After a year of duty in Dong Ha, Vietnam, he was sent to Argentia, Newfoundland for the remainder of his service. He received the National Defense Service Medal, the Vietnam Campaign Medal, and the Vietnam Service Medal.

Bottom: Allen (Pat) Malone Jr., Yeoman 3rd Class E4, U. S. Navy, 1965-1968. On the destroyer, USS O'Bannon DD-450, he participated in shore bombardment of the Vietnam coast and Saigon River. He also served in the Philippines and Guam.

Vietnam Era Veterans *(See Appendix II for complete list)*

Top: Peter W. Goss, Corporal, U. S. Marine Corps, 1969-1971, foot soldier and later supply NCO1C Company Driver of H. S. Co. 2nd Battalion, First Marine Corps in Quang Nam Province, Vietnam. He was awarded the Good Conduct Medal, the Combat Action Ribbon and the National Defense Service Medal.

Bottom: Terry N. Snow, Lieutenant, U.S. Navy, 1966-1974. He served as Main Engines Officer from 1966 to 1969 aboard the guided missile cruiser USS Chicago in the Tonkin Gulf off North Vietnam. He is pictured here in November, 1968 as officer in charge of the boat detachment for 1UWG-1. He served in the Navy Reserve, 1970-1974.

Top: Bruce E. Hilton (1945-2006), Machinist Mate 2, U. S. Navy. He served three tours aboard the USS O'Hare off the Vietnam coast in gunfire support. He earned the National Defense Service Medal, the Vietnam Service Medal, and was a life member of AMVETS and disabled veterans organizations.

Bottom: Albert H. Blackstone Jr., 3rd Class SK, U. S. Navy, 1965-1967. He was with the Sixth Fleet Special Company, on the USS Neosho, USS Mississinowa, USS Truckie and USS Tidewater. He was on the USS Liberty when she was attacked during Israel's Six-Day War.

Top: Wendy Menchen, Captain, Registered Nurse, U. S. Air Force, 1968-1972. She was stationed at Clinton Sherman AFB 8th Air Force Support Group until June 1969, then at RAF Upper Heyford, England with the 66th TAC Support Group, and later with the 20th TAC Support Group.

Bottom: Arnold F. Blackstone, ADR2, Aviation Machinist Mate 2nd Class, U. S. Navy, 1962-1966. He served aboard ship stateside, and in Morocco and Spain. He was awarded the National Defense Service Medal and the Good Conduct Medal.

Brothers-in-Law Remember Vietnam

In late 1968 in the central highlands of Vietnam, two young men with Pownal connections were doing their military service. Although their paths never crossed and they didn't know each other at the time, they were destined to become brothers-in-law. Thirty-eight years later they shared their experiences in separate interviews.

Stephen Litchfield, who was raised on the Brown Road, graduated from Freeport High in 1966 at the age of eighteen. The war was on, and without an exemption, Steve was drafted in December of that year. After boot camp and training, he got orders to Vietnam, returned to Pownal to marry his high school sweetheart Janice, and flew to Vietnam in September of 1968.

James Daniels, meanwhile, had graduated from Portland High School in 1967. Born in New Hampshire, he had moved to town when his father became railroad station master at West Pownal. Then the family moved to Yarmouth, and his Pownal connection ended, temporarily. Out of school, facing the draft, and hoping for favorable assignments options if he volunteered, Jim enlisted in the Army in April of 1968. By October of that year, he too was off to Vietnam.

Initially Steve and Jim experienced similar service patterns and comparable duties. For a few months, they both served not far from Da Nang. Steve was assigned to helicopter bases. His assignment was to obtain the necessary parts for maintaining and repairing the "choppers." This put him in small forward bases which were frequently under attack. Not far away, Jim's unit maintained

Jim Daniels in 1968. "Driving the dump truck, you'd go to the quarry, get a load, drive up there… A good day was 150 miles."

Steve Litchfield with Cobra. "When they got hit out in the field and they came back crippled, we would tear them down and replace all the broken parts."

Route 1. He participated in daily sweeps along the road for mines and also drove dump trucks. Then in early 1969 their respective units moved south. Steve's base was not far from the huge US facility at Long Binh, while Jim moved to a small base close to Can Tho city.

Although they worked as support personnel, they were exposed to constant danger and witnessed much bloodshed. Steve remembers pitch black nights spent alone on a mound between bunkers, on alert for attack and praying that the scorpion that just crawled onto his arm would move on peacefully. More than once he narrowly escaped injury or death from booby traps or incoming ordnance. Jim had to stay overnight one week per month at a small camp near a Marine base where Route 1 crosses Phu Bai Pass This area was frequently attacked. After one heavy nighttime assault, he remembers, "I spent my twenty-first birthday pulling [Vietnamese bodies] off the wire."

Jim Daniels with the Americal Division at Hawk Hill near Chu Lai, 1970. Bunkers can be seen in the background.

Steve Litchfield. "When we were in Bien Hoa, I think we got hit every hour, every day, for two months."

In August of 1969 after nearly a year in Vietnam, Steve was sent home and discharged. The next month, Jim also returned Stateside. But he was not done with the Army, since as a volunteer he wouldn't be discharged for another eighteen months. He was sent to Fort Carson in Colorado but found life there so tedious that he put in his papers to return to the war. The second tour brought him back to the central Vietnam highlands, now as a demolition man, even more exposed to battlefield hazards. A typical assignment was to detonate unexploded 2,000-pound American bombs. The purpose was to deprive the enemy of the explosives contained in such a bomb, which they could extract and use for mines and booby traps. He was wounded on one of these missions and later suffered a second wound when hit by shrapnel from an enemy mortar. His military service ended in March, 1971.

Both men returned to civilian life, marked by war. Only gradually did Steve stop diving under the bed whenever he heard a loud noise at night. But he was relatively fortunate in coming back to a home, his wife Janice, and a good job. Jim, on the other hand, had spent twice as long in Vietnam. Back in Yarmouth he was at loose ends, jobless, and still single. It took time, but eventually he moved to Florida, got work, and started his own family. Still, Vietnam lingered. He suffered PTSD. Then in 1986, when he returned to Pownal, now divorced, he discovered that he had hepatitis C, probably contracted during the war. That disease presented life-threatening symptoms, and eventually required a liver transplant. Back in Pownal, he met and married Nancy, who happens to be Steve's sister. Today Jim lives next door to Steve on the Brown Road. They never discuss Vietnam.

Familiar Vistas Reflect Pownal's Agricultural Heritage
Barns Saved, Barns Lost

This early homestead on well-traveled Elmwood Road is shown here as it looked in 1969 when owned by Charles "Bill" and Wilma Knight. In 1989, through the efforts of the Pownal Land Trust, Wilma Knight's heirs, and Land For Maine's Future, this property was protected from future subdivision and development. The home, with its classic federal lines, the stately barn, and the rolling meadows will remain a prominent vista as one comes up the hill toward Pownal Center.

As viewed from the Merrill Road in 1970, this landmark homestead owned by George and Minnie Bradbury Sr. had a rich farm history. It is currently owned by granddaughter, Jane Bradbury Carr.

This homestead, built by Cyrus Libby in 1850 on the Hallowell Road near the Pownal-Durham town line, is shown here in 1973 when owned by Kenneth and Dorothy Harlow. At that time, the Harlows operated the Golden Acres Country Store from their home. Unfortunately the barn was destroyed in a storm on December 18, 1978, robbing Pownal of one of its grandest barns.

Toward a Third Century

In the early 1970s, Pownal's selectmen, Ed Menchen, Joe Mitchell, and Fred Stasinowsky, met every Monday evening, in time-honored fashion, in Mallett Hall's small and drafty office. Ed and Joe were long-time residents while Fred had lived in town less than ten years. They were, respectively, the local mail carrier, an insurance adjuster, and a service station manager. Road Commissioner Carl Knight always came by, and occasionally Fire Ward Earle Blake, with his distinctive white crew cut, appeared. The room was blue with smoke from roll-your-own cigarettes, as they paid bills and considered town problems in a low key manner around the wood stove.

Despite the apparent small town ease, these officials were aware that change was in the wind. After all, they knew that most surrounding towns had already moved with the times to update their municipal offices and operations, and that many had recently passed zoning ordinances. Indeed, the introduction of zoning in Pownal was a current hot topic of debate. But they could not have imagined the wide range of changes, and how profoundly various new pressures would challenge the town.

During the period from roughly 1970 to the present, Pownal, like small towns across Maine and the United States, was subjected to multiple pressures, that had the potential to drastically alter the town's way of life. The questions were: How much would Pownal change? Would the town, like so many places in Maine, be swallowed up by encroaching urban and suburban landscapes? Could Pownal manage to preserve important parts of a lifestyle with roots going back more than a century?

The role of the authors of this history is neither to judge whether the pressures which we will discuss were critical, nor to proclaim the ultimate outcomes as satisfactory. Such judgments will certainly vary with each person's perspective. What is presented here is a dispassionate summary of the pressures felt by the town and the ways that natives and newcomers negotiated the challenges.

Hallowell Road (Route 9) and Elmwood Road crossroads looking south in 1976 with Bradbury Mountain Garage and Marion's Market in the distance.

Hallowell Road (Route 9) looking north past Albert Blackstone Jr.'s excavating business and Mallett Hall in 1976.

Aerial view (taken from the steeple of the Congregational Church in 1976) of the Center crossroads, picturing Bradbury Mountain Garage and Napier's General Store and Lunch. The area behind the garage shows the site of the intermediate school that had recently been sold and moved to Cousins Island.

What were these pressures? One, which has continued unabated from 1970 to the present, was the growing population. As the 1970s dawned, Pownal's population of 800 began a steady increase, reaching 1,496 by the census year of 2000. The number of households more than doubled to 567 over the same time period. This unprecedented growth rate was a contributing factor behind many of the pressures for change.

Who were the newcomers that started Pownal's population on this growth curve in the 1970s? Many hailed from more urban areas in and out of state. Some had been exposed to a broad offering of educational opportunities, and many brought with them social and economic patterns quite different from the town norm. Quite a few were young families with children, and the elementary school enrollments quickly grew. Typically, the parents brought with them high expectations of what schooling should provide. In general, whether they originated from near or far, they desired a rural life style and valued open spaces and woodlands.

They moved to Pownal for many reasons, some simple, some complex. Not a few had been caught up in the nationally prevalent "back-to-the-earth" movement of the day. They were individuals and families who had become dissatisfied with urban life and longed for a simpler lifestyle. Many saw Pownal as a town that offered much of what they desired — open fields, uncut woodlands, land for gardening and farming, and, in addition, a brand new elementary school building. Given the good roads and relatively cheap fuel, they could live in a rural setting yet work in cities like Portland, Lewiston, Auburn, or Brunswick. The prosperity of these cities had created many jobs, and even Augusta, with its expanding number of state jobs, was not too far away. And land was available in Pownal at relatively low prices. In some cases the land came with an old house and barn, and many of the newcomers delighted in the challenges of restoration. Even new houses were available for reasonable prices, as contractors like Fred York and Bill DeWitt helped spur a local building boom.

Report of the Planning Board, 1971

During the past year, the major effort of the Planning Board has been preparing a zoning ordinance that would be acceptable to the Townspeople.

It is a fact that any ordinance imposes certain restrictions, but we believe that the one recently adopted by the Town of Pownal imposes a minimum of restrictions compared to the benefits that may be realized in years to come.

We must remember that an ordinance such as this is but a tool to regulate the future growth of the Town of Pownal and if changing it in any way would benefit the Community, it is your right to do so.

One concern of all should be the ever increasing shortage of open space. At the present time, we have several parcels of Town Acquired property. We ask that you give serious thought to the future use of this land.

The Planning Board meets on the last Monday evening of each month at 8:00 P. M. at the Town Hall. We invite anyone interested to attend. It is from your ideas that our course of action materializes.

Respectfully submitted
LAURENCE W. SNOW, Chairman

It should be noted that not all who arrived were really newcomers. Many were returning from military service during the Vietnam conflict, where, although no one from Pownal had been killed, some had experienced the brutalities of war. For the most part, they picked up the pieces of their lives quietly, with little inclination to share their experiences.

Whatever their reasons for coming and the attitudes they brought with them, the newcomers arrived in a town largely inhabited by natives. The latter, typically, were long-time residents, many of whom had generational ties to Pownal's first settlers. They had been raised among these fields and hills, had received their early education in the town's one-room schools, and perhaps owned a local business or farm. Some practiced a trade locally. Most remembered with deep appreciation the strong teachers who had instructed them under a system with much lower administration and operation costs. Many had already served the town over the years in elected positions as selectman, clerk, tax collector, treasurer, or road commissioner. They had worked as crew on winter and summer road projects, had volunteered to serve on the budget committee, and had organized and run the volunteer fire department and auxiliary.

But they were not necessarily mired in the past. Quite a few had recognized the need for, and had fought for the new elementary school building. Indeed, the more visionary among them had begun planning for Pownal's inevitable growth back in the late 1950s, hoping, even as the town grew, to preserve its rural character and protect its open spaces.

In addition to in-migration and the resulting social stresses, Pownal was not immune to the cultural upheavals that were sweeping the nation. It was the era of President Johnson's "Great Society." Civil rights, racial equality, and women's liberation were related movements that impacted the town with their own pressures. Mandates from state and federal government arrived at the town office and the office of the Superintendent of SAD 62 with somewhat alarming frequency. What did not always arrive was the money to fund them, or to cover incidental costs. As an example, Title Nine of the federally mandated Education Amendments of 1972 required changes in school academic and sports programs to equalize opportunities for boys and girls. Despite partial funding, administration, personnel, and equipment costs were borne by the town and paid for by property taxes.

Pownal Volunteer Fire Department Muster Team, organized in 1975 under the leadership of Lester Blake, displays trophies won at muster competitions in 1976. Front row l. to r.: Charles Gowen, Lester Blake (team captain), Jeremy Best. Back row l. to r.: Conrad Morrison, Steve Gowen, Conrad Spaulding, Vernon Brower, and Fire Ward Earle Blake.

Another set of pressures also began to appear during this period, which come under the heading of "Environmental Protection." Across the country, Rachel Carson's book *Silent Spring* (1962) and the many books and studies that followed raised alarms and concerns about the environment. April of 1970 marked America's first "Earth Day," established largely through the efforts of Maine's Senator Edmund Muskie. Predictably, state and federal mandates addressing environmental concerns began to affect local municipalities and their budgets.

As an example, Maine decreed that the phased closing of all open dumps must be completed by 1989. For many years, the town had been paying North Yarmouth a modest sum to secure dump privileges for Pownal residents. In 1980 this sum was $8,000. With the dump closed, the town was forced to institute curbside pickup at a much higher cost. Eventually in 1992, a solid waste reduction and recycling committee was appointed, both to promote recycling and to mitigate the town's financial burden by reducing hauled-waste tonnage. They did what they could, but this mandatory change in the handling of waste was costing the town $76,000 by 1992 and $116,472 by 2007.

These pressures for change were not necessarily perceived differently by newcomers and natives, and interesting alliances arose on different sides of different issues. However, there were some prevalent feelings among the natives. Many suspected that the newcomers were critical of the way the town had been run in the past, and feared that some of their new ideas would infringe upon privacy and raise taxes, this just when the costs of new state and federal mandates were hitting their pocket books. Tensions increased, and voices were raised at public meetings.

Two of the more contentious issues were zoning and the school budget. A proposed zoning ordinance was voted down in 1969. Then in 1971, amid renewed cries of privacy infringement on one side and predictions of wanton development on the other, the town's first zoning ordinance passed by a narrow margin. Revisions of this ordinance have occasioned spirited debates ever since. One of the first school budget confrontations occurred in 1975. After two hours of heated debate, the voters at a well-attended meeting cut $23,500 from the SAD 62 budget. The school board had no choice but to make cuts, resulting in what they called "an impossibly austere" budget.

The tensions described, however, fell well short of creating an unbridgeable divide. In fact, even though many issues were, and continue to

Edward Dresser Menchen (1915-1990). In 1976 when each town in Cumberland County was asked to name an outstanding citizen to be honored with a named seat in the new Civic Center, Pownal selected "Eddie" Menchen as its choice. He had served as selectman, school board member, town treasurer, and tax collector, and he continued to hold posts for many years thereafter. (See page 192.)

This period was also marked by a healthy spirit of community. New groups were created and existing ones rejuvenated. The community helped celebrate the seventy-fifth anniversary of the Granite Grange in 1974. Long-time Grange member Doris Carter Blackstone became the first female Grange Master in 1979, and the Granite Grange remained one of the most active in southern Maine throughout the 1980s. The Improved Order of Redmen continued to meet regularly. A new group, the Pownal Scenic and Historical Society, was founded in 1970 under the leadership of Marjorie Mason, and progress was begun toward their ambitious goals of scenic improvement and historic preservation. *Pownal: A Rural Maine History* (1977) was their first publication.

Senior citizens organized to become the Bradbury Mountain Owls in 1974 and met monthly for programs and lunch. The volunteer fire department underwent a modernizing expansion in the 1970s with the purchase of a new truck with new gear, and the establishment of a reliable dispatch system. The fire department ladies' auxiliary reorganized under new leadership and expanded their fund raising efforts. In 1986, the town celebrated the centennial of Mallett Hall. Meanwhile, both the First Parish Congregational Church and the North Pownal United Methodist Church had undertaken major construction projects and were expanding their youth groups. The Saturday night bean suppers continued to grow in popularity.

For the young people, Girl and Boy Scouts troops began to be formed. Over time several came into and went out of existence. Starting probably in 1927, 4-H clubs made their first appearance in Pownal, in step with the national 4-H movement that accelerated in 1914. Subsequently various boys and girls clubs were formed. Also during this period, the school took steps to better serve the needs of the junior high students. A building project added a gymnasium-auditorium plus several classrooms.

In the case of school expansion, the pleasure of seeing the new facilities was set off against the realization that it cost a lot of money. The

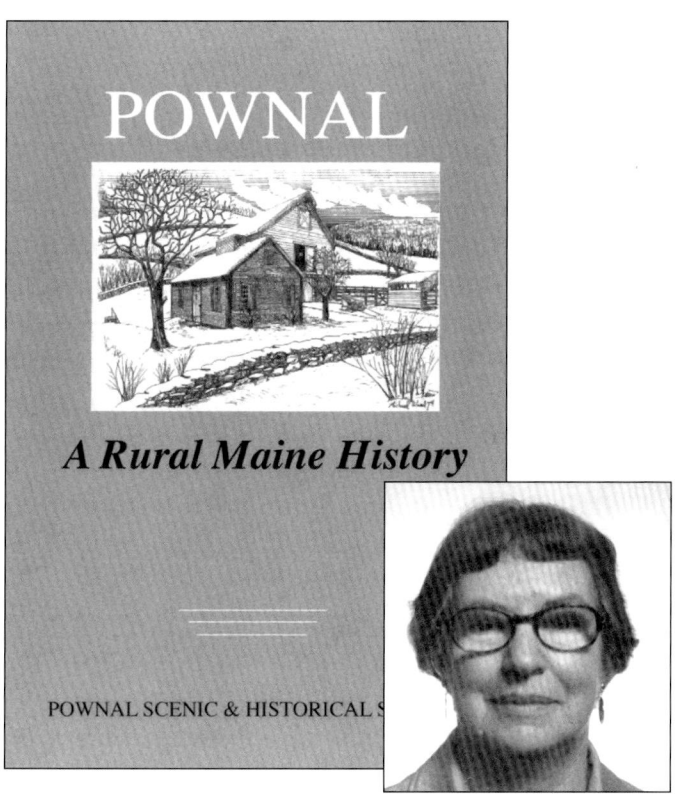

Historical Society founder Marjorie Mason (1914-1982) realized a dream in 1977 when, together with Donna Boyles, Sherilyn Dietrich, Mary Goodwin, and Kathryne Moore, she wrote and published Pownal: A Rural Maine History, *the first comprehensive history of Pownal. It was reprinted in 2006, along with Ettie Latham's 1908* History of Pownal. *Both are currently available as companions to this book.*

be contentious, the town as a whole managed to keep all sides talking and cooperating, as most realized that good people and good ideas defy labels. Many newcomers and natives together infused the town with a civic spirit not seen in some time. It is especially interesting to note that women were beginning to play a more active and visible role on town committees and boards, often as chairs. In 1976, Sherilyn Dietrich became the first woman appointed to the planning board and the budget committee. In 1980, Jane Mittel became the first woman chair of the school board. And the town once again had a resident physician, a woman. Patricia Searfoss, known professionally as Dr. Patricia Adams, had established her practice in her home on the Libby road. She became the town health officer.

Linda Seminick proudly displays her winning entry in the town seal contest sponsored by the Pownal Scenic and Historical Society in 1986. Her pen and ink drawing was judged by voters to best reflect Pownal's past. Her design was adopted as the Town's official seal, and has since been used on all official town documents and vehicles.

Throughout the 1970s and 1980s, the town planning board proposed changes in the zoning ordinance designed to both clarify and strengthen it. Some of these changes were crafted in response to state mandates, while others derived from a desire to retain the town's rural character, in part by controlling development. That Pownal managed to retain much of its rural character was due in no small part to these efforts.

Despite the changes noted above, by around 1990 Pownal still retained many features of an earlier age. Much of the operation of the town government was little changed from the previous century; procedures and equipment were outdated; officials were still working out of their homes; the organization and preservation of town records was haphazard, and threats of legal action for non-compliance were real; there had been no attempt to move toward computerization; and there was no system in place for officials to communicate with all citizens. Besides wood stoves, Mallett Hall had a large, noisy, inefficient oil-fired furnace, and lacked indoor plumbing, except for the attached, and unique, two-story outhouse.

town's share of the school budget approached eighty percent of the total tax commitment. Nor was municipal spending standing still. In 1987 for the first time, an elected office became an appointed position. Carl Knight resigned as road commissioner after twenty-three years of service, and Darrel Thurber was appointed. The town now had to provide its own road equipment, having previously rented it from Carl. Routine maintenance required an expanded garage, soon followed by a state-mandated covered salt shed, as salt had polluted several local wells. The town took out a bond for $250,000 to help cover these costs.

Some people saw these things not as deficiencies but as charming aspects of this small Maine town, while others seemed reluctant to move

(continued on page 60)

Happy Birthday, Mallett Hall 1886-1986. September 6, 1986 was a picture-perfect day with displays, flowers, bunting, and period-dressed participants lending an air of gaiety to the event, sponsored by the Pownal Scenic and Historical Society. Mallett Hall's interior hallway had been newly painted and the antique hearse was on display. The Granite Grange mounted an exhibit about their many activities, and the Improved Order of Redmen displayed ceremonial costumes. Other contributions to the event were made by the North Pownal United Methodist Church B Naturals, the Boy and Girl Scouts, and Pownal school children. The featured event was a fashion show highlighting period dress with modeling done by local adults and children.

Meanwhile, across Hallowell Road on the same day, the First Parish Congregational Church celebrated its 175th anniversary. This photograph shows people attending special services.

At the festivities, Arthur Stackhouse proudly displays the 1878 town hearse to the late Harriet Blackstone (left) and Theona Blackstone.

Pownal Pumpkin Festival
Successor to Old Home Days

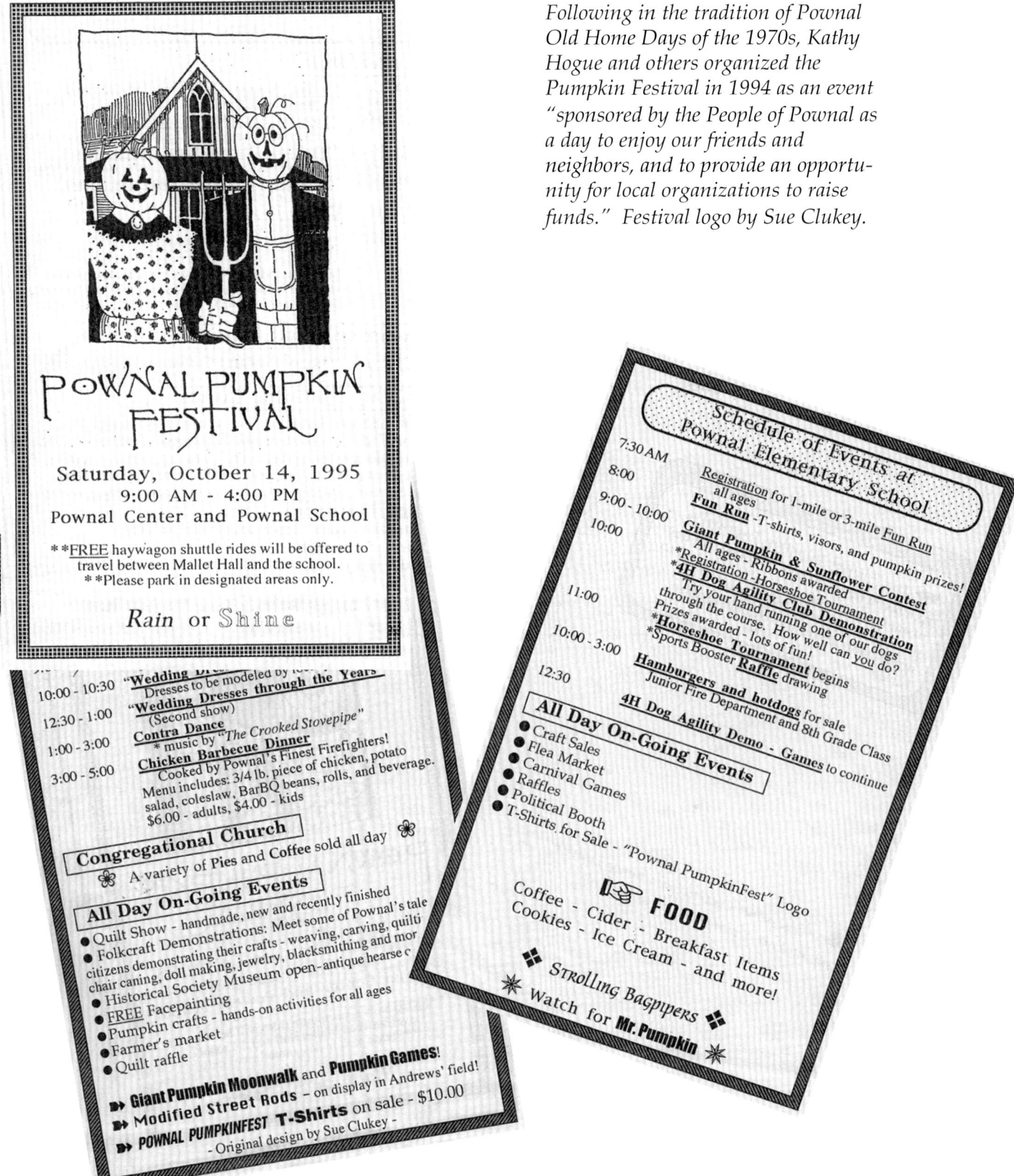

Following in the tradition of Pownal Old Home Days of the 1970s, Kathy Hogue and others organized the Pumpkin Festival in 1994 as an event "sponsored by the People of Pownal as a day to enjoy our friends and neighbors, and to provide an opportunity for local organizations to raise funds." Festival logo by Sue Clukey.

Dedication of the Mallett Hall Addition
1999 Pumpkin Festival

Making dedication opening remarks are l. to r.: Susan Mack, Chair, Board of Selectmen; William DeWitt, Chair, Mallett Hall Addition Committee; James Boyles committee member and Master of Ceremonies.
Photos: Christopher Ayres.

Crowds pour in.

Sue Mack displays plaque, signed by Governor Angus King, declaring October 9, 1999 as "Pownal Day."

The Great Ice Storm of '98

"A monumental storm struck Pownal on January 7, leaving most of us without electricity for two weeks. At first it was fun… potluck dinners with neighbors by candle light… but after a few days reality began to set in… We tired of thawing ice on the wood stove for dishwater… We desperately sought baths and showers… But soon we began to worry about others who might not be as fortunate as ourselves… Neighbors helped neighbors… Some cut trees to clear driveways… some hauled and stacked wood…some delivered candles and food to those in need." Susan Mack, Chair of the Board of Selectmen, from the 1998 Annual Town Report.

The ice storm began on January 7, 1998. Downed poles blocked Hallowell Road and Brown Road. A police cruiser monitored the situation. Photo: Paul Cunningham, Brunswick Times Record.

Sue concluded by recognizing "all those who helped out… the members of the Volunteer Fire and Rescue Department, the Road Commissioner and crew as they worked with the Board of Selectmen to provide emergency services… the staffs at Cumberland County Emergency Management Agency, Freeport Community Services, the American Red Cross… as well as countless volunteers. Even two local businesses… Village Candle donated 'candle lights' and Dominoes Pizza kept emergency crews fed." It was an experience none who were there will forget.

Above: Trees and utility polls snapped like toothpicks, ice-covered branches fell like autumn leaves. Many lost power and telephone.

Right: January 18, 1998, after eleven days Central Maine Power restores electricity on Poland Range Road.

Mallett Hall was entered into the National Register of Historic Places on October 16, 1991, through the efforts of the Pownal Scenic and Historical Society. According to State Historic Preservation Officer Earle Shettleworth Jr., the building is "recognized as a part of the Historical and Cultural Heritage of our nation and should be preserved as a living part of our community life and development in order to give a sense of orientation to the American people."

away from familiar and comfortable routines. But pressures to modernize had built to a point where they could not be ignored. The comprehensive plan, completed in 1992 by a citizen committee, recommended action to address many of these problems. Significantly, it also urged preservation of the town's rural character.

And changes did occur. In 1994 the town elected its first woman, Susan Mack, to the board of selectmen. The selectmen became more involved with regional issues. The budget committee established more rigorous procedures and initiated studies before making recommendations. The town began mailing a quarterly newsletter to every household.

The most visible and dramatic change occurred at town hall. The 1992 comprehensive plan recommended that Mallett Hall be renovated to become a more effective seat of government. The decision on whether to do this, and in what manner, was made at a town meeting where there was considerable difference of opinion. Should the town add on to the existing building, or construct a new facility elsewhere? In the end, the citizens voted to retain Mallett Hall as the focus of government and to construct an addition, modern on the inside with an architecturally compatible exterior. This would allow town officials to work out of centralized, computerized offices.

The town hall committee was appointed in 1990 to oversee the project and its funding. A vigorous fund raising campaign was begun, and ultimately the voters authorized the town to expend $150,000 for construction and furnishings. Several citizens wrote a successful grant proposal for a Community Development Building Grant (funded by the federal government and administered by the state). This source funded all handicapped accessibility construction as well as the building's first elevator, at a total cost of $138,000. An architectural firm, Barba Associates, was engaged. Although some of the construction was contracted out, the building process also involved an unprecedented number of hours donated by volunteers. The new addition was dedicated in 1999 and opened for business in 2001. The town now boasted a handsome, award-winning space, with up-to-date facilities, where all municipal business could be conducted and where civic meetings and gatherings of many sorts could take place.

Late in the twentieth century, Pownal faced yet another threat to its open spaces. As part of the effort to find and deliver more energy supplies, Maritimes and Northeast Pipeline L.L.C. proposed to lay a pipeline through Pownal, to bring natural gas from Canada to the northeastern United States. They proposed to place this line in the existing corridor, but Central Maine Power Company refused to grant easements. This refusal was eventually rescinded, but not until the energetic opposition by a Pownal activist group, "No New Corridors," had spurred reviews by the state and by the Federal Energy Regulatory Commission.

Mallett Hall Wins Maine Preservation's Historic Preservation Award for 2000

On May 19, 2000, Maine Preservation announced that "the renovation and addition of Pownal's Mallett Hall has been selected as a recipient of a Maine Preservation 2000 Statewide Historic Preservation Honor Award." Executive Director Roxanne Elfin said, "This is an outstanding example of the successful partnership between a municipality, the community, and a preservation architect to preserve an important historic resource. By creating an addition to the original structure instead of building a new Town Hall, Pownal has found a way to hold on to the past while accommodating the future." Photos: Christopher Ayres

Pownal Center crossroads at Hallowell (Route 9) and Elmwood Roads in 2005. A building just off camera on the right, which for decades housed a country store, is currently occupied by Rousseau Builders. A stop sign and flashing red light control traffic at this now busy intersection. On the right, a part of the First Parish Congregational Church can be seen as well as the homestead at 481 Elmwood Road, both obscured by trees. Off photo to left is the Short Stop Filling Station and Convenience Store. The utility poles carry not only telephone lines, as in 1908, but also electricity and cable. Maple trees, rather than elms, line the paved roads. (Compare with the picture on page 5.)

As the twenty-first century dawned, Pownal's population stood at 1,491, an 18.5 percent increase in ten years. Such a growth rate did not seem to threaten the town's rural character, as expressed in the existing comprehensive plan. There were few major subdivisions, and the houses being built did not encroach overmuch on the abundant open space.

The selectman form of government remained in place and continued little changed from 2000 to 2008. But it was constantly stressed by citizen demands for better services amid rising costs, while at the same time state and federal aid declined. The decrease in federal and state funding, direct and indirect, resulted largely from policy changes effected by Congress and the Administration, and to the drain of the Iraq war on fiscal resources. New requirements aimed at curtailing local spending, such as those imposed by the state's "LD 1" tax cap legislation of 2005, also added to the pressure.

Amidst these broader currents, some significant changes occurred locally. A specially appointed compensation committee developed an up-to-date employee benefit package that was adopted by the town in 2003. For the first time, clear written job descriptions were adopted for all elected and appointed positions. An administrative secretary was added in 2005 amid increasing talk of the eventual need to hire an administrative assistant to aid the overburdened selectmen. In 2006, the office of town clerk became appointed rather than elected. Similar changes affected the offices of tax collector, treasurer, and fire chief in 2008 and 2009. In 2007 voters approved a large expenditure to purchase a new fire truck. At that same town meeting voters authorized the selectmen to seek a one-million-dollar bond to cover reconstruction of the Allen Road, a move initiated by the recently formed capital projects planning committee to address the town's deteriorating roads.

It was abundantly clear by 2008 that the consolidation of town offices in the new Mallett Hall addition had improved operations and citizen access to services. As a bonus, the DeWitt general purpose room directly above the business offices was heavily used for meetings and social events. In this same time frame, the Mallett Hall Building and Grounds Committee worked hard to initiate and oversee renovation projects in the original town hall. With financial support from both the town and individual donors, the list of accomplishments grew long: windows restored, electrical wiring upgraded, new heating units installed, ceilings repaired, new lights and blinds installed, and the stage and voting rooms painted.

For the directors of SAD 62, the last decade has been a challenging one. Faced with slowly declining school enrollment, rising operating costs, and decreased state aid, they worked hard to keep their budget within reasonable bounds, while maintaining a sound educational program. Then in 2007, this hard working board had to deal with state legislation requiring school administrative consolidation and reduction of "school administrative units" to fewer than eighty. At this writing the complete story here has yet to be told. Planning and negotiations continue (see page 261).

As we conclude this overview of Pownal's last one hundred years, the town is looking forward to the bicentennial celebrations in 2008. Will they be as special and meaningful as those of 1908? We think so. Pownal was born in a spirit of true community, and proudly retains this spirit in the face of daunting pressures. How successfully this sense of community can flourish in the future remains to be seen.

North Pownal crossroads at Lawrence and Fickett Roads in 2005. The North Pownal General Store on the left closed in 2006. On the right, one-hundred-year old maple trees obscure the view of the Captain Joseph Small homestead at 73 Fickett Road. Stop signs control traffic at this busy paved intersection. (Compare with the picture on page 6.)

The West Pownal business district no longer exists. However the Allen Road underpass, built in 1912 (see page 12) remains virtually unchanged. Pictured here in 2005, the underpass still requires careful single file travel for safe negotiation. On the right is unpaved Dow's Lane, that once led to the business district and train station.

Recent Veterans

Mark Ingerson, U. S. Air Force, 1990-1992 and Massachusetts Air National Guard, 1992-2000, served stateside as an aerospace ground mechanic. Through his military service, loans and scholarships, Mark graduated from the University of Massachusetts in 1997, then earned a masters degree in education from Virginia Tech in 2000. In 2005, Mark won the National VFW High School Teacher of the Year Award for helping his students appreciate the efforts and sacrifices of this country's veterans.

Sergeant Charles S. Snow, U. S. Marine Corps, 2001-2005, served in the 3rd Battalion, 8th Marines Weapons Company in Japan, Korea, and Haiti. He earned the following medals and awards: National Defense, Sea Service Deployment, Korean Defense Service, Global War on Terrorism, Navy Meritorious Unit Commendation, Expert Rifle 3rd, Expert Pistol 1st, Meritorious Mass, and three Certificates of Commendation.

Lance Corporal Brain Randall, U. S. Marines, 1990-1994, served aboard the amphibious transport dock USS Trenton in the Persian Gulf, was deployed in Operation Desert Storm and Operation Desert Shield, participated in the evacuation of the American embassy during Desert Storm, and was awarded the National Defense Service Medal.

James W. Hart, U. S. Marine Corps, 2001-2005, served as a digital wideband transmission equipment operator in Iraq. He earned the following medals and awards: Iraq Campaign, Sea Service Deployment Ribbon, Global War on Terrorism Expeditionary Iraq, National Defense Service, Rifle Sharpshooter, Pistol Marksman, Certificate of Appreciation and Good Conduct.

Christopher Z. Farrington graduated in the top ten of his Cheverus High School class of 2004 and accepted an appointment to the United States Military Academy at West Point. While at West Point, he represented the academy at several national sports competitions and received the Superintendent's Award given to cadets who are in the top fifteen percent in the academic, physical, and military programs. Named to the dean's list every semester, Christopher graduated on May 31, 2008 with a B.S. degree in mechanical engineering. He is a commissioned 2nd Lieutenant in the United States Army, serving in the infantry branch.

Chapter 2

Using Our Natural Resources

"View from the Ridge" Pownal Land Trust 2004.
Tryon land included in the Bradbury-Pineland Protection Corridor Project.
Photo: Christopher Ayres

"Protect our rural character: the open fields; the forested woodlands; the wetlands, rivers, and streams; and our wildlife habitats." This was both a goal and a plea enshrined in the 2006 Town of Pownal Comprehensive Plan, as it had been in the plans of 1969, 1980, and 1992.

From the beginning, residents of Pownal have used the local natural resources for sustenance, profit, and enjoyment. During the first one hundred years of the town's existence, the exploitation of land, minerals, forests, and waters centered around survival and economic gain. But as the town entered its second century, commercial agriculture was in decline across Maine, mineral extraction had passed its peak, and second- and third-growth forests were encroaching on land previously cleared for farming. The following sections present some of the trends, practices, and people who played a role in the shifting uses of our natural resources.

Land

When one contemplates land use, the first thing that comes to mind is farming, or "that which sustained us," as *Pownal, a Rural Maine History*, expressed it in 1977. However, land may serve other purposes besides soil for crops or fields for grazing. And certain other uses have played a considerable role in the life of the town. Scenic and recreational activities have centered especially on Bradbury Mountain State Park and the recently created Bradbury-Pineland Corridor. Other spaces have been appropriated for the utility corridor that traverses the town.

Farming — That Which Sustained Us

"That [separation] will entirely shut out the inhabitants of the new town from all the benefits and advantages arising from the several landings and flats in [Freeport]." This was one of several strong points raised by Benjamin Soule in 1807, as he argued against the jurisdictional separation from Freeport of the area destined to become Pownal. And it was a point of no little concern, since at that time travel and transport by sea were as important as today's use of railroads and highways. Soule and others doubted the future viability of a town with no direct access to the ocean. Nonetheless, Pownal did separate from Freeport, and, denied this access, its residents increasingly focused attention on their large tracts of undeveloped land. The town gradually developed as an interior semi-isolated farming community. The often swampy and rocky land was cleared, homesteads were built, and crops planted. In 1840, thirty-two years after its founding, Pownal reached its nineteenth-century peak population of 1,300, at which time 344 heads of families called themselves full-time farmers. Subsequently throughout the nineteenth century, even as the population gradually declined, generation followed generation operating viable farms, often in conjunction with supplemental sources of income.

Some general observations will set the stage for the discussion of farming in the twentieth century. For at least the first half of this century, farmers in Pownal seldom concentrated

The Cyrus Libby (1811-1903) homestead. This two and one-half story Federal style homestead located at the current 796 Hallowell Road was built by Cyrus Libby in 1850. Hazel Libby Whitcher related in 1974 that "Cyrus was a cousin of my grandfather... was a captain of a small ship... When he came back he farmed for quite a few years... built that barn in the 1880s." The barn was destroyed in a windstorm in 1978.

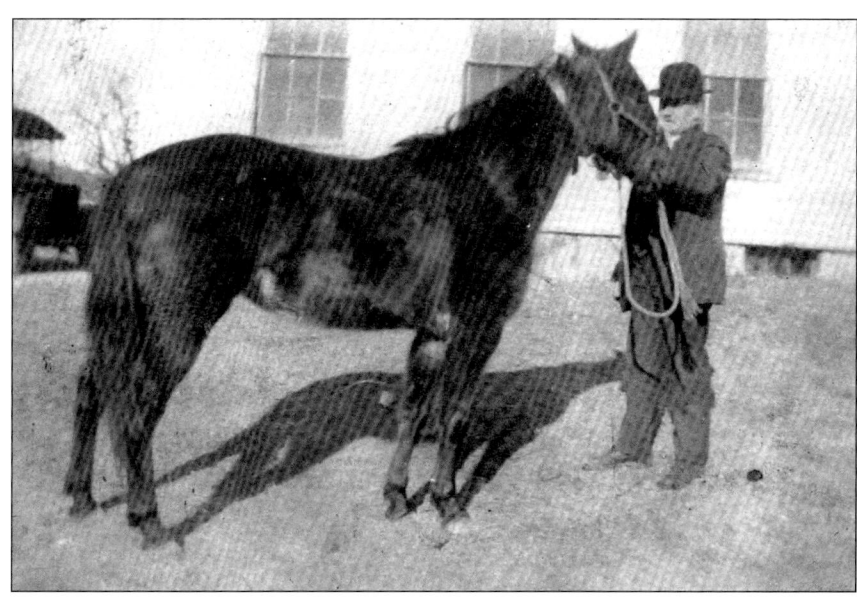

Reverend Daniel Tuttle (1861-1927) sold horses for transportation. For twenty years prior to his call to the ministry at Pownal's First Parish Congregational Church, Rev. Tuttle practiced veterinary surgery and participated in ox-pulling contests, winning more than seventy-five blue ribbons at the Lewiston State Fair.

exclusively on any one crop or animal product. Rather, they developed a necessary and admirable flexibility. At any given time, markets existed for several cash crops, and each exhibited its rise and fall. Over time, demand for some products declined, whereas new cash crops looked promising. The savvy Pownal farmer kept his knowledge of the markets up to date and adjusted his operations to maximize returns. This pattern rested on the wisdom of diversity. Almost all farm families raised multiple secondary crops and animals for their own use and for local markets. Such sales provided a reliable income.

This diversification and adaptability secured the success of many farms. Families lived in company of hard work, but the results of their labor were tangible. Their needs were modest and most were content with their lives, friendly with their neighbors, and active in their community.

Most farms in the early 1900s boasted a few cows, several pigs, a flock of poultry, and perhaps a team of oxen and a horse or two. Their larder was also supplied from their kitchen gardens of squash, corn, beans, potatoes, and peas. Pigs were raised on many farms, some for farm stock piglets, others for hams, bacon, and salt pork. "We always had chickens, hens and always raised a pig. They killed it for winter... Had bacon and smoked hams. Yes, it was smoked at home. My father kept cows and horses. We always had a garden, vegetables, hay enough to feed his stock. Didn't have to buy much at the store. Grew our own pea beans and yellow eyes. He kept a few cows. I made butter." So recalled Maude Marston Tuttle in a 1973 interview about her father's farm.

During this early period, farming for self-sufficiency and profit remained an important part of life in Pownal. Typically, operating expenses were not large, as little commercial fertilizer was used, feed grain was not too costly, and taxes were low (it was common to "work out" taxes on road repair). Often labor-intensive work such as the threshing of grain was hired out to an operator who made the rounds of local farms with his machine. On many places, motor-powered trucks and tractors didn't begin to replace oxen and horses until the 1940s. And invariably cords of firewood for heat and cooking were cut directly from the woodlot.

Complete self-sufficiency was of course impossible. Whether the farm was used primarily to produce for home consumption, or became the family's cash business, it was common that the husband and wife would each

(continued on page 71)

The Andrew and Rachel Hodsdon homestead pictured in 1993. This Greek Revival cape with attached ell and barn was moved by teams of oxen in 1840 from Turner, Maine to its present site at 255 Hodsdon Road. The Hodsdon family owned and operated extensive granite quarries behind this home from the early 1800s to 1908.

Hodsdon homestead: the house and ell.

Dairy farmer George Hodsdon (1867-1940) transports children and farm products in his horse-drawn wagon in 1920 at the farm originally owned by his grandparents, Andrew and Rachel York Hodsdon. George and his wife Sarah raised dairy cattle and chickens and sold milk, butter, eggs, and hay to Portland markets. He also sold corn, squash, pumpkins, and beans to a cannery in Gray.

Four Generations of Hodsdons have lived and farmed here: Andrew Hodsdon (1811-1899) and Rachel York Hodsdon (d. 1878); George Hodsdon (1867-1940) and Sarah Johnson Hodsdon (1881-1973); Robert Hodsdon (1904-1987) and Mabel Blackstone Hodsdon (1910-1996); and, currently, Robert and Mabel's son Ronald and Mary Ann Bailey Hodsdon.

The barn, scheduled to be dismantled in 2008.

Threshing grain at George Hodsdon's farm, c.1920. Philip Knight (1892-1981), well known in the area, owned a horse-drawn threshing machine that helped farmers process their grain. Philip was born and raised in Pownal. When he married Eva Crocket, they resided just over the border in North Yarmouth, where Philip later ran a sawmill business employing local men. Back row l. to r.: unknown, Harold Hodsdon, Charles Knight (Phil's father), George Hodsdon (with moustache), unknown, and Philip Knight. In front are George's sons Robert (sixteen) and Joe (twelve). The farm is currently owned by the son of Robert and Mabel, Ronald "Hutch" Hodsdon, and Mary Ann Hodsdon.

Eliab Latham (1848-1923) and Esther "Ettie" Johnson Latham (1854-1934) ran a highly successful farm at the current 541 Hodsdon Road, pictured here during the early 1900s. The homestead, dating to 1800, is the original home of John T. and Eunice Lawrence, Ettie's parents. The barn dates to 1887. A news article dating to 1929 stated: "Her apple orchards were known as the cream of the land, raising a wide variety of Baldwin, Wagner, and Black, down to the new-old apple which she has cultivated called 'Golden Royals.'" In addition to farming, Mrs. Latham was a featured speaker at the 1908 town centennial celebration, where she read from her newly published history of Pownal.

The Ernest Tuttle (1870-1935) and Maude Marston Tuttle (1882-1981) homestead, pictured at the turn of the century, was built prior to 1850 in the Greek Revival style. It is located at the current 133 Hallowell Road. The barn is no longer standing. The Tuttles farmed here until Ernest's death in 1935. He served as the town's road commissioner for twenty-three years between 1907 and 1933, and as the first fire warden, elected in 1914 and 1915.

be employed in part-time jobs. He might be a carpenter or shoe shop worker. She might work in the sardine packing plant or corn shop. Also "piecework" assembly, especially for the shoe shops, was often done at home.

Pownal farmers at that time were producing chickens, eggs, butter, cheese, and seasonal vegetables including potatoes, squash, and apples, for sale at Portland markets or locally. Some sold flowers. Josephine Pervier Allen recounted the following in her 1997 book, *The Remarkable Couple*: "In addition to the dairy farming there were a number of money crops (sometimes they did not bring much money). Potatoes were the most stable of the crops Dad grew. He usually planted Cobblers for an early crop and Green Mountains for the later. Sweet corn and string beans were grown for the canning factories. Squash was another cash crop." Etta Marston Starling remembered in a 1973 interview, "Father. raised his own corn, hundreds of bushels of Red Rose potatoes which turned white after they were cooked. [He] kept some for seed but sold the rest. We had cows... made butter... Mother sold butter in Portland... Father would load up with vegetables and butter and cheese and he'd go to Portland about once a week."

The cultivation and use of fruits, corn, and hay had their own stories of rise and decline. Many Pownal farmers sold apples: Baldwin, Red Astrakan, Ben Davis, Nod Head, Snowball, and Wolfe River varieties, among others. The Cotton family was raising grapes, terraced on the hillside of Bradbury Mountain. In an interview in 1975, Austin Cotton recalled the

The homestead of Henry Warren Loring (1857-1937) and Cornelia Warren Plummer Loring (1859-1923), one of Pownal's earliest farms, was located on the extension of Dows Lane (now closed). The homestead burned in the late 1920s or 1930s. Henry was known as one of Pownal's most enterprising and progressive farmers. He married Cornelia in 1885, and in 1887 at age thirty, purchased the 160-acre estate of Cornelia's father, Moses Plummer. He specialized in dairy farming, raising a herd of ten Jersey cows including a registered Jersey bull. Mr. Loring was a participant in the 1908 town centennial celebration. He served in the Maine State Legislature in 1903-1904 and 1907-1908. (For his service to the town, see page 186.)

The Josiah Libby (1847-1912) and Luella Frost Libby (1856-1906) homestead, pictured here in 1890, was located at the corner of the Libby and Goddard (now Poland Range) Roads. The farm burned in 1943. The Libby family owned a hay press and made hay poles.

following: "My father worked in Yarmouth for S. D. Warren. He was [also] a farmer...a big grape farmer. The land was covered with grapes. We'd sell tons of them. They'd come from Portland, drive out on Sundays to pick grapes. There were also apple orchards." Hazel Whitcher in 1973 also remembered the Cotton family farm: "I can remember my father telling us...Cotton had the most marvelous orchards. He had everything: apples, pears, peaches, strawberries and grapes. People used to come from all around."

Maude Marston Tuttle said that her father "had an apple orchard (Ben Davis variety), and when they got to bearing, a packer would come and pack 'em and ship them places." Sadly, just as the Great Depression hit, there was an unprecedented freeze in 1933-34. It delivered a massive blow to growers, as it wiped out two-thirds of the apple trees in Maine. Apples never recovered as a cash crop in Pownal.

Two Pownal women produced another commercial crop: wild blueberries. Over one hundred acres of blueberries were harvested in 1939 on Letha Edwards' farm on the Goddard (now Poland Range) Road. Her fields were raked for Burnham and Morrill Canning Company of Portland. In 1941, Josephine Snow, wife of Harold, used her earnings from teaching to purchase seventeen acres of wild blueberry land on the Milliken Road in North Yarmouth.

The Josiah Libby family on the front door steps of their home (1890). Back row l. to r.: Luella Frost Libby (wife of Josiah), Ada, and Alice. Middle row l. to r.: Josiah Libby, Alberta, Amy, and Almeada. Front row l. to r.: Elmer, Alzada, and Leroy.
Photos and information courtesy Luella Libby Merryman.

Their son, Luther, in a 2007 interview, remembered: "She managed it by herself. Father would mow and cut brush. Eddie Allen would burn it. She sold the berries in quarts, packed in crates, to Hannaford on Market Street in South Portland." By the 1950s, when Luther was in high school, he would drive half-bushel boxes to the Monmouth Canning Company in South Paris every night during harvest season. Luther and his brother Gordon continued to work in these fields well into the 1960s.

The Thomas J. Vosmus blueberry fields were commercially harvested for Clarence Harmon of Portland from 1944 to 1975. Frank A. Knight Jr. owned and raked several blueberry fields in Pownal and nearby towns from the 1950s to the 1970s, typically producing twenty tons of fruit per year. During the same years, Albert Blackstone Sr. also maintained blueberry fields at the corner of the Libby and Goddard Roads.

Better tasting sweet corn was introduced to New England markets in the early 1900s. The Burpee Seed Company continued to improve sweet corn cultivars, introducing the popular Golden Bantam and White Crosby varieties during these years. Advances had been made in the safe canning of agricultural produce, and sweet corn grown for canning quickly outpaced field corn as a cash crop. Local corn shops appeared. There the ears were husked and prepared for canning. Harmon's Corn Shop, located on Route 9 at the Pownal-North Yarmouth line, provided employment for local men, women and children for four to six weeks

The Samuel L. Tryon (1819-1905) and Abby Bedell Tryon homestead, built in 1853 on the Lawrence Road, as it appeared in 1905 when owned by Samuel's son, Samuel Augustus Tryon (1855-1943) and his wife Cora Metcalf Tryon (1860-1945). They had three sons: Earl Augustus (1886-1972), George (1889-1963), and Carl (1892-1984). Carl and George would inherit the family estate in 1943. Samuel Augustus was one of Pownal's most successful farmers and also established a slaughterhouse across the road from his home in 1913. This business, continued by Carl into the 1960s, operated for almost fifty years. At Carl's death in 1984, the property was willed to Earl Haven Tryon (1913-2006), who was Earl Augustus' only child and closest family relative. All buildings on this farm were destroyed in 1994. A significant portion of the land became a part of the Bradbury-Pineland Corridor Protection Project in 2004.

in late summer. The prepared corn was shipped from corn shops to canneries, and by the 1930s plants in Portland, Yarmouth, Lisbon, Gray and Monmouth were preserving sweet corn, string beans, squash, and blueberries.

Local farmers, however, didn't completely switch to sweet corn. They continued to grow some field corn, which they chopped (ears, leaves, and stalks) and "blew" into silos. Silos had been introduced prior to 1930. They were usually tall round structures of wood or concrete in which fodder was converted through anaerobic acid fermentation into silage, a succulent feed for livestock.

Hay, as fodder for cattle and horses, was an early cash crop. Demand reached its peak during World War I, when the military was using large numbers of horses both at home and abroad. During an interview in 1976, Joe Pervier recalled, "They would take [the horses] into Portland and load them on the ships to ship them across. And, of course, they had to ship the feed with them, the hay. Hay was quite a commodity, you know what I mean. [They] did use a lot of hay." After the war, the market for hay grown in Pownal consisted of local dairy farms.

(continued on page 76)

Canned vegetables from 1897 Sears Roebuck Catalogue (1993 republished edition).

Haying in the 1920s at the Lauren Tuttle Sr. (1888-1958) and Jesse Foster Tuttle (1908-1983) homestead at the current 711 Hodsdon Road. In addition to farming, Lauren served as superintendent of schools for fifteen years, as selectman for eighteen years, and as a representative in the Maine State Legislature for two terms. (For more on his public service, see page 187.)

Corn Shop Workers, September 1935

Harmon's Corn Shop, located on Route 9 at the Pownal-North Yarmouth town line provided seasonal employment for area men, women, and children. The H. L. Forhan Canning Company was taxed for the property. In her book, The Remarkable Couple, Josephine Pervier Allen wrote, "The ears of corn were hauled in by the truckload. The corn was husked and cut from the cob and stored in five gallon cans... Then it was shipped to the factory for canning. Mom (Emma Loring Pervier) worked there cutting corn from the cob... with a moving blade. The ear had to be held up to the blade and cut corn fell into a container. One had to be careful to keep from being cut. The season lasted only a few weeks." All workers had to cover their hair.

Corn Shop Workers, as identified by Marion Knight Reed: 1. Alice Kimball (Morrill); 2. Belle Fuller; 3. Charles Dunn, foreman; 4. Clarence Harmon, owner; 5. either Gertrude York or Gladys Thurber; 6. Richard Loring; 7. Emma Loring Pervier; 8. Clara Small; 9. Eva Knight with dog; 10. Irene Blair; 11. Fred Upton; 12. Fred Royal. All others unidentified.

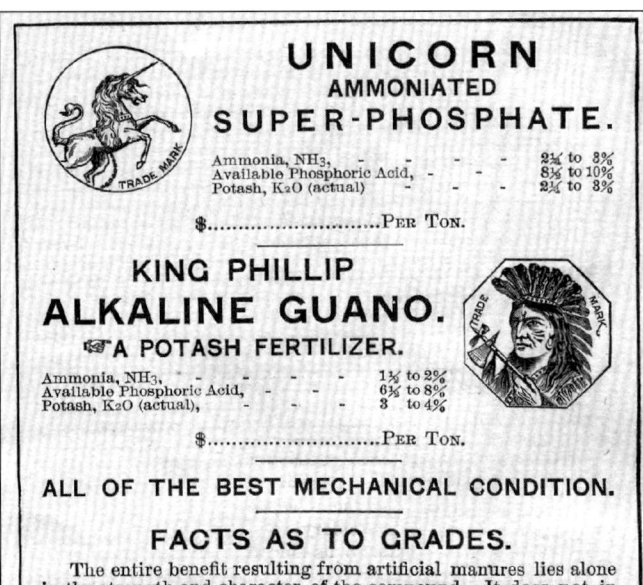

Clark's Cove Fertilizers of New Bedford, Massachusetts advertised three guano-based fertilizers for sale, "adapted to all soils and crops." This product, as well as grain, could be purchased locally at Henry Loring's farm in the early 1900s.

Little attention had been paid to fertilizing hay fields beyond the occasional application of farm manure. Consequently, many of the fields were quite simply "worn out." Too few farmers heeded the advice of the Maine Board of Agriculture which for years had been encouraging farmers to begin upgrading their depleted soils. The board of agriculture was joined by the Maine Farm Bureau Federation and the national Grange in advocating increased use of fertilizers.

On his 1907 promotional calendar, Albion K. P. Dresser of West Pownal advertised "Pacific Guano Fertilizers, Unexcelled in Quality." In the 1920 Maine Register, Emery W. Parker of Pownal was listed as a fertilizer dealer. Guano, which is the composted droppings of sea birds or bats, was shipped from Peruvian islands, and its sale in Pownal increased as its benefits were recognized.

From 1900 through 1965 poultry raising and egg production played a role in Pownal farming. Rhode Island Reds and Plymouth Rocks were preferred breeds, because of their brown eggs. Almost all farms raised chickens for home use and to sell around town. But some also undertook commercial production. Early 1900s tax records indicate that fifty-five local farmers had flocks of birds, some as large as 250. Poultry

North Yarmouth farmer John Britt Jr. is pictured here in the early 1900s using his insecticide sprayer, possibly to treat his potato crop. Mellen Tryon, in his 1900 diary, tells of spraying Paris Green, an arsenic-copper insecticide, on his potatoes during the growing season. Photo: North Yarmouth Historical Society, 2006.

was sold as meat, market eggs, hatching eggs, and day-old chicks. The 1920 Maine Register indicates that Alroy Noyes and Robert Smith were selling poultry and eggs commercially. Heinz Koenig was taxed for his chicken farm in 1934. After World War II, tax records indicate that there were many flocks of over fifty broilers in Pownal. New breeding techniques and disease controls made larger operations possible. In 1959 Frank Haney, who farmed on the Hallowell Road, was taxed for over 8,000 broilers, most of which he sold to Lipman Poultry in Augusta. However, eventually northern New England found itself unable to compete with the warmer states to the south, and by 1965, large-scale poultry operations had disappeared from Pownal.

Larger meat animals were raised for both home consumption and market. The 1936 Maine Register lists Christopher C. Sawyer and Alvirdo H. Best as meat dealers. Some farmers specialized in one animal. Shirley Thurber Verrill remembered, "In the 1930s Mr. Sawyer, who lived in Bill Knight's house, had a meat wagon and delivered meat regularly to area houses." Writing in his journal in 1922, Samuel Augustus Tryon said that Eliab Latham, who operated the farm now known as the Bradbury farm, also sold meat to markets in Portland and Boston.

For butchering services, from 1913 through the 1960s, most Pownal farmers called on Carl Tryon. Carl, who was living with his father

"Orchard Crest Farm 1920" was owned by George Frederick "Fred" Loring (1860-1917) and Olive Marston Loring (1861-1932). It was one of Pownal's most successful early farms. The barn and the square two-story outbuilding were built in the 1880s. This Greek Revival style house is located at the current 249 Hallowell Road. Josephine Pervier Allen wrote in her book, The Remarkable Couple, "Grandfather Loring had dairy cattle, pigs and hens... He did a lot of gardening... cared for large apple orchards raising Baldwin, Nodhead, and Wolfe River varieties... traveled with his horse and wagon to Portland at least once a week to market his goods. The trip started wee hours in the morning and didn't end until the dark hours of evening. Grandfather was progressive for his time... had mechanized equipment (which was located in the two story building thought to be the silo) for separating milk...gas engine with connecting belts...cream was churned into butter... skim milk made cottage cheese but most of it went to the pigs."

Samuel Augustus, operated a slaughterhouse across the road from the Tryon farm on the Lawrence road. He charged for "killing" or for "killing & cutting." In 1923 hogs cost seventy-five cents or one dollar, depending, and cows and calves were seventy-five cents or three dollars. An extra charge of fifty cents was added for home delivery. One of Carl's prominent customers was the State School for the Feebleminded located in New Gloucester (later renamed Pineland State Hospital and Training Center). Hides were sold to a tannery in Lewiston.

Many farms raised pigs, which were usually slaughtered in the late fall. The meat and by-products lasted the family through the winter. Since most households had no electricity until the 1940s, pork was often smoked. Etta Marston Starling remembered in a 1973 interview, "Father was a farmer. raised white Chester hogs. They were chunky and filled out good... made good hams. Raised about half dozen... Would sell them when small at six dollars apiece. Kept what we wanted and sold the rest in the fall and winter." Albert Blackstone Jr. remembered in a 2006 interview, "My father [store owner Albert Sr.] raised 200 to 300 pigs at his farm on the Elmwood road during the mid-1960s." As a teenager, Albert Jr. made a name for himself in 4-H circles by winning a trip to Chicago in a hog raising contest. Percy Wentworth raised pigs at his farm on

Harvest Time

I think of what we used to do
When it was Harvest Time.
So, I'll try to tell you just some of it
As I complete this rhyme!
Such a busy time for us
To gather the Harvest in
To place the many vegetables
In their own special bin!
Also, things that wouldn't keep
We had to always can,
Mincemeat and pickles were put up
Besides a lot of jam!
The oats were thrashed of course
The straw used in the barn
For animals' fresh bedding
To keep them safe from harm!
We had juicy apples
We picked all that we could
Cider made from some of them
Tasted like it should!
The dry beans kept for winter
Was brought in last of all
We could not do without them
For baking in the fall
The wood was sawed in pieces
To fit the stoves just right
For soon the parlor stove
Would be going day and night!
Many jobs had to be done
Before we felt we'd win
Then it made us very happy
When our "Harvest" was all in!

"Harvest Time", a poem by Minnie Cates, was published in Farmer's Wife *c.1930 and* Portland Press Herald, Clearing House, *September 13, 1994. Used with permission of her daughter, Virginia Cates Davis.*

Henry Allen is pictured at the Allen-Snow farm at the current 180 Leighton Road in 1920 with his ox team. Descendant of Job Allen, an original settler, Henry was a third generation dairy farmer. In 1942, the farm was willed to Harold "Bill" Snow and Josephine Bacon Snow. It is currently owned by fifth generation Luther and Evelyn Snow.

The Cumberland County Farm Bureau met at Mallett Hall on November 7, 1935.

the Lawrence road through the 1970s. Today, the one remaining operation belongs to Howard Cushman on the Hallowell Road, where he raises and sells piglets and meat locally.

Farmers who specialized in raising cattle for veal and beef found a ready market during and following both world wars. Until more recently, the handling of meat on a Pownal farm without electricity was a challenge, usually met through smoking or cooling with locally cut ice. Josephine Pervier Allen described a tempting solution to the problem in her book: "One of the most memorable events of the thirties was the `Hamburg Parties.' These involved the Vosmus family along with ours. When an animal was slaughtered by either family, there was an abundance of meat. We did not have freezers to store the meat, so we ate. We usually had the party at Aunt Abbie's [Tom and Abbie Vosmus' home on the Merrill Road] whether it was their meat or ours. This made for a great evening. We had a full tummy plus fun playing games and listening to stories."

William "Bill" Whitcher, upon returning from Navy service in World War II, resumed farming at the family place, called Branch Brook Farm, on the Beech Hill (now Tuttle) Road. But he and his wife Barbara soon abandoned the dairy operations of his father, Algernon, and uncle, Milton. They turned to raising Charolais cattle, a breed from France that had attained international importance following the war.

Charolais are known for their large frame and choice meat. Today Deborah Whitcher Cheney continues to raise these animals on the same site.

Albert Blackstone Jr. remembered, "After the war [World War II], meat was hard to come by. We owned twenty-five to thirty head of cattle, both beef and milk. My father would take his beef cattle and some veal calves to Carl Tryon for butchering at the old Perry place [next to the school on the Elmwood road]. He'd also buy cattle to slaughter. The meat was sold in the store along with the milk and cream. The excess was fed to the pigs."

In 1982, Paul Randall and his wife Sandie moved back to the farm that Linwood Randall had started in 1946 with fifteen milking cows.

Threshing machine typical of those used in Pownal in the early twentieth century.

Four years later they switched to raising cattle for meat. Today they have Black Angus and Black Baldies (an Angus-Hereford mix) in a herd numbering over one hundred. They sell feeder calves as "natural beef" (no hormones or antibiotics) twice a year at auction nationwide through the Maine Beef Producers Association. Theirs is one of the area's largest beef herds.

Currently, there are two other farms raising cattle commercially in Pownal. Stephen Litchfield raises a large herd of Herefords at his farm on the Brown Road. The Litchfields have worked this farm for five generations. Upon Steve's return from Vietnam, he and his father, Victor Litchfield Jr., also switched from primarily dairy to beef. E. Leonard "Lennie" Allen, the fourth generation to work his farm on the Hallowell Road, also raises beef cattle. He markets primarily through the Maine Beef Producers Association. Several others, including Dennis Blaisdell, Howard Cushman, and Kathleen Harlow, raise a small number of beef cattle. Their income derives from local sales.

Dairy farming was practiced during most of the last one hundred years, whether as a specialty or as part of other operations. During the early 1900s, many Pownal producers thrived. Farmers milked small herds of six to ten (Guernsey, Holstein, and Jersey were favorites), meeting the local demands by peddling milk and dairy products. By 1924, refrigerated railroad cars had become common, allowing milk to be shipped to Portland processors. It became an evening ritual for farmers to haul

(continued on page 82)

Albert Blackstone Sr., center store owner and farmer, is pictured here in front of his home on the present 484 Elmwood Road in 1940. Locally known as the Reverend Perez Chapin homestead, this Federal style, two-and-a-half story house was built in 1811 for Reverend Chapin, the first minister of the newly-established First Parish Congregational Church. The Blackstone family raised dairy and beef cattle and pigs. Meat and dairy products were sold at their country store. Teams of horses and oxen were kept to work the fields and woods. The Blackstones grew potatoes, oats and corn for animal feed, and blueberries, most of which were sold at the store.

Josephine Bacon Snow managed blueberry fields commercially from 1941 to 1960. Here she winnows blueberries in 1949 with her son, Luther (right), and his friend, Kenneth Tryon.

One of the most entertaining events at the Cumberland County Fair is the pig scramble. Pictured here in 1958 are Paul Randall (left, who won the pig) and his brother, Stephen. (Looking Back, File photo, Portland Press Herald, Sept. 28, 2005.)

Dairy cattle graze at the farm of Harold "Bill" and Josephine Snow at the current 180 Leighton Road in 1959.

their full milk cans to the station in West Pownal or the Walnut Hill station in North Yarmouth. As Josephine Pervier Allen remembered, "Dairy farming had changed, there was no more peddling of dairy products in Portland. The whole milk was sold to Old Tavern Farm Dairy in Portland. sent by train. Every evening the milk cans were taken from the tub of ice water and loaded into the back of the car and were taken to the Walnut Hill Station to be shipped to Portland. Dad [Joseph Pervier] also picked up Grandpa [William] Pervier's milk. A dairy farming family never got the chance to go very far away from home. Those cows had to be milked every morning and night." She continued, "When Dad was kept away for many hours during a snowstorm [driving the town snowplow], a neighbor was asked to milk the cows. Emma [Joe's wife] did not like to rely on someone's generosity. She learned to milk. It was not long before she was involved in most of the outside duties of the farm."

Most of the dairy barns in existence in the 1920s and 1930s had been built during the previous century, and much of the lore of dairy farming had been passed on from that time as well. But expert advice was beginning to affect dairy farming. The same national and state organizations that had advised increased fertilization, also urged dairy farmers to adopt more scientific methods. And the Grange helped spread the word through local meetings and programs designed to inform the entire family. Among other things, farmers were told that they could increase production and profits if

Menchen barn restoration. The aging barn at the farm of Edward and Edna Menchen at the current 359 Hodsdon Road had the entire foundation and sills replaced in 1975.

they took advantage of new breeding techniques, increased the size of their dairy herds, made and used more silage, and managed the farm more efficiently.

Throughout the 1940s and 1950s, many smaller farms ceased their dairy operations. Those that remained had begun to modernize. These were run by farmers whose names are still familiar today: Laurence Snow, Harold "Bill" Snow, Linwood Randall, Joseph Pervier, Noyes Mitchell, Victor Litchfield (Sr. and Jr.), Roy Tufts, Walter Rossbach, Walter Hustus and Robert Forbes. Noyes Mitchell was also the local distributor of feed grain obtained from a Freeport store managed by George Hunter of Durham. Another source of grain was the store at Dunns Corner in North Yarmouth owned by Charles Heywood.

Modernization took many forms. During the 1950s farms became completely electrified, and used milking machines, refrigerated bulk tanks, and large freezing units. Herd sizes grew to thirty or forty, and better breeding programs led farmers to concentrate on one breed. The farms operated with more power equipment such as tractors, trucks, and conveyors. Tank trucks transported milk daily to local dairies such as Old Tavern Farm and Oakhurst Farm.

Rural electrification was virtually complete by the 1950s, and this was a true turning point, particularly for dairy farmers. It might surprise us of the twenty-first century to realize how important ice once was in farm operations. Prior to the 1950s dairy farmers relied on ice cut from local rivers and ponds for cooling and preservation. An ice-cooled milk room, an ice chest in the kitchen, and an icehouse located out by the barn were essential.

Shirley Thurber Verrill related in an interview in 2006: "Dairy farmers relied on ice cut from local rivers for cooling their milk and other dairy products. They would cut ice on the rivers in winter and store it in icehouses packed in sawdust. They would cut it on Chandler River and had a bigger operation at Runaround Pond. The men would have an auger and drill into the ice and insert an ice saw, similar to a crosscut saw, and saw the ice into cakes. A team of horses with a low sled would haul it home. My mother made ice cream on the Fourth of July and we purchased a cake of ice from a neighbor. Many homes had ice boxes so ice was an important part of living." In her 1929 diary, Mrs. Elizabeth (Lizzie) Palmer noted that the men were hauling ice on a pleasant day in February. One hundred twenty-two cakes were hauled, she wrote, weighing 194 pounds each.

Milk cans used by three generations of dairy farmers displayed at the current Luther and Evelyn Snow farm. L. to r.: cans used by Harold "Bill" Snow, Henry Allen, and Greenfield T. Allen.

Pictured here in 1979 are the children of Gerald and Joan Rolfe, all 4-H Sheep Club members. L. to r.: Jonathan and Thomas with their Suffolk sheep, and Christopher and Katherine with Dorsets. They are wearing wool sweaters knit by their mother, Joan, who was a leader of the 4-H group.

As the 1970s and 1980s unfolded, it was obvious that forces in the larger U.S. economy, such as transportation costs and economies of scale, were making commercial agriculture all but impossible in places like Pownal. Many once-open fields were filling in with weedy growth and trees. Aging barns and outbuildings were falling into disrepair. Limited farming persisted as a new generation came of age, most of whom had worked alongside their parents. Some built new homes on family land, while maintaining the farm tradition and haying the fields. Their limited numbers, however, presaged the approaching end of farming in Pownal.

The 1980s did bring new entrants into limited-scale farming. Many in-migrants came with a desire to restore or build barns, often spurred by a somewhat romantic notion of traditional farming. They planted large gardens and many fruit trees, and began raising sheep, chickens, ducks, and rabbits. In some instances these activities continue as pleasant pastimes that can produce some income. But this is hardly farming as Pownal once knew it.

Today, although no dairy operations susrvive, Pownal has four reasonably large commercial cattle farms. There are several families raising animals such as sheep, goats, chickens, and turkeys for market, and a few keep bees for honey and its by-products. There are alpacas and llamas being raised as a hobby and for wool. Maintaining horses for pleasure and show is on the rise. As in days gone by, large vegetable and flower gardens can be found all over Pownal, and canning and preserving continue in local kitchens. However, farming as a singular lifestyle has disappeared.

William Ginn and June LaCombe framed their barn in one day in 1979 by organizing an old fashioned barn raising. The Ginns have raised sheep and currently keep horses at Hawk Ridge Farm on the Minot Road.

Walter "Wally" and Jill Rossbach purchased Snowfields Dairy Farm on Lawrence Road from Laurence and Clara Snow in 1966. Wally operated the farm until 1987, when he sold the land to David and Patsy O'Brien. Wally and second wife Elise, whom he married in 1974, then retired to live in Tennessee. Wally is pictured here in 1986 with a double-decker load of hay, on his way to feed his herd. Photo by Bonnie Scott.

David and Patsy O'Brien purchased the property on the Lawrence Road known as Snowfields Dairy Farm from Walter and Elise Rossbach in 1987. They built a new home, restored the original homestead that had been seriously burned in a 1975 fire, and created a riding facility used for "eventing" competitions. Eventing, an Olympic sport since 1912, tests riders and their horses in three events: dressage, cross country, and show jumping. Under the auspices of the United States Eventing Association and the Maine Combined Training Association, Snowfields horse trials have been held every August since 1992. The level of competition is high, as riders and horses vie to represent the United States at the Olympic Games.

The Kivela family of 22 Leighton Road moved to Pownal to enjoy its rural lifestyle. In 2004, they added a barn and began raising llamas to give their son Owen the experience of caring for farm animals. They also use the llamas as pack animals for family hiking trips. L. to r.: Owen, llamas Cadet and Time Out, Richard, and Carrie.

Paul Randall (left) and his father Linwood, together with Paul's wife Sandie, raise one of the largest herds of beef cattle in the area on their farm at 132 Hallowell Road.

Venture Farm, 400 Hodsdon Road, has been owned and operated by Michael and Virginia "Ginger" Albert since 1994. Head instructor Ginger has thirty years of professional horse training experience. She has shown and trained at all levels. Private and semi-private riding lessons are offered year-round to local and out of state students. The Alberts' forty-eight acre farm has a fully insulated barn, indoor and outdoor riding arenas, board-fenced paddocks, and a heated tack room with viewing area. The owners emphasize that, "in order to develop into confident thinking riders, individuals need a solid foundation with knowledge of fundamentals, flatwork, horse care, and safety."

Holly Morrison and Susan Mack of 44 Leighton Road are establishing a farm in the Scottish tradition. Holly is pictured here with Scottish Highland cows, a thousand-year-old, low maintenance, hearty breed. The cattle and an old English breed of pastured pigs are both raised for meat. A flock of Old English Game Bantam chickens provides eggs and insect control. Holly and Sue are active in the St. Andrews Society, Sue serving as president in 2008. Holly serves as chaplain and teaches Gaelic language and songs. Sue, a well-known musician, performs with, and teaches the bagpipes.

Drew and Melissa Victory, 78 Leighton Road, moved to Pownal with their daughters in 2004. They were seeking a place with a rural lifestyle where they could raise their five Icelandic horses, breed Boxer dogs, and be close to their daughters' school. L.to r.: Melissa and daughters Brynne, Katyja, and Freyja (riding Lolka).

Gregory "Greg" and Nicole Bowman Carter of Upper Farm Alpacas and Wood Products, 362 Allen Road, raise alpacas for breeding stock and for fleece that is spun into locally-sold yarn. Greg is pictured here holding Triton, a male, while Nicole holds Ella Mae, a female, both born in the summer of 2007. The Carters' herd numbers over twenty.

Farm Profiles through the Century

The Elmer and Bertha Edwards Libby Farm
Gone but Fondly Remembered

The Elmer F. and Bertha Edwards Libby homestead on the Upper Minot Road, c. 1915.

Elmer Libby (1886-1966) and Bertha Edwards Libby (1886-1961) married in 1909 and moved into the farm known as the Levi Knight Jr. homestead, built around 1826 on the Upper Minot Road. Granddaughter Virginia Libby Sanborn remembered in an interview in 2007: "My grandfather was a dairy farmer who raised a mixed breed of Holstein cows. He transported the milk to the railroad in West Pownal where it was shipped to a Portland dairy. The farm was never electrified. Ice was cut on the Chandler River and packed in sawdust in the icehouse in the shed. They also had an icebox in the kitchen. Grandma made butter and cheese at the farm that was stored in the cold room. My father, Kenneth, would help Grandpa cut wood for heating and cooking out back each winter, probably ten cord or more. They did have two Round Oak parlor stoves that were used for special occasions. Upstairs in the ell, grandpa made furniture and did wood carving. For cash, from 1910 through the 1920s, Grandpa would close the farm after the fall harvest was 'put by' and would take the whole family to Denmark [Maine] where he would

Elmer and Bertha Libby in 1915 with son Kenneth (1915-1988) and daughter Mertie [Bowden](1910-2000).

lumber in the woods for the winter. Later, he also worked with Philip Tryon for the state highway department.

"In the summer, they had huge gardens, raising corn, beans, and tomatoes, which would be canned. The root cellar was full of cabbages, turnips, beets, carrots, squash and potatoes. Blueberry fields across the road, raspberries, cranberries and a huge rhubarb plant supplied the family with the ingredients for pies, cakes, jams and jellies. They loved flowers and grew rows and rows of gladiolas and sweet peas. My grandmother was a teacher and was also a professional dressmaker who had worked in a shop in Auburn. She made beautiful fancy clothes but she also made most of our clothes (no patterns) including our snowsuits from second-hand wool coats, and dance costumes with ruffles out of grain bags. She also played the pump organ. Her extra farm income came from clerking at Merton Larrabee's General Store in North Pownal."

The farm was sold following Elmer's death in 1966. The house, barn, and outbuildings are no longer standing.

Bertha and Kenneth in 1926.

In a 1925 photo captioned "Ain't We Got Fun," ten-year-old Ken Libby cuts hay on the family farm. Eighteen years later a photo shows Ken on his father's 1931 John Deere tractor, holding Janet and Joyce, twin daughters of his sister Mertie Bowden. His father Elmer holds a hand cultivator.

Everett and Minnie Turcotte Cates, Farmers and Poet

Cates "Old Homestead Farm" in 1931. Everett and Minnie Turcotte Cates.

From 1931 to 1940, Everett Cates (1900-1968) and Minnie Turcotte Cates (1907-2002) farmed at this early homestead, currently located at 259 Libby Road. In an interview in 2006, Virginia Cates Davis remembered: "Our farm was primarily a dairy farm but we had every animal there was… chickens, geese, goats, horses, and cows… a whole barn-full. Father had a tractor. Used his horses a lot when he was haying. We had a big hay rack in the barn and the hay fork (which is still in the barn) would come down and the horses would haul it out until it went up. We also had pigs.

"In the summertime, father went to the public market in Portland on Federal Street. Sold butter, eggs, dressed chickens, and vegetables from the garden. We had an ice box in the kitchen and an ice house by the barn where the meat and butter were packed in ice. We never had electricity at the farm. Had kerosene lamps and an outhouse."

Virginia, daughter of Everett and Minnie Cates with her pet chicken, Chickie.

Minnie Cates was a well-known poet

Minnie wrote for the Farm Bureau News *in the 1930s. Her poetry was also published in the* Portland Press Herald, Clearing House *in 1986 and in* The Shopping Notes *piece entitled, "It's a Minnie–Minnie World – a Nostalgic Look at the Past."*

"OUR FARMHOUSE KITCHEN"

The kitchen was heart of our home
A bright and cheerful one
It also had three windows
That let in lots of sun!

It had a lot of cupboards
With space for everything
And a great big iron sink
That just made my heart sing!

A big cast iron stove
That had a brilliant sheen
Gave us warmth in winter
And never acted mean!

It baked our bread, cakes and pies
Our beans and casseroles
And all sorts of muffins, too
Besides the light raised rolls.

It had a friendly atmosphere
A pleasant place to work
Made one eager at their tasks
So did not want to shirk!

Besides one of our windows
Was a comfy Morris chair
My mending basket was close by
I used it sitting there.

That room was made for living
And was the reason why
People like to sit there
When ever they stopped by!

Now, I have a kitchenette
For I'm alone you see
But, I'll remember always
What the other meant to me!

By Minnie Cates

WOMEN ON THE FARM

On the farm, a woman has
 A place that's hard to fill,
Her duties call her everywhere,
 Her feet are never still.

Her household needs attention
 So she stops to clean and sweep,
Because she wants her home to be
 A place that's always neat.

She has washing to be done,
 She irons most things too,
Clothing has some tears and holes,
 Which means mending she must do.

Cooking takes up part her time,
 Her folks must have their meals.
The time she spends means nothing
 When she hears delighted squeals.

She tends the children's wants
 With an ever watchful eye,
And tucks them safely into bed,
 When eventide is nigh.

No, it matters not to her
 How much she scrubs and bakes,
Because she knows to them
 She has just what it takes.

To be a help to all of them,
 She is wife and kindly Mother,
She keeps them all so happy
 That to them there is no other.

She keeps a cheerful outlook
 As the days go winging by,
Does her best and is contented
 Living under country sky.

MINNIE E. CATES,
Member Pownal Farm Bureau.

Three Snow Generations Farm on Lawrence Road

Jonathan A. and Lydia "Nellie" Lyon Snow's homestead on the Lawrence Road, pictured here about 1890.

Jonathan A. Snow (1842-1920) and Lydia "Nellie" Lyon Snow (1859-1938) purchased the homestead pictured above in 1880 and established a dairy farm with a herd of eight to ten cows. They also raised prize-winning potatoes, beans and squash. With its flock of poultry and large family garden, their farm was described as one of the most practical and successful, with neat and tidy buildings that bespoke their thrift. Jonathan was a member of the Grange, and he served as selectman in 1899 and as town treasurer from 1890 to 1893. The couple's only child Claude Snow (1888-1974) and his wife Villa Fogg Snow (1892-1985) acquired the farm upon the death of Jonathan in 1920.

Although Claude and Villa had one cow, sold butter, and raised potatoes and squash for markets in Portland, farming was never their primary source of income. Claude did not enjoy farming. He preferred working with figures in a position at Philip Knight's sawmill and serving as selectman for six years and town clerk from 1930 to 1971. Villa, a teacher in Pownal's one-room schools from 1912 until her marriage in 1915, began clerking for the postal service in West Pownal in 1939. She was named post master in 1951, a position she held until 1963. Claude and Villa had three children, Laurence, Edna, and Carleton. Laurence would acquire the family farm.

Third generation farmers, Laurence Snow (1915-1995) and Clara Keith Snow (1920–) took over the farm in 1942 and later changed its name from "Willow Farm" to "Snowfields Farm." More substantial changes were to come, driven by the availability of electric power and an ill-fated son's passion for farming.

Laurence and Clara had three sons: Keith, Terry and Duane. All worked on the farm during their youth, but it was the eldest, Keith, who set his sights on becoming a thoroughly modern dairyman. Keith coupled his 4-H experience with techniques he learned at the University of Maine. It was his knowledge and energy that encouraged his father to modernize old practices. The entire operation was electrified. The herd grew to forty, and breeding became central. A new forage crop, alfalfa, was planted, and this, along with corn, provided nutritious silage from a new silo. A first-of-its-kind (in Maine) "loose-housing" barn was built. In 1958, Arthur Hawkins wrote in the "Lifestyles" section of the *Sunday Telegram*, "By working together, the Snows have conceded to the ways of progress. Their farm is the largest and most modern in Pownal."

Electrification also was a boon for Clara. Her daily chores became easier as she cooked and baked for family, friends, and work crews. Her extensive food preservation was now more easily accomplished. Meanwhile, she sewed clothing and did handwork for the family. She led the Bradbury Mountain Girls 4-H group, was a member of the Grange and Farm Bureau, and was active in the North Pownal Methodist church.

Laurence W. and Clara Keith Snow on their fiftieth wedding anniversary, June 1989.

By 1964, the operation of Snowfields Farm had grown so large that consideration was given to hiring additional help. However in the fall of that year, tragedy struck when Keith was killed in a farm accident. The family struggled with his loss, and no other relative was qualified or physically able to manage the growing business. With much regret, the farm was sold to Walter and Jill Rossbach in 1966.

Laurence lived thirty years beyond his son's death. His activities and contributions were many. In addition to farming, Laurence worked for the postal service and for the North Yarmouth Mutual Fire Insurance Company. He was a member of both the Granite Grange and the Farm Bureau, and remained active in the North Pownal Methodist church. Laurence remained faithful to the Pownal fire department. He is remembered for serving several terms as selectman, as moderator of town meetings, as one of the original framers of the zoning ordinance, as a member of the planning board, and as a director of the SAD 62 school board (see page 192).

Keith E. Snow (1940-1964), first son of Laurence and Clara Snow, was a graduate of Greely Institute. He is pictured here in 1958, his senior year. He was active in sports, played Junior League baseball, and was an independent member of the 4-H and tractor workshop. He graduated from the University of Maine College of Agriculture where he was director of the Dairy Herd Improvement Association and was recognized as an outstanding young farmer of the year. Keith was a volunteer fireman and a member of the North Pownal United Methodist church. He was the fourth generation to operate Snowfields Farm, until a tragic accident took his life. Photo by Sayward, Maine Sunday Telegram, Sept. 14, 1958.

The Tryon Farm, Home to Seven Generations

Original settler Simeon Tryon built this brick house, now 539 Lawrence Road, in 1806. It is pictured here in the 1970s with Philip on a ladder clearing snow from the roof. The ell and out buildings are no longer standing. Photo by Christopher Ayers.

In 1800, Simeon Tryon (1778-1844) purchased and began developing land in Pownal that would become a family farm for generations. Two years later he married Mercy Cook (1780-1825). The fascinating story of their life is told in *Pownal, A Rural Maine History*. Of Simeon's nineteen children, ten by Mercy and nine by his second wife Jane Cook (1800-1888), it was Andrew Jackson "A.J." (1827-1906) who would inherit the property. A. J. and his wife Lucinda Corliss Tryon (1832-1916) brought this well-established and productive farm into the twentieth century. By all accounts, he was a superior farmer who found time to be active in town affairs and in the Methodist church. He was well known for his carpentry and shoemaking.

The now very prosperous farm deserved to be inherited by someone who would continue to make it flourish. And such did appear in the persons of Mellen Tryon (1867-1941) and his wife Lillian Allen Tryon (1869-1956). Mellen was one of the eight children of A. J. and Lucinda.

Mellen and Lillian continued the family's tradition of raising and marketing farm products, maintaining equipment and buildings, and meeting the challenges of a self-sufficient life without electricity. Mellen kept a diary in which he noted farming activities and weekly entries about going to Grange, Redmen, and Golden Cross meetings, attending church, and transporting Lillian to Ladies Aid meetings. Mellen served as town clerk from 1915 to 1930, and intermittently as selectman for six years. He served in the state legislature from 1913 to 1914. He was employed by the legislature as messenger and sergeant-at-arms from 1920 to 1938 (see page 185).

Mellen and Lillian Allen Tryon, 1897.

Mellen and Lillian had three children, of which the eldest, Philip (1898-1983), and his wife Arleen Hodgdon Tryon (1906-1994) inherited the farm. In their early years together Philip and Arleen lived on farm income exclusively. They sold dairy products, hayed the fields, and kept cows and oxen. Eventually it became necessary to seek outside employment. Philip found work at Knight's sawmill and with the state highway department. Arleen returned to Pownal's one-room schools, devoting forty-one years to teaching. Philip served intermittently as selectman for fourteen years between 1928 and 1961. He also acted as moderator of many town meetings (see page 189).

Farming as a way of life on Tryon land effectively ended in the 1950s. Of Philip and Arleen's two children, it was Kenneth (1935-1994) and his wife Connie Enos Tryon who inherited the property. The farm was no longer active, but the brick house, built so long ago by Simeon, continued to be the home of the fifth generation. Today, Connie, her son Andrew, his wife Melissa, and their children reside there. These two children, Anna and Sarah, are the seventh generation of Tryons to live on this land.

Philip and Arleen Hodgdon Tryon with daughter Phyllis Arleen, 1930.

In 2004, Connie Tryon (wife of Kenneth) and Haven Tryon (nephew of Carl) transferred a large parcel of Tryon land to the Bradbury-Pineland Corridor Protection Project, an initiative of the Pownal Land Trust with help from Land For Maine's Future and the State of Maine. In recognition of this gift, a town celebration, called "Two Hundred Years of Giving," was held at the site.

"Two Hundred Years of Giving," a celebration honoring the Tryon Family. To the left of monument, l. to r.: Arleen Rackliffe, Philip Tryon, Tammylee Tryon, Seth Rackliffe, Llacey Tryon, Mary Rackliffe, Joseph Rackliffe, Caleb Rackliffe (holding Elisha Rackliffe). Behind monument: Isaac Rackliffe. To the right of monument, front row l. to r.: Connie Tryon (benefactor), Jeanne Tryon Rackliffe, Anna Tryon, Andrew Tryon; back row l. to r.: Millard Rackliffe, Melinda Rackliffe, Greg Rackliffe, Melissa Tryon.

Branch Brook Farm
A Working Cattle Farm Through Three Generations

Algernon and his son Danny, 1926.

Algernon Whitcher (1893-1963) and brother Milton (1885-1944) farmed on the Tuttle Road beginning in the 1920s. Even after Milton's death, Algernon and wife Hazel Libby Whitcher (1892-1983) continued the operation until Algernon's death in 1963. They raised dairy cattle, selling milk to Hood Dairy. Free-range broiler chickens went to local markets along with pigs not needed for family consumption. Fields of wheat, oats, and silage corn provided animal feed. Algernon and Hazel had four children: Daniel (who lost his life in World War II), Margaret, William, and Josephine. Josephine Whitcher Goss remembered in 2006 that, even though the farm was one of the first to get electricity, her father continued to cut ice by the Tuttle Bridge on the nearby east branch of the Royal River. Tending the farm was a full-time family occupation. Meat and vegetables were preserved for winter use. Beans and sweet corn were sold to a local cannery. Algernon and Milton supplemented their income by selling cordwood, Christmas trees, and holiday wreaths to markets as far away as Boston.

From the second generation, William (1930-2001) returned home to help his father farm, after serving in the Navy in World War II. Unlike his father and uncle, William and wife Barbara raised Charolais beef cattle. Later, William raised Standardbred race horses, and according to his obituary in *The Portland Press Herald* of April 26, 2001, "was most proud of Branchbrook Mystic, a harness racer who tore around tracks throughout the North East and won 30 of 38 career races, earning more that $81,000 in 2000."

In the third generation, Deborah Whitcher Cheney, daughter of William and Barbara, continues the family business today, raising a large herd of Charolais beef cattle on the farm once owned by her grandparents.

Algernon and Danny (one and a half years old) dig potatoes, 1926.

Algernon and Hazel Libby Whitcher c. 1950.

Second generation, William Whitcher exercises trotter Branchbrook Mystic in a photo captioned, "First Day at the Track — May 28, 1997."

Third generation cattle farmer Deborah Whitcher Cheney raises Charolais cattle on the family farm on the Tuttle Road. Charolais are a medium- to large-framed breed with a very deep and broad body. White-to-cream with a pink muzzle and pale hooves, they yield excellent beef.

Five Generations Farm at the Allen-Snow Homestead

The Allen-Snow homestead in 1942 when owned by Harold and Josephine Bacon Snow. The large barn was destroyed by a storm in 1960.

The Allen-Snow farmhouse, 180 Leighton Road, dates from 1820 when it was built by original settler Job Allen Jr. (1800-1890) and Sarah Strickland Allen (1807-1844). The original barn, built in stages, endured until 1960 when it blew down in a windstorm. It was not replaced. Over its long lifetime it housed dairy cows, beef cattle, horses, oxen, pigs, and innumerable tons of hay. The large ell, still standing, provided shelter for farm equipment, carriages, and wagons. Its second level provided storage for grain, primarily oats. Several hen houses stood beside the farmhouse. Ice was cut from the nearby river each winter and stored in the ice house behind the barn.

In the late 1800s, ownership passed to son Greenfield (1833-1909) and his wife Malvina Snow Allen (1850-1943). They were the second generation to operate a dairy farm. Of their three sons, Henry (1874-1945) would be the third generation to continue the family tradition. Henry Allen never married and, according to Luther Snow in 2007, he relied heavily on the help of his cousins Vern and Harold "Bill" Snow (sons of Conrad and Harriet Haskell Snow) who lived nearby on the Elmwood Road. Bill was of the greater help, spending many summers living with Henry and his mother. Henry was quite innovative. In 1900 he purchased and installed one of Pownal's first windmills. This unit pumped water seven hundred feet from a spring to the kitchen and to a large storage tank in the upper section of the barn. On particularly windy days, this tank would overflow giving rise to the strange sight of the barn apparently "weeping" from its eaves. This system served until the 1950s when modern plumbing was installed.

Bill Snow, dairy farmer, and Josephine Bacon Snow, teacher.

When trucks replaced the railroad for shipping milk, Bill Snow used his 1939 Dodge to transport milk from area farmers to Old Tavern Farm Dairy.

The farm was willed to Harold "Bill" Snow (1911-1990) and Josephine Bacon Snow (1907-1965) in 1942. For the next thirty years, Bill and Josephine, with the help of sons Gordon and Luther, would operate a successful dairy farm with a herd of thirty milking Holstein cows. They sold milk to Portland dairies and also green beans to a local cannery. Bill exhibited his own flair for innovation when he built a silo for ensilage (a relatively new idea). Josephine was a teacher throughout the school year, but she evidenced a lively entrepreneurial aptitude. She owned and operated blueberry fields from 1941 until the 1960s.

Luther and Evelyn Lowell Snow acquired the property in 1990 after Bill's death. Today, they continue to operate the farm on a much reduced scale, selling seasonal fruits and vegetables to local markets, delivering firewood locally, supplying Christmas trees, seasonal wreaths, and decorations, and marketing a new line of rustic garden furniture. Their large perennial-flower and vegetable gardens are exceptionally fine. They enthusiastically and proudly share memories of a rich family history. Luther has served on many town committees, and both he and Evelyn are faithful supporters of their church. They can always be counted on for their generous help.

Luther and Evelyn Snow relax at their farm after hosting a garden tour in 2005.

Two Hallowell Road Dairy Farm Families Unite

Original settler Benjamin Mitchell built this two and one-half story Federal style, center-chimney house at what is now 153 Hallowell Road. William and Nellie Pervier purchased it in 1914.

It was March of 1914 when William J. Pervier (1869-1950) and Nellie Webster Pervier (1871-1949) left Ipswich, Massachusetts, with sons Joseph, Philip, and Lewis (aged fifteen, ten, and four). Their belongings had been loaded into a boxcar and they were headed to Walnut Hill station in North Yarmouth. Their daughter Abbie (1892-1973) was already living there. From the railroad station, a hayrack, pulled over snow-covered roads, carried their goods to a new home on the Hallowell road in Pownal. William, at age 45, had established a reputation as a fine carpenter in Ipswich, and the move to Maine marked a decided change in the life of the family. Soon, however, with the able help of Joseph (1899-1980), they established a successful dairy farm. In addition, William continued his career as a carpenter. He later found time to serve as selectman (1921-26) and town sheriff. (See page 187.)

Adjoining the Pervier farm, another dairy farm had been successfully established by George and Olive Loring in 1897. George and Olive had children Roy, Leigh, Fred Perley, and Emma. At the time of the Pervier's arrival, the Loring farm was known as one of the best in Pownal. Its dairy operations and well-established orchards had made the Lorings prosperous. One can imagine that the Pervier family had much to learn from their neighbors, as they began to live side-by-side. The death of George Loring in 1917, followed by Olive's extended illness, meant that running the farm fell on the shoulders of their sons. The two families continued helping one another over the years, with Joe and Emma bear-

William J. and Nellie Webster Pervier at their fiftieth wedding anniversary in 1940.

Joseph, age sixteen, and Philip, eleven, sons of William and Nellie Pervier, at the family farm in 1915 with horses Dick and Ned.

ing a lion's share of the burdens. Soon the lives of the Pervier and Loring families officially intertwined when Joe and Emma married in 1923. They joined the Loring household. Ultimately, it proved impossible to sustain both farms, and in 1937 the decision was made to sell the Loring farm. It was during the Great Depression, and the property sold for less than had been paid for it in 1897. Relieved from keeping two farms going, Joe and Emma moved into the Pervier homestead.

Second generation farmers Joe and Emma with daughter Josephine, born in 1924, and son Felton, born in 1928, continued dairy farming in the family tradition. Additionally, Joe helped his father with carpentry, found seasonal employment in woods work, and, with a newly purchased secondhand dump truck, began hauling feldspar from the local mine and gravel for town roads. Changes in dairy farming practices and possibilities were in the wind, however, and the Perviers had to work hard to keep their operation viable. Through it all, Joe and Emma found time for civic service, the church, and many town social organizations. Joe is fondly remembered for his work in establishing Pownal's first fire department, when, as he put it, he and his brother Lewis ("Lewie") "invented the town's first fire truck." Emma, a teacher in Pownal's one-room schools from 1914 to 1923, tended to home, farm, and fire department, while engaging in seasonal employment in area corn shops and blueberry fields. (See Chapters 4, 5, and 6.)

Daughter Josephine fondly remembered her years growing up at the farm in her memoirs, *The Remarkable Couple*. In 1953 she returned to her childhood home with husband Edward and children Marion, Ronald and Edward Leonard Jr. ("Lennie"). This third generation continued operating the dairy farm while living with Emma and Joe. Emma died in 1970 and Joe ten years later. Market forces forced fourth generation farmer Lennie to abandon dairying in 1992 and move to raising beef cattle. He continues this operation today.

E. Leonard "Lennie" Allen Jr. fourth generation Pervier-Allen farmer.

Litchfield Farm Has Seafaring Roots

The Scioto, captained by William Alexander, was built by the Skolfield brothers of Harpswell in 1849. This painting by Martin Duffy, husband of Josephine E. Litchfield, is a copy of the original.

The Diary of Betsey Alexander – September 25, 1856 to January 17, 1858 is a fascinating record of life at sea. Its connection with the history of Pownal's Litchfield farm began when Betsey gave birth to Catherine Alexander at sea on August 9, 1857. Catherine (1857-1937) would eventually marry Veazie Litchfield (1850-1933).

At the time of Catherine's birth, Betsey Merriman Alexander (1817-1895) was off the coast of Peru in the ship "Scioto," captained by her husband Thomas (1813-1858). In her diary, Betsey wrote, "Sunday August 9 [1857]: This morning fine and pleasant. Afternoon, wind blowing and very rough. Evening, sick and am confined to my bed. Twenty minutes past seven, Cate Cleavland was born." On January 17 of the next year she wrote, "This day commences with fine weather but rather cold for comfort. Thomas and Cate are both sleeping and it is rather lonesome, but a fair wind makes me think we shall get in soon as I long to get on the land once more and smell the earth, it would be a treat to me."

Family history has it that Thomas promised Betsey that after this voyage he would make only one more journey before retiring. Lumber was sorely needed in San Francisco, and there was money to be made shipping it there. Thomas had sailed "round the horn" several times, but unfortunately this was to be his last passage. On the return

Veazie and Catherine Litchfield Family, c. 1898. Front row l. to r.: Edith (1890-1911) and Victor Scott. Back row l. to r.: Josephine O. [Marr] 1883-1959, Catherine C., Veazie B. and Thomas A. (1877-1898). Another son, Samuel (1879-1895) had died before this picture was taken.

trip from California he contracted yellow fever and died. His son Eli (1847-1921), who had accompanied him, brought the vessel home and later became a sea captain like his father. The widow Betsey bought the sixty-five acre farm on the Brown Road in Pownal in 1865. Eleven years later, nineteen-year-old Catherine married Veazie Litchfield (1850-1933). Catherine and Veazie inherited the homestead, raising a family of five children while operating a successful dairy farm.

The homestead eventually passed to their youngest son Victor Scott (1892-1965) and his wife Iona Osgood Litchfield (1895-1964). They continued dairy farming while modernizing and enlarging the cape-style house for their growing family. Daughter Arlene L. Bradbury, one of the couple's eleven children, remembered in 2006 that her parents were wonderfully hard-working. Records show that in the 1920s Victor Sr. had one of the first hay presses and one of the first tractors in town. Arlene fondly remembered the entire family working together during haying time. The farm's primary income came from dairy products (milk and over one hundred pounds of butter per week). Corn and beans also were raised for sale to local canneries. The farm was not fully electrified until the 1950s. The depression years and World War II made life difficult, and Victor Sr. supplemented their income by working as the school bus driver (see Chapter 6) and as the town snowplow operator. He also worked at L. L. Bean in Freeport. From 1932 to 1936 he served as a town selectman.

Left: Victor S. and Iona Osgood Litchfield Sr., married October 16, 1915.

Right: Victor S. and Vina Vosmus Litchfield Jr., married June 25, 1946.

Of their eleven children, Victor Scott Jr. (1920-1994), with his wife Vina Vosmus Litchfield (1919-2004), continued dairy operations at the homestead. Both were also employed at L. L. Bean for many years. However, by the time their son Stephen returned from army service in Vietnam in 1969, market forces had made small dairy farms unprofitable. Steve and his father turned to raising beef cattle. Today, Steve Litchfield represents the fifth generation to farm the land that Betsey acquired in 1865 when she returned home from the sea.

Stephen and Janice Golding Litchfield, married August 10, 1968.

The Thomas and Abbie Vosmus Farm Depended on Blueberries

"Tom Hen and kids in hay wagon." Thomas and Abbie's son, Tom Henry, their daughter Winnie (in the doorway), and other children on the Vosmus farm, currently 188 Merrill Road, about 1930.

Blueberries were the main cash crop on the one-hundred-acre farm of Thomas J. Vosmus (1882-1968) and Abbie Pervier Vosmus (1890-1973). For thirty-one years, their fields were annually dusted, burned, and raked by the Clarence Harmon Company of Portland. Local townsfolk also participated in the harvest from 1944 to 1975. A hand-written bill of sale from 1944 records that 17,535 pounds of blueberries were raked for a total of $589.19.

Lois Vosmus Sanders related in 2005 that the farm consisted of the blueberry fields, a small wood lot, hayfields, a large family garden, and an apple orchard out front. She remembered "[apple varieties of] Baldwins, Nodheads, and Snows [probably Snowballs] that were so white inside and so red outside. Dad also kept five cows, two horses, a few pigs and some chickens. The big garden out back gave us all the vegetables the family needed: potatoes, carrots, turnips and squash, all kept in bins in the cellar. Mother canned corn, tomatoes, beans, and made pickles, relish, jam and jellies… We had no freezer… We had no electricity."

In addition to farming, Tom was road commissioner intermittently from 1948 to 1964 and also served on the town cemetery commission for eighteen years. Abbie worked as book keeper for the Freeport Shoe Company for many years, while raising six children: Vina [Litchfield] (1919-2004), Thomas H. (1920-2007), Winnie [Carter] (1922-2003), Lois [Sanders] (1924-), Ralph (1925-1993), and Kenneth (1927-). Both parents were active in the First Parish Congregational Church where Abbie was the organist for fifty years.

Thomas J. and Abbie P. Vosmus, October 1958.

From The Kitchen of Lois Vosmus Sanders
Blueberry Cake

¾ Cup Sugar
¼ Cup Shortening
1 tsp Vanilla
2 Eggs
1 1/3 Cups Flour
2 tsp Baking Powder
¼ tsp Salt
½ Cup Milk
1 Cup Blueberries

Cream sugar and shortening, add eggs and mix well, add vanilla, add sifted dry ingredients alternately with milk. Fold in blueberries. Sprinkle with topping (1/4 cup sugar & ½ tsp cinnamon). Bake in 9x9 pan at 350 for 30 Min.

Lois Vosmus Saunders shares a favorite family blueberry recipe.

Blueberry Ridge Farm of Dick and Kathy Hogue

Kathy and Dick Hogue and the house they built.

Dick and Kathy Hogue, 167 Loring Lane, acquired the land once known locally as "the town blueberry field" in 1977. They built a saltbox style house, began raising their two children, Erin and Jon, and embarked on their dream of becoming self-sufficient in a rural setting. Today, they are well on their way to realizing this dream. Their large gardens produce rhubarb, asparagus, strawberries, raspberries, grapes, and a wide variety of vegetables. They manage a small apple orchard, and continue to maintain and harvest the namesake blueberry fields.

They built numerous outbuildings, some of which house lambs, turkeys, and chickens. They sell much of their abundant produce and most of their turkeys (prized locally for Thanksgiving). They have been raising honeybees since 1982, and their six hives produce between sixty and two hundred pounds of honey each year. Honey, its by-products, and other organically grown produce are sold at their farm stand during the summer and fall.

Dick has recently built a small shingle mill, mating traditional machinery with his own novel design. He plans to produce custom-made shingles. Kathy has added to the creative atmosphere with her extensive flower and herb gardens, featuring rustic trellises, arbors, and benches of her own design and construction.

Off the farm, Kathy serves as the town selectmen's administrative secretary and is a member of Bradbury Mountain Arts. She is a member of two town committees, chairing the town's two-hundredth birthday committee. She has also teamed with daughter Erin to make unique gemstone jewelry marketed under the "Tree Of Life Designs" label. Dick is employed full-time, but also serves the town as an emergency medical technician and deputy chief of the Pownal fire and rescue department.

Dick examines a frame from one of his beehives.

The Gerald and Joan Rolfe Sheep Farm

Above: February is lambing month on the Rolfe farm. Eighteen were born in 2007. Right: Joan and Gerry with a pair of newborns.

In 1972, seeking a rural lifestyle, Gerald "Gerry" and Joan Rolfe moved their family from Connecticut to 1 Loring Lane, Pownal. They acquired open fields and a large barn, but as Joan admits, "We knew nothing about gardening or raising sheep." Undeterred, they acquired two bottle-fed lambs that their children (Thomas, six, Chrisopher, four, and twins Jonathan and Katherine, two) excitedly helped nurture. Thus began thirty-five years of raising sheep.

From the start the entire family was involved, learning the sheep business and raising market lambs. Joan joined the Cumberland County 4-H Sheep Club, as did all the children when they reached the minimum age of nine. Joan became an assistant leader of the club and started her own breeding program. Until they graduated from high school (the last one in 1988), the children could be found with Joan at jamborees and area fairs, winning their share of ribbons for market lamb quality, showmanship, blocking, and shearing. They joined the Maine 4-H sheep team and attended the Eastern States competition in Springfield, Massachusetts. During the 1980s, Joan became the leader of the sheep club, and also turned her talents to spinning and knitting. She knitted hundreds of sweaters from their wool, and sold extra wool to Bartlett Yarn Co. in Harmony, Maine.

In 1994, Joan was given the Outstanding Leader Award for distinguished service by the Cumberland County 4-H Cooperative Extension of the University of Maine. The Friends of the Extension cited her in 2006 for her outstanding leadership and service in support of 4-H. In addition to her long-standing involvement in 4-H, Joan has been a member of the board of directors of the Maine Sheep Breeders Association. Joan has served on several town and school committees. Gerry was town treasurer for seven years and selectman for nineteen years, sixteen as chair (see page 194). They love their rural life and continue to sell lamb locally in the fall.

The Rolfe flock in 2007 consisted of both breeding ewes and rams: Suffolks (shown here) and Oxfords, as well as several naturally colored sheep prized for their wool.

Kathy Harlow: Purveyor of Hay, Tender of Fields

Left: Kathy on her John Deere 2750 tractor and, above, with other haying equipment.

It is not unusual to see fields being hayed in Pownal. Today much of this work is being done by a young mother of two. Kathy Harlow, 554 Poland Range Road, fell in love with haying in 1972 when she was a little girl in West Cumberland on the farm of her grandfather, Hollis Thurlow. As she remembers it, "I couldn't throw the loose hay to the top of the hay wagon, so the boys would toss me up and I would tread the pile." This love has grown into a business, with Kathy contracting with owners to maintain their fields by applying lime and manure every two or three years and harvesting two crops annually.

Kathy began farming twenty years ago with her then-husband Tim. Today, her daughters Chelsea (eighteen) and Katie (twelve) work with her during haying time and help with their farm animals. Kathy raises and sells Shorthorn-Black Angus cross beef cattle. She owns four horses and boards others. She sells hay and composted manure, does garden mulching, and somehow finds time to hold down a full-time job at L. L. Bean in Freeport. However, haying remains her joy and passion.

She explains, "Square-baled hay is used mostly for horses, while dry hay in round rolls is used mostly for cattle. Plastic coated round rolls, rolled up wet and called "baleage," have higher protein content, since it ferments. It is fed to cattle only." With her large tractor, baler, front-end loader, and five hay wagons, Kathy is a familiar sight in summer fields in Pownal and surrounding towns. Clearly, her goal is not just to take the hay. She views her role as tending the fields for posterity.

Daughters Katie (left) and Chelsea help with barn chores, 2007.

> *"And when the question arises what to do,*
> *Bradbury Mountain is the place for you."*
> From Benjamin H. Britt, *"A Rambling Rhyme by Park Ranger,"* c. 1940

The hill just north of Pownal Center rises to its full 485 feet as the town's most prominent landmark. How it came to be called "Bradbury Mountain" is puzzling. Benjamin Britt, the park's first ranger, wrote a brief *Ranger's History of Bradbury Mountain State Park* for interested visitors. In it he stated that Samuel Bradbury, a "young explorer and hunter," got lost and perished there in 1710. He does not say where he learned this. He also included a poem, "A Rambling Rhyme," which he calls "part... history, perhaps part fancy too." It reads, "Young Bradbury, so the story is told, Lost his life on its summit bold." This suggests that it was a story he heard from local people.

Could the name have become attached to the hill through property ownership, as with Tryon Mountain? Again there is no evidence to indicate that this was the case. *Old Times of North Yarmouth, Maine* (a facsimile of magazines from 1877 to 1885) provides the genealogy of a North Yarmouth Bradbury family, going back to 1736. Some daughters married into other families, and some sons established lines, but the latter moved to New Gloucester and Auburn. The 1790 census records no Bradburys in either North Yarmouth or Freeport (of which Pownal was then a part). In 1908 when Ettie Latham wrote her history, she included a section on Pownal's early

"Devil's Seat" looking toward Hallowell Road about 1880. Note the treeless landscape.

Mary Sibley Sweetser (1872-1962) visits the summit with her children in 1907. L. to. r.: Helen, William, Elsie, and Marjorie. In the background, treeless fields and slope.

families back to 1775, without mentioning any Bradburys. Thus neither the "young explorer" story nor property ownership can be documented. Still (except for Abenakis, who probably camped on the summit and surely had their own name) people always called it Mount Bradbury or Bradbury Mountain.

The hill and adjacent land on either side of Route 9 were privately owned up into the 1930s. The Cotton family had a house and lands north of the summit. They grew apples and grapes. The iron hooks that can still be seen imbedded in the cliffs near the "Devil's Seat" are said to have been used to secure supports for the vines. On the Cotton land, the town constructed the cattle pound, one of a very few such structures still extant in Maine today. In 1929 the house burned and the family's farm operations presumably stopped. The property was sold to Everett Larrabee.

Meanwhile, in 1916, the Robert Smith family acquired what is now the park superintendent's house and acreage on the west side of Hallowell Road. They raised chickens and later added land on both sides of the road. A small feldspar deposit was discovered not far from the cattle pound, and from the late 1920s into the early 1930s, mining operations were carried out. Mr. Britt said that there was a narrow-gage railway to carry ore from the mine to Hallowell Road, but there is no surviving physical or documentary evidence to verify this.

This was how things stood until the 1930s. Then the Great Depression sparked the first phase of transforming these fields and forests into a state park. Among the New Deal programs, the Soil Conservation Service was organized in 1935 under the Department of Agriculture. The Service in turn established districts in each state. In Maine these soil conservation districts acquired land for public enjoyment.

The first parcel purchased by the government for this purpose was Mr. Larrabee's twenty acres in Pownal. He received sixty-nine dollars. Mr. Smith died in 1935, and in the subsequent two years his heirs sold the dwelling and land on both sides of the road. The federal government now owned about 173 acres. In 1936 the WPA funded a project to develop a trail to the summit and to construct picnic and parking facilities. In 1940 the government leased this land to the state, and the Maine State Park Commission created Bradbury Mountain State Park, one of five new state parks.

Park entrance and ranger's home in 1950.

Left: During the 1940s, the park ranger's sons, Donald and Bernard "Micky" Britt, climbed to the summit each morning before school to raise the American flag, then lowered it each evening.

Below: Picnic shelter constructed by the WPA during the 1930s.

In the early years, usage included hiking on the single trail, enjoying the view from the summit (which was outfitted with a binocular device), picnicking among the tables and fireplaces or under the rustic pavilion, and camping at the sites on the east side of the road. There was also some skiing in the area of the old feldspar mine, as well as occasional snowshoeing. In 1941, Ranger Britt estimated that by year's end 2,500 visitors would have used the park. There was also a flag pole at the summit; each morning and evening Mr. Britt's sons Donald and "Mickey" had to go raise and lower the flag.

During and for several years after World War II, the park continued to provide these rustic pleasures. Cars arrived via the broad gravel road that was Route 9. Benjamin Britt, ranger from 1940 to 1948, and Henry Darkis, his successor, enthusiastically welcomed visitors and did what they could to develop trails and other amenities. For several seasons, starting in 1946, Darkis operated a rope ski-lift, powered by an old automobile engine that was housed in a structure near the cattle pound. Skiers could grab the rope and be dragged part way to the summit. A day pass cost fifty cents, later raised to one dollar, but once a year it was free, and instruction was provided and contests held. This ended by 1954, since it did not prove profitable.

The 1950s and 1960s saw the park's first expansion. In 1955 the federal government gave all of the approximately 173 acres outright to Maine. Three private gifts and one purchase brought the total to around 300 acres by 1968. Usage, although fluctuating year to year, grew to around 11,000 day-use visitors and 9,000 campers by the mid-1960s. To accommodate the increasing traffic, an expansion of facilities was undertaken in 1954 or 1955, according to Luther Snow who, fresh out of high school, was hired for the project. Parking, toilets, fireplaces, etc. were all upgraded.

One fascinating footnote to the park's history relates to efforts in the late 1960s to create a small lake just west of Bradbury. A few civic leaders got the idea of creating a mile-long body of water fed by Thoits Brook. This would offer recreation and possibly municipal water. It was no mere passing fancy. The planning board strove for about three years to actualize this idea by working with and seeking support from federal, state, and county agencies. Sadly, in the end, what might have been 140-acre Lake Pownal never got off the drawing board.

Visionary thinking resumed in the 1980s. Prosperity in southern Maine and expanding tourism further increased park usage. Meanwhile, some citizens, many being recent arrivals, began to fear that development could consume what had attracted them here, the town's open spaces. Joining with established town families, they began to seek land acquisitions and easements which would increase public land and provide more ways to enjoy the park. They founded the Pownal Land Trust in 1989. Meanwhile, the state created the Land For Maine's Future Program in 1987, funded by a $35 million bond (a second $50 million bond was passed in 1999). Also the Libra Foundation acquired Pineland, located mostly in New Gloucester. The

Henry Darkis, the park's second ranger from 1949 to 1964. His hand-carved sign was the model for all later park signs.

Park Ranger Benjamin Britt and family, c. 1939. Front row l. to r.: Beverly Atkins, Elsie Atkins, Donald Britt, Bernard (Mickey) Britt, Winona Britt, Emma Britt. Back row l. to r.: Edith Britt Atkins, Arthur Atkins, Benjamin Britt, Nellie Wilson Britt, Robert Britt, Harry Britt, Roy Britt.

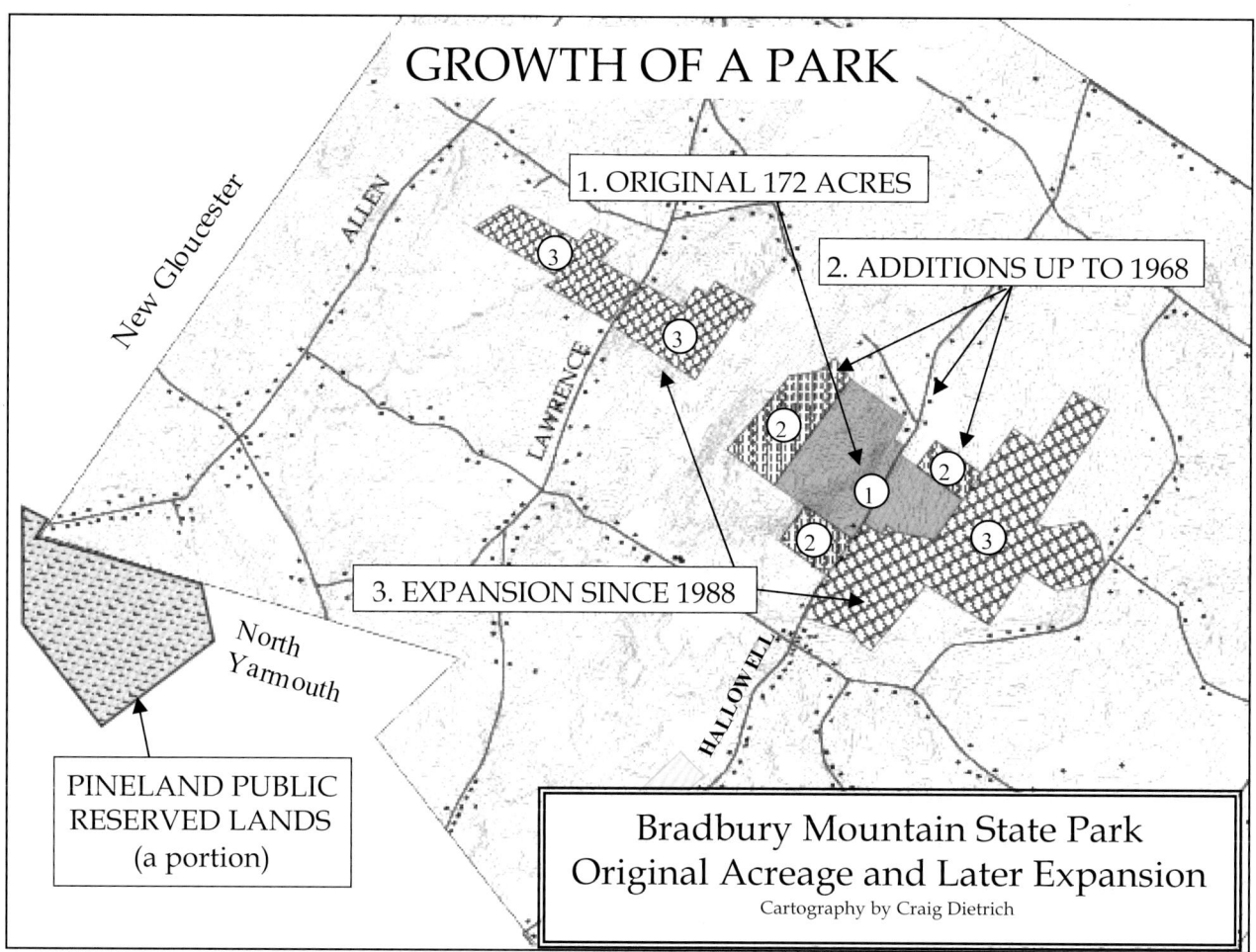

Growth of a park. As the map indicates, the original 173 acres grew to almost 900 acres through acquisitions.

former mental institution campus, now known as Pineland Farms, was extensively renovated and converted into an office complex, equestrian center, visitors facilities, hiking and skiing trails, and even a primary school. Libra also gave over 600 acres in New Gloucester, North Yarmouth and Gray to the state as "public reserve lands."

These developments fueled expansion of the park. Two families (the heirs of Wilma F. Knight and Jack and Anne Spiegel) gifted or sold a total of 250 acres to the state. Adding in other donations and purchases, the park grew to about 590 acres by the turn of the century. In 2001 the Pownal Land Trust celebrated a huge success, as the Land for Maine's Future program awarded $840,000 to fund efforts to link the park with Pineland through acquisitions or easements. The aim was to create a "corridor" of multi-use trails to help meet the recreational needs of southern Maine. Under this program the Connie Tryon and Earl Haven Tryon families gifted 185 acres to the park, including Tryon Mountain, west of Bradbury. Additional acquisitions and easements brought the total of land added to the park in 2003 and 2004 to over 300 acres. Negotiations with other land owners to link these parcels to create a "corridor," and to acquire land or easements between older park lands and the newer section around Tryon Mountain, continued and were virtually complete by 2007.

Usage of the park and the corridor kept pace with the physical expansion. Day use reached over 63,000 in 2005. The simple activities of the original park continued to be important: hiking, scaling the summit, picnicking, visiting the cattle

(continued on page 116)

A new shelter with toilet and shower facilities, which opened in 2007, improves the camping experience. It was financed largely through additional revenues from increased park usage, especially by mountain bikers.

Park Manager Michael "Mick" Rogers and wife Cynthia "Cindi" with their three daughters. L. to r.: Jamie, Danica, Cindi, Mick, and Krista. Mick took over the operation of the park in 1994. He supervised Park Ranger Bryan Kalleberg and three seasonal employees. The park's recent expansion in size and function was carried out under his leadership. Mick served in Pownal's fire and rescue department from 1997 to 2008, and as its deputy chief from 2005 to 2008. In January 2008, Mick was named Supervisor of Outdoor Recreation at the Maine Bureau of Parks and Lands. Frank Appleby replaced him.

pound. But the trail system had grown from a single path to include at least twenty trails by 2006. Guided nature walks were instituted. In 2007 the Bradbury Mountain Raptor Migration Project, sponsored by the Wild Bird Center of Yarmouth, inaugurated a spring migration hawk count, with an official counter stationed at the summit every day from March 20 to May 20.

Snowshoeing and cross country skiing were greatly expanded. Around 6,000 skiers used the park in 1988. Snowmobiling and horseback riding were permitted on some trails. Most significant was the advent of mountain biking. In 1997 Supervisor Mick Rogers began working with biking organizations to open trails to individual riders and to offer a venue for organized rallies and races. For such events a thirty-mile loop could be assembled. By 2007 the usage had grown dramatically, as 20,000 to 30,000 mountain bikers came annually. The bikers, who had access to very few trails in southern Maine, now enjoyed twenty-two miles of beautiful woods trails, with more being developed. Their patronage significantly boosted the park's revenue.

One beneficiary of this increasing use was camping. Primitive camping had been promoted from the beginning. But unfortunately, lacking shower and washing facilities and in competition with more luxurious recreational vehicle parks, Bradbury's campground was attracting fewer and fewer campers. By 2005 visits to this section were only half what they had been forty years earlier. However, thanks to new revenue, the upgrading of the tenting area began in 2006, with every expectation of reversing that trend.

Above: Pownal resident Jon Hogue participated in the June 2005 Bradbury Mountain Bike Race, winning third prize in the Novice Men's Senior 1 division.

Left: Local resident Rosemary Whitney astride her horse Sonny frequents park trails.

Birder Lionel Quirnon, official counter of the Spring Hawkwatch, at the summit of Bradbury Mountain in 2007. The full-time hawk watch was sponsored by Pownal residents Derek and Jeanette Lovitch, owners of the Wild Bird Center of Yarmouth. In its inaugural year, Lionel reported on migrating hawks each day from 9 AM to 5 PM from March 20 through May 20, weather permitting. According to Jeanette, "In its pilot season with the weather not being very cooperative, fifteen species were recorded with a season total of 2,123 migrants. The most frequent species was the Broad-winged Hawk, with 805 reported. The surprise hawk noted was a Black Vulture, a visitor from more southern ranges."

In the summer of 2007, Pownal residents Michaela Goldfine and Kirk Niese enjoy an afternoon walk to the summit with daughter Cecily and their dogs.

In Search of Jones' Inn

by Sue Clukey
A Report in fulfillment of a Maine Humanities Millennium Matching Grant

"Jones' Inn," as painted in 1892 by Clara L. Dyer, artist and granddaughter of Cyrus Jones, was located on Hallowell Road across from the Pownal cattle pound. The buildings burned prior to 1892 and a marker on Bradbury Mountain State Park land marks its site.

"Jones' Inn," on Hallowell Road, "is an intriguing part of Pownal's past — still very much an enigma."
Pownal: A Rural Maine History (1977)

Three decades have passed since those words were written, but Jones' Inn has continued to arouse curiosity. The structure existed for most of the nineteenth century, but little documentation survives. A watercolor representation was painted in 1892, after the house was gone. Only a photograph of this image now survives. Just what was it? Was it an inn? A store? A tavern? A farm? No conclusive written evidence exists.

Members of the Pownal Scenic and Historical Society wondered, "Could archaeology solve the riddle?" Perhaps physical remains could be unearthed to verify or contradict the stories and fragmentary records. A Maine Humanities Millennium Matching Grant was obtained, and SAD 62, the Pownal Foundation, and the Pownal Scenic and Historical Society enthusiastically matched the grant.

The dig took place in the Fall of 2001. Sue Clukey was project director, and Norman Buttrick was site archaeologist. The excavators included twenty-six dedicated Pownal middle school students, historical society members, and interested citizens of the community.

What did they find? Did archaeology answer the Inn-igma? No. And yes. Here is what was learned: The house measured thirty by forty feet. It was sided in wood, as shown by a large number of machine-cut nails. This supports an ac-

Pownal Scenic and Historical Society
Pownal, Maine 04069

November 18, 2008

Maine Humanities Council
Attn. Trudy Hickey
674 Brighton Ave.
Portland, ME 04102

Dear Trudy,

In 2001 the Maine Humanities Council awarded a Community History Grant #21717:00-01-CH-06 to Project Director Sue Clukey of the Pownal Elementary School (SAD#62) titled, "Getting to Know Jones' Inn – A School and Community Collaborative." The Pownal Scenic & Historical Society was one of the co-sponsors of the grant. According to one of the terms of the contract, the historical society would include a final report in a proposed town history to be written to coincide with the town's bicentennial in 2008. The project was of great interest to the school, the historical society and the community.

Sue Clukey informed me that her final report to the council was submitted December 2001. The societies publication, *On Pownal Time, One Hundred Years in a Rural Maine Town,* was published this summer and it includes the final report of the project in pages 118 to 121. We are sending you a copy of the book for your archives.

Sincerely,

Donna F. Boyles

Donna F. Boyles, President and Chair of the book committee
584 Poland Range Road
Pownal, ME 04069

"enhancing and preserving our rural heritage"

count that Jones' Inn was "constructed of the finest lumber of which the forests abounded at the time." A chimney arch was unearthed, easily massive enough to support the large center chimney shown in the painting. The foundation was native granite blocks. In it were shards of hand-blown window glass and the aforementioned nails. There was evidence of a possible ell on the northeast side. As of 1923, a massive granite entry post survived as the only remaining artifact. This has long since disappeared, but a large post hole and mold were excavated in the front yard. Was this evidence of the entry post?

One- to two-inch layers of charcoal and ash were found in every test pit outside the cellar hole. This might seem to affirm oral interviews with the grandson of the last owners and Ettie Latham's 1908 history. They said the stand of buildings burned after being struck by lightning. Buttrick, however, found it odd that there were few if any artifacts beneath the burned layer and very few scorched household objects. If the buildings had burned, there should have been artifacts representing the life of the house for the ninety previous years. Now we have another mystery!

The excavation provided, as archaeologists say, "negative evidence." Nothing was found to confirm or refute its use as an inn, store, or tavern. If the building had served a public use, one would expect to find litter dropped by customers around the doorways. Common items excavated from contemporary public buildings include clay pipes and bowls, mug fragments, shot, brass pins, food preparation ceramics, wine bottle glass, and common pins and buttons. Here very little was found except remnants of building materials such as brick, window glass and machine-cut nails, domestic objects such as ceramic and glass, and farm implements. Maybe someday trash pits will be found containing evidence of public use.

Sometimes in attempting to answer one question, unanticipated questions get answered. When the students explored some test pits inside

(continued on page 121)

Father and daughter Calvin Ryder Jr. and Heather Ryder participated in the dig.

Above: Pownal middle school students eagerly looked for clues to Jones' Inn's past.

Below: Sue Clukey, project director, demonstrated proper excavating technique.

the cellar hole, things took an unexpected turn. They unearthed a 1900-to-1930s dump so deep that they never reached the bottom. This dump yielded a wonderful microcosm of early twentieth- century rural culture. Artifacts revealed clues to foodways (sardine cans, a juicer, pickling crock shards, ceramic dishes, condiment bottles, a goblet, and bones), personal hygiene (tins of tooth powder, cold cream jars, a mirror, and perfume bottles), home decorating (bits of wallpaper and linoleum, an arts-and-crafts vase), clothing (buttons, overall clasps, suspender clips, rivets from jeans), lighting (oil lamp parts and early electric bulbs), manufacturing (leather shoe parts, possibly home piecework from the shoe shops in Freeport), and farm tools. These materials come from before the time the park was created in the 1930s.

Principal investigator Buttrick wrote, "I would have to say that for most of its history, the house was a farmstead rather than any of the other classifications that tradition has pinned on it." He added, "Even though the Jones site did not turn out to be the traditional 'Jones' Tavern,' it is an important historic site for the town of Pownal in the nineteenth century."

Thus Jones' Inn remains something of a mystery. Perhaps a future dig will investigate the suspected ell, an area between the foundation and the well, and the front entrance. Perhaps further written documentation will turn up. In any case, this site is too interesting to abandon, and perseverance may reveal more secrets in time for Pownal's tri-centennial in 2108.

Historical Society member Arthur Stackhouse looks for archeological evidence to confirm the existence of Jones' Inn.

A Corridor Runs Through It

Land resources take various forms, from farm fields, to pasture, to the subsoil from which minerals may be extracted. Land also provides space, whether for buildings and roads or for recreation. In the twentieth century, another spatial use became very important and even hotly contested in Pownal, namely, land for facilities to move energy and communications.

The first instance arrived innocently enough. Roadside poles appeared with the advent of the telephone, early in the century. Electrification was spreading elsewhere in the nation, but not yet in Pownal, although privately-owned electric generators began to appear in town by the 1920s. The young electrical industry in the state was composed of many small generators, and by the early 1930s three larger companies were bringing power into parts of town, coming from different directions. One of them, Walter Wyman's Central Maine Power Company (CMP), absorbed the others one by one. By the early 1940s, CMP had a switching station on the Elmwood Road, and by the end of that decade was providing service to most homes. The space occupied by its poles seemed inconsequential, and the energy and communication service they carried were in great demand. That was how things stood for the next twenty years.

In 1967 CMP began to acquire property in north and west Pownal to be involved in creating a large regional power grid. The company needed land for the high tension lines that would bring power from plants in Maine, New Hampshire, and New Brunswick through numerous Maine towns, including Pownal. In addition, CMP constructed a large transformer on the Allen Road. Named the Surowiec Substation, it was dedicated in 1972, the first of its size in Maine. Also in 1972 the Maine Yankee nuclear power plant in Wiscasset went on line and began delivering power to Surowiec. Later, plants in Orrington, Buxton, Cousins Island, Maxcy's, and South Gorham were added. This Pownal transformer reduces 345 kilovolt (kV) power down to 115 kV. From Surowiec, seven 115 kV lines then carry the electricity to consumers throughout much part of the state.

In Pownal the corridor passed mainly through farm land. The path chosen happened to lie over a moraine—more easily excavated glacial till as opposed to granite bedrock. Although eminent domain could have been used if owners had resisted, they willingly sold the re-

Transmission lines in the utility corridor along Allen Road.

Electric Power Comes to Pownal

In the 1930s, Lewis Pervier built a garage next to the Pervier farm on the Hallowell Road and started an auto repair business. At the time, the nearest towns that had commercially supplied electricity were Freeport and Yarmouth. "Lewie" knew that electricity could help his business by providing lighting and power, and he purchased a 32-volt generator. This was better than nothing, but he wanted more. He and his brother Joseph discussed the situation and decided to contact the power company. The rest of the story is told by Josephine Pervier Allen in her book, *The Remarkable Couple*:

```
The power company said they could not afford to put up lines in the out-
lying areas.  At that time the minimum charge was $1.00 per month.  The
company offered to put up the lines if it could be guaranteed money
enough to cover the cost.  This could be done if enough families signed a
contract to guarantee the needed amount.  Joe and Lewie canvassed the
area from the nearest line through to Pownal.  They got enough signers
who would be willing to pledge a reasonable rate for the convenience of
electricity.  They took their list of hopeful consumers to see what the
company would offer.  They found if each family guaranteed a minimum of
$2.66 per month for five years the line could be put through.  This deal
was accepted at once.  I expect the customers had no problem in using
enough power so their minimum was covered.  So it was in 1935 electric
power [through commercial lines] made its way to Pownal.  I believe it
only went as far as Pownal Center that year.  Joe bought a book entitled
Wiring Your Own House.  Thus Joe added another skill to his ever broaden-
ing [capabilities].
```

However, it would not be until the 1950s that the entire town became electrified.

---

quired parcels. At the time Pownal had a great deal of relatively cheap farm land, and the grantors were allowed ten years' access to all the timber on the parcels sold. There was little open opposition. Soon the high tension lines and the substation became a normal feature of the landscape, although some people began to complain about the unsightliness, humming noise, and herbicide use.

Twenty years later, another CMP project came to the fore. This time there was local resistance, although it was limited, possibly because no additional land was needed in Pownal. In 1987, CMP announced plans to create a new corridor to transmit direct-current hydropower from Quebec to Jay, Maine. In Jay, it would be changed to 345 kV AC power and sent on to the Surowiec substation. Although the company said (in the Sunday newspaper) that its new transmission lines would have "the least impact possible on area ecology, aesthetics and land use," the proposal nevertheless triggered opposition from affected homeowners and camps in northern Maine. In Pownal, a meeting of some fifty residents raised objections to expanding the substation. Some worried about health risks from electromagnetic radiation and from herbicides applied to the corridor. Others objected to the substation noise and the prospect that expansion would further degrade the rural tranquility. "Some of us live out in the country because we like that quiet," said one resident in the evening paper. CMP also faced numerous regulatory hurdles, Canadian and domestic. It ultimately abandoned this plan. However the local resistance foreshadowed responses to yet another project a decade later.

Surowiec substation on the Allen Road as pictured in 2006.

"This has to be the most explosive issue ever to hit Pownal," said Selectman Susan Mack in the summer of 1997. She was speaking about a new corridor use, one not envisioned in the 1960s. A consortium of energy companies, had announced plans to construct the Maritimes and Northeast Pipeline through Maine to carry natural gas from fields near Sable Island, off the coast of Nova Scotia, into Massachusetts. In Pownal the original plan proposed a seventy-five foot right of way next to CMP's existing corridor.

A complex interplay of local, regional, and international interests was set in motion. In Pownal the big question was whether the pipe would be laid in CMP's existing corridor, which that company resisted, or in a new adjacent corridor, which Pownal residents strongly opposed. Local reaction was immediate and intense. Protest meetings were organized, speakers dispatched, signs painted, and letters sent. In November a large crowd of protestors gathered in the as yet unfinished Mallett Hall addition. Speeches were made, and Jim Hale sang a folk ballad, composed for the occasion, likening the protestors to Minute Men and urging Pownal, "Don't give up the land to no damned pipeline."

In the end, CMP allowed Maritimes and Northeast to run the pipeline in the existing corridor. Construction began in 1998, and in 1999 large quantities of natural gas began flowing through Pownal underground. A second pipeline bringing gas from Quebec was not laid, nor was a proposed spur through Yarmouth to supply the Wyman plant on Cousins Island. This spur would have passed through Pownal along the edge of Elmwood Road. Vigorous local objections centering on safety and on the potential loss of old trees helped in the defeat of this proposal. By 2007, the story was taking another turn. The Sable Island gas fields were being rapidly depleted. To replace this source, gas from a liquefied natural gas (LNG) terminal at Saint John, New Brunswick was scheduled to begin flowing in 2008. Another proposed LNG facility near Calais seemed doomed to failure because of Canadian and American concerns for the maritime environment.

Collectively, utilities own 431 acres, or three percent of Pownal's taxable land. Who benefits from this type of land use, where no crops, animals, trees, or minerals are produced? Of course consumers and businesses across the northeast

(continued on page 126)

The Mouse That Roared

Residents of Pownal, the smallest town on a proposed 350-mile-long pipeline route, took up verbal arms in 1997 against cutting a proposed new corridor through town. They wanted Maritimes & Northeast LLC to lay its natural gas pipeline within the existing utility corridor. "No New Corridors" became their battle cry. The campaign succeeded, showing once again that individuals can sometimes influence the outcome of large-scale events.

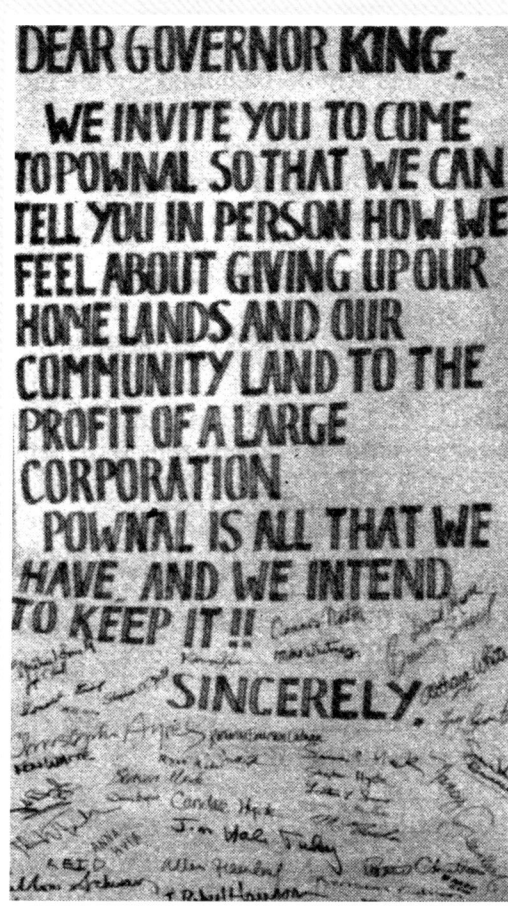

Selectwoman Susan Mack addressed townsfolk at an anti-pipeline rally.
Permission: James Saunders, reporter and photographer, "Pownal Residents Join Pipeline Protest," The Northern Forecaster, November 27, 1997.

receive the energy they need. Large corporations profit from the energy they transport along the corridor. The town can only benefit financially through levying taxes. The amounts paid by these companies have been significant, but they have varied widely over time. As a proportion of the town's annual total commitment, they rose from under ten percent in the 1930s, to over fifty percent in the 1970s, and then steadily back down to below 10% in the 2000s. There are other ways in which the existence of the utility corridor can be said to benefit Pownal. Maintained as a large swath of non-forested space, it provides opportunities for snowmobilers, hikers, and hunters. In places, hay and blueberries can be taken from the land. Moreover it provides an open wildlife habitat.

In the 1990s yet another type of resource came to the town's attention, namely air space. The issue was whether cell towers that might be erected in Pownal would blight the rural landscape. The experience of nearby towns with towers, some as high as 300 feet with lights flashing at night, caused alarm and led to the drafting of an ordinance to limit the height of cell towers to thirty-five feet. A special town meeting passed a temporary ordinance in late 1997, and a permanent ordinance in 1999. The engineering, location, and design standards specified in this ordinance are quite explicit and extensive, requiring co-location on existing towers where possible. Currently there are no communications towers functioning in town.

In the developments just described can be seen a profound change in the relationship of the town to its land. Back in the early twentieth-century, when poets sang of the rural landscape, the fields that they admired were still those of working farms. Their beauty was tied in with the rural life they made possible. In the later twentieth century, as agriculture retreated and urbanization advanced, Pownal land was no longer used primarily to grow crops. Its principal purposes were increasingly to provide a scenic, private, rural setting for the town's residents, and to accommodate outdoor recreations of many kinds. Evan Richert has examined this trend statewide and describes it as a change from land being organized "for the primary purpose of production," to being organized "for the primary purpose of consumption." When the industrial projects described in this section threatened this new use of the land, town residents rose up in protest and succeeded rather well in protecting their interests.

Central Maine Power lines, looking east from the Lawrence Road in 2007.

Forests

Lumbering and the use of forest products became Pownal's first industry. The Reuben Haskell sawmill, located on the East Branch of the Royal River on the Hodsdon Road, was established as early as 1795. It is pictured here in the early 1900s when owned by Frank A. Knight Sr. and Charles H. Knight Sr.

One of the first visual impressions the early European settlers had of New England as they approached from the sea was a rugged shoreline backed by seemingly endless forests. This was confirmed as they moved inland, for, with the relatively rare occurrence of Indian-cleared land, the forests indeed covered a vast area. This abundance of trees was both a challenge and a gift. Clearing the land for living space and farming tested settlers' energy and perseverance, while the abundant wood provided a ready source of building material and fuel. Thus began a cycle of over-harvesting, depletion, and renewal, culminating today in more enlightened forest management. A recent statewide survey by the Maine Forest Service shows Maine forests to be an amazingly self-renewing resource. In the year 2000, Maine was as heavily forested as it was in 1600, after being severely cut in the 1850s. Today, Maine is the most forest-covered state in the Union. Forests are now sensibly managed to provide lumber, pulp, and fuel. They are also managed for recreational activities such as camping, hiking, hunting, and snowmobiling. Wildlife habitat protection is also very important. Pownal residents have always relied on their forests and woods as a renewable resource. In this section we describe who used this resource and how it was used over the last one hundred years.

Early History

Lumbering and the use of forest products became Pownal's first industry. As early as 1795, two sawmills were functioning on the east and middle branches of the Royal River. By this date, coastal areas had been cleared of their forests, and trees from Pownal became an immediate cash crop. They were in demand locally and beyond for the construction of houses, barns, and carriages as well as for heating and cooking. Hemlock bark processed for the tanning industry and wood processed for potash were forest products that added to the economic base of the town.

By 1908, most of Pownal was deforested, with the exception of a few well-managed lots. However, renewal was in evidence. As large-scale farming declined and farmers withdrew land from cultivation, secondary tree growth began inexorably to take over. Farmers were still harvesting hardwood for heating and cooking, but kerosene and coal were beginning to replace wood as fuel. Thus the stage was set for a resurgence of forest growth.

The two mills that had opened in the late 1700s were still in operation. The Reuben Haskell mill on the Hodsdon Road on the East Branch of the Royal River was operating in 1908 as a sawmill. It was then owned by Frank A. Knight Sr. and Charles Knight Sr. By 1918, this mill had been sold to Emile Deslauriers who operated it as a dowel mill until its final closing in 1936. The Jacob Randall mill on the Lawrence Road on the Middle Branch of the Royal River (locally called Chandler's Brook) functioned seasonally until 1940. Owners during the early twentieth century were Rufus Harris, Enoch Shaw, Herbert Merrill, and Delmar Sylvester.

Logging was a seasonal occupation. Cutting began in November after the first light snow. Trees were felled and "twitched" to yards along a main road. Later from December through February, the logs would be hauled to convenient landings, there to await the spring rains that provided the rivers with enough flow to power the

(continued on page 130)

The Reuben Haskell sawmill in 1908, the year of the town's centennial celebration. Emile Deslauriers operated it as a dowel mill from 1918 to 1938, after which time it ceased operations.

The Jacob Randall sawmill, located on the Middle Branch of the Royal River (also known as Chandler's Brook), was established in 1795, originally as a grist mill. This mill was the center around which the North Pownal village grew, and it provided sawn lumber for the area for one hundred and forty years. It is pictured here after the hurricane of 1938. Channing Penley (seen in the photo) remembered in an interview in 2003 that "the flood washed out the top of the sluice-way and pressure took out the water wheel." It was owned at the time by Herbert Merrill and Delmar Sylvester and ceased operation after the flood.

The Jacob Randall homestead was listed in the National Register of Historic Places in 1979 through the efforts of the Pownal Scenic and Historical Society. It was listed for its Federal-style architecture and its association with early industry in Pownal. Jacob Randall (1770-1829) moved here from Durham to begin a grist and sawmill operation by 1795. He built his home of brick across the road from the mill around 1800. The home, currently 725 Lawrence Road, is pictured here during the winter of 2005, one of Maine's snowiest.

mills. Oxen were generally preferred for this hauling as they were more sure-footed than horses. During a 2006 interview, Shirley Thurber Verrill remembered seeing "logs lined up along Lawrence Road waiting to be rolled over the bank to be sawed."

The Whitcher brothers, Algernon and Milton, were dealers in wood and wood products in town from 1900 to the 1940s. Others appeared on the tax records during this period as operating portable saw mills and providing lumber for building. They were John T. Lawrence, A. H. Parker, Wallace Polley, Ernest Tuttle, Howard Kimball, and Herbert Merrill. Through the 1940s, wood remained the primary or only source of heating and cooking fuel for some households. One could always find local men to cut and deliver firewood.

Hauling out wood in 1930. Harold "Bill" Snow (1911-1990) and Verne Snow (1907-1976) use their team of horses and a pung to bring in cordwood for cooking and heating the Allen-Snow farm, currently 180 Leighton Road. The farm, totally heated by wood, required sixteen cords per year.

Philip Tryon (1898-1983) hauled cordwood at his farm, currently 539 Lawrence Road, during the winter of 1935, using a team of oxen and a pung.

Elmer Libby (1886-1966) and son Kenneth "Chub" (1915-1988) haul lumber to their farm on the Upper Minot Road in 1926.

Joseph Pervier's portable sawmill located behind the family homestead on the Hallowell Road was used by son-in-law Edward Allen to saw the lumber for the home he built on Loring Lane for himself and his wife, Josephine, in 1980.

The Whitcher brothers, Algernon (1893-1963) and Milton (1885-1944), were dealers in cordwood, Christmas trees, and wreaths, selling their products at Portland and Boston markets. This photo shows trees bundled for loading into the truck box.

Forest Health: A State and Local Concern

Preparing to make Christmas wreaths, a seasonal event at the William and Nellie Pervier farm on the Hallowell Road in the 1920s.

As early as 1920, the state recognized tourism as a growing industry and began to promote it. Rural resorts opened as more people from out of state used their increased mobility to reach the hunting, fishing, and outdoor recreation available in Maine. Locally, the Poland Spring Resort employed many Pownal residents. Even some abandoned farms opened as summer homes. There were problems however. Deforestation of the previous century had led to unsightly and scrubby second growth in many areas. Streams, deprived of the drainage buffer of surrounding trees, were no longer dependable sources of power generation. Serious forest fires were not uncommon. The Maine Forest Service was forced to increase its management efforts to meet the new demands that tourism placed on the forests, and fire suppression practices were developed.

As early as 1908, a serious threat to trees had been recognized in the form of a brown-tail moth infestation. It is the caterpillar stage that causes defoliation damage, but the hairs from the caterpillars and moths also cause skin irritations in humans. The town helped meet this threat by paying individuals a small sum for each brown-tail moth nest verifiably destroyed. Money was allocated for this annually from 1908 to the end of the infestation in 1919. The total spent in this way is not known, but it ranged from a few dollars in 1908 to $750 in 1915, the apparent height of the infestation.

In 1926 a new threat to forests was recognized, one that lingered into 1969. This was not another defoliating caterpillar, but rather a fungus disease deadly to white pines. White pine blister rust threatened forests statewide, and all local communities were asked to help in its eradication. The fungus lives alternately on white pine trees and adjacent currant bushes. The infection cannot pass directly from tree to tree. Rather, it must live for a period of time on the leaves of surrounding bushes before moving onto the trees. Control involves eliminating currant bushes from any stand of white pine trees, a control that is effective for five to ten years. At the time, Pownal had 4,256 acres of white pine trees requiring protection, with the total area

(continued on page 134)

K. W. SMITH, PRES.
EARLE W. MOODY, VICE PRES.

ALPHEUS G. DYER, TREAS.
PAUL L. POWERS, COUNSEL

Casco Shipbuilding Co., Inc.

Freeport, Maine

FRED F. PENDLETON,
MASTER BUILDER

August 28, 1942

Dear Sir:

Regarding to your application for employment, which we have on file at this office, we are in need of men.

If you wish to report for work we will arrange your pay according to your classification.

Bring what tools you have available.

Very truly yours,

CASCO SHIPBUILDING CO., INC.

By
N. B. Emerson, P. A.

Letter sent to Milton Whitcher in response to his request for employment with the Casco Shipbuilding Company of South Freeport in 1942. Milton (1885-1944) and Pearl Greene (1884-1968) Whitcher lived and farmed at the current 78 Merrill Road. Milton and his brother, Algernon, operated Whitcher Brothers, a successful dairy farm and wood products business, from 1910 until Milton's death.

that needed to be scoured of currant bushes approaching 10,000 acres. During this period, Pownal appropriated an annual average of $200 for this eradication, money that was matched by both state and federal agencies.

Another pathogen hit New England's forests hard during the 1950s. Dutch elm disease proved to be unstoppable, as it destroyed millions of the great vase-shaped elms that graced roadways and shaded houses and barns. The trees in Pownal were devastated. Elmwood Road, named for the stately trees that lined it, lost all of its namesakes. Ultimately, the town appropriated $100 to remove the dead elms.

The Philip E. Knight Lumber Company, located on Route 9, Crockett's Corner, North Yarmouth, began in 1935 and closed in 1952. Pictured here are local men employed at the sawmill in 1945. Front row l. to r.: Kenneth "Chub" Libby (truck driver), Philip Knight (owner), Linwood York, Oscar Johnson (woodsman), Linwood Randall, John Menchen. Middle row l. to r.: Ralph Babbin, Lawrence Yates, Bob Locklin, Arthur Atkins, Fred Upton (woodsman), Ed Menchen, George York. Back row l. to r.: Leland Arris, Leon Hanscom, Tony Tucci. Not pictured: Carl Tryon, Laurence Snow, and Claude Snow (truck driver). Identified by Marion Knight Reed, 2005

Local Conservation Efforts

The first conservation commission in Pownal was established by a town vote in 1979. The chair was William Ginn, and other members included William DeWitt, Leonard Allen, Marjorie Mason, Albert Blackstone Jr., Stephen Hyde, and Sherilyn Dietrich. A town meeting the following year authorized the commission: "To give Selectmen authority to develop and implement a management plan for town-owned land, such plan to be limited to forest management and recreational uses, and pay any expenses associated with such plan but not in excess of any income derived there from." On this authority, the commission proceeded to carry out selective tree harvesting, supervised by a forester. Additionally, they clearly identified all forest tracts, removed fallen trees from streams, and planted new trees in village centers.

The Southern Maine Forestry Services developed a ten-year-cycle harvesting plan, with the first harvest to be completed in 1984. Robert McMahon, commission chair from 1986 to 1990 and from 1998 to 2000, was responsible for implementing most of this plan. Town-owned land on the Elmwood, Dresser, and Poland Range Roads was harvested between 1984 and 1999, yielding a $28,127 return to the town.

Throughout this period, the commission addressed its other tasks, adding water quality and environmental impact to their areas of concern. The commission became inactive after 2000, but not before it had played a major role in establishing the first "Pownal Pride Day" in April of 1992. This has endured, under the direction of the recycling committee, as an annual event during which roadside litter is removed by volunteers, metal recycling is encouraged, and pick up of large-item household waste is provided by the town.

In 2007, a new conservation commission was created by the selectmen. Thomas Cushman was appointed chair, and other members included Ruth Hannan (secretary), Robert McMahon, Jeff Raymond, Matt Welch, Derek Lovitch, Shawn Bennett, and alternate Robert Hanson. It was charged with monitoring all open areas, public or private, including wetlands. It was authorized to recommend conservation programs to any local or state official or agency.

According to the Maine Forest Service, ninety-one timber harvests were conducted between 1991 and 2005, covering a total of just over three thousand acres. Almost all were selective harvests.

Niki Mains, 4-H Collars and Leashes member, plants flowers around the base of newly planted maple trees in Pownal Center. The trees were planted by the Conservation Commission in 1987.

Philip E. Knight (1892-1981)
Known and Respected throughout Area Towns

Philip E. Knight, son of Charles and Mary Jane Soule Knight Sr., was born and raised on the Hodsdon Road in Pownal. Educated in Pownal's one-room schools, he grew up amid the granite quarry operations of his father. These quarries spanned the border between Pownal and North Yarmouth near the intersection of the Hodsdon and Royal Roads. As a young man Philip spent some years working in Boston, returning in 1918 to join his father in the quarry. He spent the next ten years there, often engaged in hauling stone to various projects (see page 144).

Seasonally during these years, Philip turned to sawmill work. As his daughter, Marion Knight Reed, related in a 2005 interview, "Dad ran portable sawmills in the area and as far away as Naples, gaining an impressive knowledge of timberlands in the area… He knew where to find various species of wood including red oak and hemlock. And he knew who to hire. Oscar Jordan, Fred Upton, and Carl Tryon cut the wood, while Norman Reed and Waldo Bickford used their teams of horses and wagons to hall it out. Dad also threshed grain for area farmers at harvest with his portable threshing machine."

Philip married Eva Crockett, a North Yarmouth farm girl, in 1916. They established their home at Crockett's Corner crossroads in North Yarmouth, and raised two daughters there, Marion and Irene. Philip established a sawmill business at the same location, where it became a well-known landmark for many years. According to Marion, "To establish a permanent sawmill business, Dad knew he needed electricity [which had arrived in Yarmouth] and he brought it into North Yarmouth in 1935. He hired local men to work for him. Some traveled from Pownal: Laurence Snow tallied the board feet of lumber sawed each day. Ken "Chub" Libby and Claude Snow, who drove trucks, hauled lumber as far away as Massachusetts and Rhode Island."

By 1942, Phil's sawmill boasted a large saw and powerful planer. This mechanical capability, coupled with his broad knowledge of where the best timber could be found, landed him in the middle of a little known World War II project. The goal was to build four 194-foot cargo barges out of oak. These would replace metal barges in areas where enemy magnetic mines (triggered by

Truck driver Kenneth "Chub" Libby is pictured here in 1947 as he hauled logs for the Philip Knight Lumber and Building Materials Company.

steel hulls) might be a problem. The Casco Bay Shipping Company of South Freeport was commissioned to build these barges. The call went out for shipwrights to begin construction at the Soule-Bliss yards, and Philip began "cruising" the area for proper oaks.

In a November 2000 *Down East Magazine* article titled "Red Oaks To The Rescue," William David Barry wrote, "At the height of the project more than forty individuals worked the woods and lumber yard while 250 worked at the South Freeport yard… Three Red Oak barges did enter the service, though exactly where they went remains cloudy." By 1944, four oak barges had been built for the war effort.

By 1952, Philip Knight had retired, but his active life was far from over as he continued his involvement in civic affairs. Notably, he vigorously supported the work of local historical societies. His winning smile, sharp memory, and keen sense of humor made him a favorite program speaker. To those who worked for him, he is fondly remembered. As his daughter Marion expressed it, "Dad always worked with the men. He'd tell them how to do it and then he'd help them do it."

From the Six Towns Times *February 13, 1948.*

-See KNIGHT lumber for RIGHT prices-
Will furnish Carpenters for Shingling or Repair Jobs
ESTIMATES GIVEN—FHA PLAN IF PREFERRED

PHILIP E. KNIGHT
ROUTE 9 IN NORTH YARMOUTH
Tel. Cumberland 76-2 or 76-21

The Current Scene

How many acres of forests does Pownal have today? Ken Canfield, district forester for the Maine Forest Service, said in a recent interview that the agency has no relevant records specific to Pownal. Overall, the state is seventy-five percent forested and twenty-five percent cleared, while in 1850 the reverse was true. He further stated, "Well-managed wood lots are less susceptible to disease in general, and white pine blister rust is no longer a problem."

For many years, harvesters have been required to file annual notification of acres harvested in each town. Gregory Lord, Planning and Research Associate II of the Maine Forest Service, has reported that, from 1991 to 2005, Pownal had ninety-one timber harvests involving a total of 3,002 acres. It appears that the forests of Pownal are being well monitored and sensibly managed.

Today, there are seven recognized dealers in forest products in town. Their operations include logging, processing of cut timber, and production of salable items.

Maine Custom Woodlands is owned by Thomas Cushman, a certified "Master Logger." He manages a full-service mechanical logging operation and has been providing forest management and harvesting services since 1993.

Luther Snow bucking firewood.

Kermit Wentworth has been supplying firewood locally for thirty years.

Housed in a shop built by Richard "Dick" Hogue in 2004, this c. 1900 shingle saw has cut the shingles which cover the roof and walls of the building's exterior. Dick uses locally harvested red and white pine. The bark and shavings are used to mulch the family gardens. He plans to sell homemade shingles locally.

Maine Custom Firewood is owned and operated by Thomas Cushman and Alan Curry. They prepare seasoned firewood that is delivered to area homes, campgrounds, restaurants, and small stores.

Luther and Evelyn Snow have been working with forest products for over fifty years. Luther, working with son David, cuts and sells firewood locally. Prior to 1978, when his sawmill burned, he made lobster traps and fish boxes that were marketed along the northeast coast and Canada. Luther and wife Evelyn have been making seasonal decorative wreaths, roping, kissing balls, and centerpieces for forty-two years. These are marketed locally along with a new line of bentwood lawn furniture.

Kermit Wentworth has been a cordwood dealer supplying firewood locally for thirty years. He also works with son Eric clearing land.

Upper Farm Wood Products is owned and operated by Gregory Carter who has thirty years experience in logging. He offers custom portable sawmill services, firewood, lumber for custom projects, and land clearing.

SLB Enterprises, Inc. is owned and operated by Stanwood Burnham. He sells firewood and bark mulch to homes and area businesses.

David W. Coffin provides portable sawmill service in the local area.

Above: Maine Custom Woodlands owner Thomas Cushman holds a degree in forestry from the University of Maine.

Right: His Caterpillar forest machine pictured in 2006.

Frank A. Knight Has Deep Roots in Pownal's Forest and Granite Industries

Frank A. Knight, celebrates his one-hundredth birthday in 2008, just as the town in which he was born celebrates its two-hundredth. What's more, Frank's family roots go back two hundred years to Pownal's original settlers. Frank's father, Frank (1870-1912) was co-owner of the sawmill on the Hodsdon Road, as was his uncle, Charles H. Knight Sr. The senior Knight was also the owner of the granite quarry along the Hodsdon and Royal Roads. Frank's mother, Kate Coolidge Hodsdon (1876-1913) was a daughter of Charles and Eliza Mitchell Hodsdon who owned extensive granite quarries along Hodsdon Road. (See page 144.)

As Frank related in 2006, "My father ran the mill and my grandfather ran the stone." Following the deaths of his father in 1912 and his mother in 1913, Frank went to live with his grandmother, Eliza Hodsdon, at the family farm, currently 234 Hodsdon Road. Frank said, "I got into the wood business in 1921 when I was twelve years old. I had learned all I could learn

attending the Hodsdon one-room school and was too young to go to North Yarmouth Academy, so Emma Loring [later, Pervier], the teacher, designed a special program for me where I would attend school two days a week and would work on the farm three days a week. I got ambitious... Got Harry Sweetser to help me... We cut twelve cord of hard wood pulp... Then Uncle George Hodsdon helped me haul. He double-team hauled [horse and sled] two cord, and I hauled one cord until we hauled all twelve cords to Forest Paper Company in Yarmouth. I got a check for $144.00, twelve dollars per cord, pretty good, and gave the check to my grandmother. I can remember that so well. The stone came later."

Frank graduated from NYA in 1925 and from the Forestry School at the University of Maine at Orono in 1930. During the summers while in college, Frank worked for his Uncle Charles at the granite quarry. These were the days when the Bailey Island bridge was being built. Later, his first job was cruising (surveying) the Allagash for Great Northern Paper Company. During the depression years he supervised the Civilian Conservation Corps camps in Lewiston. By 1940, the demand for wood of all kinds was great and Frank decided to go into business for himself. He found a ready market and began to build a reputation as a pulpwood dealer. During this time, he worked with his cousin, Philip Knight, cruising for wood to build the red oak barges at the South Freeport yard. (See page 137.) Eventually he became foreman of a planking crew during the construction of these barges.

By the 1950s, Frank and his crew had begun clearing lands to build Interstate 95, the Portland Jetport, and Valhalla Golf Course, cutting 10,000 cords of pulpwood per year. Frank experienced an industry in transition from the horse and wagon to the use of motorized vehicles and automatic loaders. He retired in 1974.

When Dutch elm disease hit the trees of the area in 1956, Frank was appointed tree warden of Yarmouth, an unpaid position. As he managed the twenty or so remaining elms, one survivor caught his attention and received special care. Known locally as "Herbie," this 240-year-old tree is twenty feet around at the base and 110 feet tall, with a crown of 120 feet. In 1987, Frank entered it into the Big Tree Register, where it remains today as the New England champion American elm.

Residing today in Yarmouth, Frank maintains close contact with area family and friends. He attends many local functions, where his charming smile and quick wit assure him of a warm welcome. Particular favorites are the local church bean suppers. He delights in sharing his memories—memories that span one hundred years of the life and times of a generous and much-honored man.

Right: "Herbie," the largest American elm tree in New England, in 2007. It is located at the Route 88-Yankee Drive crossroads in Yarmouth. The Elm Historic Institute of Nashua, New Hampshire has declared Herbie an historic elm to be preserved.

Left: For over fifty years Frank Knight has been monitoring the health of Herbie and Yarmouth's twenty-plus remaining elms. Over 700 of these old trees were lost to Dutch elm disease in Yarmouth. Frank explained in 2007, "It is like a cancer. We look for signs of disease in the summer noting limbs with wilting leaves that quickly turn brown. The treatment is to cut out the diseased limb and then inoculate against the disease. Herbie has been treated fourteen times… Don't know if we caught it all this year."

Pownal's Big Trees

Hophornbeam 5'10"
Kevin Rodel - Sue Mack
Leighton Road

White ash 15'8"
Arleen Tryon
Lawrence Road

Red Oak 17'9"
Fred Stasinowsky
Merrill Road

1988

This project was carried out by members of the Collars and Leashes 4-H Dog Club Rita Ryder, Allison Hewett, Heather Blackstone and their leader Sherry Dietrich.

As reported in *4-H Earth Connections News*, Winter, 1989, "Sherry Dietrich, leader of her dog obedience club, called the 'Collars and Leashes,' created a youth activity called 'Tree Search' for nine- to fourteen-year-olds… Armed with only tape measure, Sherry and three 4-Hers (Heather Blackstone, Allison Hewett, and Rita Ryder) tromped over acres and acres of woods, fields, and lawns in search of large trees… The largest were a red oak at 17'9", a white ash at 15'8", and a hop hornbeam at 5'10". The Department of Conservation verified the measurements and confirmed that they had found a State Co-Champion with the hop hornbeam… [The children] also learned about trees and how a small number of people can create community awareness." The hop hornbeam is listed in *Maine's Big Tree Register*.

This hop hornbeam, nominated to the Maine Big Tree Register in 1988 by Sherry Dietrich, is being re-measured in 2007 by Maine State Forester Rebecca Tavani. Assisting are Lindley Saffeir, left, and her sister Jesse. It remains a co-champion on the 2007-2008 register.

Minerals

*The Charles Knight Sr. quarry on the North Yarmouth side
of Royal Road, inactive since the 1930s,
pictured in 1981.*

Vast changes in the earth's structure and climate over geologic time have placed certain mineral deposits near the surface of the land we call Pownal. Residents have been quick to take advantage of this, from the town's founding through its second century. Quarried granite takes pride of place in any discussion of Pownal's use of mineral resources. But its smaller forms, gravel and sand, have established their own importance as well. Also, feldspar mining flourished briefly as a local commercial venture.

Granite: The Everlasting Foundation

"Without doubt more dollars have been made in our town from the quarrying of granite than from any other industry." This statement by Ettie Latham in her 1908 book, *History of The Town of Pownal*, may have been true, but by 1908 it was clear that this industry was in a continuing decline in Pownal as well as in the entire state. The glory days of granite, when vast quantities of Maine stone were shipped to many cities in the U.S. and around the world, were over. Architectural styles were changing and granite, a less adaptable building material, was being replaced by steel, concrete, and composites. A mild recovery in the mid 1920s, based largely on a demand for paving blocks, helped, but in another two decades the last quarry in Pownal would be closed.

It was noisy, dusty, dangerous work. During a 1974 interview, Philip Knight recalled, "On a long sheet, we'd drill six or seven holes in there and you'd fire them all at once with an electric battery... We didn't use any dynamite any more than we had to, 'cause it destroys everything... When you use [black] powder, the powder just lifts, that's all... We put in just a spoonful, just a little powder in each hole; fire it; then put in a little more; fire it again; lift again, and sometimes three or four times." As Philip remembered it, the air in the stone cutting shed, where twenty-five men might be working at one time, was particularly unhealthy: "The shed was full of dust, you know, an inch and a half deep of dust, and the air was full of stone dust and everybody was apoundin' it. A lot of 'em died, you know, from stonecutter's consumption back in those days."

The Charles Hodsdon quarry on the Hodsdon road closed in 1908. However, the Charles Knight quarry, which Mr. Knight had purchased from Dudley Freeman's heirs around the turn of the century, remained in operation. It was located on the southwest side of the Hodsdon Road and extended into the adjacent towns of North Yarmouth and Freeport. This quarry continued to produce granite stone for many uses. Chief among them were the 1920 construction of the Sacred Heart Church in Yarmouth and the

Philip Knight is pictured at the Charles Knight quarry in 1974 explaining how granite was harvested. "A Fordson tractor ran a compressor to power jack hammers to drill three-inch holes. When [they were] filled with black powder [and] detonated – a big whump and a seam opens."

1926-1928 building of the Bailey Island cribstone bridge.

Master stonemason Charles Knight Sr. and his son Carl, a blueprint specialist, (both of Pownal) began construction of the Sacred Heart Church in 1920. However, Charles' other son, Philip, actually began work on this project three years earlier when he started hauling the granite stones from the Knight quarry. He reached the site by taking the Royal Road to the Ledge Road, then to the North Road, to East Elm Street, and to Main Street in Yarmouth. He remembered, "The stone was hauled by horses… every day of the week but one… Started in the fall with wagon… Went to sleds… Hauled stones steady three trips a day… Never missed but one day (with) snow blowing and twenty-five below zero… [One winter] I had the whole town to myself, everyone stayed in 'cause three people had smallpox. Thought it would kill you… I handled every stone in that building that's above ground… You had to pick these up all by hand to load and unload them… I had two, three pile of stone the whole length of the place up eight, ten feet high before we even started to build the building there… I guess I hauled stone there for

Sacred Heart Church, located on Main Street, Yarmouth, as it appeared in 2005.

(continued on page 148)

The Bailey Island cribstone bridge, completed in 1928, was said to resemble "a string of pearls." Photo by Maine Department of Transportation.

Hodsdon-York Family Role in Quarrying and Town Affairs Extends over Many Generations

Andrew Hodsdon (1811-1899) and Rachel York Hodsdon (d. 1878)

The Hodsdon-York families owned and operated extensive granite quarries, from the early 1800s to 1908. They were located behind their homes on the Hodsdon Road and extended over to the Royal Road. These families played leading roles in the granite industry as well as in the early history of the town. The quarrying began with original settler Captain Joseph York who cleared the land of tree growth to begin farming and uncovered the large expanses of granite. Andrew Hodsdon married Rachel York, Joseph's daughter, and operated the business alone throughout these years, until he was joined by his son, Charles, just returned from serving in the Civil War. With the increasing demand for granite paralleling the growth of the railroad, the industry reached peak production from the 1850s to the 1890s. Sometime during this period, Charles Hodsdon had a derrick at Yarmouth Junction that was used to load paving and curb stones for shipment by rail to the distant cities of Minneapolis, St. Paul, and Cincinnati. Charles also served as superintendent of the Fred Greene quarry, located in Pownal but owned by Pownal benefactor Edmund B. Mallet Jr. George, son of Charles and Eliza, continued to operate the family quarry until it closed in 1908.

The Charles Hinkley Hodsdon (1838-1911) and Eliza Mitchell Hodsdon (1843-1925) family, pictured in 1887 on the porch of their home, currently 234 Hodsdon Road. Charles and Eliza are seated with their daughter, Florence. Their other children stand in the back row l to r.: Ella, Rachel, Josephine, Elizabeth, Edith, Kate, and George.

In a speech given to the Granite Grange in the early 1900s, Josephine Hodsdon Small noted that the first significant amount of material quarried was used to pave the streets of New Orleans. Orders were then taken for paving stones for Portland and for other cities nationwide, as well as for curbing stones and for covering municipal fire-protection reservoirs. Other projects across the state included major bridges and dams; foundations for mills, schools, and churches; and the Masonic Hall in Yarmouth. Granite was used locally for similar applications.

Following his service in the Civil War, Charles became active in town affairs, serving as selectman for eleven years (1877 to 1901), as town clerk for two years, and as district school agent for District 3 (later known as the Hodsdon School). Four of his seven daughters became school teachers: Florence, Rachel, Elizabeth, and Josephine. Son George (1867-1940) and his wife, Sarah Johnson (1881-1973), took over the original Andrew Hodsdon farm, where they raised their family. It was located across the road from the home of Charles and Eliza. Later, George and Sarah's son, Robert (1904-1987), and his wife Mabel Blackstone Hodsdon (1910-1996) continued to live on this homestead. Today Robert and Mabel's son, Ronald, and his wife, Mary Ann Bailey, reside in Andrew's original house. They are the seventh Hodsdon-York generation to live here, and, following family tradition, they continue to actively serve their community.

Three generations: Ronald "Hutch" Hodsdon and Family. Front row l. ro r.: Mary Ann Bailey Hodsdon, Malia Hodsdon Morin (granddaughter), Robin Hodsdon Morin (daughter). Back row l to r.: Robert (son), Samuel (grandson), and Ronald Hodsdon. Not pictured: daughter, Lisa Marie Hodsdon Bernstein.

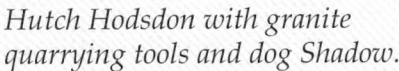

Hutch Hodsdon with granite quarrying tools and dog Shadow.

Each granite block used in the bridge construction was numbered and lettered.

two winters." When the first service was held in the church on June 25, 1923, those in attendance found themselves in a beautiful slate-roofed Romanesque building further accented with mosaics over the windows. Following an extensive interior renovation in 1977, the exterior stone was renovated in 1994.

Perhaps the largest and most extensive building project involving Pownal granite in the twentieth century was the construction of the Bailey Island cribstone bridge located in Harpswell. Many of the freestanding blocks that form this unique bridge were mined in the Knight quarry. Each block was numbered and lettered. These huge pieces were hauled on horse-drawn sleds during the winter to Marsh Bridges on the Cousins River in Yarmouth, there to await the spring thaw for loading onto barges and transport to the bridge site. (See page 150.)

Philip Knight and his father were running the quarry during these years, and working conditions for these and other projects must have been much as Philip remembered: "In the summertime, of course, around all the ledges, it would be two, three hundred men altogether from all around... Everything was done by hand. A stone quarryman got a dollar a day, a stonecut-

(continued on page 152)

WINTERS HE WENT WHERE THERE WAS WORK

I can remember as a child sitting quietly listening to my Grandmother reminiscing about the old days with my Mom and Dad. One particular evening she was telling about my grandfather working in the winter in a quarry. It seems that he would get up at 4:00 A.M., go out to the barn and feed the horses, and get their feed for the week loaded onto the wagon. He then would return to the house for breakfast that Grandmother had been preparing along with everything in a satchel for his week away. He would go back to the barn, hitch the horses to the wagon, and off they would go to the very southern end of town about ten miles away. A working quarry was there and someone would have shelter for the horses, and Grandfather would find a place to board. Meanwhile, back home on the farm, Grandmother was left with four sons and an invalid. The boys would milk the cows and take care of the barn, then be off to school.

At the quarry, the stone would be cut and loaded onto skids, and the horses would haul the stone over the snow to the ocean in Yarmouth, where it would be stored until spring then put on a barge and taken to Orrs and Bailey Island to build the cribstone bridge. They probably made one trip a day. The quarry was about three miles or more from the ocean. On Friday, Grandfather and the horses would return to the farm for the weekend. I would guess that this was extra income for the winter.

2003 Remembrances of Mary Mitchell Strong about her grandfather, George P. Mitchell (1881-1938), and grandmother, Goldie Noyes Mitchell (1883-1969).

Historic Pound

The cattle pound, built in 1818 and pictured here in 1900, is one of Pownal's rare historic treasures. It is located on the Hallowell Road on Bradbury Mountain State Park land. Early homesteaders built stone walls around cleared property to keep stray farm animals out. If animals were caught damaging crops, they were taken to the pound and kept to such time as the owner claimed them. There was a fee schedule for keeping animals for twenty-four hours or more, and all animals had their ears notched for identification. John Tyler was paid fifty dollars to build the pound. Thomas Cotton, whose land abutted, was the first town pound keeper.

Through the efforts of the Pownal Scenic and Historical Society, the Pownal cattle pound was entered in the National Register of Historic Places on July 28, 2004 by the National Park Service. The remaining structure is pictured here in 2005.

Bailey Island Cribstone Bridge Receives Another Honor

On July 19, 1984, the Bailey Island Cribstone Bridge, then fifty-six years old, received national recognition as a "Historic Civil Engineering Landmark." It was recognized that no other similar structure has ever been built in the State of Maine or possibly in the world. The public was invited to the dedication ceremonies during which two plaques marking the historic landmark were erected, and following which a social hour was held at Cook's Lobster Pound Restaurant. This was not the first honor for the well-known bridge, as it had been placed in the National Register of Historic Places in 1974.

Construction of this unique bridge began in 1926 using a plan designed by Llewelon N. Edwards, Maine State Engineer from 1921 to 1928. The plan would connect Bailey and Orrs Islands without impeding the tidal currents and seasonal ice flows. It would also provide an opening to allow boat passage under the bridge by area lobstermen and recreational boaters. His plan called for hauling twelve-foot granite slabs by barge to the bridge site, and laying them in crisscross fashion with a steam derrick, for a length of 1,111 feet. Workmen constructed a rail system on the bridge deck to move the derrick and other heavy building materials during construction. The deck was topped off with a concrete roadway. The completed bridge, costing $120,000, was opened to traffic in 1928. Later, in 1935, the state installed a narrow walkway on the east side of the bridge.

In the 1990s, repair work was done on the bridge, as many of the granite slabs were broken and some had shifted. The stones were reinforced with concrete. Nevertheless, in 2003 Ben Foster, State of Maine Engineer, cited conditions that made the bridge un-

Huge granite pieces were hauled on horse-drawn sled to Marsh Bridges on the Cousins River to be hauled on barges. Photo: MDOT 1926.

Steam derrick placed the granite in crisscross fashion. Photo: MDOT 1926.

safe. They included broken and shifting granite slabs, deterioration of the narrow sidewalk beams, and the too narrow width of the bridge. He stated that the Maine Department of Transportation (MDOT) is bound by state law to provide for safe and efficient bridge traffic and would be held accountable should accidents occur. Harpswell citizens and others interested in preserving the bridge advocated maintaining its unique historical integrity. Public hearings were held. An in-depth study was done by MDOT with the assistance of the Lichtenstein Engineering Company, a firm which has experience in historical preservation.

Rachel Ganong reported in the *Times Record* of October 25, 2005 that MDOT and utility company officials had met with local officials to discuss preparations for temporary wire crossings so that bridge repairs could begin in 2008. The project, estimated to cost between five and eight million dollars, calls for widening and roadway replacement; rehabilitation of the supporting bottom stones; and construction of a temporary bridge. Harpswell residents and others interested in its preservation have been reassured that all efforts will be made to restore this historic landmark and maintain its usefulness for traffic of the twenty-first century.

MDOT engineer Jim Wentworth underlined Pownal's connection to this bridge in 2007, when he indicated that replacement granite will come from a quarry next to the Pownal site that supplied the original material. He added, "The stones we use will match the grain of the stones already in the bridge. They will come from the same vein."

2005 view of the bridge.

ter got three, and the engineer (the guy who ran the boiler) got two dollars a day. The stonecutter was the highest paid, they were scientific guys, darn good too. One was George Monroe, one was Moses Blackstone, and one was Harlan True. They worked from seven to five with no breaks except for lunch."

Stonecarvers were skilled craftsmen who worked with the cut stone. Many were of Italian ancestry. Such was Francis Latty, an Italian immigrant, who moved to Pownal from Stonington in the early 1900s. He purchased the Reed Quarry, named after its first owner Josiah Reed, an original settler of Pownal. Located where the Hodsdon Road meets the Ledge Road, this large quarry spreads over Pownal, Freeport, and North Yarmouth. Mr. Latty was known as a fine stonecarver, and he operated this quarry with his sons Elvin (known as Jack) and Basil until the mid 1930s. They produced high quality monument stones and other carved stones for public buildings. Tax records indicate that from the mid- 1930s through the mid-1950s, this quarry supplied much sand and gravel for road construction. Current heirs and owners, Mark and Denise Latty, no longer operate the quarry.

By the 1940s, the last granite quarry in Pownal had closed, and the daily sounds of hammers and black powder explosions were heard no more. Today, in addition to the church and the bridge, many structures made with this stone survive. At its peak prior to 1900, Pownal granite had been shipped all over the state and beyond for use in large public buildings, bridges, and roads. Many of these are still standing. Locally, surviving structures include the Yarmouth Water Works building, the Key Bank building in Yarmouth, and the Pownal Cattle Pound. The Cattle Pound is one of two in Maine that has been placed on the National Register of Historic Places. Only a handful of such pounds have survived in the state, whereas once they were working structures found in many rural communities. They played a central role in the control and return of straying livestock.

The visible heritage of Pownal's granite production continues to pervade our immediate sur-

The Tuttle (or Toothaker) Bridge, built of Pownal granite, is pictured in the early 1900s spanning the East Branch of the Royal River (Branch Brook). It has been replaced with a modern structure.

Stone mason Dennis Peaslee Jr. constructs a dry stone garden wall at the current 584 Poland Range Road in 1996.

roundings in the form of house and barn foundations, steps, posts, and paving stones. And then there are the many miles of granite stone walls, the early settler's enduring answer to perishable wooden fencing. These walls, hand laid using the abundant "crop" of stone "harvested" from the land's surface, are daily reminders of how much of Pownal was once cleared and cultivated. Early farmers made good use of granite fieldstone, and a well-built wall was often equated with prosperity and plenty. In many places the woods have now reclaimed the land, but the walls endure. They stand as mute evidence of previous open vistas traced with walls delineating boundaries and enclosing fields of crops and livestock.

Jordan A. Smith is an artist and designer who has worked increasingly in three dimensions over the past decade. He is the owner of Rocksmith, Inc., a landscape and construction company, which he founded in 2003. He creates high quality stone walls, patios, walkways, and ponds and art to go with them. Many of his projects use Pownal granite as raw material, acquired from an abandoned local quarry. He is shown here with his display at the 2008 Portland Flower Show, whose theme was "Urban Retreat." He won the show's award for best hardscape.

Charles Henry Knight Sr. (1857-1947)
Quarry Man, Stone Mason, Contractor, Farmer

The obituary of Charles H. Knight Sr. begins: "The community was saddened this week by the death of one of Pownal's oldest citizens, on January 30th after a month's treatment in Maine General Hospital for a broken hip." It seems, as one reflects on Charles' life, that the community must have thought he would endure forever, like the granite that he worked. He truly became a man with more lasting monuments to his life than his gravestone.

His granddaughter, Marion Knight Reed, recently remembered him as being "very tall and rugged, with not a bit of fat; he was a quiet man who was always known as a 'hard worker' both at the quarry and on his farm." Born in 1857 at the Hodsdon Road home of his parents, Edward and Mae (Mary) Augusta Brown Knight, Charles attended local schools. In 1884 he married Mary Jane Soule of South Portland and they settled on a farm, currently 172 Hodsdon Road, where they raised seven children: Carl, Clinton, Elsie, Philip, Donald, Helen,

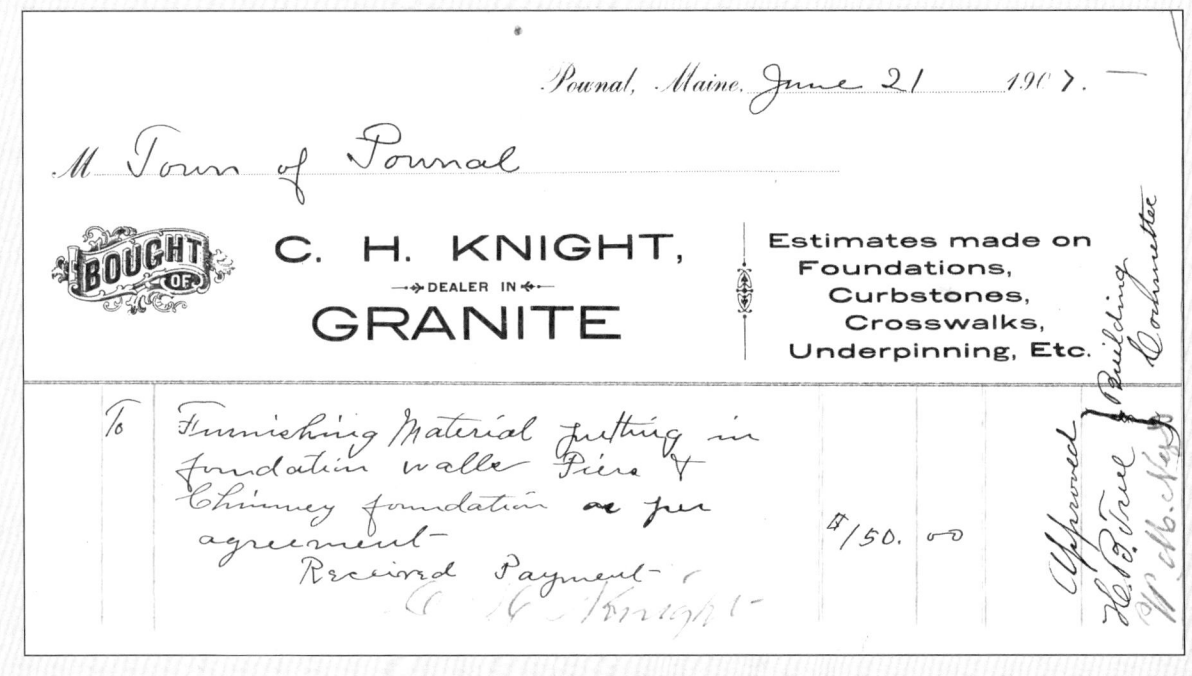

and Charles H. Jr. His wife, Mary Jane, died in 1931 and in 1936 he married Zona Soule (no relation to Mary Jane). Charles was a descendant of Jeremiah Knight, who was listed in 1808 as an original taxpayer.

Charles worked as quarry man for many years before purchasing the Dudley Freeman quarry around 1900, following the death of Mr. Freeman. His quarry, crossing the Pownal-North Yarmouth border along the Royal and Ledge Roads, provided granite for building many fine buildings and homes in surrounding communities. The granite used in the construction of the Sacred Heart Church in Yarmouth and the Bailey Island cribstone bridge was quarried here.

The archives of the Pownal Scenic and Historical Society contain newspaper accounts describing a man who never retired to live an easy life. In 1932, at his surprise seventy-fifth birthday party, he celebrated with family and friends after "chopping a cord of wood." For his eightieth birthday, press coverage by Louise Rogers headlined: "Puts Up Half-Mile of Stone Wall—Knight Claims He's In Spring of Life And Proves It." In her article, Rogers continued, "Instead of sitting by the fire with a book and his pipe, he is building a dry stone wall, one-half mile long, on the Philip Payson Estate (along Route 88) at Cumberland Foreside." Charles continued to lay stone until he retired at age 85, thereafter maintaining an active life until his death in 1947.

Charles was a founding and lifelong member of the Knights of Pythias, and a member of both the Granite Grange and the Westcustogo Lodge. His hobbies were hunting and fishing, and he particularly enjoyed angling for trout from a brook near his home.

Stone wall built along Route 88 in Cumberland Foreside by Charles H. Knight Sr., still sound seventy-one years later.

Feldspar's Rapid Rise and Fall

Feldspar is the name given to a group of crystalline minerals consisting mainly of aluminum silicates and containing other trace elements. Found as a constituent of nearly all crystalline rocks (including granite), feldspar was mined in Pownal during the 1920s and 1930s.

Pownal had two active feldspar mines. One was located on Bradbury Mountain, while the other was on nearby Tryon Mountain. The June 22, 1935 obituary of Robert A. Smith states: "Feldspar was found on his property [currently Bradbury Mountain State Park land] and was mined extensively for some time." Tons of feldspar were removed from these mines during the 1930s, trucked to the West Pownal railroad station, and freighted to New Jersey where it was ground for use in the composition matrix of pottery, dishes, enamelware, and bathtubs. It also found use in glazes as well as certain abrasives and soaps (Borax).

This activity mirrors developments in the entire state as indicated in the Maine Department of Conservation Geological Survey Report of October 6, 2005. This report documents that the statewide production of feldspar peaked in the late 1920s and almost ceased during the depression. Local workers profited from the brief active life of these mines, and Josephine Allen recounts that, during the depression years, her father, Joseph Pervier "picked up work with his truck hauling feldspar that was mined at Bradbury Mountain."

The *Geological Survey Report* of 2005 further indicates that feldspar, a mineral of variable composition, remains relatively abundant in Pownal and elsewhere. Less abundant, but still found in Pownal, are several other minerals of more specific composition, namely: beryl, columbite, fluorapatite, magnetite, microcline, monazite, muscovite, pyrite, quartz, uraninite, and zircon. Today any "mining" activity is limited to visitors to the two former sites, where they pick over the feldspar scree, and to hobbyists searching for the more pure crystalline minerals just mentioned.

Tryon Mountain, accessed by foot trail from the Lawrence Road, still offers mute testimony to the brief heyday of feldspar mining in Pownal. The site features a tall derrick pole, still standing and supported by five guy wires which are secured to the trunks of large trees. The picture to the left, taken in the winter of 2005, shows the quarry pit, which is presently partly filled with water.

Sand and Gravel: Small Pieces of Great Importance

As the glaciers melted and receded thousands of years ago, they left behind an outwash of rocks, gravel, and sand in the lower terrain. This readily accessed debris was destined to play an important role in road, bridge, and other construction across the state, and most certainly in Pownal.

In Pownal's 1905 town report, Road Commissioner Henry Sweetser wrote, " In some parts of town, even where there's gravel within the road limits, it is costly and difficult to get the job done. I would suggest that the town buy two or three gravel pits in different parts of the town… First it would be much cheaper than buying by the load, second we need a good deal of gravel on our clay roads." It would be eight years before Henry's advice was taken. In 1913, the town purchased its first gravel pit located on what would become Bradbury Mountain State Park land. Later, in 1942, a second pit was purchased at the intersection of the Hallowell and Tuttle Roads.

(continued on page 159)

Above: Naturally occurring, bank-run sand from the Brown Road pit. This sand has not yet been stockpiled. The layers are still visible.

Below: In the foreground, a pile of "tailings" is left over from the screening process. These stones, along with the larger ones in the background, will be crushed into "rip rap," an 8- to 10-inch stone used for erosion control. The pile in the mid-ground right is 4-inch gravel. The machine on the right is an 892 John Deere excavator.

Blackstone's Brown Road pit handles materials from fine sand to huge boulders. The rocks seen in the foreground will either be used for retaining walls or crushed into gravel. Equipment from left to right: John Deere loader, screening plant, 892 John Deere excavator, and a Kamatsu loader. The material emerging from the screener is screened loam. Looking on are Albert Blackstone Jr. and his grandson, Able Kaplan.

From left to right: a pile of screened loam, stumps (background) that will be re-screened and ground up for compost, John Deere loader, tailings from the screening process (foreground) that will be crushed for gravel.

Apparently the town-owned pits were never quite sufficient, and throughout the period between 1908 and the 1940s, the town purchased gravel from private pits. Charles Knight, George Hodsdon, Kathryne Sturtevant, Horace Merrill, and Mellen Tryon were among those who sold sand and gravel to the town during these years.

Indeed, sand and gravel have been quarried and used in Pownal almost from its founding. Many pits, both large and small, have opened and closed over the years. In a 2006 interview Carl I. Knight said, "There were little pits everywhere… As it was mostly done by hand, they'd just move on when the digging got hard." Eventually, the advent of powered mechanized equipment made the extensive quarrying of large pits feasible. Located on the Libby road, one of the earliest was owned by Charles Henry Knight (1857-1947). Ownership of this pit passed through his son, Charles (Bill) Knight Jr., to Carl I. Knight who sold it to Scott Dugas of Yarmouth in 1978. Nearby, on the Elmwood road, is a pit currently owned by Albert Blackstone Jr. who acquired it from his father in 1968. These two pits are the only ones, currently, with commercial potential in Pownal.

Today, two other large, active gravel pits are owned by a Pownal resident, but they are located in Durham. Bill Knight Jr. purchased the Big Sky pit in 1950, then passed it to his son Carl in 1978. This was sold to Albert H. Blackstone Jr. in 2005. On the Brown Road, Albert also runs a large gravel pit that he purchased in 1985, after leasing it for fifteen years. Both of these deposits continue to supply sand and gravel for projects in the vicinity.

An overview of the Brown Road pit shows stockpiles of processed gravel, crushed stone, leaching sand, and winter sand.

Albert Blackstone Jr., Excavating

Albert Blackstone Jr. has been in business in the heart of Pownal for almost fifty years. His father, Albert Sr., owned and ran the general store in the center, but always supplemented his income with a woods operation.

In 1953, when Albert Sr. purchased a bulldozer for his woods operation, Albert Jr. was ten years old. He operated the dozer, building woods roads. Albert Jr. often used the dozer in the winter to plow snow for a steady group of clients. At his young age, he even helped the town with culvert work. Often the machine was used to pull their hay bailer through the fields. When his father bought a crawler/loader in 1957, Albert Jr. hauled sand out of the family's Freeport Road pit. "We did what was needed... I never made it a point to go into the sand business. If someone had needed me pulping, I'd be pulping now."

But the sand business grew, and Albert Jr. bought his own equipment: a 1957 Chevy truck in 1960 and a new bulldozer in 1962. Just as the business started to take off, however, Albert was drafted, serving until 1967. After his return to Pownal, it took a year before the business was resurrected. Albert bought the Freeport Road pit from his father in 1967, and soon after started hiring his first full-time crew. Business has been steady ever since. "We'll be out straight with work for a few years, and then it'll take a bad turn. Always the same, but we average a twelve-man crew today, same since 1979."

What are the qualities that have allowed this 40-plus year business to thrive? "I just keep going and stay numb to what people think. I knew business meant working seven days a week, and I just kept my head down. Plus, you just gotta have a supportive spouse... You just can't get on without a supportive spouse." And who was his most influential business teacher? "My father taught me the most. The [three] things were: being sensitive to people, knowing what people needed, and being loyal to his workers. He'd do anything for them."

Above: 2003 Mack dump truck with a 12-14 dump body.

Right: Standing in the bucket of a 644 John Deere loader: Ronald Newell, pit supervisor (left); Albert Blackstone Jr. (right); and Able Kaplan, grandson of Albert Blackstone Jr. and Sharon Blackstone.

Chapter 3

Businesses Change with the Times

By 1908 it was clear that Pownal's two early major industries, sawmills and granite quarries, were in decline and would not remain viable very far into the twentieth century. The businesses destined to continue were primarily purveyors of goods and services to meet local needs. Such enterprises, most classified as home occupations, have comprised the town's economic base over the past one hundred years. The Grand Trunk Railroad with its station in West Pownal played a major role in setting the business climate up to mid-century. For as long as it remained in operation, the railroad provided key transportation services. It brought local businesses raw materials and carried their goods to market. This chapter presents a gallery of pictures, documenting the broad array of businesses that have flourished in Pownal during the past century. Since there have been so many of them over the years, this is a selective overview rather than an exhaustive listing.

George D. Daniels (1883-1958) worked for the Grand Trunk Railroad for fifty-two years. He is pictured here at the Gilead, Maine station where he worked for thirty-four years until the station closed in 1946. The Pownal station called him to service from 1947 to 1952 when the station officially closed. George Daniels also served as a town selectman from 1952 to 1955.

The Grand Trunk Railroad Station, Pownal, Maine is pictured as a train arrives during the winter of 1910.

Pownal Center Store
True Warren, Owner, 1886-1914

The Pownal Center General Store, located at the northeast corner of the busy Hallowell and Elmwood (previously Dyer) Roads intersection, was purchased by True Warren in 1886. Since 1832, when Hosea Newell owned it, it had been providing daily necessities for the nearby residents, and goods for people who passed through the village. Early commodities sold included grains, groceries, dry goods, dried fish, bulk items such as lard, molasses, and vinegar, tin and hardware, yard goods, sewing notions, clothing items, tobacco, candy, and medicines.

True Warren also repaired shoes and harnesses. By the early 1900s, kerosene and gasoline were sold. The store functioned as the center for town news and notices, and housed a post office until 1907. True Warren also served as town clerk from 1893 to 1915. In 1975, Henrietta Marston Starling remembered the candy counter with glass windows when she was a child. "I used to climb up there with my pennies in hand and point out what I wanted. A stick of this and a stick of that, you know. He [True Warren] was awfully nice."

Above: Pownal Center General Store is pictured around 1908, when it was owned by True Warren.

Left: Interior of the center store, showing True Warren mending a leather harness. He also repaired shoes.

Pownal Center Store
Albert H. Blackstone Sr., Owner, 1926-1972

Albert H. Blackstone Sr. purchased the Center Store in 1926. It had been sitting vacant for eight years and required extensive renovations. The photo below reveals that he sold "Ice Cold" Coca Cola, Hires Root Beer, Ingleside beverages, S&H Ice Cream, groceries, candy, tobacco, and refreshments. Sacony gasoline (at twenty-two cents per gallon) and motor oil were available for the increasing number of motor vehicles. The sale of beer began in 1944, and with the advent of refrigeration, the sale of meat and perishables increased.

The Blackstone General Store witnessed many changes over forty-six years, before closing in 1972. The store continued to operate until 1978 under owners Norman and Faye Napier, and its last owner, Paul Bessey. During that period it also featured a lunch counter. Currently, the building is owned by Albert and Sharon Blackstone Jr. and is occupied by Rousseau Builders.

Although difficult to make out in this picture, Albert is pictured around 1930, standing on the porch of his newly renovated store. The attached living quarters are on the right.

Albert H. Blackstone Sr. (1907-1980) and Christina Bradley Blackstone (1905-2005) in 1956.

The store as it appeared in 1960.

North Pownal General Store
William J. Sawyer, Owner, 1900-1919

North Pownal had two general stores, established in the early 1800s, to meet the needs of the village and people passing through. The principal one, located at the intersection of Lawrence and Fickett Roads and referred to as the North Pownal General Store, supplied groceries, dried fish, tinware, clothing, sewing supplies, tobacco, candy, and medicines. It also was a post office until 1907. Joseph N. Small (1871-1934), a farmer and house painter who lived next door at the current 73 Fickett Road, worked there as clerk and barber. As in Pownal Center, by 1926 the North Pownal stores also began selling gasoline and motor oil to the rapidly growing number of automobile owners. In the 1940s the store began to sell beer.

The North Pownal General Store in 1908, when it was owned by William Sawyer.

Interior of the North Pownal General Store, c. 1908, with tinware display and customer seating close to the woodstove. The store carried all the necessities of daily life.

North Pownal General Store
Roland and Joyce Morin, Owners, 1978-1996

After 1919 the North Pownal General Store passed through numerous hands. The list of owner-operators includes D. F. Danforth, B. W. Penley, Merton Larrabee, O. H. Winn, Owen Farwell, Theodore Hathaway, Earle Babbidge, Richard Haskell, Roger Bolduc, John Baert, Anna Slocum, Roy Tufts, and James Salisbury.

From 1978 to 1996 Roland and Joyce Morin owned it. They sold the usual groceries, ice cream, beer, wine, sundries, fuel and motor oil. During the hunting season the store operated as a game inspection station, and "hunters breakfasts" served by Joyce became very popular.

Many improvements were made during their ownership. Joyce ran a small restaurant serving deli sandwiches, pizza, "Italians," crab meat rolls, pepper steak sandwiches and homemade desserts.

Roland also operated a filling station and small engine repair business here until 1990. Video tape rental was added in the mid 1990s.

James Daniels operated the store and restaurant from 1997 until 2005. Currently, the property is owned by Leslie and Samantha Hanscom, but the store has been closed.

Above: the store as it appeared in 1996.

Below: Edward Morin, son of Roland and Joyce, managed the store during its last years in operation. The customer is Cecil Burtt.

The Second North Pownal General Store
(or Ben Randall General Store)
Lemuel F. Sawyer, Owner, 1886-1900
Merton Larrabee, Owner, 1919-1941

Benjamin Randall (1803-1870) opened a second store in 1826 across the road from his home at the current 856 Lawrence Road. He also ran a shingle-making business at this site. From 1862 to 1873, this store was owned by Ben's son, Elmer and was known as the Ben Randall General Store. From 1886 to 1900, it was owned by Lemuel F Sawyer.

During certain periods, both North Pownal general stores were owned by the same person, although they were probably not always in operation at the same time. Merton Larrabee (1877-1941) owned and operated both stores from 1928 until his death. The second store building briefly came into the possession of Owen Farwell, who sold it in 1941 to the North Pownal Community Club, a non-profit organization established for the purpose of maintaining the building for public use. This arrangement has continued up to the present.

The second store in 1900 when owned by Lemuel F. Sawyer. The open porch was later removed. The building's rather crude construction is evident in the porch's loose stone foundation.

Above: the store in 1928. L. to r.: owner Merton Larrabee; store clerk and family friend of Mr. Larrabee; Bertha Libby; children of Reverend Earle and Elizabeth Vosmus Steeves, who lived in the home across the road; and Kenneth Libby, Bertha's son.

The store in 1940 when owned by Merton Larrabee.

West Pownal General Store
Charles Dow and Walter Libby, Owners, 1890-1918
Francis C. Handy, Owner, 1919-1933

West Pownal General Store c. 1930, when owned by F. C. Handy.

Francis C. Handy (1888-1952).

The West Pownal Store was owned by Francis C. Handy from 1919 to 1933. Carl Wing, grandson of Mr. Handy, remembered in an interview in 2006 that the railroad depot was a busy center. Dairy farmers brought their milk for shipping each evening, teams of horses and wagons loaded pulpwood into railroad cars for transport, and grain was processed at the nearby mill. He said that "the store sold everything: flour by the barrel or twenty-five pound bag; molasses, you carried in your own jug; medicines, such as sulfur, were sold to treat yourself or your animals; shoes were 'sewed, fixed, soled'; and on the right side of the store on entering was the post office." Mr. Handy was postmaster from 1919 to 1933. He also served one year as selectman in 1928. In 1933 the building burned. A private dwelling occupies the site today.

A contemporary drawing of the Dow & Libby General Store. An 1898 billhead announces that the store dealt in groceries, flour, grain, dry goods, boots, shoes, hardware, crockery, etc.

Fred and Jean Worden Store and Diner 1937-1949

Fred Worden's General Store and Diner (1937-1949) was located on the Allen Road on the New Gloucester town border. Four years after F. C. Handy's store at the depot burned, the Wordens began serving the West Pownal area, especially workers at the State School, now known as Pineland Center. It was operated by Fred until his death in 1941, then by his wife Jean until it closed in 1949. Fred's mother, Laura Worden (1881-1964), ran the diner section.

Dolores Worden Greer remembered in a 2006 interview what was sold in the store. "For groceries, let me see... cookies in bulk boxes with no plastic gloves. You reached in and got your cookies and put them in a bag. Then you walked over and there was bread. The lower shelves had macaroni, string beans, Franco-American spaghetti, tea bags, coffee. Then there was on the next shelf pink and red salmon, pink for pussy cats and red for people. And canned corn. Sometimes canned orange juice of that day which was quite the thing. Nearer the top shelf, toilet tissue, cereal, Wheaties, Ralston, Wheatena and Aunt Jemima pancake mix. Then you went around the corner and there would be shoe laces and white shoe polish (all staff working at Pownal State School wore white uniforms and white shoes)... Behind the counter was the opening to a glass display case for candy which was low and I could reach it. Mary Janes, Squirrel Nuts, lollipops, wafers, Skybar, Hersheys... Then there was the cash register which you added with a paper and pencil... Some people we would allow credit... particularly those of Pineland because they'd get paid every twenty-four days, and mom would cash their checks minus their store bill, which generally consisted of ice cream, pop, cigarettes or pipe tobacco... We even had chewing tobacco. And oh, the ice cream cooler... always chocolate, vanilla, strawberry and the flavor of the month... Did I love the month they had banana nut... could have eaten the whole five gallon drum.

"Standard fare from the diner, where Grammy [Laura] Worden did most of the cooking, was hot dogs, hamburgers, cheeseburgers. Special occasions was crab meat rolls. Once in a while a roast beef or pot roast. Always coffee. Always home fried potatoes. Always eggs. Always cheese. We did not sell beer, as we were too close to the State School. But tobacco. Anyone who had eighteen or twenty cents could buy a pack of cigarettes. And the prices: hot dogs five cents a piece or two for eight cents. And we had a juke box with records changed once a month by a man from Gray. Customers would be locals and those employed at Pineland (then known as the Pownal State School)."

Fred Worden (1905-1941).

Jean Snow Worden (1909-1975).

Marion's Market
Keith's Garage

Marion's Market was operated by Marion Davis Irish (1910-1983) from 1969 to 1975 for owners Arlene Best and Melva Farley. The store was opened in 1946 by Charles "Bill" Knight and Virgil Best, and was then one of two stores operating in the center selling groceries, meat and gasoline. The building is now owned by Rose Edwards and, over the past ten years, has been leased as a restaurant by a series of operators who opened Hannahs, then Morgan's Diner, and then JB's. Its most recent tenant, Cross Roads Pizzeria, closed in 2005.

Marion's Market. Hallowell Road, Pownal Center, c. 1970.

No photos of Donald L. Keith's (1916-2001) garage are available. From 1938 until 1950, Donald repaired and rebuilt motor vehicles at his shop, first located on the Hodsdon Road, then later on Hallowell Road at the Pownal-North Yarmouth town line. Brother Scott Keith remembered during a conversation in 2007, "Don was a good mechanic who learned his trade on hand... During the war years... vehicles were not being produced and tires were running awfully thin... Folks came from all around for his service."

Bill for Carl Thurber for installing shock absorbers and a used coil, 1944.

Repair Shops Straddle the Century

Hathaway J. Fickett's blacksmith shop was located at the North Pownal crossroads. Hathaway's original shop burned in 1917, and a new one was constructed the following year from materials of the recently dismantled nearby cheese factory. Mr. Fickett was known to be able to "straddle the century," servicing both horse and wagon as well as newly arrived motor vehicles.

Hathaway J. Fickett (1873-1933), far right, with unidentified associates in the 1920s.

Pervier's Garage, an auto repair shop and filling station at the current 153 Hallowell Road, was built by Lewis Pervier (1910-1943) following his graduation from Freeport High School in the early 1930s. "Lewie" operated it until his death in 1943. It was then purchased by his brother, Joseph, for the latter's son, Felton, who operated it until 1965. According to Josephine Pervier Allen, Lewis was known for his mechanical abilities, was available anytime day or night, and worked to bring electricity to the center of town in 1935.

Lewis A. Pervier (1910-1943).

These photographs, apparently from the 1930s or 1940s, show Pervier's Garage as a filling station, dispensing Sacony-Vacuum Mobilgas regular and Mobilgas special. The picture of Lewis Pervier appeared in a newspaper about 1932.

Hibbard's Airport
Browercraft Wood Products

Harold E. Hibbard Jr. (1938-1984) was self-employed at his garage and airport hanger near his residence on Hallowell Road. He learned repairing and inspecting planes while in the U. S. Navy. Earning his pilot's license in 1964, Harold had five years' experience with the Civil Air Patrol and was a float plane pilot at Naples, Maine before starting his business in Pownal. Mr. Hibbard owned three planes, a 1956 Cessna Skyhawk, a 1957 Piper Pacer, and a Classic 1946 Fairchild. He died tragically in an airplane accident in August, 1984.

Harold Hibbard Jr. with his Piper Pacer. Photo Don Hinkley, Brunswick Times Record, *October 24, 1983.*

A lobster boat model, one of thousands produced by Vernon C. Brower and Sons over the years.

Vernon C. Brower (1924-2002) established a family business in 1950 in his home in West Pownal. Vernon C. Brower and Sons Industries produced model fishing boats and marine objects, both finished and in kit-form. The business continues today as Browercraft Wood Products.

Garden Spot Farm
W. A. Machine Company

Garden Spot Farm, 896 Lawrence Road, was started in 1972 by Dennis C. Peaslee Sr. (1941-2001) offering a wide selection of vegetable and flower plants and seeds. Over the years, Garden Spot Farm has become a full-service nursery, offering annuals, perennials, herbs, vegetable and flower starts, potted plants, hanging baskets, rose bushes, trees, shrubs, and seeds. They also sell other plant-related products and garden accessories. Following the death of Dennis Sr. in 2001, the business continues to be owned and operated by his wife Patricia Vosmus Peaslee and son, Dennis Jr. Building on the latter's skills in masonry and stone work, landscaping services have been added.

Dennis C. Peaslee Jr.

Robert and Janice West, 2006.

W. A. Machine Co., 614 Elmwood Road, a small metal products manufacturing business, has been owned and operated by Robert and Janice West since 1974. The business was first located in the basement of their home where they assembled golf shoe hardware for MacNeill Engineering in Waltham, Mass. They moved to their current location in 1990 where they manufacture fasteners for wire lobster and crab traps, hog rings, head hoops, aluminum clips, and a line of patented tools. Currently they have eight employees.

DeWitt Real Estate Agency
Arnold Blackstone Excavation

William "Bill" DeWitt, 303 Hodsdon Road, received his real estate license in 1968 and began a career that has spanned forty years. Soon after starting to sell properties, Bill recognized a growing market for people wanting to move out of the cities into affordable housing in a country setting. He established a separate partnership with Fred York, York and DeWitt Builders, Inc. According to Bill, "We built hundreds of New England expandable Cape Cod style homes in the area from 1970 to the mid 1980s. At that time, home construction costs averaged $20,000 to $40,000, while lot prices for one to two acres averaged $2,000 to $6,000." He continues to sell properties, manage rental units, and do consulting and development on building projects with his son Jeffrey W. DeWitt and son-in-law Dennis Dyer.

This expandable Cape Cod style home with single car garage, located at 562 Poland Range Road, was built by York and DeWitt Builders, Inc. in 1970. Left: Bill DeWitt in 2007.

Upon his return from military service in 1966, Arnold Blackstone worked in several areas while continuing his education and building a home for his family. Although he earned a B.S. in biology, his love of machinery and mechanics led him into the contracting business. In 1976, Arnold set up a one-man company. He gradually acquired equipment and grew into an operation with as many as seven employees. Although still active as a general contractor, he has downsized his operation in recent years, spending more time as a certified airplane mechanic at the Auburn-Lewiston Municipal Airport. Among his many contributions to the town, Arnold served many years on the school board and was a selectman. He is remembered for his volunteer work excavating for the foundation, water lines, and septic system for the Mallett Hall addition.

Arnold Blackstone, 2007.

Blueberry Pond Campground
Blueberry Pond Observatory

Blueberry Pond Campground, 218 Poland Range Road, was established and operated by Donald and Patricia Searfoss from 1973 to 2002. Since 2003, new owners William "Bill" and Donna Hooper have been welcoming visitors "to the peaceful deep-green environment of Maine woods handy to both Portland and Bath-Brunswick areas," as their brochure states. The campground's forty sites are open from May 15 to October 30. Secluded primitive sites are available for tenters, back packers, and cyclists, as well as full hook-ups for recreational vehicles. A two-room cabin is also available. The campground provides toilet and shower facilities, tables, fire pits, grills, firewood, and ice. Other attractions include a forty-two foot swimming pool, a ball field, table tennis, swings and a sand pile with toys for the children. Special Saturday night suppers are scheduled throughout the season.

Bill, Donna, and daughter Shannon have been sharing their love of Maine (and Pownal) with guests since 2003.

Thurston Searfoss with twelve-inch Meade LX200 Schmidt-Cassegrain telescope, 2007. The attached high resolution camera takes pictures which are comparable to visual observation through a much larger thirty-inch telescope.

Blueberry Pond Observatory, 355 Libby Road, the home of Thurston Searfoss, has been offering tours of the night skies since December 1999. The moon, planets, and stars can be viewed through a twelve-inch telescope that also allows images to be digitally photographed. With a life-long passion for astronomy, a degree in computer science, and software development experience, Thurston has built an observation system accessible to families, students and vacationers. Two-hour "observation tours" of the night sky are available for small groups, who may then use their digital cameras to capture unforgettable images. The observatory also offers Star Parties for groups of twenty to forty, including programs for students at all levels to compliment their classroom studies. Thurston also owns Fogstone Games, a company which markets "Lost Admiral" and other computer games over the internet.

Vosmus Builders
Hanley and Yost

After military service in a Seabee battalion, Craig Vosmus returned to Pownal in 1976 to build his home (136 Libby Road), raise his family, and begin his construction business, Vosmus Builders. Over the past thirty-two years, Craig has worked as an independent general contractor, building customized houses, barns, and outbuildings. He carries a well-deserved reputation for his restoration and remodeling skills. Craig frequently works with his sons Donald and Al at his side. For many years, his late father Thomas H. Vosmus, electrician, and his uncle Kenneth Vosmus, plumber, complemented the team.

This addition with porch was constructed by Craig as he renovated the early homestead at 532 Elmwood Road.

For twelve years, Craig served on the committee which oversaw the town hall addition. During construction, he often supervised volunteers or did work himself. The offices and lobby, the stairway, the clerk's counter and window, and the recognition plaque in the lobby are some of the places where his craftsmanship can be admired.

Dennis Hanley and Greg Yost met at Southern Maine Technical College in 1978. Later, they worked for the same construction company for five years before deciding to start their own business. Hanley and Yost Custom Builders, Inc., 383 Hallowell Road, formed in 1986, has grown to include four employees in addition to the owners. They specialize in building custom houses, often of their own design, and pride themselves on high-end craftsmanship. While most of their work has been in Southern Maine, they have also built homes in other areas.

Office of Hanley and Yost Builders.

Farrell and Company
Rousseau Builders, Inc.

Charles "Charlie" and Mary Ellen Farrell, 505 Hodsdon Road, own and operate a company that specializes in construction of structurally authentic timber-framed buildings. The company's impact on the Maine construction scene began in 1976, as Charlie established his reputation for timber-framed houses and barns featuring English and Colonial American joinery. His work has been featured in *Down East*, *Maine Boats*, *Homes & Harbors*, and *Fine Home Building*. The company, backed by Charlie's thirty-nine years of experience and with a full-time crew of three, builds throughout Maine and in a few other states. In addition to many dwellings, barns, and outbuildings, their recent work in Maine includes a new addition to the Maine Maritime Museum in Bath and the Rose Pergola at the Maine Botanical Gardens in Boothbay Harbor.

The Farrell Barn designed and built in 1989.

Rousseau custom-built dwelling at 123 Leighton Road.

John Rousseau, 469 Elmwood Road, has been building custom homes and additions in Southern Maine for over thirty-five years. Offering design/build services for those clients who choose to work directly with a builder, John has developed an outstanding reputation for quality workmanship coupled with innovation and fine detailing. His signature style, called "shinglow," incorporates natural elements with Arts and Crafts features. In addition to homes, John and his five employees have completed projects that include renovations, kitchens, baths, barns, and outbuildings. The company's work has been published in *Custom Builder* and *Fine Home Building*.

The Wood Wizard
Short Stop Gas Station and Convenience Store

In 1985, leaving a professional position, Alan Bradstreet began a second career, designing and producing small decorative boxes, post cards, and novelty items, all made from fine woods. He marketed his creations at craft shows. Soon his cherrywood bookmarks became a hit. Here was an unusual article of high quality, reasonably priced, that had wide appeal. As Alan said, "It came out of the blue, because I had some leftover stock from box making." He experimented until he got the system just right. He designs numerous cut-outs of animals and objects, obtains scrap cherry from cabinet shops, rips the blanks, scroll-saws the piercings, and sands, using jigs of his own design. An oil finish completes the process. Alan also creates and teaches every summer at the Haystack Mountain School of Crafts in Deer Isle, Maine.

Alan's wife Susan manages the business from their home at 856 Lawrence Road, shipping thousands of bookmarks all over the country and to England. The L. L. Bean store in Freeport accounts for much of their business.

Alan and Susan Bradstreet, co-owners of the Wood Wizard business, display their signature bookmarks.

Interior of the Short Stop with owner Rose Edwards at the cash register in 2006, as she has been for the past twenty-three years. When she opened for business, regular gasoline had fallen to under $1.25 per gallon from much higher levels. As this book goes to press, the price is threatening to exceed $4.00.

The Short Stop gas station and convenience store, at the Pownal Center crossroads, has been owned and managed by Rose Edwards since 1985. Short Stop serves as a place where locals and travelers along Route 9 may purchase regular or diesel fuel at a fair price. Rose also sells convenience store items, groceries, beer, wine, soda, juices, ice cream and cigarettes. Propane tank refills, local newspapers, ice, hot dogs, and coffee are also available. Her business is open from 6:30 A. M. to 8:00 P. M. seven days a week. Currently this is the only convenience store in Pownal. It also provides a place to hear the latest town news and post notices.

Kevin Rodel, Furniture and Design
June LaCombe, Sculpture

Kevin P. Rodel and Susan C. Mack, after working for eight years in other small furniture shops, opened Mack and Rodel Cabinetmakers in 1986 at 44 Leighton Road. There they handcrafted high-end furniture in the Arts and Crafts style. In 2002 the business became Kevin Rodel Furniture and Design Studio, and currently operates in Brunswick.

Kevin's distinctive work has been featured in leading magazines, such as *Fine Woodworking* and *Home Furniture*. He also teaches Arts and Crafts design at the School for Furniture Craftmanship in Rockland. In 2003, he and Jonathan Benzen co-authored *Arts and Crafts Furniture - From Classic to Contemporary* (Taunton Press). More recently he was made design and project manager for the interior of the visitors center at Maine Coastal Botanical Gardens in Boothbay Harbor.

The "Argyll Server," a sideboard, featuring a tiled counter top and leaded stained glass.

June LaCombe with "Spirit" by Gary Haven Smith, 2007.

June LaCombe, artist, educator and independent art consultant, has been exhibiting and selling sculpture for the past fifteen years at Maine Audubon Society's Gilsland Farm in Falmouth, at Meeting Hill Farm in Yarmouth, and at Hawk Ridge Farm, her home on Minot Road. She recently began placing the sculptures at Maine Coastal Botanical Gardens in Boothbay Harbor. Her support of sculptors from across New England has provided a wider audience for an art form not fully appreciated in the past. June believes that "the best way to support art is to sell it," and that her job is to "show pieces off to their best advantage." The sculptures are displayed in gardens or along inland and coastal trails, "to awaken the senses and make us more mindful of our connections to the Earth."

Town Physicians

Dr. S. Addison Vosmus.

As a small town, Pownal was fortunate, in some periods, to have its own medical professionals serving the community. At the turn of the twentieth century the town's doctor was Dr. S. Addison Vosmus (1858-1927). He received his doctor of medicine degree from Bowdoin College and practiced from his home at the current 856 Lawrence Road.

He traveled by horse-drawn carriage or sleigh to care for the sick and dying all hours of the day or night and in all conditions. It has been reported that he would deliver a baby for five dollars or would accept payment in food and firewood.

Dr. Vosmus served as supervisor of schools for seventeen years and as the town health officer from 1913 until his death in 1927. He was elected to six one-year terms as first selectman, from 1912 to 1918. (See also page 240.)

Mrs. Patricia Searfoss, known professionally as Dr. Patricia Adams, moved to Pownal with her family in 1972. After graduating from Windham High School and the University of Maine, she received her M. D. degree in 1959 from the University of Vermont, specializing in pediatric medicine. She received further degrees and did internships at hospitals in Baltimore, Ann Arbor, and Los Angeles. She practiced pediatric medicine in Hawaii and California before returning to Maine.

Her practice, located on the Libby Road, offered care for area families from 1972 until she retired in 1996. In addition, she provided night care coverage for Pineland Hospital and Training Center from 1976 until that facility closed in 1996. Pat also served on the SAD 62 board of directors from 1973 to 1976.

Dr. "Pat" Adams ministers to one of her tiny patients.

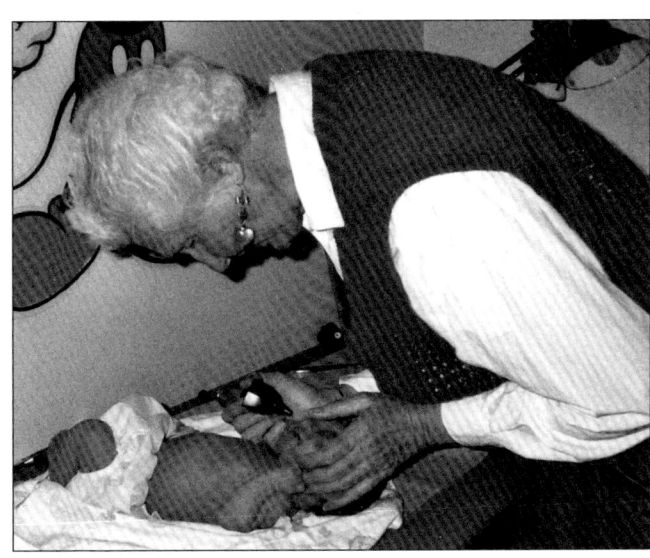

U. S. Postal Services, Pownal, Maine 04069

During the latter half of the 1800s, Pownal had postal centers in each of the town's three main general stores. A postmaster was appointed for each. By 1907, all the mail arrived by rail at a central post office in the West Pownal general store, under direction of one postmaster. Charles Dow, owner of the store, was postmaster from 1898 to 1914. His wife Alice then took over the position, until 1919. Francis C. Handy purchased the general store and post office in 1919 and operated them until the building was destroyed by fire, following a robbery, in June 1933.

After the fire, temporary structures were built in the West Pownal area to service the town's postal needs, until 1969 when the current post office on Allen and Chadsey Roads was built. Postmasters who served during these years were: Fred Allen 1935-1951, Villa Fogg Snow 1951-1963, and Laurence Snow (Villa's son) 1963-1966.

In 1966, postmaster Robert Forbes convinced postal inspectors that a post office lacking indoor plumbing was inadequate to meet the town's needs. By 1969, a new facility was under construction by builders Laurence Snow and his son, Duane. This building continues to serve as the Pownal Post Office. The current postmaster is Pownal resident Jean Seely.

Villa Fogg Snow (1892-1985) postmaster 1951-1963. She was elected to the superintending school committee from 1927 to 1930.

Laurence Snow (1915-1995) postmaster 1963-1966. He was also a leader in town government (discussed in chapter 4).

Robert Forbes (1925-1995) postmaster 1966-1986.

Pownal Post Office, winter of 2007.

PART TWO
GOVERNING IS A CHALLENGE

THEN

NOW

THEN: Mallett Hall, July 4, 1918 – Motor vehicles parked along Hallowell Road as town folk attend Fourth of July celebration.

NOW: Mallett Hall, Saturday, March 10, 2005 – Town meeting begins as voters elect the moderator for town meeting and town officers for 2006.

Chapter 4

Enduring Form – Increasing Complexity

"Town Meeting"
hand-colored pen-and-ink drawing
by Andrea van Voorst van Beest

The fundamental form of Pownal's government has remained unchanged during the past one hundred years. Naturally, there have been many changes with respect to the issues and challenges that must be addressed. Governing this small town today involves more critical decisions and forward planning than in 1908, and a steady acceleration of pace is evident, when one examines all the years in between. In this chapter we focus on governmental details of three representative years: 1908, 1958, and 2006. Certain developments that occurred in other years are mentioned when they seem particularly significant. Of special note are actions taken in 2006 and 2007 that authorized changing the offices of Town Clerk, Tax Collector, and Treasurer from elected to appointed positions. Also noteworthy is the departure from long-standing practice: in 2007, the town voted to operate on a fiscal rather than a calendar year. Thus from 2009 onward, the annual town meeting will occur in June rather than in March, when it has been held every year since the town's founding. Town officials pictured here include some that have served multiple terms in office. A more complete listing of officials is given in Appendix I. This chapter ends with a review of the many active committees that increasingly carry out much of the town's business.

At the Centennial Year 1908

Warrant for Annual Town Meeting, 1908: "To Alroy Noyes, a Constable of the Town of Pownal, in the County of Cumberland. GREETING: In the name of the State of Maine, you are required to notify and warn the inhabitants of said town of Pownal qualified by law to vote in town affairs, to assemble at the town-house in said town on Monday, the ninth day of March, A. D. 1908, at nine o'clock in the forenoon to act on the following articles, to wit: ..."

This photo captures Mallett Hall and the Center one-room school with a forty-five star American flag flying. Part of the town tractor shed can be seen on the left. The picture has been dated between 1905 and 1907. Telephone poles first appeared in Pownal in 1905. Utah became the forty-fifth state in 1896, and the forty-sixth was admitted to the union in 1907. Note the gravel road.

So began the 1908 annual town report, summoning all registered voters to vote for town officers and to attend the annual town meeting for Pownal's centennial year. This format was nothing new to those gathered here this Monday morning in March. It had been followed since 1808. This year, Moderator Harlan B. True called the meeting to order. Three selectmen, a town clerk, a collector of taxes and treasurer, three school committee members, and a road commissioner would be elected, each to serve a one-year term. The meeting recessed at noon for a lunch that was prepared and served by women of the town, citizens who would not get the right to vote until 1922.

After recess, those gathered (from a town population of 600) would hear selectman reports by Harlan B. True, Mellen Tryon, and William Brown; treasurer reports by Alroy Noyes; and the school report by Superintendent Oliver Stover. The town's valuation totaled $261,523, as calculated from real estate taxes ($216,500) and personal property taxes ($45,023). The selectmen annually assessed personal property taxes on livestock, bank stock, money at interest, stock in trade (stores), logs and lumber (mills), wood and bark (dealers), musical instruments, and machinery. When automobiles, tractors, radios, and televisions appeared, they also were taxed. This method of adding to the revenue base continued until the mid 1970s. Poll taxes assessed on 157 males age 21 years and older and living in town that year would add another $392.50 to the town's treasury.

Budget recommendations for 1908 totaled $5,619. The selectmen appointed a sealer of weights and measures to monitor scales in town, a fence viewer to settle boundary disputes, and a surveyor of logs, wood, and bark to monitor the mills and logging in town.

A major area of concern for the taxpayers at this time was one that would persist throughout the century — how to provide the best education for children and how to pay for it. The average number of students attending school between the ages of five and twenty-one was 115 in 1908. The school budget warrant articles included requests for money to cover: common schools, high school tuition, repairs on school buildings (three new schools plus four very aged schools), textbooks and blanks, insurance, apparatus, appliances and "other necessary charges." For 1908, the town's share of the $2,160 school budget was $1,730, or thirty percent of the total town budget for the year. The balance of the school's revenue came from state subsidy. The town's contribution to education was destined to remain the largest part of the overall town budget for the next one hundred years. In a money-saving effort, Superintendent Oliver Stover expressed the need to move from seven one-room schools to five by closing two of the oldest ones. This focused parental concerns on

Mellen Tryon (1867-1941): Representative, Maine State Legislature 1913-1914; House of Representatives Sergeant at Arms 1921-1937; Selectman for nine years between 1895 and 1914; Town Clerk for fifteen years, 1915-1930; Centennial Committee Secretary; town and county Republican Party Chair, twenty years.

William A. Brown (1864-1928): Selectman for eight years between 1907 and 1922; Superintending School Committee member for six years between 1912 and 1928; Board of Health member 1923-1928; Road Commissioner 1917-1918.

loss of neighborhood schools and increased the cost of "conveyance." Thirteen older students had their tuition paid to local high schools, but no transportation was provided. Meanwhile, some citizens continued to champion the establishment of a local high school, perhaps in the newly-built Mallett Hall.

Another area of concern to 1908 taxpayers, as is the case today, was the roads and bridges account. The number of automobiles and trucks using town roads was increasing, and all roads needed to be widened and many surfaced. Road Commissioner Ernest Tuttle presented his articles on the warrant, requesting money to cover the following accounts: repairing roads, repairing bridges, cutting bushes, and snow bills. His budget of $1,250 amounted to twenty-two percent of the annual budget. Fifty-eight local men had worked as road crew, as a way of "paying off their taxes." Voters gave Commissioner Tuttle permission to purchase a new road machine from the Good Road Machinery Co. for $207.90, the money to be taken from his budget for that year. In response to a related area of concern, Selectmen Harlan True and Mellen Tryon agreed

Henry W. Loring (1857-1937): Representative, Maine State Legislature 1903-1904 and 1907-1908; Selectman for three years between 1896 and 1914; Moderator for seven years between 1915 and 1922; participant in the centennial celebration.

to journey to Augusta to confer with the railroad commissioner about constructing a railroad underpass on the Allen Road for vehicle safety. However it was not until 1912 that this project would be completed.

After paying state and county taxes amounting to fourteen and four percent of the town budget, respectively, the remaining balance was spent on care of the poor ($500) and contingent expenses ($500). The care-of-the-poor account, administered by the selectmen, paid for board and care, clothing, and, if needed, hospitalization at the Maine Insane Hospital. All those receiving such aid found their names in the town report. The 1908 contingency expenses included: paying town officers' salaries, running the town office, caring for cemeteries, paying off loans, and miscellaneous items. (The cemetery commission, as it exists today, was not established until 1923, and its first request for town monies was $100.) Certain other 1908 town expenses are unfamiliar to us today. Individuals were paid to collect browntail moth nests. And a few with productive wells were each paid four dollars to allow those whose wells had run dry to collect water; this was called "public watering privileges." The town also paid a small monetary reimbursement to those whose chickens had been killed by foxes.

At a time when health insurance as we know it did not exist, the 1908 selectmen were responsible for appointing a health officer to monitor the general health of the community. Vaccines to prevent communicable diseases such as chicken pox, measles, whooping cough, diphtheria, typhoid fever, small pox, tuberculosis, polio, and *la grippe* (flu) were unknown, and antibiotics to treat infections had yet to be discovered. An observant health officer was critically important. Dr. S. Addison Vosmus served in this capacity from 1893 until his death in 1928. The state of the community's health was reported each year in the town report. By 1923, the town had established a three-member board of health to oversee this area.

As we approach the town's bicentennial celebration year, two items that the voters approved on the 1908 budget are of particular interest. One was the appropriation of $100 to fund the centennial anniversary celebration, and the other

Alroy Noyes (1848-1939): Representative, Maine State Legislature 1899-1900; Tax Collector and Treasurer for forty-seven years between 1884 and 1933; Constable and Truant Officer between 1908 and 1934.

was an appropriation of $200 to build "a toilet on the back of the town house." This rather unusual two-story attached outhouse was subsequently constructed. It survived almost until the bicentennial year but succumbed to the wrecker's ball in 1996, to make room for the new Mallett Hall addition.

Above: Alvin L. Tryon (1900-1958): Tax Collector and Treasurer for eight years, 1933-1941; Cemetery Commissioner for six years, 1943-1949; Budget Committee member 1946-1948; Constable and Truant Officer between 1935 and 1943.

Left: Charles P. Heywood (1874-1938): Selectman for five years, 1915-1920; Superintending School Committee member 1911-1912; Cemetery Commissioner for twelve years, 1926-1938; Moderator for three years between 1923 and 1929.

Below: William J. Pervier (1869-1950): Selectman for five years, 1921-1926; Superintending School Committee member for five years, 1927-1932; Truant Officer 1921-1924.

Lauren H. Tuttle Sr. (1888-1958): Representative, Maine State Legislature 1943-1944 and 1953-1954; Selectman for eighteen years between 1936 and 1958 (fourteen years as Chair); Health Officer 1930 to 1958; Superintendent of Schools for three years; and teacher for fifteen years.

At the Sesquicentennial Year 1958

Warrant for Annual Town Meeting, 1958: "To Joseph H. Pervier, a Constable in the Town of Pownal in the County of Cumberland and the State of Maine. Greetings: In the name of the State of Maine, you are hereby required to notify and warn the inhabitants of said Town of Pownal qualified by law to vote in town affairs, to assemble at the town house in said town, on Monday the 10th day of March, A. D. 1958, at 1:30 o'clock in the afternoon to act on the following articles to wit:"

So began the 1958 annual town report, summoning all registered voters to vote for town officers and to attend the annual town meeting for Pownal's sesquicentennial year. The selectman-town meeting form of government had been serving Pownal for one hundred and fifty years. Philip R. Tryon, Elbert K. Babbidge, and Lauren H. Tuttle Sr. (who died January 23, 1958) had been serving as selectmen, assessors, and overseers of the poor for the past year. Their report would be given at the meeting along with those of Joseph H. Pervier, tax collector and treasurer, and Claude L. Snow, town clerk. Others elected to serve that year were: Evangeline T. Lee, Dorothy Emmertz, and Earle Blake for the superintending school committee; Road Commissioner Roy C. Tufts; Cemetery Commissioners Roy C. Tufts, Joseph H. Pervier, and Thomas J. Vosmus; and Fire Ward Joseph H. Pervier. The town's valuation totaled $308,883, as calculated from real estate assessments ($290,818) and personal property assessments ($18,065). The budget committee's recommendations for 1959 came in at $39,038.

At 8:00 P.M., after voting was complete, Moderator Philip R. Tryon called the meeting to order. The town had experienced many changes during its previous 50 years. Population had grown to 725, as men and women returned from military service in World War II and found area employment. The interstate highway system was expanding, and society had become more mobile. Most families owned cars. Electricity had arrived in town along with almost universal indoor plumbing. Farming was in decline. Developments noted in nearby towns prompted local leaders to address planning issues.

Seen in 1966, newly-paved Hallowell Road, Mallett Hall, and the grammar school (two years before it closed). The fire escape was added to town hall in 1925, and dormers surrounding the chimneys were added in the 1930s.

The major area of concern for taxpayers was, once again, the high cost of education. Forty-five percent of the total town budget would be appropriated to this end, even as the state was picking up fifty-five percent of the total school budget. The five one-room schools, some of which were one hundred years old, had become more costly to repair, and multi-level classrooms were crowded. Certified teachers were hard to find. High school students still had no transportation provided. The warrant asked voters to authorize the selectmen to appoint a school planning committee, five members or more, to study the implications of the Sinclair Act recently passed by the state. This act was intended to close one-room schools and organize larger school districts, thereby improving student achievement and lowering costs. Over the next ten years, until the present elementary school opened in 1969, the school planning committee, the superintending school committee, the parent-teachers club, and town citizens would work together to create SAD 62.

The roads-and-bridges account in 1958 stood at thirty percent of the total town budget, reflect-

Claude L. Snow (1888-1974): Selectman for five years between 1919 and 1927; Town Clerk for forty-one years, 1930-1971.

ing continual growth since 1908. Roadways had never been adequately surfaced, mud season brought traffic to a standstill, and equipment costs were increasing. An equipment building was needed. Road Commissioner Roy C. Tufts, elected yearly, hired twenty-nine local men to work throughout the year as crew. The aging

Left: Philip R. Tryon (1898-1983): Selectman for fourteen years between 1928 and 1961; Moderator for ten years between 1945 and 1972; Superintending School Committee member for three years, 1928-1931; Budget Committee 1967-1972, Chair, four years; Planning Board member 1965-1969.

Right: Joseph H. Pervier (1899-1980): Selectman for five years, 1927-1932; Tax Collector and Treasurer twenty-three years, 1941-1964; Cemetery Commissioner for forty-three years, 1938-1981; Moderator for twenty years between 1925 and 1955; Fire Ward for thirty-three years, 1926-1959; Town Constable 1942-1964.

town grader needed constant repairs, with "breaking roads" in winter inflicting the most wear and tear. Excise tax receipts would be added to the grader account until 1962 when a new grader was purchased.

Fire Ward Joseph Pervier reported, in part, "This year we have responded to five chimney fires, two woods fires, and three grass fires... We have added a new Indian pump and tanks... There was enough money to add about 250 feet of hose." The Fire Department, organized under his leadership in 1948, needed equipment and a station. Up to this time, all fire apparatus had been housed in private structures. It would not be until 1960 that the current Center fire station was built by members of the Granite Grange, using $1,000 appropriated by the town. Ironically, this was the same year that Joseph Pervier retired after thirty-three years as fire ward.

The town appropriated $100 in 1958 ($150 in subsequent years) to provide public health programs for all citizens. The parent-teacher club of

J. Noyes Mitchell (1908-1986): Selectman for three years, 1943-1946; Cemetery Commissioner for ten years, 1940-1950; Board of Appeals 1965-1968.

the Center schools assumed responsibility for organizing these events. Immunizations were provided free of charge for diphtheria, typhoid, pertussis (whooping cough), and small pox. Salk vaccine to prevent polio was newly available, as was testing for tuberculosis. Physical examinations as well as dental and eye clinics were organized to provide much needed preventative care. Summaries of the state of the town's health were to appear in the annual town report until 1970.

By 1958, town leaders had realized that, without a plan for orderly growth, one of the town's greatest resources, open land, was in jeopardy. It would take many years and much legislation to address this concern, but a first step was taken in 1959 with the adoption of a building and house-trailer code, later amended in 1964 and 1965. In 1964, a planning board was established, with members Edward Mitchell, Philip Tryon, Laurence Snow, Donald Knowlton, Lawrence Smith, Raymond Spencer, and Joseph Ryan. That same year, a board of appeals was established with members Walter Hustus, Ralph Vosmus, J. Noyes Mitchell, and associate Andrew LaFreniere. The town's first building inspector, Robert H. Norton, was appointed in 1958. Its first plumbing inspector, Kenneth Vosmus, would not be appointed until 1968.

Thomas J. Vosmus, Cemetery Commissioner from 1950 to 1968 (standing), and Michael Menchen place a flag on the grave of Revolutionary War soldier Edmund Cleaves, as the town prepares to pay tribute to its eighty-three deceased war veterans on Memorial Day, 1965. Tom was elected to serve as commissioner for eighteen years, from 1950 until his death in 1968. Michael Menchen would replace him on the commission from 1969 to 1976.

Throughout the late 1950s, the selectmen realized they were facing responsibilities and duties requiring knowledge gained only through experience and continuity. Neighboring towns were beginning to add administrative and supportive positions to aid in this regard. Pownal's eventual solution to this problem did not result in new positions, but rather in a reorganization of the selectmen's terms of office. In 1965, it was voted to extend each selectman's term from one to three years. The elections were then phased so that only one was elected each year.

In preparation for the 1958 sesquicentennial celebration, the town voted to spend $300 on planned festivities. Additional monies were appropriated to modernize Mallett Hall. The hall received a new heating plant ($1,500) and new coats of interior and exterior paint ($1,000). This "modernized" Mallett Hall then had central oil heat on demand for social events, although the selectmen's office continued for many years to be heated by a wood stove.

Frederick W. Stasinowsky (1925-2004): Selectman for twenty-four years, 1970-1994; Cumberland County Deputy Sheriff for twenty-nine years; Town Constable for twenty-nine years.

Robert Slocum (1926-1994): Selectman for five years, 1961-1966; Tax Collector and Treasurer for one year 1969-1970; Moderator for eight years 1963-1970; Superintending School Committee member for nine years between 1950 and 1968; SAD 62 School Building Committee Chair 1968-1969.

Lawrence E. Carter (1914-1993): Selectman for seven years between 1953 and 1966; Superintending School Committee member for three years, 1967-1970; SAD 62 School Building Committee member 1968-1969; Budget Committee member 1967-1990; Building Inspector 1978-1980; Board of Appeals member 1977; Planning Board alternate for seven years.

Laurence W. Snow (1916-1995): Selectman for seven years between 1943 and 1961; Moderator for six years between 1942 and 1991; Planning Board member for fourteen years 1965-1978; original framer of the zoning ordinance; SAD 62 School Building Committee member; Superintending School Committee member for four years, 1966-1970. He received the North Pownal Community Club Community Service Award in 1994 and was honored in the 1995 annual town report for over fifty years of service.

Edward L. Mitchell (1911-1978): Selectman for four years, 1966-1970; Superintending School Committee member for seven years, 1965-1972; SAD 62 School Building Committee member 1968-1969; Moderator for two years between 1973 and 1975; Budget Committee member 1949-1964, Chair nine years, Secretary one year.

Edward D. Menchen (1916-1990): Selectman for seventeen years between 1951 and 1973, Chair thirteen years; Tax Collector for twelve years, 1978-1990; Treasurer for sixteen years, 1974-1990; Cemetery Commissioner for five years, 1959-1964; Moderator for five years, 1978-1982; Planning Board member for many years; Superintending School Committee member three years, 1944-1947. In 1976 he received the Cumberland County Civic Center Honor Award as Outstanding Town Citizen.

Nearing the Bicentennial Year— 2006

Warrant for annual Town Meeting, 2006: "To Kathleen A. Hogue, a resident of the Town of Pownal, in the County of Cumberland and the State of Maine: Greetings: In the name of the State of Maine, you are hereby required to notify and warn the inhabitants of the said Town of Pownal, qualified by law to vote in town affairs, to assemble at the Town Hall in said Town of Pownal on Saturday, the tenth day of March, A. D. 2007, at 8:00 o'clock in the morning to act on articles one and two of this warrant to wit:

Mallett Hall "all dressed up" for dedication of the new addition at the Pumpkinfest, October 6, 1999. With the exterior completed, professionals and volunteers under the direction of Interior Sub-Committee Chair James Boyles labored for another two years to ready the offices for opening in December of 2001.

So began the 2006 Annual Town Report, summoning all registered voters to vote for town officers and to attend the annual town meeting just two years short of Pownal's bicentennial year. By 2006, the selectmen-town meeting form of government had been serving Pownal for almost 200 years. The population had increased to 1,491 (doubling since 1970) with 570 residential units spread along the same roads that had been present in the nineteenth century. At 2:00 P.M., after voting for officers was complete, Moderator James Boyles called the meeting to order. Of the 1,100 registered voters, just one hundred and nine would take their seats in the school auditorium to begin considering thirty-nine warrant articles. In their opening report on the state of the town, Selectmen James H. Briggs, William E. Crain, and Philip M. Wentworth lauded the efforts of many who had helped the town maintain its unique character while meeting local needs and expectations. They particularly mentioned the Comprehensive Plan Update Committee and the newly formed Capital Projects Planning Committee as two efforts to look ahead, set objectives, and lay plans for the future.

The town's valuation, as calculated from real estate stood at $70,438,620. The budget committee's recommendations for 2007 totaled $1,024,869 for operations of the town, excluding any town commitment to SAD 62. The fiscal process had grown more complex over the years, and the budget committee was meeting throughout the year, meticulously examining each pro-

Gerald H. Rolfe: Selectman for nineteen years, 1974-1993, Chair sixteen years; Treasurer for seven years 1995-2002. The 2001 annual town report was dedicated to him recognizing twenty-six years of community service.

jected expense before recommending its inclusion in a warrant article. Budget Committee Chair Thomas Godfrey wrote in his report that the committee was frustrated by having to recommend a tax appropriation increase, in spite of its success in meeting the expenditure cap established by the recently passed state law known as LD 1. This apparent contradiction, he pointed out, could be traced to the fact that excise taxes were down and state revenue sharing had been relentlessly declining for several years.

Not surprisingly, the town's share of school expenditures was again the largest piece of the overall town spending. The town contributed $1,333,194, or fifty-four percent of its budget, toward the SAD 62 budget of $1,971,418 (which was passed in June with only sixteen citizens present and voting). There were 165 students in grades pre-kindergarten through eight, the largest enrollment since 1998. The school board, led by Chair Paul Schumann and Vice Chair Jennifer Blackstone Kaplan, had worked hard and successfully to realize savings through cost sharing arrangements with the Freeport school system, and through in-house innovations. New on the board's agenda was consideration of the recently announced statewide school consolidation plan, a plan that was then unclear and in a constant state of flux. The students meanwhile were doing well as evidenced by their solid performance on Terra Nova, a national test that compares student reading and math scores across the U. S.

Road Commissioner Shawn Bennett discussed the proposed budget for the highways-and-bridges account. These expenditures, totaling $479,049, were authorized by the voters. Ultimately they amounted to seventeen percent of the town's actual expenses. Although this account and the name "road department" had not changed over the years, given its expanded role in providing town services, it was perhaps better described as a "public works" department. The department included the commissioner and three employees.

At the 2006 meeting, the commissioner's report gave a clear picture of Pownal's deteriorating roads and what this implied for the future. He supported a proposal put forward by the capital projects planning committee (endorsed by the selectmen and the budget committee) to seek a bond to cover much needed initial work. The voters authorized bonding for $1,182,500. Fire Chief David Malone spoke to the need for a new fire truck, and the voters authorized floating a bond of $300,000. The total bonding for

Joseph R. Mitchell: Selectman for six years, 1971-1977; Moderator 1974.

$1,482,500 was the largest ever entered into by the town.

Town officials were now comfortably settled in their offices in the completed addition to Mallett Hall. Two years previously, the hiring of a part-time administrative secretary, Kathleen Hogue, had been the town's response to the need for providing assistance to the selectmen with their ever-increasing list of responsibilities.

Many of the challenges facing the town continued to be addressed by committees and boards staffed by volunteers. Year-end reports were included in the annual report from the following: Road Commissioner Shawn Bennett, Fire Chief David Malone, First Responders Deputy Chiefs Dick Hogue and Mick Rogers, Cemetery Commission Chair Lorraine Merrill, Animal Control Officer Allison Whitaker, and Planning Board Secretary Elizabeth Nichols. Committee reports included were: Budget, Tom Godfrey; Capital Projects Planning, James Boyles; Mallett Hall Building and Grounds, James Boyles; Bicentennial, Kathy Hogue; Veterans Memorial,

James A. Sanders (1919-2002): Selectman for six years, 1966-1972; Moderator eight years 1983-1990; Superintending School Committee member for five years between 1963 and 1977; Budget Committee Member 1972-1992, Chair nine years; Planning Board original member and Chair 1970-1997; Zoning Ordinance Committee original member; Mallett Hall Addition Committee member 1990-1993. He received the North Pownal Community Club Community Service Award in 1992, and the annual town report dedication 1997 for fifty-eight years of service to the town.

Craig Vosmus: Selectman for twelve years, 1977-1989; Codes Enforcement Officer 1993-2008; Plumbing Inspector 1987-2008; Building Inspector 1995-2008; Electrical Inspector 1995-2008; Cemetery Commissioner 1993-2008; Town Constable 1977-2008. The 1998 annual town report was dedicated to him in recognition of his twenty-five years of service.

Sherry Dietrich; and Solid Waste Reduction and Recycling, Mary Lee Fowler. The Pownal Scenic and Historical Society also included its annual report.

Two new ordinances were enacted by the voters in 2006: The Addressing and Road Naming Ordinance and the Emergency Management Ordinance. Robert McMahon accepted the newly-created position of emergency coordinator. The expanded role of the town health officer, Carrie Kivela, was seen in her closer interaction with the fire department and with the new emergency coordinator. She also continued working closely with county officials as they prepared for a possible flu pandemic. At a special town meeting in 2006 and at the annual town meeting in 2007, actions were taken that collectively changed the offices of town clerk, tax collector, and treasurer from elected to appointed positions. Henceforth, only the selectmen and the cemetery commissioners would be elected officials.

The Pownal Bicentennial Committee, chaired by Kathy Hogue, was hard at work by 2006 planning for the celebration in 2008. Much of its work had been assumed by an executive subcommittee composed of Chair Kathy Hogue, Sherry Dietrich, Ted Walsh, Kelly Wentworth, Diana Passmore, and Mary Ann Hodsdon. The predecessor committee, the Bicentennial Steering Committee, had done its work well. Begun in 1998 with $500 seed money from the town, this committee consisted of Sherry Dietrich, chair; Donna Boyles, secretary; Kelly Wentworth, treasurer; James Boyles; Alan "Bo" Chesney; Kathy Hogue; and Tom Bowen. By 2006 they had raised an additional $3,455. Before it disbanded in 2006, the steering committee turned over to the bicentennial committee all funds, with the stipulation that at least $3,000 be used for constructing a veterans memorial. An additional grant of $4,000 from the town, added to $3,011 earned at a silent and live auction, increased substantially the financial support for this much-anticipated program of events.

Susan C. Mack: Selectman for nine years (she was the first woman elected to that office), Chair six years 1994-2003; Conservation Committee member 1990-1993, Chair three years; Budget Committee member 1991-1993; Solid Waste Reduction and Recycling Committee member 1992-1993; Coordinator, Community Development Grant for Mallett Hall Addition 1998; Originator, Maine Department of Transportation Community Development Gateway Project Grant 2002.

James H. Briggs: Selectman for eight years, 1999-2007, Chair two years; SAD 62 School Board member for six years between 1991 and 1999.

Lauren H. Tuttle Jr. (1931-2002): Selectman for fourteen years, 1989-2003, Chair three years; Town Constable for fourteen years; SAD 62 School Board member for two years, 1975-1977; Mallett Hall Addition Committee member for twelve years, 1990-2002.

Edna S. Menchen: Town Clerk for twenty-seven years, 1975-2002; Deputy Tax Collector for twelve years, 1978-1990; Deputy Treasurer for sixteen years, 1974-1990; Tax Collector for eleven years, 1990-2001; Treasurer for five years, 1990-1995. In 1991 the North Pownal Community Club presented her with its Community Service Award. The annual town report for 1996 was dedicated to her in recognition of twenty-one years of service, and the 2002 annual town report recognized her twenty-seven years of community service.

Kelly M. Wentworth: Town Clerk for five years, 2002-2007; Deputy Town Clerk for one year 2007-2008; Treasurer for six years 2002-2008; Tax Collector for seven years 2001-2008; Bicentennial Steering Committee member 1998-2005; Bicentennial Executive Committee member 2005-2008.

Town officers and staff, February, 2008: seated l. to r.: Administrative Secretary Kathleen Hogue, Selectman Matthew Allen, Town Clerk and Deputy Tax Collector Kathleen Malloy, Selectman Timothy Giddinge. Standing l. to r.: Health Officer Carrie N. Kivela, Registrar of Voters Mary Ann Hodsdon, Tax Collector and Treasurer Kelly M. Wentworth. Insert: Selectman Chair William E. Crain. Not pictured: Animal Control Officer Allison Whitaker. (Composite photo)

Members of the Cemetery Commission are elected to three-year terms, one member elected each year. L. to r.: Craig A. Vosmus; Lorraine S. Merrill, Chair; Duane Snow.

Town Meeting Reconvenes, March 14, 2005

Ballot counter Joan Rolfe reports to Moderator James Boyles on a warrant article hand vote at the annual town meeting, held in the Pownal Elementary School auditorium.

Moderator James G. Boyles calls the town meeting to order. Jim served as Moderator for seventeen years, 1992-2008. He was a member of SAD 62 School Board for three years, two as Chair, 1974-1977. He served on the Mallett Hall Addition Committee from 1995 to 2002, chaired the Mallett Hall Building and Grounds Committee from 2002 to 2008, chaired the Capital Projects Planning Committee for three years, 2006-2008; and was a member of the Bicentennial Steering Committee. The dedication of the 2005 annual town report expressed appreciation for his thirty-one years of community service.

Selectman Chair James Briggs and Selectman Philip Wentworth preside at the meeting. Selectman Sean O. Bennett resigned his position that evening due to illness. In the election prior to the meeting, William Crain was elected to fill out the term from 2005 to 2008.

Outstanding Service Acknowledged

Althea Blake with grandson Jared Blake after receiving a State Recognition Plaque for Volunteer Service to the Community from State Representatives David Webster (District 106) and Susan M. W. Austin (District 109). The 2004 annual town report was dedicated to Althea for her fifty-six years of service to the community.

Gerald "Gerry" Rolfe (left), Selectman from 1974 to 1993 and Treasurer from 1995 to 2002, received a town recognition plaque and flowers at town meeting on March 10, 2003. He also received a State of Maine Legislature Citation from Freeport-Pownal Representative Thomas Bull (pictured on the right) for his twenty-six years of community service.

Edna Snow Menchen received a town service recognition plaque and flowers from Moderator James Boyles at town meeting on March 10, 2003. Edna served as Town Clerk from 1975 to 2002, as Tax Collector from 1990 to 2002, and as Treasurer from 1990 to 1995. She also received a State of Maine Legislature Citation from Freeport-Pownal Representative Thomas Bull for her twenty-seven years of community service.

Kermit Wentworth, recently-retired Pownal solid waste hauler, received an Eco-Excellence Award for Recycling at the August 21, 2006 selectmen's meeting. Mary Lee Fowler, chair of the town's recycling committee said, "Kermit has increased citizen awareness of the work and responsibility involved in keeping our town beautiful,... kept the town's trash hauling costs down,...set high standards in reducing waste, and encouraged recycling." The 2006 annual town report was dedicated to Kermit for his forty-plus years of service to the town.

Town Hall Addition Committee (1990-2002)
Oversees Project from Conception to Completion

William "Bill" S. DeWitt chaired the Town Hall Addition Committee from 1990 to 2002. Members of the committee were: Sherry Dietrich, secretary; Lilyan Forbes; Christine Phelps; James Boyles; Lauren Tuttle Jr.; and Craig Vosmus. The committee engaged architect Nancy Barba, raised $70,115 from various private sources and events, hired professional contractors, and supervised volunteer work. They also managed a $138,000 Community Development Block Grant that covered the cost of an elevator, entrance ramp, and handicapped accessible bathroom. In 1999, Bill received the Governor's Service Award for "his outstanding commitment to volunteerism and his dedication to service within his community." In 2004, the DeWitt Room was named in his honor.

Left: Local contractor Arnold Blackstone (pictured with backhoe) contributed equipment and many volunteer hours to the project.

The unique one-hundred-year-old, two-story outhouse succumbed to Arnold Blackstone's backhoe as construction began in March of 1996. For the first time in its history, Mallett Hall was about to acquire indoor plumbing.

Craig Vosmus inspects roof trusses as they are put into place with help of Lester Loeschner, operating a crane hoist. Craig, a professional builder, often led volunteer crews and generally supervised the project.

The masonry crew, led by Walter Schmidt with tender Tom Bowen and mud mixer Bill DeWitt, laid hundreds of cinderblock for the interior walls of the foundation and for the elevator shaft.

After the exterior walls and roof were completed by June of 1998, volunteers framed the interior walls and office space. Between 1996 and 2002 over 3,368 hours of volunteer labor had been donated by more than 116 people. Three of them are seen here l. to r.: Alan Greenleaf, Paul Schumann, and Craig Dietrich.

The year 2001 was busy for the interior subcommittee and volunteers. Chair James Boyles, Donna Boyles, Kathy Hogue, Craig Dietrich, Lilyan Forbes, and Susan Mack led efforts to trim out and paint offices and lobby, select furniture, hang blinds, and complete wiring for security and computers (putting the Town of Pownal on line for the first time). In December the offices in the new addition opened for business.

Committees Render Invaluable Service

Committees, both standing and ad hoc, have helped govern the town from its beginnings. Over the course of the last century, their numbers and importance have increased, and since the early 1990s, many critical functions have been delegated to committees. They now play an integral role, assisting elected and appointed officials in running a modern municipality. It is not an overstatement to say that governing the Town of Pownal could not succeed without the active participation of its committees.

Budget Committee

The first town Budget Committee was appointed by the board of selectmen in 1933. Since that time, members have always been appointed and served for an indefinite term. For the first sixty years, the committee met once each January to review the selectmen's budget. They critiqued it and then presented their recommendations to the voters at the March annual town meeting. In 1993 with budgetary issues becoming more complex, Chair Sherry Dietrich recommended that the committee meet four times annually to plan for the following year's budget. By 2006, under the leadership of Chair Tom Godfrey, the committee was meeting more than a dozen times a year to thoroughly review each line item, working closely with Treasurer Kelly Wentworth. Tom wrote in the 2006 Annual Town Report that the committee would "make certain that the municipal budget strikes the right balance in getting the work done and keeping taxes in check while starting to plan for the future."

Seated l. to r.: Nancy Doble, Carlene Harvey, Chair Tom Godfrey, Marsha Martino. Standing l. to r.: William DeWitt, Sean O. Bennett, Alan Bradstreet, Mary Lee Fowler. Not pictured: Scott Kaplan, Robert Humphrey, and Ronald Hodgdon. Sherry Dietrich retired in 2006 after thirty years of uninterrupted service on the committee.

Ordinance Review Committee

The Ordinance Review Committee was established in 2006 in response to a recommendation in the 2006 comprehensive plan to review all land use ordinances as they relate to commercial and residential development. Its scope was broadened when it was charged to examine all existing town ordinances and recommend to the board of selectmen changes as deemed necessary.

L. to r.: John Bourassa, Co-Chairs Don Arnold and James Briggs, William Schmidt. Not pictured: Sean O. Bennett and Mike Pocock.

Housing Committee

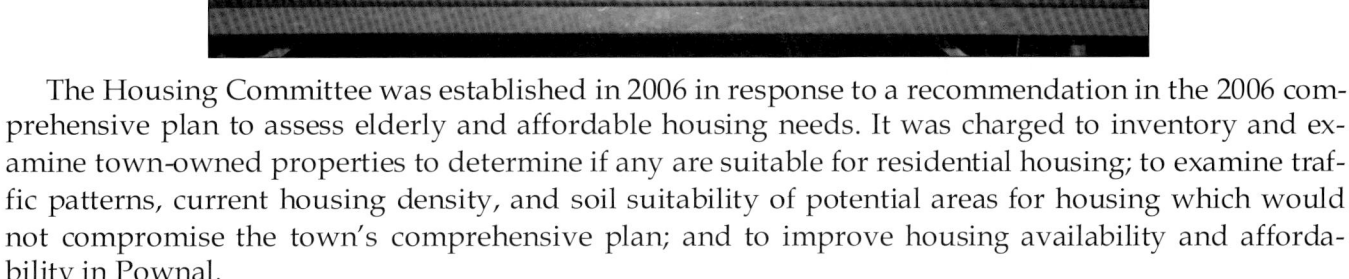

The Housing Committee was established in 2006 in response to a recommendation in the 2006 comprehensive plan to assess elderly and affordable housing needs. It was charged to inventory and examine town-owned properties to determine if any are suitable for residential housing; to examine traffic patterns, current housing density, and soil suitability of potential areas for housing which would not compromise the town's comprehensive plan; and to improve housing availability and affordability in Pownal.

L. to r.: John Harvey, Co-Chairs Don Arnold and Sharon Townshend, Lois Pervier. Not pictured: Secretary Rosemary Whitney.

Comprehensive Plan Committee 2004-2006

At the March 2004 town meeting, voters appropriated $4,000 for the selectmen's request to review and update the 1992 Comprehensive Town Plan. The town plan would set "goals and policies to develop a vision for the town by recommending measures to guide growth using both regulatory and non-regularity strategies." The resulting comprehensive plan was adopted at a special town meeting in September of 2006.

L.to r.: Secretary Joan Mueller, Chair Lin White, Liza Nichols, Sherry Dietrich, Ronald Hodsdon, John Bowdren. Not pictured: Lois Pervier, Scott Pollock, and Intern Wendy Carter.

Planning Board

This board was formed in 1964 to review site plans and subdivision plans for the town, to respond to state laws, and to keep abreast of state planning initiatives. Members are appointed by the board of selectmen and serve five-year renewable terms.

Seated l. to r.: Chair Ronald Hodsdon, Vice Chair Russell Allen, Secretary Liza Nichols. Standing l. to r.: William Jordan, Joan Mueller. Not pictured: Kelly Welch, Eric Dube. Sherry Dietrich retired in 2006 after twenty-nine years of service on the board.

Board of Appeals

This board was formed in 1964 to hear and decide administrative appeals and requests for variances filed in response to decisions made under local ordinances. Members are appointed for three-year terms.

L. to r.: Chair Richard Hogue, Joseph Raymond, Vice Chair Lois Pervier, Matthew Kennedy. Not pictured: Robert Farrington, Stephen Litchfield, and Philip Wentworth.

Solid Waste Reduction and Recycling Committee

The Solid Waste Reduction and Recycling Committee was formed in 1992, with members appointed by the selectmen. It examines all aspects of solid waste, recycling, and hazardous waste collection. It organizes Pownal Pride Day in April, a day when the community engages in roadside cleanup and metal recycling. The committee's goals include educating the community on the need to reduce the volume of household rubbish and encouraging residents to recycle and compost. Pownal is a member and participating owner of Ecomaine, a non-profit waste management company. The town's recycling "silver bullets" are located behind Mallett Hall, and curbside collection of non-recyclable trash occurs weekly.

Seated l. to r.: Jamie Welch, Chair Justin Nichols, Mary Lee Fowler. Standing l. to r.: Kirk Niese, Alan Bradstreet.

Conservation Commission

Members of this commission are appointed by the selectmen and serve for three-year staggered terms. Their duties and responsibilities as outlined by state law are: to maintain meeting and activity records and make an annual report to the town; to conduct research in conjunction with the planning board; to seek to coordinate with the activities of other conservation bodies with similar goals; and to keep an index of all open marshlands, swamps, and other wetlands for the purpose of obtaining information relating to the proper protection, development, or use of those open areas.

L. to r.: Matt Welch, Secretary Ruth Hannan, Chair Tom Cushman, Jeff Raymond, Robert McMahon. Not pictures: Derek Lovitch.

Capital Projects Planning Committee

This committee was formed in March, 2006 and was given the following charge: to define what constitutes a capital project in the Town of Pownal; to identify all capital projects that the town can anticipate in the next fifteen years, to determine funding schemes for the above-named projects; and to recommend to the selectmen the funding schemes they develop.

Standing l. to r.: Chair James Boyles, Jan Pieter van Voorst van Beest, Fire Chief Scott Pollock. Seated l. to r.: John Harvey, Secretary Tom Godfrey. Not pictured: Road Commissioner Shawn Bennett.

Bicentennial Executive Committee

This committee began as an ad hoc body in 1998 when members began to plan for, and raise funds for the town's bicentennial celebration in 2008. In 2005 after the ad hoc committee disbanded, selectmen appointed this committee to continue the work of financing and planning for the specific events of the celebration. Members of the committee are: Chair Kathy Hogue, Treasurer Kelly Wentworth, Donna Boyles, Sherry Dietrich, Mary Ann Hodsdon, Erica Giddinge, Ruth Hannan, Nancy Malone, Linda McMahon, Jane Mittel, Diana Passmore, Mavis Peaco, Jeff Raymond, Joe Raymond, Luther Snow, Cheryl Vosmus, Craig, Vosmus, Ted Walsh, and Marie Wendt.

Pictured are members of the executive committee of the whole, front row l. to r.: Chair Kathy Hogue, Sherry Dietrich. Back row l. to r.: Ted Walsh, Diana Passmore, Kelly Wentworth, Mary Ann Hodsdon.

Mallett Hall Building and Grounds Committee

This committee was formed in 2002 after the Mallett Hall Addition Committee was dissolved. It is charged with oversight of any changes to the interior, exterior and grounds of Mallett Hall. The committee has overseen several renovation projects of the original building including: restoring the windows, hanging window blinds, installing new heating units, effecting ceiling repairs, upgrading the electrical system, incorporating period-appropriate lighting, and painting the stage and voting rooms. The committee plans to continue renovation efforts throughout 2008.

Seated l. to r.: Chair James Boyles, Kathy Hogue, Jane Mittel, Luther Snow. Seated on floor: Marie Wendt. Not pictured: Jan Pieter van Voorst van Beest, Lilyan Forbes (resigned), and Doris Blackstone (appointed February 2008).

Veterans Memorial Sub-Committee

The Veterans Memorial Sub-Committee is a sub-group of the bicentennial committee. It works closely with the elected members of the cemetery commission to plan for the creation of a memorial in Elmwood Cemetery honoring Pownal's veterans. They are tasked with the design of the memorial and its location, preparation of the site, fund raising, and planning for the dedication ceremony scheduled for Memorial Day, May 26, 2008.

Seated l. to r.: Chair Sherry Dietrich, Cheryl Vosmus, Secretary Mary Ann Hodsdon. Standing l. to r.: Cemetery Commissioner Craig Vosmus, Luther Snow, Joe Raymond, Consultant Rosemary Whitney, Cemetery Commissioner Duane Snow, Alan Chesney. Not pictured: Cemetery Commission Chair Lorraine Merrill.

Sketch of the Pownal Veterans Memorial plan designed by Rosemary Whitney.

Chapter 5

Town Services Are Essential

The town Cletrac tractor with snowplow attached refuels at Pervier's Garage c. 1945. Pictured on the right is Joseph Pervier; on the left is wing-man Steve Libby. The man in the center is unidentified.

Public Works

"To open roads to their full width and prohibit lumber from being twitched across bridges." This motion was voted at Pownal's first town meeting in 1808. Road construction and maintenance have occupied a position of prime concern ever since. By 1871, all of the current town-managed roads had been built, following paths hewn out of the wilderness by hand. Their roadbeds of rock, grave sand, and clay were laboriously laid down by farmers and laborers, none of whom had studied road or bridge engineering or soil mechanics. These early roads were, understandably, narrow. It would take the advent of the automobile before the town widened roads to allow carriages or cars to pass one another safely.

In 1905, State Highway Commissioner Paul D. Sargent urged all towns to improve roadbeds, cut brush to the margins, and place trained men in charge. He advised towns to create a plan, maintain a regular schedule, and schedule necessary work immediately. Pownal responded as best it could. By 1908 the town was annually electing a road commissioner. Some state-aid money for a few roads came in, but most road expenses were borne by local taxpayers. Throughout the first third of the twentieth century the nature of the work remained essentially unchanged, with the jobs accomplished by manual labor, aided by horses or oxen. The town had owned a horse-drawn road machine since before the turn of the century, and in 1908 a new one was purchased from the Good Road Machine Company for $207.90.

Summer months saw road surfaces dragged smooth, gravel added, bushes cut, ditches and

Ernest Tuttle (1870-1935) served as road commissioner for twenty-three years between 1907 and 1933. He lived and farmed with his wife Maude Marston Tuttle (1882-1981) at the current 133 Hallowell Road. He also served as Pownal's first elected fire ward in 1914 and 1915

were purchased at local stores. Blacksmiths Hathaway J. Fickett and Rufus Skillin were paid for repairing machinery and sharpening tools. "Snow Bills" that year would amount to one-third of the total road budget. Eighty-eight men shoveled snow, or used either horses or oxen to drag a road-clearing plank. The year's budgeted "Snow Account" of $500 was overspent by $220.

In 1907 Earnest Tuttle became road commissioner, a post he would hold for twenty-five years. Toward the end of his tenure, in 1930, the town purchased from the Portland Tractor Company its first crawler tractor for $4,685, a Cletrac, built by the Cleveland Tractor Company. Road crews now had a powerful machine, complete with a snowplow attachment for winter duty.

By the 1930s, the more mobile town folk with their increasingly numerous cars and trucks, de-

culverts cleaned and repaired, bridges repaired, and stone work "set aright." Winter brought many challenges. Chief among them was "breaking roads," opening them to traffic after snowstorms. Snow fencing was deployed to limit drifting, since there were few trees forming natural windbreaks. During a 1974 interview about winter work, Carl Tryon recalled, "We broke roads one winter here with oxen...two pair of oxen. We had sleds. You'd put a stick under the front sled...and break the snow down. [The oxen] would wallow through the snow. It didn't bother them any... We shoveled it first down to a foot. It used to drift here quite badly, it did. We shoveled down to a foot and left that on the road." The roads were rarely cleared bare, since a layer of packed snow allowed sleighs and pungs to move more easily.

The records for 1908 provide a glimpse at typical details. During that summer, twenty-two men were paid to labor on the roads and six to work on bridges and culverts. Their "pay" usually took the form of credits toward their yearly property taxes. Bridge stringers and new culverts were shipped in by rail, but hemlock planks came from several local farms. Sand, stone, and gravel were obtained from local quarries, while nails, bolts, spikes, lime, and cement

Town folk have stories about the many hardships they faced during "mud season," but the archives contain few photographs of what it looked like. This photo, by Villa Snow, inscribed "Lawrence Road past the Jonathan Snow farm during mud season c.1920," says it all.

manded wider and better-maintained roads. Moreover, the consolidation of one-room schools brought about increased transporting of students. Pownal got its first school bus in 1934. This was another impetus for improved roads.

The town, however, still did not own its own trucks to haul sand and gravel. Many men working on the roads were paid for the use of their trucks. Their labor was still compensated by tax credits. Teams of horses were sometimes used, but increasingly the Cletrac was put to work on the more difficult projects. By this time, the nature of roadwork support services had moved away from blacksmiths and farms toward the local garages that had been newly established. The garages of Lewis Pervier and Donald Keith now provided gas, oil, and mechanical service for trucks and tractors.

Even with constant attention, the town's gravel roads were all but impassible at times.

(continued on page 213)

Henry T. Sweetser (1868-1956) about 1915. Henry and his wife Mary Sibley Sweetser (1872-1962) operated telephone central in their home at the current 554 Elmwood Road from 1905 through 1948. Henry did line work and collected monthly bills for the company while his wife, daughter Marjorie, and daughter-in-law Kathrine worked as switchboard operators.

The Old-Fashioned Way

Henry T. Sweetser, road commissioner from 1905 to 1907 and 1919, is pictured here with the town road machine and his team of four horses. The date of the photo is unknown. An American Champion, a horse-drawn road machine, was acquired in 1898 for $235. Another was purchased in 1908 from the Good Road Machine Company for $207. In 1907 Henry Sweetser noted that "[the] King Split Log Drag is a valuable machine on clayey roads."

"In 1915, the State Highway Commission again issued advisory instructions to town road crews. Among them were: DON'T use six horses on a road machine when four can do the work and even two are sufficient in some cases; DON'T use a road machine when a split log drag will do the same work and save money; DON'T place eight men around a car to load gravel when four is the most economical number to use; and DON'T build a split log drag so heavy that it will take more than one pair of horses to haul it." Sherry Dietrich. The Notes, July 5, 2005.

A road crew surfacing the Fickett Road with gravel c. 1938, taken from inside the North Pownal General Store then owned by Merton Larrabee. Clarence "Cad" Fickett served as road commissioner for nine years between 1919 and 1943. Possibly he was in charge of this project. Note the Cletrac pulling a simple hand-guided plow. To the left in the distance is Mr. Larrabee's second store. On the near right is the building where Alan Bradstreet now houses his Wood Wizard business.

Road crew at work c.1938. Viewing this photo in 2008, Kenneth Vosmus stated that he believed the truck belonged to Joseph Pervier. Indeed, the 1939 Town Report lists $46.90 as spent on Fickett Road repairs and lists Joe Pervier as being paid for the use of his truck. To the right in the background stands the Golden Cross Hall which was later demolished.

Spring thaws and rains brought on mud season, and schools declared a two-week mud vacation when the roads were impassable. Lois Vosmus Sanders remembered in 2005, "We called mud holes in the roads 'honey pots'... Got stuck on Ledge Hill road when George Hodsdon had to get the horses out to pull the cars out of the mud... Spring vacation or mud vacation would last at least two weeks... Busses could not get through."

During the depression years, local road efforts were bolstered by a $12,000 WPA project grant that employed forty men and seven trucks to surface the Pownal to Freeport section of what is now the Elmwood Road. Generally, however, throughout this period the nature of both summer and winter roadwork stayed much as it had always been. "We worked as long as money held out," said Kenneth Vosmus during a 2008 interview.

A new item began to appear in the annual road budgets: funds for "tarring and patching." The town was beginning to move beyond purely gravel roads. In 2005, Carl Knight (who would become road commissioner in 1964) said, "Take Poland Range Road: [They] would dump piles of

Everett Cates (1900-1968) was road commissioner from 1943 to1947. Daughter Virginia Cates Davis remembered in 2006 that "we used to have awful snow storms... My father would walk from West Pownal where they were living to the center to get the plow equipment out... He was so conscientious."

Pictured here during a winter in the 1950s with the second Cletrac are l.to r.: Roy Tufts, driver Kenneth "Chub" Libby, and wingman Victor Litchfield Sr. Louis Haskell related during a 2005 historical society program that this Cletrac with snowplow would have been the "new orange one purchased secondhand from Durham that had hydraulics for lifting the wings and could travel at four miles per hour."

Roy C. Tufts (1913-2003) served as road commissioner from 1954 to 1959. Roy and his wife Dorothy (1917-2001) lived at the current 878 Lawrence Road and owned the North Pownal General Store from 1968 through 1972. Roy served as fire department captain of the North Pownal fire station and was instrumental in rebuilding the station after it burned in 1969. Dorothy Tufts served as president of the firemen's auxiliary in the 1950s.

sand along side the road, then he would spray liquid tar over the surface, then all of us kids would shovel the sand by hand over the hot-top tar. It would last several years... Traffic in those days wasn't very heavy."

In 1949, a new (second-hand) Cletrac was purchased along with a power grader (pulled by a truck). Kenneth Vosmus remembered his father Thomas J. Vosmus, road commissioner at the time, operating this grader. The new Cletrac was in for a severe test when the blizzard of 1952 hit. Louis Haskell remembered in 2005, "The phrase 'stuck on the flats' makes me remember the blizzard of '52. Before they had this orange [Cletrac], they had a gray one... The wings didn't work with hydraulics... My dad walked behind it before he was ill... You pulled the ropes by hand to lift the wings. The orange one was purchased from Durham, second hand. [It] went four miles per hour while the old gray one went one mile per hour." Then in 1954 a natural disaster occurred in the form of hurricane Edna. Many of Pownal's roads and bridges were destroyed, and it took $25,559 in Federal relief funds to rebuild them.

By the middle of Pownal's second century, changes affecting the road department began to come quickly. For one thing, people were increasingly looking outward. The horizon-expanding experiences of World War II and the postwar industrial boom had created a populace willing and able to move about the country. The farm no longer provided adequate incomes, and people routinely sought out-of-town employment. Economic expansion brought a boom in the automobile industry. Millions of cars and trucks rolled off Detroit's production lines, as tourism was being promoted state- and nationwide. Expanding volumes of freight were increasingly being hauled by trucks, rather than railroads.

This increased traffic and heavier usage demanded more and better roads. Nationally, the tipping point came in 1956 when the Highway Revenue Act created a trust fund derived from fuel taxes and dedicated to expanding the nation's roads. This resulted in the creation of an interstate highway system of more than 46,000 miles. Like every other state, Maine received its share of this outpouring, but had already been busy on its own, constructing the Maine Turnpike from Kittery to Portland (1947) and Portland to Augusta (1955). Town road departments

Cletrac and plow pictured from rear showing the pulley and hydraulic system.

increasingly found themselves at the center of community concerns, while federal and state revenue sharing, state-aid funds, and excise tax revenues poured into local coffers to be used to upgrade roads and bridges.

In Pownal, how the road department approached its work and how the community viewed the department were beginning to change. During the 1960s, the warrant at a town meeting would contain separate articles asking voters to raise and appropriate money for "common roads," "winter roads," "bridges and culverts," "purchase snow fence," 'tarring and patching," "grader upgrades and repairs," "equipment building," and "special road construction." By the turn of the century this format had morphed into a more general request to raise and appropriate funds for highway maintenance. When needed, special road construction items or requests for new equipment would be added. No longer was there an item "to purchase snow fencing," as trees and bushes had now filled in once-open fields. "Tarring and patching" became "paving," and "grader repairs" and "equipment building" were absorbed into the overall maintenance budget.

Thomas J. Vosmus (1882-1968), road commissioner for eight years between 1948 and 1964, attended the Sweeney Automobile School in Kansas City, Missouri in 1915. This training greatly added to his skills as commissioner, particularly when equipment required repair. Tom was commissioner during the Hurricane of 1954, and family records indicate that he was the foreman of a state road project for reconstruction of the Sweetser Road and bridge in 1961.

Thomas J. Vosmus is dwarfed by the town's new Gallion Road Grader, purchased for $24,000 in 1962. The grader was kept at the commissioner's residence, the current 188 Merrill Road, since the town had no large equipment building or garage until 1967.

Route Nine Bids Open Are Called Satisfactory

Bids were opende this week on construction of route nine by Bradbury Mountain State Park in Pownal and along a stretch of the same route across the Androscoggin county line.

The state highway commission informed Rep Ben S Crockett that all bids were satisfactory and that while the work has not been awarded yet, the lowest bidder will probably get it.

Separate bills were passed in the last legislature appropriating funds for these two stretches of work. Rep Crockett was sponsor of the $21,400 bill for construction work in Pownal on route nine and co-sponsor of the $18,000 bill for work on route nine in Androscoggin valley.

Arthur D Ingles entered the low bid on both projects. He bid $16,259.50 for the Pownal piece and $16,230.50 or the Androscoggin county piece.

Next lowest bids were entered by O & M Taylor and C W Quarlie. Second lowest bids were for $16,425.70 and $16,273.10.

The bids do not cover the payment of the inspector.

Route 9 (Hallowell Road) had been paved with asphalt up to the Pownal Center crossroads by 1955. Many are surprised to learn that, beyond this point, this state road still had a gravel surface at that time. The section past Bradbury Mountain State Park was to be asphalted by Arthur D. Ingles for $16,259.50, as reported in the Freeport Press, *October 6, 1955. Later, under separate bids, the surfacing of Route 9 would continue through the Androscoggin valley.*

Town officers, road commissioners, and budget committees began exerting tighter control over the road department's budgeting process, in order to keep property taxes as low as possible. They attempted to identify all possible outside funding before asking voters to "appropriate from taxation," but over time the local burden increased. In the 1960s seventy-five percent of the highway budget was funded from external sources, while twenty-five percent came from property taxation. By the 1980s, outside support had dropped to fifty-four percent, leaving Pownal to pick up the balance. Another problem was that, because of federal and, especially, state funding, major thoroughfares were inevitably the first to be paved, while many town roads went unpaved for lack of resources.

In the middle of much of this change was Carl Knight. Carl was elected road commissioner in 1964, and was reelected yearly until his retirement in 1987. Carl grew up in Pownal, a descendent of the Knight family that dates to Pownal's earliest settlers, and his father and grandfather played prominent roles in the town's granite and lumber businesses. He had worked on the road crew since 1947, owned a sand, gravel, and loam business, and knew the needs of roads and bridges. He provided the department, not only with leadership, but also the necessary equipment.

Two years after Carl's election, the town voted funds to build an equipment building beside Mallett Hall to store the town-owned grader and snow blades. The town rented trucks, a backhoe, and other tools from Carl, who fueled and maintained them. Not until 1979 did the town hire a full-time employee (John Dobson). And it continued to hire part-timers as the need arose, especially for snow plowing. The days of "working off your taxes" were over.

When Carl retired, the lead for an article in the *Evening Express* of February 10, 1987 declared, "Retirement Leaves Town Unequipped." This referred to the very real sadness at the departure of its trusted road commissioner. But it also, perhaps unwittingly, highlighted a problem: the rental arrangements with Carl were ending. At town meeting that year, voters approved a bond for $250,000, the largest ever up to that point. From the proceeds, $170,000 would purchase two dump trucks, a backhoe and front-end loader, and tools for the department. The remainder would be used to build a covered salt and sand shelter. The previously uncovered salt and sand pile had contributed to the contamination of several nearby private wells.

Selectmen Gerald Rolfe, Fred Stasinowsky, and Craig Vosmus appointed Darrel Thurber road commissioner, inaugurating a permanent change from election to appointment. Darrel would serve faithfully for the next sixteen years. In 1999 a second full-time crew position was added.

Throughout the 1990s demands on the department greatly increased. Pownal's population grew to 1,100 by the turn of the century, and the traffic from more and heavier automobiles, trucks, and construction vehicles was damaging roads never engineered or surfaced to bear the added weight and usage. Roads deteriorated markedly. At the same time, some residents were asking for more gravel roads to be paved. The paving account of $50,000 per year could not even meet current needs, let alone support the surfacing of even more roads. Additional costs were on the horizon as the price of new equipment was escalating along with compensation (salaries, health care insurance, and pension plans) for the full-time crew. Meanwhile, money

The 1987 Town Report was dedicated to Carl I. Knight in recognition of, and with thanks for, his many years of service to the Town of Pownal as a member of the road crew beginning in 1947 and as road commissioner from 1964 to 1987. Carl was the last elected road commissioner; all subsequent commissioners have been appointed.

for the highway budget from outside sources was dwindling.

At the urging of many residents, the selectmen responded in 1997 by appointing a road committee to take a comprehensive look at these issues. Some of its more important recommendations were: to increase funding for road reconstruction, to establish a needs-assessment process for prioritizing future construction projects, to complete Lawrence Road construction, and to establish written job descriptions for the road commissioner and the crew. The committee also recommended that a separate line item of $35,000 be included in the annual budget for ditching and erosion control—a preventative measure long ignored. Some, but not all, of these recommendations had been implemented at the time of the committee's disbanding in 2003.

By 2000, it became obvious that the town needed to provide all its employees a benefit plan that addressed health care, insurance, and retirement. It was prompted in large part by the imminent move of town offices from private homes to the new facilities in town hall. An ad hoc compensation committee was appointed to

Highway truck acquired in 2004 working on the Sweetser Bridge project during the summer of 2005. The cost of the truck with plow gear, sander, body, radios, and lettering was $115,887.

Left: Shawn Bennett, road commissioner 2003 through 2008, has had with many years experience in construction and public works, with broad experience in road maintenance and construction. In 2005, he was elected to the board of directors of the Maine chapter of the American Public Works Association.

Right: Pownal highway department employees in 2008. L. to r.: Road Comomissioner Shawn Bennett, mechanic and equipment operator Philip Wentworth, equipment operators Benjamin Porter and Donald Randall.

recommend policies and procedures for implementing a benefit plan at a fair cost to the town. Their recommended plan was adopted at town meeting in March of 2003. Unfortunately, these changes in their existing benefits prompted the road commissioner and crew to resign. A temporary crew was hired, consisting of Rodney Richards, Eric Wentworth Sr., and Jason Best, providing interim coverage, for which they received the selectmen's grateful public thanks.

In the spring of 2003 Shawn Bennett was appointed road commissioner, with Roger Coulombe and Todd Richards hired as equipment operators. This appointment ushered in an era marked by comprehensive planning and up-to-date methods. Shawn's mission for the department is, "to plan and use our resources wisely, to maintain and protect the town's infrastructure and natural resources, and to be a respected, well-managed, financially prudent department." He oversees the work of three employees: mechanic and equipment operator Philip Wentworth and equipment operators Donald Randall and Benjamin Porter.

The department has under its care twenty miles of paved roads, fourteen miles of gravel roads, and seven bridges. The town maintenance building and salt shed are located behind Mallett Hall. Nearby are stored four dump-plow trucks, a motor grader, a backhoe-loader, a hydraulic sweeper, an excavator, and a twenty-ton equipment trailer.

Shawn attends workshops on road management and professional gatherings, in order to stay current with best practices. His thorough report on the state of Pownal's roads convinced the capital projects planning committee to recommend that the town begin rebuilding some of its crumbling roads. At the March 2007 town meeting, the town voted to begin with part of the Allen Road. The $1,182,500 price tag became part of the largest bond obligation ever accepted by the town.

Recently, the department has broadened its role to include some general maintenance of town-owned buildings. Also they plow the parking lots of Mallett Hall, the fire and rescue stations, and the elementary school. They help with construction projects as needed by the cemetery commission. In these ways, they have become, in effect, a public works department—a forward-looking change that appears both efficient and fiscally sound.

Sweetser Road Bridge Project Wins Award

In the 2003 annual town report, Road Commissioner Shawn Bennett introduced himself and the new road crew members and outlined the projects that were imminent. He reported that the Sweetser Road bridge had been declared unsafe by the state and that the road would be closed until further notice. Shawn's $40,000 replacement plan was accepted by the voters at the March 2004 town meeting. A Pownal native, Shawn was sensitive to the town's commitment to preserve its history and rural character and he knew the uniqueness of the Sweetser Road landscape. His plan would in his words, "preserve the look of the granite abutment built sometime in the 1800s, yet construct a bridge strong enough to carry today's heavy loads."

Work on the large project continued throughout 2004 with a small crew (mechanic-operator Roger Coulombe and equipment operator Travis Merrill). The road was again open to traffic in the spring of 2005, with sedimentation pools in place, vegetation planted, and approaches to the bridge reconstructed. A special part of Pownal's heritage was preserved and a very prestigious award earned for the town.

For quality, innovation, value, and community satisfaction, the Sweetser Road bridge project was awarded the First Place Public Works Excellence Award by the Maine Chapter of the American Public Works Association in conjunction with the Institute for Mechanical Engineering. The engraved green marble plaque is displayed in the Mallett Hall lobby.

Road Commissioner Bennett explained, "To establish structural integrity, the existing granite abutments had to be modified. Rocks were drilled through and pinned, then all joints between rocks were grouted. Concrete caps in existing abutments preserved the old look and would carry unlimited weight."

The completed bridge during the winter of 2008. As Sean Bennett described it, "In the end we have a strong steel-framed bridge with a pressure treated deck that looks very similar to the previous wooden structure." Another step has been taken to preserve Pownal's rural heritage.

The snow removal plan of the Pownal highway department includes: pre-treating road surfaces to prevent ice and snow from bonding to the pavement; keeping main roads continually plowed for safety as soon as there are two to three inches of accumulation; plowing secondary roads with three to four inches of accumulation; plowing the driveways of the fire stations, the school, the town hall, and the dry hydrants. When the storm subsides, the roads are plowed and treated a final time.

Ditching and Culvert Replacement: According to Shawn Bennett, "The most important factor in road maintenance is drainage. Without good drainage the best of road construction methods could be wasted. Seventy-five percent of our old culverts are completely rusted and are collapsing." The picture shows the Chadsey Road after a ditching and culvert replacement project was completed in 2006.

Conservin' Energy
by June Tucci

At the March 2003 Pownal Arts Evening, sponsored by the Bradbury Mountain Arts Society, June Tucci read the following story to the great amusement of everyone. A prolific poet, June has been writing verse for many years and frequently give readings of her work. Here she combines the theme of Yankee frugality with the universal experience of jarring spring roads into a classic piece of Maine dialect humor.

Now, down home we're quite mindful of conservin' energy. You wouldn't think so, though, the way the light comp'ny keeps on includin' them cute little remindahs in the bills they sends out! For quite awhile they was puttin' out what they thought was a nice little gesture, you know, to sorta soften the blow of the metah readin's. They was puttin' in them little recipes ... or as our Uncle Lou used to call them, "Re-*sipp*-eez".

Well heavens-to-Betsy, we know how to boil a lobstah and bake beans an' scratch up a batch of buttahmilk biscuit! Ayuh! Well somebody musta set them guys wise, cuz they don't include that stuff no more. No, now the've took to puttin' in them confusin' little graphs tellin' us what time a day we should turn on the 'lectric stove, open the 'fridgerator door and use the washah and dryah. That's to make us *think* they really care about us savin' money by conservin' energy... Oh shu'ah!

Well now, Chummy, I'm gonna tell ya somethin'. Up he'ah in good ol' Pownal we are way aheada them boys cuz Virgil (that's Maw Beasley's youngest, and a right smaht young fella he is, too), he thought up the most ingenious way to get th' washin' done without makin' that metah needle on the side th' house go spinnin' round like droppin' a dollah bill down the flush. "Yep," he says to Maw Beasley, "They want consahvation, we'll show 'em what consahvation really is!"

Well you know, he got the idea from goin' up and down the Chadsey Road on his way to and from the post office. Now, in case you don't know, that Chadsey Road is about as rough, rugged and wrinkled as any washboard road you evah did see. So, Virgil, he hauls down the old galvanized washtub from the bahn chambah, sets it up in the back of Paw Beasley's old Ford pickup, fills her up with hot watah and soap powdah (the washtub, that is), and gets Maw's old scrub board off the shed wall. Then he takes the big ol' rockah off th' side th' porch and sets his Maw right up on that and off they go down the Chadsey Road!

Well now, Chummy, them bahn-overalls of Paw Beasley's was caked up with mud, crud and stuff enough to stand alone, but all Maw had to do was hold them overalls up against the washboard while Virgil drove up and down. The Chadsey Road done the rest and Paw Beasley had the cleanest overalls in the whole town of Pownal!

Cou'se, they did get kinda ragged lookin' and Virgil, well, he did spend a whole week's wortha gas money in one aftahnoon, but the light bill went down. Only thing is, it's been about a month since poor Maw Beasley did that washin' – and she's still a-goin' like this: ～～～〰︎

Public Safety

On a fine spring day in 1905, a coal-fired steam locomotive passed through West Pownal, dumped its ash box and moved on. Wind-whipped sparks settled on dry tinder. Flames begin licking their way through brush and trees. This was the likely cause of a huge fire that consumed 234 acres in ten hours. Some 200 men using only shovels and buckets were required to quell the blaze. Barely four years later, twenty men, paid by the town, battled a large fire on the Hodsdon Road for three days, again armed with nothing more than shovels and buckets.

Such was the nature of fire fighting in the early part of the twentieth century. There was little equipment, and no tested fire fighting techniques. As early as 1900 the University of Maine Agricultural College stressed fire prevention in its forestry courses. But not until after devastating fires struck throughout Maine between 1903 and 1905 did Maine forestry districts implement fire protection programs. Contributing to these blazes were the loss of watersheds, reduced stream flows, and tinder dry brush, all resulting from the extensive denuding of Maine's forests.

In Pownal, chimney and building fires were also of great concern. One of the first fire fighting improvements in those days was more rapid communication following the arrival of the telephone in 1905. In a 1973 interview, Hazel Whitcher said, "Mrs. [Mary] Sweetser was telephone central and the arrangement went by (and it worked well in those days) was one long ring. That meant fire! Everyone would take down their receiver and listen. She'd tell them where the fire was and from all over town they'd go. They would do the best they could. Still the fire got the best of them lots of times." As for town buildings, the only expense for fire prevention

Left: Leigh W. Loring (1887-1962) was fire ward for three years from 1923 to 1926.

Right: Joseph H. Pervier (1899-1980) was fire ward for thirty-three years from 1926 to 1959. (See chapter 4 for Joe's years of town service.)

equipment seems to have been the purchase of a copper fire extinguisher for Mallett Hall in 1905, and it was not until 1919 that fire insurance was taken out on the building.

Ernest Tuttle became Pownal's first fire ward in 1914. He was conscientious in his duties, but it was one of his successors, Leigh Loring (serving from 1923 to 1926), who is credited with bringing the town's fire fighting capabilities close to the standards of the time. Through his efforts the town acquired more soda-acid fire extinguishers, paid men to guard or watch fires, and agreed to elect fire wards annually, paying them a stipend. Mr. Loring wrote in the 1925 town report, "The fire equipment owned by the town consists of six pyrene extinguishers, three rough rider extinguishers of the soda type, and twenty pails. We need more of the soda type extinguishers and a suitable extension ladder. Our greatest menace to public safety is Mallett Hall; here the outer doors should be made to swing outward and a fire escape provided, if large gatherings are to be permitted in the upper hall." Voters agreed to spend $225 for fire escapes, and eventually the doors were changed to

As Pownal had no fire stations in 1941, Pownal's fire truck and equipment were kept at the Pervier farm at current 153 Hallowell Road.

open outward. But at the same time the voters turned down a request to purchase a modern chemical fire truck for $2,400.

Joseph Pervier, Mr. Loring's brother-in-law, was elected fire ward in 1926, beginning what would become thirty-three years in that position. He was forced to move slowly with improvements, especially once financial crisis and depression hit and made budgets even tighter. Even so, in 1929 he was able to persuade voters to allocate $150 for a truck, "to speed necessary equipment to a fire." By 1937, Mr. Pervier was recommending that, "everyone have a ladder that will reach the eaves of the house and a roof ladder that will reach the length of the roof." This he felt would be a very good precaution, since the large majority of the town's fires were in chimneys. Indeed, between 1929 and 1939, eighty-six of the reported one hundred and thirty-five fires were chimney fires. They were often easily extinguished, but there were also very serious fires. One consumed the store and post office in West Pownal, and a grass fire resulted in the death of a small child.

Fire truck built by Joe and Lewis Pervier in 1941 for $300.00 appropriated by the town. Mickey, the family pet, became Pownal's first firedog

Joe asked the town in 1940 for a sum of money that, "would not be excessive—two to three hundred dollars," to equip a fire truck. The money was granted. A used truck was pur-

Pervier Fire-Fighting Team

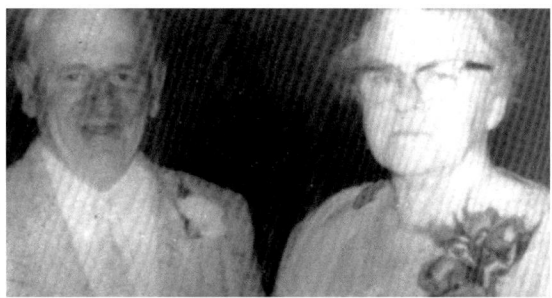

Fire Ward Joseph Pervier (1899-1980 and Emma Loring Pervier (1893-1970).

Joe and Emma Pervier worked as a team—Joe as Fire Ward and Emma as his assistant. Josephine Pervier Allen remembered in 1998, "My mother Emma was the only girl in a family with three brothers who as a young girl desperately wanted to help the 'boys' fight fires. [Her brother Leigh Loring had been fire ward from 1923 to 1926.] After she married my father, she assumed an active role in fire fighting. She drove the truck to the scene of a fire…[and] would tell the 'boys' how the truck worked… She manned the red phone at our house…and she stoked the fires in our garage where the truck was kept, to keep it from freezing in the winter." Josephine further recalled that, "When my mother was pregnant with me, she carried a ladder while helping fight a fire at Blackstone's barn [on Elmwood Road] which many said led to my birth a month earlier than expected." Perhaps Emma Pervier should be called Pownal's first woman volunteer fire fighter. As Josephine related, "One year she even got votes for fire ward at the town election."

chased, along with a 500-gallon tank, a pump, and 175 feet of hose. Joe and his brother Lewis assembled the "fire truck" at Pervier's Garage, or as Joe put it, "We invented it." Thus did the town acquire its first fire truck even though it still had no formal department. "We have made a start toward a more efficient fire department," Joe said, but his dream of creating an official town organization didn't materialize until 1948.

It came about following the state-wide conflagrations of 1947. In 1948, Joe urged the organization of a fire department, and the town agreed. They appropriated $500 to get it off the ground, and increased the fire ward account to cover operating expenses. At the next year's town meeting, Joe reported, "The Volunteer Fire Department has been formed and it has regular monthly meetings and it has a membership of fifty-three." However, it did not have a station or barn for storing the fire truck and the equipment that Joe and Lewis had worked so hard to acquire. All would be kept at the Pervier farm until 1959 when Joe retired.

In 1998 Sherry Dietrich wrote a series of articles in *The Notes*, looking back on the fire department's first fifty years. On May 26, she wrote, "In 1958 Fire Ward Joe Pervier announced his retirement. His reign of thirty-three years began when the fire department still clung to nineteenth century fire fighting methods and concluded with his having organized a formal volunteer firemen's unit and buying modern (for the times) equipment. Mr. Pervier was also successful in having voters realize a tax-supported fire department was absolutely necessary for the safety of the citizenry. His foresight and devotion to fire safety and prevention made Pownal a better place."

Joe Pervier's successor was Earle Blake, also destined to have a long career as ward. He would continue to support upgrading equipment and providing training. Among the new initiatives he championed were the inclusion of a civil defense program within the department and construction of a new fire station in Pownal Center. In 1960 the town appropriated $1,000 for the project and leased land from the First Parish Congregational Church. Members of Granite Grange 14 set to work constructing a two-bay station, complete with a meeting room on the second floor. This effort earned the Granite Grange first prize in the Community Service Contest sponsored by the Sears Foundation and the National Grange. The award lauded its "Real Service and Contribution to the Community." The structure, its exterior little changed, continues to house the department today.

Also during Earle's twenty-three years of leadership, the North Pownal fire station was rebuilt, following its destruction by fire in 1969. Several second-hand oil trucks were retrofitted for use as water tankers. Then in 1975 the town purchased its first commercially built fire engine—a new 1975 pumper with a 750 G.P.M.

Earle A. Blake (1914-1988) was Fire Ward for twenty-three years from 1959 to 1982. Earle served on the superintending school committee from 1951 to 1963 and as town constable for many years. He and his wife Althea were founding members of the Pownal Scenic and Historical Society.

pump, high pressure fog unit, and 750-gallon tank. Equipped, it cost $35,000.

Earle was particularly proud of the fire prevention education program he helped start at the school. Meanwhile, his son Lester, a member of the department, organized a firemen's muster team in 1975. This team went on to win sixty-six trophies in local and state competitions. Their successes were occasions of pride for the community, but perhaps more importantly the muster team attracted many young men to join the department.

When Earle ended his tenure as fire ward in 1982, he could reflect that the department was much better equipped. Retrofitted tank trucks had been replaced by newer units; volunteers were outfitted with coats, helmets, and Scott Air Packs; and two-way radio communication had been provided. However, looming on the horizon were an increasing number of state regulations and insurance requirements, all of which would severely impact the town's budget.

Lester Blake was elected fire ward in 1982 and began a tenure that lasted twenty-one years,

Ralph A. Vosmus (1925-1993) served as a volunteer fireman for over thirty years, and later as a department captain. He was a member of the budget committee from 1962 to 1992; was elected to serve on the cemetery commission from 1964 to 1993; and was a member of the board of appeals from 1964 to 1968, and from 1974 to 1993.

Lester Blake served as fire chief from 1982 to 2003.

only two less than that of his father. His immediate goals were to modernize fire trucks and to meet the ever-increasing state and federal regulations. Newer (although still second hand) tank and auxiliary trucks were purchased over the next twenty years, but the addition of a second fire engine would have to wait until 1998. Safety equipment was upgraded and volunteer firemen were outfitted with individual pagers.

Lester oversaw the construction of several dry hydrants at water sources around town. The department also installed two "red phone" base stations, one at Assistant Fire Ward Vernon Brower's house, staffed by Vernon and his wife Geraldine, and the other at the North Pownal General Store, staffed by Captain Roland Morin and his wife Joyce. The phones, which were attended at all times, would ring when the fire department was called. The base station radios would then send a call to the pagers of individual fire fighters. This "dispatch" system continued until 1994.

In annual town reports, Lester continued to appeal for more volunteers. He especially wanted people who were available during the day and could learn how to operate the increasingly sophisticated fire fighting equipment. He wrote in 1982, "[I] want to thank officers, members of Ladies Auxiliary, and fire fighters who give up their time to make the Fire Department." Of the twenty-two individuals he listed, one was Kathy Harlow, the first woman to officially serve. In following years, other women would sign on. But state and federal regulations were becoming more exacting. They dictated that volunteers, men or women, could no longer be recruited off the street in time of need. They now had to undergo a formal training program and be fully equipped. These requirements and their associated time commitment made it ever more difficult to recruit volunteers.

As early as 1993 the department recognized that it had outgrown the facilities at the Center fire station. The meeting room was too small, there was little storage space, there was no toilet, and OSHA-required washing facilities were non-existent. A study committee was formed, but it would not be until 2003 that these issues started to be addressed. At the same time town residents were beginning to agitate for more reliable fire response as well as response to medical emergencies. With Vernon Brower's resignation

Vernon Brower (1924-2002) began his service in the fire department in 1963 and served as captain in the North Pownal station. In 1981, he was promoted to assistant fire ward and department safety officer. He and his wife Geraldine operated the red phones, an early form of dispatch, from their home until 1994.

in 1994 and the consequent loss of his red phone base station, these issues came to a head. The town addressed the first of these by contracting with Freeport for dispatch service. The second was addressed by contracting with Freeport Rescue for $1,000 and North Yarmouth Rescue for $500. These contracted services continue today, albeit at greater cost to the town.

In 1995, Lester recommended to the town that it support a First Responders Medical Team, trained and equipped to work with the Freeport and North Yarmouth rescue units. The town initially funded this program with $4,300 in 1996, and by 1997 Mari Smith, deputy chief and head of the team, reported that they had received state licensing. She also noted that the twenty-two members had received first responders and basic EMT training, and that the unit had responded to forty-five emergencies in town. That same year, the town appropriated $140,000 to purchase Fire Engine 2. This truck was housed at the North Pownal station, while Fire Engine 1 remained at the Center fire station.

The year 1998 was a special one for the fire department. The whole town celebrated the fiftieth anniversary of the department's official founding. Much progress had been made during these fifty years, and the town appropriately recognized and lauded the accomplishments. One year later, in 1999, the town finally and officially changed the title Fire Ward to Fire Chief, the name already long in common use. By 2000, a new policy of compensating volunteers on a pay-per-call basis had been instituted. That same

---

Blake Fire-Fighting Team

Earle and Althea Blake worked as a team — Earle as a fireman and later as fire ward with Althea as his "right-hand-man." In 1998, remembering department growth and modernization over the years, Althea said, "We were both actively involved, as Earle replaced antiquated equipment and trucks, volunteers were trained, stations were built, and new regulations were implemented. I was busy as founding member of the firemen's auxiliary, later serving as president. There were many good years of families and neighbors working together, taking drinking water to "the boys" when fighting a fire, feeding the boys coffee and sandwiches after a fire, fund-raising suppers at the church, helping to clean the fire stations, and worrying over the safety of the boys when they were called to fight a fire."

Fire Ward Earle Blake (1914-1988) and Althea Blake (1914-).

During these years son Lester became involved in the department and was part of the "Blake Team." He was later elected to the position of fire ward in 1982 when his father retired. Over the next twenty years, the Blake team continued to grow as Lester's (then) wife Karen joined the fire and rescue department, along with daughter Jessica and son Jared. Althea remembered that when asked to help out, she always responded, "I don't know how good I'll be, but I'll do my best!" That she did. In 2004 on her ninetieth birthday, Althea was honored by the Pownal Scenic and Historical Society, and by the town, for fifty-six years of town service.

This North Pownal Fire Station served the area from 1950 until it burned in February of 1969. In the 1949 Annual Town Report, Fire Ward Joseph Pervier reported, "A [1947 Dodge] truck loaned by Kenneth Libby is being rigged as a unit to be housed at North Pownal. This truck with a front-mount pump, tank, and other equipment will be ready to operate in a few weeks." This truck burned with the station in 1969. Kenneth Libby also donated a 4000-gallon water tank that was installed in the ground at North Pownal with the help of members of the fire department. This tank is still in use.

year a 1979 fire engine (E-1), acquired from the New Gloucester Fire Department for $1.00, replaced the fire engine purchased in 1975. The enhanced 911 emergency response system came online in 2001, and the town was fully compliant thanks to the efforts of Robert McMahon.

In March of 2003 Lester Blake retired as fire chief. Between Lester and his father Earle, the town could look back gratefully at over forty-three years of fire department leadership by the Blake family.

In a smooth transition, David Malone was elected fire chief in March of 2003. At the same time, in addition to the operating budget, the town appropriated an additional $8,225 to be used to upgrade the department's radio communications. In his first town meeting report a year later David stated, "Members responded to sixty-nine calls for service involving over 721 hours of call time. [Collectively] they underwent 1,000 hours of training."

About this time the department began actively looking for appropriate grants to finance new equipment. Lieutenant Robert McMahon undertook the grant writing and was successful in acquiring $35,000 to update equipment, install eye-wash stations, and purchase two computers complete with administrative software. This success bolstered the department's case when they asked the town in 2004 for $10,000 to continue improvements at both stations. The town agreed. Bob's grant writing continued, and by 2005 the department had received a total of $150,883 from such sources.

These financial resources, plus donations, allowed the department to complete a variety of upgrades, renovations, and purchases between 2003 and 2007. Some of the major ones were: the addition of a dormer onto the Center fire station, creation of more usable office and storage space at the Center, installation of bathroom and kitchen facilities at the Center, and renovation of wiring and electrical services at both stations.

2004 brought with it the resignation of Mari Smith as deputy chief in charge of the first responders team. Under her leadership, starting in 1996, the unit had steadily improved and modernized its equipment and training. They had gained the respect and confidence of town residents who had come to rely on their capable services. The unit was responding to ever more calls, and their equipment had increased to include an Automatic External Defibrillator (AED) and Epi pens. Skill levels were also increasing as four members were upgraded to EMT technician. Chief Malone said that Mari had "formed the department [team] and turned it into the highly skilled professional unit it is today." Following her resignation, leadership of the team became a joint effort shared between Deputy Chiefs Richard Hogue and Michael Rogers. In recognition of the increased importance and role of the first responders unit within the fire department structure, the name of the department was changed to Pownal Fire and Rescue Department in 2005.

Since the early 1950s there has been an organized support group for the fire department. In its early days this group was known as the Firemen's Auxiliary. In 2006 the group was formally reorganized into the Pownal Fire and Rescue Company, a non-profit non-municipal organization. They sponsor social activities for the department and raise money to aid in purchasing supplies. A recent project undertaken by the organization was funding and construction of retaining walls at the Center station. Current officers are: Conrad Lausier, president; Ronald Hodsdon, vice president; Mary Ann Hodsdon, secretary; and Linda McMahon, treasurer.

By 2007 it was obvious that the E-1 fire engine acquired from New Gloucester had reached the end of its useful service. The voters were asked at town meeting that year to approve bonding for $300,000 to purchase a new modern replacement truck. The bonding article passed. It is interesting to ponder the future implications of this 757 percent increase in the price of a truck since Pownal's first purchase in 1975.

(continued on page 232)

The Pownal Volunteer Fire Department celebrated fifty years of service at the Pumpkin Festival on October 4, 1998. In the 1997 annual town report, Chief Lester Blake thanked those who made the celebration possible, including: Sherry Dietrich for the series of weekly historical notes which she researched and wrote for The Notes *from January to December, 1998; the Historical Society for assembling a memorial photo album and for organizing a museum display commemorating the event; Christopher Ayres for his excellent photographs, one published on the cover of* The Notes *on October 6; and Chris White for organizing the chicken barbeque held at the festival. As Chief Blake wrote, "A good time was had by all." Pictured in front of the North Pownal fire station are: front row l. to r. Dan Brown, David Malone, Chris White. Back row: Aaron Phelps, Scott Pollock (atop truck), and Jessica Blake Brown.* Photo: Christopher Ayres

Deputy Chief Chrisopher White served the fire department for twenty-six years from 1976 to 2002. Chris also served on the SAD 62 board of directors from 1993 to 1996 and on the planning board for sixteen years (eight years as chair) from 1989 to 2005.

Fire Engines over the Years

Pownal Tank Truck 1. Originally a civil defense vehicle, it was given to Pownal around 1960 by the Town of Yarmouth. It served until the mid-1970s and was stationed at North Pownal.

Pownal Tank Truck 2. To replace the 1947 Dodge engine that burned in the station's fire in 1969, the town purchased a 1961 fuel oil truck from Bradbury Oil Company. It was the third truck to be retrofitted by Frank Staton and served into the mid-1970s. Fully equipped with hose, ladders, extinguishers, shovels and brooms, it cost the town $4,500. It is pictured here at the North Pownal Fire Station with Assistant Fire Ward Vernon Brower at the wheel c.1972. It was replaced by the 1975 Ford fire engine that cost $35,000.

Pownal's first new fire engine was purchased in 1975 for $35,000. It was replaced in 2000 by the E-1 fire engine.

Fire Engine 2 was purchased in 1998 for $140,000. It is stationed at Pownal Center.

This 1979 E-1 Mack fire engine is stationed at Pownal Center. It was purchased for $1.00 from New Gloucester in 2000 when Pineland was sold to the Libra Foundation

The E-1 was replaced by a Ferrara Intruder 2 CAFS Pumper, in the spring of 2008.

Mari-Melinda Smith is pictured in 2008 at the Freeport Fire and Rescue dispatch center. She began working for the Freeport Rescue Department in 1987 after receiving an associate degree in law enforcement technology. She joined the Freeport dispatch team in 1988, and by 1994 was covering emergency calls from Pownal. Mari organized Pownal's First Responders in 1996, continuing to serve as deputy chief of rescue until 2004.

safe parking. Sited where it is within yards of a busy highway, safety is compromised when responding to calls, preparing the trucks, and performing after-call clean up.

Major active equipment now includes: two fire engines, one water tanker, one forest fire truck, and required fire fighting gear for both the trucks and the firefighters. Holdings also include all of the equipment and supplies for the first responders, two thermal imaging cameras, communication gear, and computers with associated software. Indeed, the Pownal Fire and Rescue Department has come a long way from its primitive beginnings with a locally made truck. What has been constant over all these years is the dedication and competence shown by the many officers and the multitude of volunteers who have devoted themselves to this important town service. Pownal is fortunate that this spirit of volunteerism continues today.

Current members of the department are: Fire Chief Scott Pollock, Deputy Fire Chief Erik Nielsen, Deputy Rescue Chief Richard Hogue, (Michael Rogers, deputy rescue chief, and his

During the summer of 2007, Fire Chief David Malone resigned for personal reasons and Deputy Chief Scott Pollock was appointed to finish his elected term. The office continues, as it has for years, to be remunerated only by an annual stipend, currently, $4,500. The responsibilities include managing the budget, purchasing equipment, scheduling training, meeting all state and federal requirements, overseeing two stations with their ongoing renovations, and moving the department forward as a modern, efficient unit. Daunting challenges indeed.

Chief Pollock has cited the department's mutual aid agreements with surrounding communities as critical elements in operating a modern-day service. He hastened to add that there is an emerging need to hire a full-time staff member to provide daytime coverage and manage the increasing volume of records, forms, and certifications. He also insists that the need for a new center fire station will not go away. The size of the current station is inadequate, and there is no

Fire Chief David Malone was elected in 2003. He served for twenty-one years in the department, working his way up from fire fighter to deputy chief under Lester Blake. Chief Malone resigned from the position the summer of 2007

wife Cindi, first responder, moved out of town in January 2008 capping ten years of service), Captain Andy Ward, and Lieutenant and Training Officer Robert McMahon. Firefighters are: Dan Brown, Jessica Blake Brown, Scott Hendee, Conrad Lausier, Brad Mallett, David Malone, Erik Nielsen, Paul Plummer, and Scott Pollock. Rescue and firefighters: Melissa Britton, Richard Hogue, Bryan Kalleberg, Marie Lausier, Robert McMahon, Linda McMahon, and Andy Ward. Fire Police are: Don Arnold, Ron Hodsdon, and Jack St. Pierre.

Fire Chief Scott Pollock was appointed to complete Chief Malone's remaining term. Chief Pollock began his service in 1992 as firefighter, and after sixteen years in the department worked his way up to the position of fire chief. He began the practice of placing memorial flags on the graves of Pownal firemen each year.

The North Pownal Fire Station in 2008. Fire Ward Earle Blake wrote in the 1969 Annual Town Report, "The town itself suffered the biggest loss when the building and tank truck burned at North Pownal for a total loss. A new two bay station with cement foundation and floor was built by volunteer labor under the direction of Roy Tufts. The cost of this building, including the new furnace was $3,400."

The Pownal Fire and Rescue Department in 2008. Front row l. to r.: Deputy Chief Erik Nielsen, Fire Chief Scott Pollock, and Lieutenant Robert McMahon. Middle row l. to r.: EMT Marie Lausier and EMT Linda McMahon. Back row: Fire Police Jack St. Pierre, Fire Fighter Brad Mallett, Fire Fighter Conrad Lausier, Fire Fighter Craig Guile, Deputy Chief Rescue and EMT Richard Hogue, Fire Police Ron Hodsdon, and Fire Police Don Arnold (behind Hodsdon). Not pictured: Fire Captain Andy Ward, Fire Fighters Mike Newman, Dan Brown, Jessica Blake Brown, Scott Hendee, Bryan Kalleberg, Paul Plummer, and David Malone, Junior Fire Fighter Jeremiah Gross, and Fire Fighter and First Responder Melissa Britton.

The 2008 Ferrara Intruder 2 CAFS (Compressed Air Foam System) Pumper, at the Pownal Center station, soon after its arrival on April 15, 2008. It replaced the 1979 E-1 Mack.

PART THREE
EDUCATION IS IMPORTANT

THEN: *The North Pownal one-room school, built in 1894 is pictured here in 1948 when it served scholars from sub-primary to eighth grade. It is the only remaining one-room schoolhouse in Pownal. Carefully preserved by the North Pownal United Methodist Church, the building is now attached to the church. It will be dedicated on June 22, 2008 as the Brooks Room, in honor of Marjorie Brooks. (See page 247.)* Photo: Louis Haskell.

NOW: *Pownal Elementary School, built in 1968 to serve pre-kindergarten through grade eight, is pictured in May 2003 with fourteen-year-old crabapple trees in full bloom. The trees are a result of a 1989 Arbor Day tree-planting project led by school board member June LaCombe, with help from teacher coordinators Joye Carkin and Ann Slattery. Many teachers, students, and parents assisted with the planting.*

Chapter 6

Schools and Schooling

Doing Our Best – But It Wasn't Easy
1908-1939

In the three decades following the town's centennial in 1908, America experienced a roller coaster economy, from the Great War boom and the Roaring Twenties to post-war bust and the Great Depression. During this thirty-year period, Pownal's economy exhibited a rather steady decline. Farming was becoming less a source of sustainable income, local granite and lumber industries faced hard times, and the town's population dropped from 625 in 1908 to 462 in 1930—the lowest ever. Viewed against this background, Pownal did what it could for its schools, but indeed it wasn't easy.

In 1908, the town was supporting seven one-room schools. Three had been built within the previous fourteen years (North Pownal 1894, Center 1896, Merrill 1907). The remaining four (Hodsdon 1875, West Pownal 1854, Paine 1813, Tyler 1813) continually required costly repair. None of the seven had electricity or indoor plumbing, and all were heated by wood stoves. These schools served 134 elementary students while thirteen others, with tuition paid but no transportation provided, attended the high schools of Yarmouth, Edward Little, and North Yarmouth Academy. At the same time, the state

The Pownal Center school was built in 1896 at a cost of $700, to serve scholars of ages three to twenty-one. This photo was taken in 1913.

Known individuals as numbered: 1. Elizabeth Scribner, Teacher; 5. Martha Grant's brother; 6. Helen Kimball? 8. Delia Jordan? 9. Emma Loring; 11. Elsie Sweetser; 16. Marjorie Sweetser; 19. Martha Grant; 20. G. Harold Kimball; 21. Austin Cotton; 22. Kenneth Knight. (Also present but not identified: Winnie Blair and Katheryne McGorman. Others unidentified.)

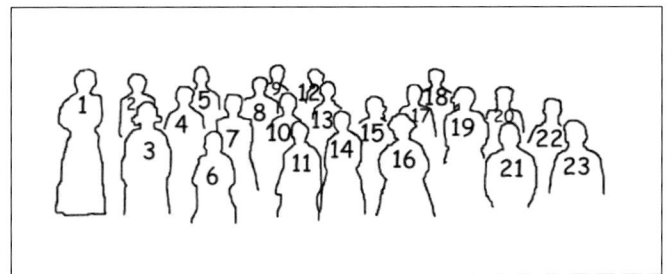

was recommending teacher's salaries of $12.00 per week for a thirty-five week school year, whereas Lauren Tuttle Sr., a highly qualified Pownal teacher, was being paid only $7.16 per week during Pownal's thirty-two week year. Pownal's teacher compensation placed it twenty-fifth out of twenty-six schools in Cumberland County.

By 1923, lawmakers in Augusta specified that a "Standard Rural School" have certain amenities, many of which Pownal schools simply could not immediately afford. Among other things, the state had specified that all stoves in schools be "jacketed", that sanitary water coolers be provided, and that outhouses be sanitary, free from markings, and capable of direct entry from the schoolhouse. The town's response to state lighting requirements was the addition of larger windows to the Center Grammar School. Throughout the 1920s and 1930s the town tried its best to meet all standards through local taxes. The school budget consistently figured at thirty percent of the total town budget. Additional local help came from School Improvement Leagues, forerunners of Parent Teacher Clubs. These Leagues funded and administered preventive health and immunization clinics, organized hot lunch programs, and purchased such fundamental items as screens, blinds, flagpoles, and swings.

Like many rural towns, Pownal's families were thinly scattered over a large area, and each school duplicated the full all-level curriculum. Transportation was costly. The state had been encouraging school consolidation for some time as a means of addressing these and other issues, but it would not be until 1931 that Pownal acted. Amidst protestations (not unlike today) that neighborhood schools should be preserved, consolidation proceeded. The Paine and Tyler schools were closed. Sub-primary, first, and second grades attended the Hodsdon school. The Merrill school, recently moved to the Center area, became the Intermediate School for grades three, four, and five. The Center school became the Grammar school for grades six, seven, and eight. The North and West Pownal schools retained their full multi-level operation.

One recurring difficulty over all these years was the hiring and retention of teachers. In 1937, the state helped in this area when it removed the ban on hiring married teachers, a ban that had affected women teachers primarily. Still, Pownal's salaries lagged behind. It was paying its teachers $500 per year less than the state mandated minimum of $1500 per year. At the close of the 1930s, 131 students were attending town schools, while another twenty-six were distributed among the high schools of Freeport, Edward Little, Greely Institute, and North Yarmouth Academy. Town folk were aware of school challenges yet to be met, but they were relatively satisfied with their children's education. A proposal to establish a junior high school in town was rejected as too expensive and unnecessary.

As America bid farewell to the Great Depression and braced for the as yet unimaginable trials of World War II, the schooling of Pownal's children had a look not very different from what it had been on the eve of World War I.

The West Pownal school, pictured here in 1968, functioned from 1857 to 1968 at the corner of the Allen and Chadsey Roads. It housed sub-primary to eighth grade. Photo Michael Menchen.

The Hodsdon School. Built in 1875, this school served all grades until the 1931 consolidation, when it was given over to sub-primary and grades one and two. The building no longer exists, but its site was deeded to the Pownal Scenic and Historical Society. A commemorative plaque marks the site. Photo: Michael Menchen 1968.

The Merrill School became the newest one-room school, when it was built in 1907 for $1,000. It was moved to this site on Elmwood Road across from the fire station in 1931. It became the intermediate school consolidating grades three, four and five. This picture was taken in 1968 when it closed. It was sold in 1972 and moved to Cousins Island to become a private residence. Photo: Michael Menchen, 1968.

The Center School after consolidation in 1931 was known as the Grammar School. It served students living in the immediate area in grades six through eight. Closed in 1968, the building currently houses a business. Photo: Michael Menchen, 1968.

The Paine School, shown here with the class of 1905, was one of the six original District Schools of 1813. Built on the site at the intersection of the Lawrence and Paine (now Leighton) Roads, it finally closed its doors in 1940.

Pictured are Teacher Nettie Blagdon and l. to r.: Earl Tryon, George Tryon, Maurice Snow, Harold Newcomb, a Libby child, Letty Mitchell, Laurice Leighton, Grace Lary, her twin sister Gladys Lary, Lula Newcomb, and John Newcomb.

S. Addison Vosmus, M.D. (1848-1927) taught District School 13 on the Royal Road in the early 1880s before receiving his Doctor of Medicine degree from Bowdoin College. Married to Elvina Libby, he practiced medicine from this home (now 856 Lawrence Road) in North Pownal. He served on the Superintending School Committee for eleven years between 1886 and 1914. He was Superintendent of Schools for sixteen years between 1894 and 1918. He also served as Selectman for six years from 1912 to 1918, and for thirty years on the Board of Health. The 1928 Town Report described him as "a man of upright character and an upright citizen. Always devoted to the interest of his town, promoting the causes of education and temperance… As a Republican he always supported the party in which he believed, serving on the town committee for many years."

Conrad S. Snow (1852-1922). After his accidental death, he was eulogized in the 1923 Town Report: "...We do hereby acknowledge him to be a man of true worth, sterling character, an upright citizen; a man devoted to the true interest of his town, always promoting the cause of education, temperance and civic righteousness. He was a Democrat of the Old School, always supporting the candidate of his party, whom he believed represented the principles he believed in. He held the offices of Selectman [1914-1915], Supt of Schools [nine years between 1880 and 1892], School Committee member, and taught a number of terms [1884 and 1885] in several different districts…" He was also a state officer of the Sons of Temperance.

"What Parents Should and Should Not Expect —

But every parent can keep in mind the few absolute necessities—honesty, accuracy, respect for authority, clear knowledge and some real skill … do not expect a school to alter the nature and capacities of your child… do not expect it to make him love good conduct… or books. You can expect this: that the school will teach your boy a few facts… some skills and will train & develop his natural capacities… will make him familiar with good conduct & good books… with high standards of intellectual, technical & moral performance… that it will demand from him honesty, accuracy and respect… And if a school does these things, and you cooperate, you may reasonably suppose that he will be better, wiser, and more well-informed with each year that he stays."

Report to the Town, 1908 by Oliver Stover (1871-1947). He served on the School Committee in 1906 and as Superintendent of Schools 1908-1909. He was a representative to the state legislature, 1933-1934. His son John later operated Stover Airport just off the Brown Road.

Emma Loring Pervier (1893-1969) graduated from Hebron Academy in 1910 and returned to teach at the Center and Hodsdon Schools. In 1923 she became a "State Certified Rural School Teacher." She served several terms on the School Committee and did substitute teaching.

From the 1923 School Report: "Miss Emma Loring was one of the teachers accepted by State Superintendent Thomas for special training for rural school work last summer. She worked hard at Eastern State Normal School [in Castine]... and came back to serve Pownal with a new vision for her work and additional skill to carry it out. By working early and late she has not only managed her own school exceptionally well, but she has also aided other teachers with their problems... Her salary has been increased this year... The previous year she taught an excellent school, but refused an increase in salary. — Frank Byram, Supt."

Lauren H. Tuttle Sr. (1888-1958) taught in Pownal's one-room schools for fifteen years, after graduating from Bridgton Academy in 1907. He was Superintendent of Schools for 15 years. (For his civic offices, see page 187.) In the 1914 Town Report he wrote that Pownal would soon need its own high school. "We are well aware of the fact that taxes are high and good schools are expensive, yet it has been truly said that, 'the chief assets of a town lie not in its costly public building, nor its good roads and bridges, however necessary they may be, but in its boys and girls,' and it has been our observation that the boys and girls of a town are in a measure what the public schools make of them."

Josephine Bacon Snow (1907-1965) moved from Wesley, Maine to Pownal in 1930 to teach in the Paine School. She taught in several of Pownal's schools for many years, ending her career as a teacher in the Yarmouth schools. She became the daughter-in-law of Conrad Snow in 1933 when she married his son, "Bill". For their life as farmers, see pages 100-101.

This simple ledger, authorized by George Hodsdon and Rev. Daniel A. Tuttle, records the salaries for spring term 1918. Except for Phoebe Flanders who earned $10.50, teachers Elsie Sawyer, Ellen Mitchell, Lauren Tuttle, Mary Brown, Emma Loring, and Eva Cushman earned $9.00 per week. Janitors Robert Small, Freddie Worden, Lauren Tuttle, William Brown Jr., Asa Blackstone, Harold Hodsdon, and Mildred and Blanche Libby received $3.00 for their services during the ten-week term.

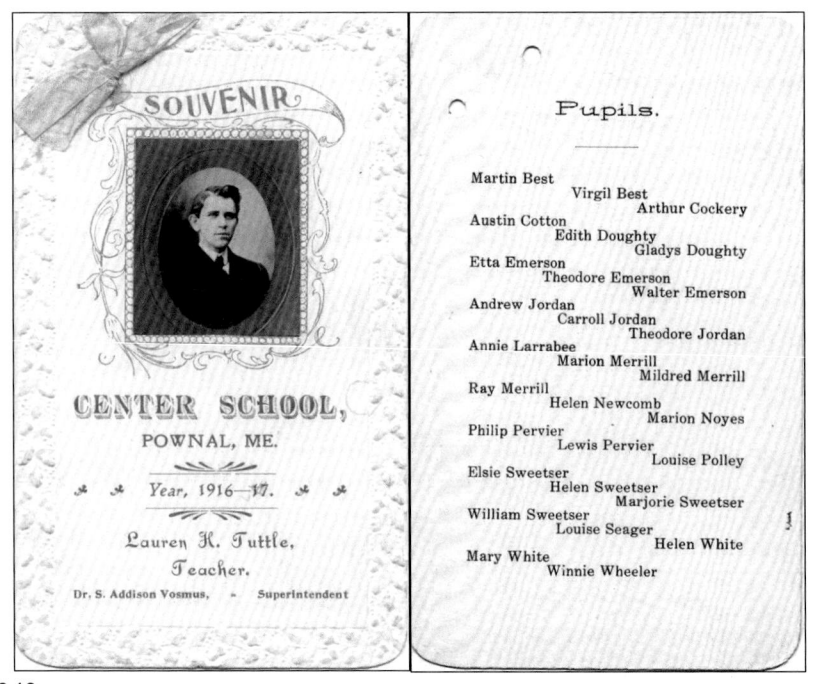

Souvenir programs such as this one from 1917 were produced by the teacher. The pupils in this example range from sub-primary to eighth grade. Typically, many of the students were brothers and sisters.

Scholars of the North Pownal school, c. 1910.

Front row l. to r.: Raymond Sawyer, Thomas Vosmus, Raymond Parker. Second row l. to r.: Carl Tryon, Willis Morton, Elizabeth Vosmos, Vina Small. Back row l. to r.: George Tryon, Earl Tryon, Teacher Annie Parker, Annie Libby, Daisy Parker, Pinkey Estes.

Scholars of the North Pownal School, 1928, taught by Maude Hodgkins Small.

Front row l. to r.: Bertrand Penley, Channing Penley, Priscilla Steeves, Raymond Steeves, Addison Steeves, Theona Penley. Back row l. to r.: Mildred DeWeaver, Thelma Fickett, Fredrick Steeves, Kenneth Libby, Edward Menchen, Nathan Fickett.

Receipt from North Yarmouth Academy for tuition, fall term, 1918, for Evelyn Snow, Stanley Wilson, Andrew Heywood, Harold Hodsdon, Robert Hodsdon, Helen Knight, and Hilda Peterson. Tuition was $10.00 per term.

The expansion of the role of the schools was accelerated in the 1919 state law which decreed that towns must "make provisions for instruction… in personal hygiene, community sanitation and physical education…" Health records were to be kept on all children. The school report of 1926 indicated that "through the efforts of Miss Myra Brown (Tryon), the helping teacher… and county nurse, a Dental Clinic was carried out. Forty-six pupils were treated… 165 fillings… 88 extractions were made at a cost of $120. The School Improvement Leagues contributed $60 and an equal amount was contributed by the State…" The 1931 report stated that, of ninety-five children examined in a health inspection, "only 18 were without defects." The principal "defects" were found in teeth and tonsils. The dental clinic shown here took place in Mallett Hall c. 1923-24.

Maintaining the one-room schools: This invoice of 1908 (from the True Warren store) records purchase of a door spring for the Center school, fifteen cents, and for the Merrill school, a pail for twenty-five cents and a broom for thirty cents. Approved by Oliver Stover, Superintendent.

This 1937 graduation program featured the theme, "Following the Gleam." Superintendent R. G. Oakes awarded diplomas to Laura Britt, Donald Hall, Floyd Keith, Janet Newcomb, Josephine Pervier, Carleton Quint, Lawrence Ryder, George Stone, Everett Sylvester, Lois Vosmus, and Daniel Whitcher, who variously delivered orations on "Following the Gleam in Literature," "Following the Gleam in Transportation," etc. Members of the school's Horace Mann Club also presented a play, and Everett Sylvester played the violin.

Moving the Merrill School, 1931: "It took all day to move the school off its foundation and to transport it to the corner of the Hodsdon and Merrill Roads. The corner was difficult to maneuver and the school had to remain there over night. There were rumors about that indicated that those opposed to the move might cause damage to the building as it was being moved, so my father [Joseph Pervier], who was also a town constable, slept in it overnight to prevent any damage. The next morning the move continued." From Josephine Allen, "Memories."

Pownal's first school bus, 1934, pictured in front of Pervier's Garage on the Hallowell Road. Through a State subsidy of $350, the body was purchased from Oxford Body Co. and placed on a truck owned by Victor Litchfield Sr. The body was easily removed, so the truck could be used for farm work in the summer. Students sat back-to-back in two parallel benches.

Running Hard to Keep Up 1940-1968

Great transformations swept the world and the nation in the 1940s, 1950s, and 1960s, exemplified by the fact that while Americans had followed the war against Germany and Japan on radio, now television brought Vietnam into their living rooms. Maine and Pownal participated in all these changes—changes that included economic recovery and an increase in job opportunities. Education came in for its share of changes as the nation placed higher value on it, spurred on to a significant degree by the advent of "Sputnik" and the perceived dearth of science, mathematics and modern language teaching in the country.

In Pownal, the population grew by thirty-nine percent during this period, rising from 574 in 1940 to 800 in 1970. The school system absorbed the accompanying increase in students, but had few answers to its lingering problems. The five one-room school buildings were showing their age and in constant need of repair. Overcrowding was a problem, with forty-five students per school in some instances. Teacher recruitment was difficult given the undesirable teaching conditions and the fact that compensation remained the lowest in the area. And the persistent problem of where and how to place secondary school students was still being solved on a year-to-year basis.

The year 1941 saw the state education commission citing Pownal's schools as having overcrowded multilevel classrooms, inadequate lighting, and unsafe playgrounds. By 1946, the lighting problem was solved when each school was electrified. Through the volunteer efforts of the School Improvement Leagues and the students themselves, lights and light bulbs were acquired at no cost to the town. Oil-fired heaters replaced wood stoves in the mid 1950s, but indoor plumbing remained nonexistent. In 1958, a School Building Fund was established with an initial $1,000. This fund had grown to $3,314 by 1964, although by that time its initial intent had been modified, overtaken by events.

Myra Brown Tryon (1895-1977) began teaching at the Tyler School near her home on the Brown Road immediately after graduation from Freeport High School. She took advanced teaching courses from Castine Normal School, Bates College, and St. Joseph's College, and was awarded a "Life Certificate" which guaranteed her a life-time teaching position. She taught at several Pownal one-room schools, ending her career in the Freeport schools.

Despite these difficulties and challenges, Pownal students were exposed to a solid elementary-level education, and many went on to excel in high school and college. Then in 1957 the state intervened in the operation of all schools when the legislature passed The Sinclair Act. This sweeping legislation offered financial incentives as it required communities to join into larger more efficient school districts. The town responded initially by appointing a five-person Citizen Study Group to study the provisions of this act and explore the advantages and disadvantages of joining a large administrative district. By 1961, the legislature had authorized Cumberland, North Yarmouth, and Pownal to consolidate. This proposal would have created a new local school for kindergarten through sixth grade, with junior high and high school students traveling to Cumberland. In total, there were seven attempts to structure such a consolidation. Ultimately, neither Cumberland nor North Yarmouth saw much advantage in joining with a system that could contribute so few assets, and voters in both towns narrowly defeated the proposal in 1964.

Stung by headlines such as "Pownal Shunned by Neighbors," the school board proceeded to negotiate a contract with Freeport High School to accept the town's secondary-school students at $256 per pupil, with Pownal providing transportation. The problem of secondary-school student placement was solved for the moment, but the larger question of consolidation remained unanswered. The school board (Robert Slocum, Earle Blake, Bruce Carroll) along with the Citizen Study Group continued to work on the consolidation issue, however prospects for a solution seemed dim.

Then, almost out of the blue, newly elected State Representative for Pownal and Freeport David Graham chose Pownal's educational plight as his cause. Coming to the aid of the school board (Bruce Carroll, Evangeline Tuttle Lee, James Sanders), he pushed through a special grant from the legislature in 1966 allowing the town to build a consolidated school. Thus was created Maine School Administrative District 62 (M.S.A.D. 62). See David Graham's account on page 251.

During the next two years, building committee and school board members labored effectively to make the new building a reality. Doors opened in 1968 on a modern structure that cost $336,000, with the state having contributed seventy-seven percent. The era of the one-room school with its many delights and many challenges was over.

Marjorie Cushman Brooks (1890-1988) graduated from Gould Academy and taught at the Pineland School for several years before coming to Pownal to teach in 1927. She taught at the West and North Pownal Schools for 28 years.

Verna Fickett Libby (1911-1991) was born and raised in North Pownal on the present Fickett Road and attended Pownal's one-room schools. She graduated from high school at Wesleyan Seminary and, in 1931, received a degree from Gorham Normal School. She taught primarily at the Hodsdon, North, and West Pownal Schools before moving to Gray.

Robert Slocum (1926-1994), Superintending School Committee member for nine years between 1950 and 1968, SAD 62 School Building Committee Chair 1968-1968. (For town service, see page 191.)

Memories of the One-Room Schools
By Sheila Menchen Merritt

The following is excerpted from "School Days," an unpublished account of her school experiences by Sheila Menchen Merritt, daughter of Edward Menchen and Edna Snow Menchen.

There were only three grades in a schoolroom... Mrs. Libby was the teacher... There were two entrances to the school with boys going in one side and girls in the other. Just inside the doors were the cloakrooms where coats were hung and probably lunches left. We entered the classroom from the front. Near the center front of the classroom there was a big wood stove. At opposite ends of the back of the classroom were separate bathroom doors for girls and boys. Behind the door was a small room, and then [a] second room was the outhouse. When one returned to the classroom, one washed one's hands at the sink.

Intermediate School – As you went in the door, you were at the back. Third grade was on the right, 4th grade in the middle, and fifth grade on the left. There was a bookcase near the center back. There were lots of books of fairy tales, which I loved... Baseball and Halley-Over were popular games outdoors, and most or all of the school played those. If there was rain, we played an indoor game, like "Gossip". Arleen Tryon was the teacher the whole three years that I was there. I remember some phonics in third grade, some Social Studies about children in foreign lands, and health in fifth grade. The three classes were taught separately in turn. One did one's assignments while the other classes were having lessons. One learned a lot by listening to the older classes.

Grammar School – As you went in the door, you were at the back. Sixth grade sat on the right side, which had no windows. Seventh grade was in the middle, and eighth grade on the left. There may have been a blackboard on the windowless wall; there was probably one up front... There was a big bookcase with glass doors in the back right corner. Every month (or was it every year?) the library got a wonderful new book; . . We did Current Events and were graded for remembering. Each row was assigned a day of the week.

Sydney Merrill was the teacher when I was in sixth grade. He was young, a wonderful change after 3 years of Mrs. Tryon. He told us about leaving college to help fight those terrible fires – was it the prior year?

We studied mythology (for social studies) in sixth grade. . . The year after Mr. Merrill, Mrs. Tryon came over from the Intermediate School to teach us. I had her for five years total...

The music teacher came regularly. I remember Mrs. Bennett who was old and Mrs. Shroeder who was large. There was a young woman whose name I do not remember. We had music every day and sang songs out of our music books. "Skaters' Waltz" was a personal favorite. Most of the songs were unfamiliar and hard

The Center Grammar School in 1968. Three windows had been taken from the south side and added to the north, giving eighth graders, who sat near the windows, abundant light. The sixth graders got less.

to sing I do not remember any of the schools having a piano. A pitchpipe was used to get us started.

A visiting nurse showed up occasionally. The traveling Bible teacher came every two weeks. Scheduling among the 5 schools in town was arranged so that it would be convenient for the mother of the Roman Catholic children to have them at home during the lessons at their schools. The teacher was young and pretty. We learned a Bible verse each lesson, and we played a game to see who could find verses the quickest. She told Bible stories and put colorful figures of the characters on the flannelboard. We learned lots of songs. If you learned 25 prescribed verses, you got a New Testament. If you learned 100 verses, you got a Bible. If you learned 300 verses, you got to go to summer camp. Memorized verses were recited to Mrs. Tryon... At the end of the year there was a big program at the Pownal Center Church.

Arleen Hodgdon Tryon (1906-1994) taught in one-room schools for twenty-four years.

We always knew when the Superintendent of schools was coming to visit because Arleen Tryon wore earrings...

Someone might have to "stand in the floor" up front for misbehaving. Mrs. Tryon was prone to belittle children with whom she was not pleased. "You'll never amount to anything!" I realize now that she probably hoped to inspire them to prove her wrong, but at the time I felt very badly for the victim of the statement.

In Grammar School, at the beginning of lunch time someone from each row would take orders and money and go the store (Virgil's) for Coke, etc.

Baseball was popular. Girls and boys played separately, except that my sister Pat was so good that she played catcher with the boys. The boys played across the road over in a little field beyond the cemetery. The girls played in the driveway in front of the school...

My favorite part of the school day was right after noon recess when the teacher read a chapter of a book to us. That's how I met The Hardy Boys.

The year that I was in eighth grade I was janitor of the Hodsdon School. Pat had been janitor the year before. Dad took me every morning along with enough water to fill the big crock beside the sink. That would provide all water for drinking and washing hands. My job included building the fire. After school I got off the bus at the school and swept the floor...

My class graduated from eighth grade on Flag Day. There was a big program at the Town Hall. We first met some of the students our age from the North and West Pownal schools at rehearsals. Because of Flag Day Mrs. Tryon said we could not choose our class colors: they would have to be red, white and blue. Our graduation Program included a play. "Columbia, the Gem of the Ocean" with the theme of America as a Melting Pot. Girls wore white dresses. I have never seen some of my classmates since; we went to a variety of different high schools.

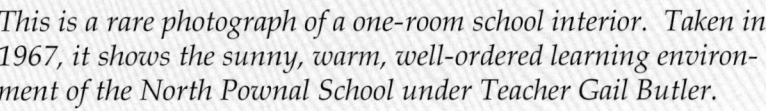

This is a rare photograph of a one-room school interior. Taken in 1967, it shows the sunny, warm, well-ordered learning environment of the North Pownal School under Teacher Gail Butler.

The Intermediate Center (Merrill) School (grades 3, 4, 5) 1949.
Front row l. to r.: Sam Greenlaw, Roland Spaulding, Ernest Townsend, Ronald Turcotte, Roger Sanders, James Hibbard, James Tibbetts, unidentified, Jack St. Pierre. Second row l. to r.: William Condon, unidentified, Ralph Carter, Arthur Tibbetts, Robert Greenlaw, Don Irish, Richard Cavanaugh, Robert Keith, unidentified. Third row l. to r.: Marla Howe, Sally Pervier, Claudia Blackstone, Patty Wentworth, Kathleen Tibbetts, Thelma Keith, Della Spaulding, Mary Lee Bigelow, Carole Lewis, Wilma Golding, Mildred Knox. Back row l. to r.: Linda Carter, Gordon Snow, Joyce Elaine Card, Harriett Morrill, Sheila Menchen, unidentified, Byron Greenlaw, Raymond Randall, Ronald Hodsdon, Robert Wentworth.

The Center Grammar School (grades 6, 7, 8) 1949.
Front row l. to r.: Dale Howe, Rich Spinney, Larry Smith, Granville Arris, Otis Taylor, George Smith, David Blake, Ray Beau, Rusty Bigelow. Second Row l. to r.: Louise Bucklin, Marion Best, Judy Sweetser, Evelyn Golding, Dot St. Pierre, Patty Hibbard, Bev Condon, Virginia Taylor, Millie Ryder, Christine Arris, Patricia Menchen. Third row l. to r.: Fred Upton, Alice Lewis, Norma Spaulding, Thelma Merrill, Glennis Huard, Joyce Wyman, Carolyn Colby, Bessie Pervier, Jean Wyman, Harold Hibbard, Teacher Raymond Allen. Back row l. to r.: Paul Turcotte, Paul Bieske, Eugene Capon, Vincent Irish, John Bieske, Paul Levesque, Gerald Arris, Calvin Ryder, Michael Greenlaw, Luther Snow.

Grammar School Graduation, 1958. pictured in the First Parish Church sanctuary.
Front row l. to r.: Cheryl LaFreniere, Sandra Ryder, Winona Edwards, Janet Colby, Nancy Smith, Portia St.Pierre, Randa Keith, Janet Sawyer. Middle row l. to r.: Arnie Bigelow, Kermit Wentworth, Betty Hawkins, Marilyn Keith, Janice Anderson, Peter Harlow, Paul Boyden. Back row l. to r.: Woodrow Irish, Douglas Wentworth, Stanley Spaulding, Harold Tenney, Terry Snow, John Carter Jr., Albert Blackstone Jr.

How a School Was Born

Excerpted from "David L. Graham, "Maine's Year of the Donkey," The Nation, *January 10, 1968.*

I had begun working on one bill even before the session started – it was to provide a decent school for Pownal, a town in my district that had nothing but five dilapidated, overcrowded, one-room schoolhouses... Only by wheedling a special grant from the Legislature could the job be done...

My first step ... was to get myself appointed to the Joint Committee on Education... The Department of Education wrote up my bill for me, the Legislative Research Committee put it in the hopper...

In due course the Pownal bill had its committee hearing and the Pownal School Board ably presented its arguments. But afterward,... the committee ... felt they couldn't make an exception for Pownal. If they approved a bill making Pownal a one-town school district, twenty or thirty other towns that were as badly off would demand like favor.

My answer to this had two parts: (1) Let them, I said; if they are as wretchedly equipped as Pownal, they deserve special help; and (2) oh, no they won't ... it's too late for any more bills to be introduced in this session...

...[Unimpressed,] the Education Committee issued a 7-to-2 'ought not to pass' report... But when Pownal came before the House, I arose in my legislative innocence and moved that we accept the minority report... I suggested that

The 1964 electoral landslide sent Edmund S. Muskie to the U.S. Senate and gave Maine Democrats control of both houses of the legislature for the first time since 1914. David L. Graham was swept in as a freshman House member representing Freeport and Pownal. This is his account of his efforts on behalf of Pownal.

outhouses had little education value, that Pownal's children were entitled to a school with plumbing, good lighting and adequate space.

...The House... went along with Pownal. The Senate did not, but the Committee of Conference -- three members of each house – which resulted from the deadlock rewrote the bill ... and then approved it unanimously.

With victory in hand, the bill was then held up in the House. Prayers and entreaties heavily seasoned with tact overcame the objections, and the hope of Pownal plunged forward once more, finally landing on the Senate appropriations table...

...during the final hours of the session, the Senate majority leader . . . rammed it through the enactment [in part as a reward for my having sponsored an unsuccessful bill to introduce a state income tax.

Pownal Elementary School under construction in 1967.

Sketch of Pownal Elementary School. Wright, Pierce, & Whitmore, Architects, Topsham, Maine, 1967. The leadership that brought this project to completion included the school building committee of Chair Robert Slocum, Lawrence Carter, Genevieve Hawkins, Felton Pervier, and Laurence Snow, working with school board members Evangeline Lee, Edward Mitchell, and Laurence Snow.

Everything So Clean and Convenient
Seeing the new school for the first time
Excerpted from Josephine Pervier Allen, "Memories"

The day came when the move to the new school was in definite view. It was decided that the children should get a preview. We boarded the bus for the half mile ride and toured the school. The kids were quite impressed, and so was I. Each room had about the same floor space as the entire old school. The spacious windows, bright, colored walls, and tiled floors were quite a change. The rooms were all in contact with the office through the intercom system. This really gave the kids something to talk about. The idea that the principal could listen in, or that the teacher could contact the office at any time seemed a bit threatening to some. They had heard talk about being sent to the principal but had yet to experience it.

There were sinks and water fountains in each room and of course, toilets with plumbing. The color of the paint in the toilets was a conversation piece. The boys' room was pink and the girls' room was blue... A writing assignment showed that most of them had mixed feelings about leaving the one-room school... and that the intercom and the color of the toilets were what had impressed them the most. The move materialized during the February vacation... a teacher couldn't ask for a nicer place to work... everything so clean and convenient... and it was more pleasant to have the company of other teachers.

Students enter their new school for the first time in 1968.

To Be the Best 1968-2008

On a snowy February day in 1968, approximately 140 students crossed the threshold of their new elementary school for the very first time. They could not have fully appreciated the scope of the changes of which they were now a part. This new era meant more than just leaving the homey one-room setting and entering a consolidated school divided by grades. The curriculum, the faculty, the administration, and the entire learning environment became part of a modern suburban school.

The elementary school population remained relatively small, but in the first years of the new school, enrollments grew as migration brought new residents to town. The school-age population of about 200 in 1967 climbed to 321 in 1984. However, by 2002 the numbers came back down to 222, following national trends toward smaller and older families. Private and home schooling options removed still others from the public school system.

Faculty and staff numbers increased in order to meet the needs of the separate grades. Before the move, Pownal had five one-room-school teachers: Marguerite Babb, Gail Butler, Phyllis Mitton, Lillian Perkins, and Arleen Tryon. Three teachers were added to staff the new school, and within three years the core faculty numbered eight full-time teachers (Josephine Allen, Marguerite Babb, Lucille Bowie, Gail Butler, Marie McCann, Alden Overlock, Alice Smith, and Theodore Walsh) and a full-time teacher-principal (Dennis Pinkham).

The elementary school building, so impressive compared to the one-room schools, was expensive to maintain. While some federal funds provided for the newly mandated "Title I" classroom aides, the school still needed many new amenities. The budget, as a consequence, rose every year. The first year, 1967-68, saw a large jump in the total budget to $104,000. By 1974-75,

Theodore J. Walsh. In 1968 Ted was hired to teach seventh grade in the new Pownal Elementary School. He had just graduated from Gorham State College. After three and a half years, he combined the roles of principal with teacher of social studies and reading. In 1980 when a full-time superintendent-principal was hired, he taught fifth grade until leaving for another career in 1982. Students and parents also fondly remember the many stage productions he directed.

the request came in at $234,000. This increase placed a significant demand on taxpayers.

Where state and local funds fell short, parents and volunteers picked up the slack. Parent-teacher clubs had been involved for years, and the new consolidated club worked hard to raise funds for new necessities. Beano games, first organized in the 1950s to help finance the new school, continued through the 1970s as a way to fund a school library. Donations of time, effort, and money helped enhance the physical surroundings through improvements to the playground, landscaping, and erosion control.

After 1965, a contract with Freeport High School had assured Pownal students of a site for their secondary education, and this arrangement continued. However, by the late 1970s amidst a

(continued on page 255)

The Alice Andrews Library at Pownal Elementary School opened in 1974. Librarian Ruth Granholm (seated) instructed volunteer staff l. to r.: Arlene Bradbury, Ann Blaisdell, Sherry Dietrich, and Donna Boyles in library protocols, as the library prepared to serve students.

POWNAL OLD HOME DAY
SEVENTH ANNUAL CELEBRATION
SATURDAY AUGUST 25

POWNAL CENTER, POWNAL, MAINE

FRIDAY, AUGUST 24

7:30 P.M. Teen Dance At the Elementary School Featuring Music By "SOUND UNLIMITED"

SATURDAY, AUGUST 25

10:00 A.M. to 4:00 P.M. WGAN REMOTE BROADCAST From Pownal Center

10:00 A.M. PARADE— Including: The Pine Tree Warriors - Floats - Bands - Parade Horses - Fire Engines - Antique Cars - Decorated Doll Carriages and Bicycles - Miss Pownal Old Home Day and her Court

ALL DAY GAMES— Ten NEW exciting game booths
- AUCTION—Old and New Items of Interest and Value
- HELICOPTER RIDES
- MOON WALK
- PONY RIDES
- HANDICRAFT SALE
- GARDEN PRODUCE SALE
- FOOD SALE
- BOOK SALE
- WHITE ELEPHANT SALE
- REFRESHMENTS— Hot Dogs - Hamburgers - Corn On The Cob - Hot and Cold Drinks Pop Corn - Potato chips
- RAFFLE TICKETS On Sale Throughout The Day 50¢ each 5/$2.00
  - 3:30 P.M. Drawings
    - First Drawing—Suzuki TC100K Blazer Motorcycle
    - Second Drawing—Two Round-Trip Tickets to Nova Scotia on the Cruiseship BOLERO
    - Third Drawing—$25 Gift Certificate at L. L. Bean

2:00 P.M. Firemen's Muster—Pownal Center

5:30 to 7:00 P.M. Baked Bean Supper - Congregational Church, Pownal Center

8:00 P.M. Adult Dance At The Elementary School Featuring The "FUDDY DUDDIES"

1973 Old Home Day Program. The Old Home Day celebrations in 1972 and 1973 were sponsored by the parent teacher club to raise funds for a school library. Jim Boyles, co-chair of the 1973 event, remembers that the day netted $2,800. It was used to install book shelves, built by local craftsman Dan Brown.

Beano games were organized by the parent teacher club in the late 1950s to help raise funds to build a new school. First held in Mallett Hall, they continued through the 1970s and moved to the new school. Paul Hamilton, Ann Cordell, Marjorie Mason, and Gary Harlow served as the organizing committee. PTC members worked the games and provided food. As this form submitted to State regulators indicates, on October 20, 1969, thirty-four people played Beano, netting $87.25.

rising school population with high educational expectations, parents began agitating for additional secondary school options. Responding to these pressures, the 1979 school board under the chairmanship of Jane Mittel successfully negotiated the addition of Greely High School in Cumberland as a second option. The resulting two-school arrangement was to last for twenty-five years. Pownal high school students adjusted well in both of these settings. Many excelled academically as well as in extra-curricular activities. Transportation was provided to both high schools, and when additional after-school transportation was provided in the 1980s many participated in sports, drama, and other pursuits.

Throughout the 1970s, Pownal and Freeport shared a superintendent, Robert Cartmill. In Pownal, the day-to-day role of principal was handled by teacher Dennis Pinkham until 1973 and then by Ted Walsh. This arrangement worked well enough until 1980 when Pownal was suddenly informed that Freeport no longer wished to share its superintendent. A new principal, Frances Hale, had just been hired, and the school board sought permission from the state to appoint her as principal-superintendent. Initially, State Education Commissioner Harold Reynolds Jr. refused, on the grounds that the district was too small. Later, finding no district willing to share a superintendent and noting Pownal's unique history, the commissioner finally agreed. Frances Hale thus became Pow-

Frances H. Hale, Principal 1980-1981, Superintendent-Principal 1981-1985.

The Class of 1979 was the first to have the option of attending either Freeport or Greely High School.

Rront row l. to r.: Kenneth Leighton, Neal Strong, Darrell Jewett, Michael Wyman. Second Row l. to r.: Diana Dietrich, Barbara Maltby, Andrea Richards, Teacher: Gail Butler, Jeanne Twomey, Kristen Boyles, Heidi Dobson. Back Row l. to r.: Martin Pinkham, Wayne Randall, Tim McMahon, Roland Coulombe, Joe Mitchell, Kim Perrine, Karen Snow, Anna Jordan, Sherry Everett, Carolyn McManus.

Almost simultaneously with the completion of Pownal Elementary School, two private schools opened their doors. One was the Harbor School, founded by Dr. Peter Bowman to serve emotionally disturbed children. Information on this institution is scarce, and it ceased to operate in the mid 1970s. The other new school occupied 110 acres and several buildings off the Tuttle (then known as Beech Hill) Road. The Collins Brook School opened in 1969 and at its peak in 1975 had a staff of fourteen with forty students ranging in age from pre-school to high school.

The founders of Collins Brook were Dick and Sharon Watson, a young couple who were inspired to create an alternative school after teaching several years at Lewis-Wadhams School in upstate New York. The latter in turn represented an effort to replicate in America the "free school" at Summerhill, England.

Among the cultural cross-currents of the 1960s and 1970s, the back-to-the-earth spirit moved many people like the Watsons to seek out rural settings where they could grow their own food and create a more authentic existence, away from the mainstream. Unfortunately the mid-1970s also brought a period of oil shocks, inflation, and recession. The school struggled to survive declining enrollments and mounting costs. Efforts in 1975 to merge Collins Brook and Lewis-Wadhams on the Pownal campus collapsed. The school closed in 1978. Later the land and buildings were sold, and Collins Brook faded into history as one of two private schools to have operated, if only briefly, in Pownal.

Dick Watson. The Times Record, *April 3, 1975.* Scanlan photo.

nal's first principal-superintendent in 1981. With her background in special education and gifted and talented programs, Fran Hale was well qualified to respond to state mandates and to oversee major changes at the school in the early 1980s.

From the first day in the new school, the existing curriculums were examined to bring them in line with state mandates. Some new programs (music, art, physical education) were added. But it was the 1980s that saw a plethora of both state and federal mandates descend on the school system. Title 1, Title 2, Project Rural, and others required compliance. Even though they were funded programs, often the funds had to be supplemented with local monies. One of the most significant mandates was the introduction of special education for children with learning difficulties. Both speech and physical therapy had to be available. Staffing for this started as a half-time special teaching position, grew into a full-time position, and ultimately into two full-time positions. Meanwhile, pre-kindergarten was added, and a federally funded hot lunch program installed.

Extra-curricular activities blossomed in the 1980s as well. After-school sports for boys and girls were added to the existing physical education program. A basketball team, a cheerleading and pep squad, and a ski club made their appearance. Science fairs, math competitions, music lessons, band, Junior Great Books, yearbook work and other activities sprang up thanks to many volunteers. Student counseling was begun, and (reflecting the realities of the time) the QUEST anti-drug education program was added. Academic assessment testing began in the 1980s, introducing the concept of student academic tracking throughout all school years.

The most outwardly visible change in the period was new construction. Growing enroll-

Linwood Randall (1919–) started driving the school bus before 1957, serving Pownal's five one-room schools. He also brought the daily supply of water to each school, since they had no indoor plumbing. The buses in those days were cold, uncomfortable and not always in good repair. After many years of driving hundreds of students over thousands of miles he was recognized in the 1984 yearbook for his excellent driving over the years and his kindnesses when taking students on field trips. Little did the editors of that yearbook imagine that he would continue driving the bus for another fifteen years, until his retirement in 1999.

ments and new programs were stressing the school's physical plant. The school board and citizens explored their options and determined that they should either limit the student body to kindergarten thru grade six, while tuitioning-out grades seven and eight, or they could expand the existing building. Voters decided in favor of an addition. Under the leadership of Superintendent Fran Hale and School Board Chair Arnold Blackstone, the district won a State school construction grant. The project added a gymnasium-multipurpose room and more classroom space along with administration and health offices. The old multipurpose room and cafeteria were converted into a library and classroom. The construction was completed in 1984 at a cost of $470,000, with local taxpayers' share at $13,000 plus interest.

In retrospect, the 1980s enjoyed bountiful state subsidies. While the state's portion varied through these years, it often approached seventy percent. Fran Hale retired from her position in 1985 and John Gale took the helm. Programs expanded at a slower pace and Pownal students continued to excel in high school. But in the 1990s as enrollment numbers dropped, the state's complex funding formula, factoring in local property values, income, and student population, dictated that its share must decrease. It went as low as twenty-eight percent in 2003.

Mary Mitchell Strong. Few staff left a deeper impression than Mary Strong, the first Director of Food Services from 1974 until 1983. Especially memorable was the delicious aroma when she baked bread and cinnamon rolls. Her hot lunch program included favorites like chicken, pizza, grilled cheese and Dagwood sandwiches. She created turkey candlelight dinners for Thanksgiving and Christmas. The hot lunch program was federally directed. It reimbursed those who qualified and also provided surplus foods for use in the program.

Alice Blackstone Smith attended Pownal's one-room schools and graduated from North Yarmouth Academy. After receiving her bachelors degree in education from the University of Maine at Orono, she returned to teach at the Hodsdon one-room school. Her teaching career spanned thirty-one years, twenty-nine of them teaching first grade at Pownal Elementary School.

Gail Butler spent twenty of her twenty-one years in teaching in Pownal, where she began at the North Pownal one-room school. In the new school, she taught mainly fifth grade and is especially remembered as an outstanding teacher of English and social studies. She retired in 1986. She is a graduate of Miami University in Ohio.

Josephine Loring Pervier Allen taught fourth grade from 1968 until her retirement in 1984. She had attended the one-room schools and her mother, Emma Loring Pervier, had been a teacher in Pownal schools in the 1920s. She holds a bachelor's degree from Gorham State College and a master's degree from the same institution, now part of the University of Southern Maine.

Marie Mason McCann. Thirty-one of Marie's thirty-five years in teaching (1967-1998) were spent in Pownal, teaching kindergarten, grades two and three, and a multi-age classroom of grades one and two. After retirement from teaching, she served for two years in administrative positions at the school. Marie holds a bachelor's degree from St. Joseph's College, a masters in education from the University of Southern Maine, and took additional studies at the Harvard Graduate School of Education. She also attended teacher study programs in England, Denmark, and Russia.

Lilyan Petkus Forbes served as Pownal Elementary School Librarian from 1981 to 2000. After raising her five children, Lilyan's life-long love of reading and education led her to begin studies in library science at Southern Maine Vocational and Technical Institute and at the University of Southern Maine. In 1980 the Maine Library Association certified her as Librarian in Charge.

Faculty and Staff 1981. Front row l. to r.: teachers Jane Donelon, Marie McCann, School Nurse Nancy Hewett, teachers Gail Butler, Josephine Allen, Joye Carkin, Alice Smith, Sandy Whitmore, Alison Pinkham. Back row l. to r.: Secretary Yvonne Desrosiers, bus drivers Larry Harlow & Linwood Randall, Principal/ Superintendent Fran Hale, teachers Marcia Gilliam, Ted Walsh, Ed McIntosh, bus driver Ed Granholm, Secretary Beverly Harlow. Not pictured: Sherilyn Dietrich.

Sue Hartford Clukey spent twenty of her thirty-eight years in education teaching special education and gifted-and-talented, as well as fifth grade, in Pownal Elementary School (1981-2001). She also drew upon her expertise in archaeology to lead her students on many "digs." The last one was the Jones Inn dig, in collaboration with the Pownal Scenic and Historical Society. She holds a bachelors degree from Gorham State College and a masters degree in American and New England Studies from the University of Southern Maine.

This class of twenty-seven students, scheduled to graduate in 1985, benefited from the expanded and modernized curriculum; the enriched junior high experience; the development of a physical education, health education, and interscholastic sports programs; and the new facilities and space provided in the 1984 school addition.

As Fourth Graders, kneeling l. to r.: Melissa Wentworth, Amy Mittel, Melanie Strait, Sasha Goodwin. Front row standing l. to r.: Becky Randall, Jenny Blackstone, Johanna Libby, Aaron Keith, Tina Jordan, Theresa Smith, Kenny Drouin, Neil Peaslee. Middle Row l. to r. Teacher Josephine Allen, Greg Merrill, Joanne Gobeil, Missy Nadeau, Ricky Spaulding, Mike Ward, Kelly Jewett, Heidi Ingerson, Tom West, Teacher Aide, Mary Ann Hodsdon. Back Row l. to r.: Becky Anderson, Todd Richards, Jason Pettengill, Timmy Kennedy, Sarah Hayes, Robin Hodsdon, Jamie Graham.

Throughout the 1990s, the school continued to win its share of federal and state grants, and the parent-teacher club assisted where it could. In 1993, June LaCombe and William Ginn formed the Pownal Education Foundation to supplement programs and projects outside the school budget. This foundation continues today to award yearly grants for deserving programs and teachers. Still, the financial burden fell mainly on property taxpayers, and despite all efforts, the realities of funding remained daunting. Teachers understandably sought salaries comparable with other area schools; expensive computers and media center facilities were deemed necessary; and secondary school tuition rates at both Freeport and Greely had almost quadrupled since 1979. The school board worked diligently to save costs without sacrificing quality. Among the changes they instituted, was negotiating an exclusive secondary school contract with Freeport High School. Thus in 2005 the secondary school arrangement had returned full circle to what it had been in 1965.

State wide ballot initiatives in 2004 sought to cap property taxes (unsuccessfully) or increase state support of local schools (successfully). However, little financial help actually materialized for Pownal, and the SAD continued to jockey for resources to sustain its vital programs and extracurricular activities. In part this was achieved through public and private grants. In 2004, the school won a $18,126 grant to upgrade its computers, and in 2005 with help from Representative David Webster, it secured a $200,000 grant for special education programs. Creative problem solving and tireless volunteers continued to keep the school on course.

Then in 2007 a statewide education shakeup occurred, such as not experienced since the Sinclair Act of 1957. Governor John Baldacci proposed a school consolidation bill married to his biennial budget. This proposal, which was amended before being passed by the legislature, required all school units, municipalities, and districts to be replaced by RSUs (Regional School Units) serving a minimum of 2,500 students each.

The school board worked with community volunteers to identify potential consolidation partners and tried to organize the details of a merger before the August 31, 2007 deadline. Freeport and Pownal continued their strong partnership throughout these efforts. Yarmouth, the other town proposed by commissioner Susan Gendron to combine with Pownal and Freeport, opted to exercise their special "high performing exemption" option, rather than consolidate. On December 1, 2007, the Pownal School Board voted to submit a progress report stating that it would be negotiating a consolidation with the schools of Freeport and Durham.

Weekly meetings of the Pownal Regional Planning Committee (Paul Schumann, Chair of SAD 62 Board; Jen Kaplan, Vice Chair of SAD 62 Board; Tim Giddinge, Selectman; Sherry Dietrich, Cliff Ruprecht, and Rhonda O'Shea, community members), with their counterpart committees of Freeport and Durham continue. Negotiations have centered on subsidized school choice, cost sharing, and reallocation of debt. The date for implementation of this consolidation is June 30, 2009. As discussions continue, the resolution of details, both practical and philosophical, remains elusive.

Although it has presented the town with persistent and often contentious funding challenges, the Pownal school system, in all its forms over the past 100 years, has provided generations of students a secure and supportive learning environment of a kind that is becoming increasingly rare. Time alone will tell if any merger under the new requirements will benefit Pownal students, let alone save on taxes for the citizens of the town.

A 1983 view of the new addition under construction. Architect: REA Associated of Auburn. Builder: McKee Co. The Times Record, *December 15, 1983, Anna Hoyt, photographer.*

The Class of 1998 ready to board a Maine Line bus for its class trip to Quebec.

Kneeling l. to r.: Sarah Bennis, Ashley Hutchinson, Matthew Allen. Standing l. to r:: Jenna Stull, Scott LeClair (behind Rebecca Carter), Rebecca Carter, Danica McKay, April Hart, Cathy Ryder, Nicholas Pascarella, Nicole Weirs, Joshua Seely, Ryan Harlow, Ryan Cleaves. The class trip was funded by student fund raisers, the Parent Teacher Club, and parents.

In 2001, President George W. Bush initiated the "No Child Left Behind" program that required schools to pass all "learning results" and show adequate progress for special needs students. By 2004, Pownal Elementary had consistently made "adequate yearly progress" according to the national standards, and in a 2007 study conducted by the Maine State Department of Education and David Silvernail, director of the University of Southern Maine Center for Education Policy, Applied Research, and Evaluation, Pownal Elementary was identified as a High Performing School.

This classification would not have come as a surprise to many former administrators and school boards. They have seen the consolidated elementary school not as merely adequate or good, but as truly exceptional. In 1984, Fran Hale wrote, "The district has a reputation of having an excellent school system." Reports in subsequent years announced that it was "A fine school," and "Equal to any elementary school in the state, [unsurpassed for its] caring and loving atmosphere." In 1995, acting Superintendent Frank Harrison and Principal Michael Wood went so far as to declare their intention of establishing "Pownal Elementary School as the best school in the State of Maine." Over the next decade, "The Best School in Maine" was often cited as the school's goal or even its claim. This excellence, hoped for or realized, is a cause for celebration and a continuing challenge for the twenty-first century.

SAD 62 Teachers and Staff, 2007-2008. Front Row l. to r.: Ann Pierce, Kari Crosman, Donelle Nielsen, Lynda Hartzell, Chake Higgison, Elaine Moore, Barbara Wentworth. Middle Row: Diana Passmore, Gayle Barschdorf, Erika DuPont, Diana Mosher, Sara Shannon, Joye Carkin, Christine Carter, Linda Woodard, Tamia Welch. Back Row: Breanne Raymond, Armon Duford, Ann Slattery, Stephen Neill, Kim Ordway, Beth Moulton, Jim Donoghue, Lisa Kimball, Joseph Feeney, Andrew McCullough. Not pictured: Kim Callnan, Diane Boucher, Melissa Russell, Cheryl Page, Karen Sylvain, and Tracy Borden.

Class of 2008. Seated l. to r.: Caleb Merrill, Nate Leonard, Morgan Brown, Savannah Spaulding, Andrea Grant, D. J. Mooney, Sadie Russell, Anna Brown, Shannon Hooper. Standing: Philip Badger, teacher Erica DuPont, Hayden Collins, Brandon Tuttle, Cory Doughty, Mattie Woodside, Natasha Dyment, and Nicole Pollock.

Joseph R. Feeney assumed the positions of Principal and Superintendent at Pownal Elementary School on January 3, 2000. Joe, a former teacher and principal from Houlton, Maine, met every challenge with great facility. After thirty-eight years in education, he announced his plans for retirement beginning June 30, 2008. Joe also filled the positions of Special Education Director, Transportation Director, and Director of Admissions. Summing up his eight years at Pownal Elementary, he said, " I tried to impress upon the dedicated staff that all children have the ability to learn, and it is incumbent upon us to make sure that they do... I invested a great deal of energy and time in training teachers in research-proven methods including assessments that can be utilized to modify and adjust their teaching. I truly believe that these efforts will enhance our overall program now and into the future."

Directors of SAD 62, 2008-2009. Seated l. to r.: Vice-chair Jennifer Blackstone Kaplan, Chair Paul D. Schumann, Rhonda O'Shea. Standing l. to r.: Carol Cyr, Karen L. Badger.

Situated at the foot of Bradbury Mountain, Pownal Elementary School and SAD 62 await an uncertain future.

PART FOUR
MEETING SPIRITUAL AND SOCIAL NEEDS

THEN: Town folk gathered at the First Parish Congregational Church for the July 4, 1918 celebration.

NOW: Town folk gathered to dedicate the Mallett Hall addition, October 6, 1999. Photo: Christopher Ayers.

Chapter 7

One Town - Two Churches

First Parish Congregational Church Steeple.

North Pownal United Methodist Church Steeple.

> *The Church's one foundation is Jesus Christ her Lord,*
> *She is His new creation By water and the word.*
> *From heaven He came and sought her to be His holy bride;*
> *With His own blood He bought her, And for her life He died.*
> *The Church's One Foundation, S.S. Wesley and Samuel J. Stone, 1864*

Entering Pownal from either north or south on any given Sunday morning, you might hear this hymn coming from one of two churches. The United Methodist Church in North Pownal and the First Parish Congregational Church in Pownal Center remain as active today as they have been throughout the last one hundred years. S. S. Wesley's music and Samuel J. Stone's lyrics have come to symbolize the spirituality of the two congregations. One other church established a brief presence in town in the 1940s. The Church of God in Christ operated a camp for African-American children on land they still own at the corner of Route 9 and Poland Range Road.

First Parish Congregational Church

In 1908 the First Parish Congregational Church lacked heat, plumbing, and electricity. Note the carriage sheds and the narrow dirt road. The sheds were dismantled in the 1940s.

From the crossroads at the center, one's eye is drawn to the visually dominating church on the corner of Hallowell and Elmwood Roads. The First Parish Congregational Church has been here since the town began. Establishing a Congregational church was a prerequisite for incorporating as an independent town in the year 1808. The church building, completed in 1811, served both as a house of worship and as a civic meetinghouse, during a time when the separation of church and state was not as pronounced as it is today. By 1908, the Federal style architecture of the original one-story building was almost indiscernible. A second story had been added in 1838, followed by full exterior remodeling in the Greek Revival style in 1851. Today, just a few remnants of the Federal style remain.

In 1908 Reverend Daniel A. Tuttle was called to serve as pastor. Thus began a remarkable nineteen-year pastorate, the longest in the twentieth century. Under the inspiring leadership of this man, the church experienced a revival both of spirit and membership. An article in the Lewiston Evening Journal on September 20, 1924 captures this well. "It is said of Mr. Tuttle that he is equally strenuous and energetic as a clergyman and that he has done wonders in building up the old church. He is not only able and eloquent as a preacher but he is popular with all classes. His congregation is by no means limited to church members and he is reputed to have the ability frequently to fill every pew. He is thoroughly imbued with the spirit and traditions of the church and has the rare faculty of attracting the confidence, affection and respect of the younger generation." During his tenure, Rev. Tuttle continued to have the active help of the Ladies Aid, an invaluable church group formed in 1893. From a low of twenty-two at the time he arrived, church membership grew until his death in 1927. This is remarkable given that the town's population was declining during these years.

The death of Reverend Tuttle marked the end of an era for the church. Pownal's population reached a low point of 462 in 1930, just as the Great Depression began. The pulpit during these years and into the 1950s was occupied by a series of student and visiting pastors. The resulting lack of strong, consistent leadership contributed to waning enthusiasm among the congregation. However, some significant physical changes did occur. In 1936, electric lights were installed in both the church and the parsonage. A kitchen was added in 1945 and enhanced in 1950 with running water piped from the parsonage. The outside of the church was repainted in 1953, financed largely through the efforts of the Ladies Aid.

Reverend Ronald W. Smith and his wife Ethel arrived in 1955. Membership stood at twelve. Reverend Smith's obligations were unique in that he preached not only for the Congregational Church, but also for the North Pownal United Methodist Church. By the time their three-year tenure was over, average Sunday attendance had grown to eighty and Sunday school participation had increased. Youth fellowship programs had been introduced under Ethel Smith's leadership. During this brief revitalization, more physical

Reverend Daniel Tuttle (1861-1927) served the First Parish Congregational Church from 1908 until his death.

The First Parish Congregational Church c. 1924, at which time the Portland Evening Express *promoted attendance to a sermon by Dr. Metcalf, "The Efficacy of Prayer." In early photos, those from 1908 through 1918, the chimney is not present. It appears in photos from 1924 to 1958, but then disappears. The steeple, apparently missing, is actually present in this image, but overexposed. Photo: David G. Coffin Collection*

enhancements were added. In 1958, an electric organ was given to the congregation in memory of Mrs. Kate Kenny. Abbie Pervier Vosmus (1882-1973) was the organist at this time, and her service in this capacity spanned over fifty years, ending only a few years before her death. The sanctuary was redecorated and central heating was installed.

The year 1961 marked the church's 150th anniversary. The event was celebrated with two days of special services and social gatherings. Patricia Menchen wrote "The 150 Year History of the First Parish Congregational Church of Pownal, Maine" for the occasion. Although this year began another nineteen-year period of relatively rapid turnover in ministers, improvements and activities continued under strong leadership from within the congregation. In 1975, the steeple was repaired, and both the interior and exterior were repainted. Having gained the reputation as the "finest around," the monthly bean suppers offered by the Ladies Aid continued to bolster the financial foundation of the church.

On June 20, 1975, the church was rededicated. William R. Gordon was the pastor and Dorothy Boyles the organist.

In 1980, Reverend John Eklund succeeded Pastor Gordon, and for the next five years he and his wife Elizabeth raised attendance and enthusiasm. Particularly popular were the new Bible study groups and the rejuvenated youth fellowship. Church membership grew, paralleling the growth in the town's population.

Reverend M. Lester Strout and his wife Betty arrived in 1985, serving the church for the next sixteen years. Most notable during this period was the "lifting" of the building. The large granite foundation blocks had been slowly sinking on the northern side for some time. By 1988, sufficient funds had been raised to allow the trustees to authorize lifting the church and creating a full basement beneath it. Trustees Stephen Litchfield, James Sanders, Craig Vosmus, Edward

(continued on page 272)

The church was rededicated on June 16, 1958. Pictured are some who participated in the service. L. to r.: Dr. Cornelius Clark, Superintendent, Congregational Christian Conference of Maine; Rev. Ronald Smith, pastor; Edward Brooks Jr.; James Sanders; Lauren Tuttle; Sr.; Percy Wentworth and Edward Menchen.
Photo and caption by Gray. Lois V. Sanders Scrapbook clipping.

The committee to plan 1958 church rededication. Seated l. to r.: Mabel Blackstone Hodsdon and Lois Vosmus Sanders. Standing l. to r.: Josephine Pervier Allen, James Sanders, Chairman, and Winnie Vosmus Carter.
Scrapbook Lois Sanders, photo by Ralph D. White, newsclipping source unknown.

Left: Abbie Pervier Vosmus (1892-1973) in June, 1968. She served as church organist for over fifty years from 1920 to 1972, using a pump organ until 1958 when an electric organ was gifted to the church in memory of Mrs. Kate Kenney. At Abbie's death, memorial donations in her honor purchased a new electric organ.

Right: Dorothy MacAllister Boyles (1907-1998) served as church organist and choir director from 1973 until 1994. Prior to moving to Pownal, she had been an organ and piano teacher as well as organist and choir director for forty-three years at churches in Pennsylvania.

As Josephine Pervier Allen expressed it in her 1990 history, The Miracle of the Eighties: *"Even in the 1998s many of us doubted the success of this operation. As Christians we know alone we are nothing, so again we turned to God with our prayers asking for success in this undertaking… After many hired and volunteer hours of labor… and after raising $50,000 for the project… the basement was dedicated October 28, 1990 with praise to God and all who contributed."*

Reverend M. Lester and Betty Strout served the church from 1986 until 2002. They are pictured here in 1988 with the church raised on I-beams as the building "lifting" was in process.

Menchen, and Wedgewood Wheeler agreed to hire Clayton Copp and Sons Building Movers from West Cumberland to begin work in the spring. The building was successfully raised and placed on I beams. The foundation work, overseen by Craig Vosmus was then completed, and the church lowered. During this work, the membership was invited to worship at the North Pownal Methodist Church, and bean suppers were suspended. By the end of July, the congregation had returned home. The new basement featured a restroom, kitchenette, several Sunday school classrooms, and much needed storage space.

On October 28, 1990, the basement was dedicated during a Sunday service. The program recognized those who labored voluntarily on this project. Thomas H. Vosmus, electrician, Kenneth Vosmus, plumber, Craig Vosmus and Donald Vosmus, carpenters, Gary Libby and John Litchfield, carpenters and dry-wallers, and Michael Menchen, oil burner mechanic, had all been instrumental in helping the church achieve this goal. Then in 1994, new front entrance doors, topped by a stained glass window designed and crafted by Gabriel Harrison, were installed and dedicated in memory of Lawrence Carter, (1914-1993).

In 2002, Pastor Strout retired and was replaced by a temporary pastor, Reverend How-

First Parish Congregational Church in 2007. Note the parking area filled with cars, the mature trees, planted in the 1950s, and the paved Route 9 (Hallowell Road).

ard Richardson. Pastor Richardson and his wife Lynda accepted a one year commitment to the congregation. He brought to the pulpit a fresh enthusiasm, and sparked a surge in membership. As of 2008, the Richardsons had continued their commitment to the church, and attendance at Sunday services and Sunday school continued to grow. Sunday worship now includes a contemporary music "pre-service," with a state-of-the-art sound system and Christian "Power Point" presentations. The worship service has become more celebratory and modern in tone.

Recently additional changes have been made to both the interior and exterior of the building. The steeple was repaired and painted in 2005, a ramp was added for handicapped accessibility, and an elevator was installed. In 2006, the kitchen was refurbished, and a restaurant-grade dishwasher installed. Then in 2007, the middle-floor windows, dating to the original building, were replaced, and new granite front steps installed, all under the direction of Craig Vosmus. The completed steps, with wrought iron railings made by James Bennis, were dedicated in memory of Winnie Vosmus Carter (1922-2003).

The formal leadership of the church in 2007 was as follows: Pastor, Howard Richardson; Treasurer, Edna Menchen; Trustees: Wayne Gerrish, Jody Hibbard, David Stewart, Craig Vosmus, Clyde White; Deacons: Jody Hibbard, Stephen Litchfield, Craig Vosmus, Wedgwood Wheeler; Deaconesses: Jackie Gerrish, Janice Litchfield, Lois Sanders, Cheryl Vosmus.

As the town's bicentennial approaches, the Ladies Aid Society, first organized on September 12, 1893, continues to be the church's primary

Interior of the church sanctuary in 2007. Lighting fixtures dating to the 1860s exist alongside a state-of-the-art electronic system, which delivers modern sound and accommodates Christian Power Point presentations.

social and fund raising organization. Bean suppers continue to provide the core financial support for church restoration and building projects. Currently, there are forty active members. Officers for 2007 were: President, Mary Ellen Farrell; Vice President, Linda Allen; Secretary, Erica Giddinge; Treasurer, Cheryl Vosmus.

Reverend Howard F. and Lynda McAllister Richardson. Pastor Richardson holds both bachelor and master of theology degrees from Andersonville Theological Seminary in Camilla, Georgia. He has forty-nine years of experience as a clergyman, administrator, evangelist, church planter and church growth facilitator in all aspects of church work. Prior to coming to Pownal in 2004, he served churches in Conway and North Conway, New Hampshire.

Bean Suppers Bring In the Bacon

It is the third Saturday in May, the first supper of the season, and all is in readiness. This has been happening in one form or another for the past one hundred years: generations of Ladies Aid Society members raising money for the church through bean suppers. The Friday night crew has peeled one hundred pounds of potatoes for potato salad, cabbage has been sliced and mixed for coleslaw, and forty pounds of kidney and yellow eye beans, plus twenty-five pounds of pea beans, have been prepped for baking. Preparations continue through Saturday. Sixteen pounds of dry spaghetti, twenty pounds of hamburger, and many cans of tomato sauce will soon be simmering. Everyone has a job and each is expert at it.

At home, "Pie Ladies" are baking ninety pies of fifteen varieties. Some make twelve and have been doing so for fifty or more years. None is reimbursed for her costs. Five kinds of tempting cakes will be donated. Summer gardens have supplied cucumbers and beets for seventy-five gallons of sunshine pickles, bread-and-butter pickles, and pickled beets, all preserved and shelved each fall. They will last throughout the six suppers of the season. Forty dozen rolls, the only food not homemade, have arrived from a Lewiston bakery.

By 4:30, cars are beginning to park near the church. Many have made reservations in advance. One hundred and seventy-five diners will be seated at 5:00 o'clock and a like number at 6:00. At 7:00, the last sitting, latecomers will eat with the workers. In total, about four hundred diners will have been fed, all they could eat for seven dollars. By 9:30, clean up will be complete. Workers will go home tired, but pleased that they have made a significant contribution to their church. In another month, it will all begin again.

Willing Hands Help Out

Bean supper pie ladies, renowned for their cooking, work in the kitchen c. 2000. These women have baked thousands of pies. Some produced as many as twelve per supper for over fifty years, carried to church in special pie carriers crafted by their husbands. L. to r.: Vosmus sisters Lois Sanders, Winnie Carter, and Vina Litchfield; Jackie York, Edna Snow Menchen, and Arlene Davis Litchfield.

A hustling kitchen crew cheerfully delivers beans, salads, spaghetti, rolls, condiments, and pies to the tables.

Evelyn Vosmus Wheeler, left, helps her aunt, Lois Vosmus Sanders prepare rolls on June 16, 2007.

Arlene Golding Smith, 86, (left) and Edna Snow Menchen, 90, take a break on June 16, 2007. They have been working bean suppers for over sixty years and have contributed incalculable delicious pies and cakes.

North Pownal United Methodist Church

Left: The North Pownal Methodist Episcopal Church, undated photograph, was built in 1844. At that time, the church sat on the corner of the Lawrence and Poland Range (or "Potash") Roads, beside Ben Randall's country store. At the time the school was on the Fickett Road.

Right: A new one-room school was built in 1894. In a photograph from c. 1910, it stands next to the recently remodeled church. The structure barely visible to the left of the church is the store, which was then doing a thriving business. In 1992 the school was connected to the church and became known as the Brooks Room.

A centerpiece of the North Pownal community is the United Methodist Church. The church fronts "four-square" on the Lawrence Road, but this has not always been so. Significant renovations and changes, including moving the building, have occurred since the original structure was built. But a church is more than a building, and the North Pownal Methodists can trace their origins to the Bowdoinham Methodist Circuit formed in 1803.

By the early 1800s, it was clear that the Congregational Church did not share the same spiritual views as much of Maine's expanding population. Spiritual alternatives, Methodism among them, found fertile ground and set their seed particularly among the backcountry residents. Methodism then embodied a worldview similar to that of separationists, anti-Federalists, and the new Jeffersonian Democratic-Republicans. By 1806, Pownal was part of the Durham Methodist Circuit in company with Durham, Danville, Lisbon, and Litchfield. Pownal and Durham families formed the Methodist Episcopal Church utilizing the Methodist Meeting House in Durham. Then in 1844, with Pownal's population at 1300, North Pownal Methodists built their first church structure. Ultimately, this congregation was reorganized as the North Pownal United Methodist Church, under which name it exists today.

The beginning of the twentieth century was accompanied by a sense of prosperity and well being generally throughout the country. In the thriving area of North Pownal, these were times to take stock, spruce up, and plan for the town centennial celebration in 1908. And the original Methodist Church came in for its share of renovations. Although detailed records with precise dates are scarce, it's clear that during the early 1900s the church structure was rotated a quarter turn so as to squarely face the Lawrence Road. Jessie Foster Tuttle in a 1974 interview recalled that, "In 1908 my father built the steeple and the vestry." By 1911, a 32-inch Blymyer church bell weighing 550 pounds had been purchased from an Ohio foundry and hung in the steeple. And the building received a fresh coat of white paint applied by Joseph Nelson Small. During these times, his father Lemuel Small wrote in the *Daily Eastern Argus*, "The Methodist church in this place has been undergoing extensive repairs. The roof has been reshingled, the chimneys rebuilt...the Ladies Benevolent Society [has] made the inside attractive by calcining the walls and ceiling, recovering the pulpit, and purchasing a fine carpet...and now the people have added a fine chandelier."

Incomplete records indicate that from the time of WWI through the great depression years to the end of WWII, the church building and church membership experienced a steady decline. These were difficult years, money and materials were in short supply, and the town's declining population was mirrored by the church membership. Recovery was to be slow, but by the end of WWII it was well underway.

The years following WWII, 1945-1969, became a period of reactivation and rededication for the church. Membership rose and baptisms increased in number. In 1950, electric lights were installed, and six years later an oil-fired heating system was purchased. That same year new drapes were purchased, and the roof and vestry floor were replaced. In 1964, a new furnace was installed, and with the help of the Women's Service Club the building was painted. A new organ was purchased in 1966. Throughout this period, conference reports indicate that no pastor remained for more than a few years. Those serving were: Rev. Gladys York, Rev. Ernest

Edward "Ed" Mitchell (1911-1978) and Dorothy Gagnon Mitchell (1914-1971) are pictured here in 1965 in front of the church they served for over forty years. Ed served as Trustee and on every committee, and was instrumental in acquiring the school for the church. He could always be found laboring on church maintenance and, along with Dorothy, working to raise monies to fund its activities.

Angeline "Angie" Baker Penley (1883-1933) was organist at the North Pownal United Methodist church from 1924 until her death. In addition to raising four children, she taught piano and organ, and played for entertainments at the Golden Cross Hall and at the local one-room school.

The obituary of Ethel Stebbins Smith (1924-1999) stated, "Music and serving her church were the great loves of her life... [She was] organist for over fifty years...lay leader, lay speaker and lay member to the Northeast Conference... counselor at Mechuwana Church Camp... served on the District Superintending Committee of the Methodist Conference." After raising four children, she received her bachelors and masters degrees in education with high honors and began a twenty-seven-year teaching career at Durham Elementary School. Photo: Olan Mills 1995.

Reverend Eva Cutler (1931-2006) served as Minister from 1990 to 2002, making her the longest serving pastor in the church's history. In addition, she received the Jefferson Award for her volunteer work as an advocate for the deaf and blind at the Barron Center, Pineland Hospital and at the Rape Crisis Center. She taught sign language and communication motor skills, and interpreted for the deaf during court hearings. Photo: Olan Mills 1995.

Roberts, Rev. J. B. Shaw, Rev. S. W. Taylor, Rev. Ronald Smith, Rev. A. Christopher Ives, Rev. Bruce McSpadden, and Rev. Evans Wilson.

In 1969, an acquisition occurred that ultimately led to the contiguous expansion of the church structure. For one dollar, Edward 'Ed' Mitchell purchased from the town the adjacent and recently abandoned North Pownal one-room school building. The town had just closed all of its one-room schools and was disposing of the buildings. Ed deeded the building to the church for Sunday school and social uses. Ethel Smith wrote in 1994, "The addition [of the one-room school] provided dimension to the life of the church that had been limited to say the least." In 1988, under the leadership of Reverend George Tripp, planning and fund raising began for a project that would connect this building to the church structure. But first the schoolhouse, built in 1894 and never modernized, underwent extensive renovations. An attached outhouse was removed, plumbing installed, and a bathroom and kitchen added. Thoughtfully, these changes were made with an effort to retain as much of the original school structure as possible – this being the only remaining one-room school building in town.

Reverend Eva Cutler answered the call to minister in 1990 beginning what would be a thirteen-year pastorate. One year later, in April of 1991, construction began of the unit that would connect the church to the old school building, with Reverend Cutler presiding at the groundbreaking ceremony. Laurence Snow was both the architect and the leading carpenter for this project. Assisting were Alvah Donnell, Harold Small, Walter Barschdorf, Philip and Barbara Wentworth, William Beasley, Henry Nichols, and members of the Brunswick United Methodist Church. This connecting structure, housing a large all-purpose room and a minister's office, was completed in 1992 and the all-purpose room

(continued on page 280)

Henry Nichols paints windows in the room connecting the church and former schoolhouse. Photo by Gordon Chibroski, possibly PPH Feb. 1992.

Church members Harold Small (1917-2008), left, and Laurence Snow (1915-1995) join in the all-volunteer effort, from 1988 to 1992, to complete what became the Snow Room. It was dedicated in 1992. Unknown source.

The Snow Room, pictured here in 2005, is the central structure which provides an all-purpose room and minister's office. It links the church to the former North Pownal one-room school or Brooks Room (right), which contains a kitchen and an area for Sunday school and other activities.

279

Allen "Pat" and Nancy Mitchell Malone continue to serve the church today much the same way as Nancy's parents, Ed and Dorothy Mitchell, did. Nancy serves as Parish Administrator, and both have served as Trustees and on all committees. They can be found working together at bean suppers, doing church maintenance, and raising funds for church activities. Photo: Olan Mills 2005.

was dedicated appropriately as the "Snow Room." The one-room school, now connected to the church, was named the "Brooks Room" after Marjorie Cushman Brooks (1890-1988), a longtime local resident and teacher at the West and North Pownal Schools from 1927 to 1963. These two new rooms soon became the centers of increased church activities and fund raising events such as bean suppers, fairs, and entertainments. In 1994, as the church celebrated its 150th anniversary, Ethel Smith wrote, "[the anniversary] is celebrated with great joy and thankfulness for all that has come about in these many years through the diligent, hard-working people of the community, who continue to faithfully worship a never-changing God."

The strong leadership of Reverend Eva Cutler from 1990 to 2002 and Reverend Richard "Dick" Sheesley who succeeded her and remains today, has proved critical in implementing needed church improvements. During their tenures, entrance paving and handicapped accessibility to the Brooks Room were completed; an off-street parking lot with stairway entrance to the Snow Room was created; kitchen facilities were updated including the installation of a commercial dishwasher; and the interior of the Brooks Room was further renovated and painted. Church membership has increased and has been reenergized under the leadership of Reverend Sheesley and his wife Ruth. A monthly newsletter informs members of church news and provides a calendar of events listing activities for all ages. It recognizes birthdays, anniversaries, graduations, and special events. The church has reached out to the community at large, offering Senior Citizen lunches, sponsoring a weekly food distribution program, and providing music to local nursing homes.

When the church bell calls members to worship in 2008, it will have been chiming for ninety-seven years. Much has changed over these nearly one hundred years, but the strong spiritual message of the church remains unaltered.

Barbara Wentworth, Music Director.
Photo: Olan Mills 2005

Church officials in 2007 were: Richard "Dick" Sheesley, Pastor; Nancy Malone, Parish Administrator; Connie Tryon, Treasurer; Barbara Wentworth, Director of Music; and Kathy Nickerson, Administrative Council, Chair. Church Trustees in 2007 were: David Edwards, Leslie Peaco, Andrew Tryon, Walter Barschdorf, Connie Tryon, Philip Wentworth, Ralph Hutchinson, C. J. Larrabee, and Kim Drew.

The Get-A-Ways, organized in September 1982 after the North Pownal Service Club disbanded, is a community service group composed of women from the North Pownal United Methodist Church and the community. It currently has twelve members who raise monies to support its programs by hosting an October Harvest Dinner, a March Spaghetti Dinner, and an annual Christmas Fair. The group awards youth scholarships to Methodist Church Camp Mechuwana, assists in the weekly food distribution program, provides support for sick and elderly, and helps financially with the needs of the church kitchen. Club officers in 2007 were: Doris Morgan, President; Lucille Wentworth, Vice President; Caron Beard, Secretary; and Connie Tryon, Treasurer.

Reverend C. Richard "Dick" and Ruth Sheesley have been serving the North Pownal United Methodist Church since 2003. Rev. Sheesley has been in the ministry for forty-five years. He earned a bachelor's degree at from Houghton College. From Asbury Theological Seminary he received both a master's in divinity and a master's in sacred theology in psychology and pastoral counseling. He is licensed as a psychological therapist pastoral counselor by the State of Maine, and prior to coming to North Pownal served for nineteen years as Director of Pastoral Care at Maine Medical Center. Photo: Olan Mills 2005.

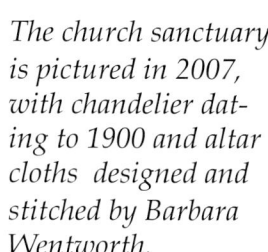

The church sanctuary is pictured in 2007, with chandelier dating to 1900 and altar cloths designed and stitched by Barbara Wentworth.

Above: Making apple butter the old-fashioned way, a fund-raiser for the church. Front row l. to r.: Mavis Peaco, Ruth Sheesley (behind Mavis), Jennifer Barschdorf, Gayle Barschdorf, Leslie Peaco, Ralph Hutchinson, Karen Hutchinson, Philip Badger, Lucille Wentworth. Back l. to r.: Rev. C. Richard Sheesley, Nancy Malone, Pat Malone. Photo: Olan Mills 2005.

Below: North Pownal United Methodist Church Choir. Front row l. to r.: Jayme Barschdorf, Barbara Wentworth, Janice Anderson, Nancy Malone. Back row l. to r.: Pat Malone, Jennifer Clark, Tom Harlow, Rev. Sheesley. Photo: Olan Mills 2005.

Bean Suppers Grow in Popularity

Diners and workers at the August 4, 2007 Saturday bean supper.

Over the past century, Saturday bean suppers have been the primary source of income for small churches like the Methodist Church in North Pownal. Prior to the addition of the Snow Room and the kitchen renovations, it was difficult to do this, and so this important source of income was not available. But since the dedication of the addition in 1992, bean suppers have been offered regularly and have grown in reputation and popularity.

The year 2007 was typical. Supper organizers Nancy Malone, Caron Beard, Karen Hutchinson, Kim Drew and Lucille Wentworth met in February to plan for the upcoming season. The previous fall, Mavis Peaco had turned locally grown cucumbers into sixteen gallons of her famous Church Pickles (her secret recipe), while Caron and Barry Beard "put by" twenty-five gallons of pickled beets, all for the upcoming year's suppers.

For the April supper, a crew of eight began preparation on Friday evening. They set up tables, soaked three kinds of beans prior to baking, and organized the ingredients for spaghetti, potato salad and coleslaw. They prepared to serve one hundred fifty to two hundred diners. Cooking continued all day Saturday and by 4:30, as the aroma of fresh-baked biscuits and brown bread filled the rooms, the first tables were served. Pie ladies had brought forty delicious pies, baked at home. Coffee, tea and punch were prepared. Those served could eat all they wanted for just $6.00. After the last diner was served, clean up began. The tired but happy crew left for home by 8:00 P. M., having fed the multitudes and brought in revenue for their church.

So it went every first Saturday from April through November, 2007 and so it continues.

Pownal Cemeteries — Places of Remembrance and Peace

The Pownal Center Cemetery (No. 1 on map, page 286) is adjacent to the First Parish Congregational Church and dates to 1824, when the land was purchased by the town. It contains 162 monuments with 192 names engraved. The town hearse house, which dates to 1834 and was restored by the Pownal Scenic and Historical Society, sits at the northern boundary of the cemetery. The centifolia roses alongside the hearse house were planted by June Tucci and historical society members in 1993.

This is the second hearse purchased by the town. It was manufactured by the Geo. L. Brownell Co. of New Bedford, Massachusetts in 1878. It is pictured here in 1997 after restoration. Carl Mason funded the two-year restoration project. Committee members included Arthur Stackhouse, Craig Dietrich, Tom and Mary Pat Bowen, Janet Roberts, and Jim and Donna Boyles.

Below: York Cemetery (No 11 on map, page 286) began as a family cemetery, but was taken over by the town in 1830. It contains forty graves. It is pictured here as members of the Historical Society's Cemetery Committee, Sherry Dietrich and Janice West, complete a second inventory of monuments and epitaphs. The Hodsdon and Mason families cleared brush and trees along with members of the Cemetery Commission prior to professional restoration by Christopher Stilkey in 2007.

Above: Lake Cemetery (No. 5 on map, page 286) served the North Pownal area from the early 1800s. It contains 279 monuments. It was named for the Eleazer Lake family, original settlers at the Lawrence and Tryon crossroads.

Warren Cemetery (No. 3 on map, page 286) began in 1819 as a family cemetery with the death of George Warren, one of Pownal's earliest settlers. It contains eighty-one monuments and was professionally restored in 2007 by Christopher Stilkey. In 2005, Shawn Teriault of Boy Scout Troop 86, Gray, Maine enlisted a group of volunteers who, with his leadership, cleared brush, replaced fencing, and cleaned stones. Shawn earned his Eagle Scout Badge in 2006 along with a commendation plaque from the cemetery commission. James Bennis crafted and donated the wrought iron sign.

The Toothaker (Tuttle) Cemetery (No. 9 on map, page 286) contains sixty-five monuments and one of Pownal's more decorative headstones, that of Andrew Adams. Scrolls and roses carved in the granite signify "completion and the brevity of earthly innocence." The epitaph reads:

*How sweet is that home where the weary rest,
No toil, no temptations are known by the blest.
A bright bow of glory will shine o'er their way,
And saints with the Angels chant a sweet lay.*

Elmwood Cemetery (No. 2 on map, page 286) dates from 1884 and is the largest and most commonly used burial ground in Pownal today. It is pictured here in December 2006 with wreaths gifted by Michael Smith of the Freeport Lions Club. In 1976, members of the Historical Society's Cemetery Committee, Ruth McCarthy, Dorothy Boyles, and Marjorie Sweetser, inventoried all monuments with dates up to 1900. Currently the committee of Sherry Dietrich, Janice West and Carrie Kivela are completing a second inventory that will include all monuments and epitaphs. When this survey is complete, all eleven of Pownal's cemeteries will have been inventoried, epitaphs recorded and information archived at the local and state level.

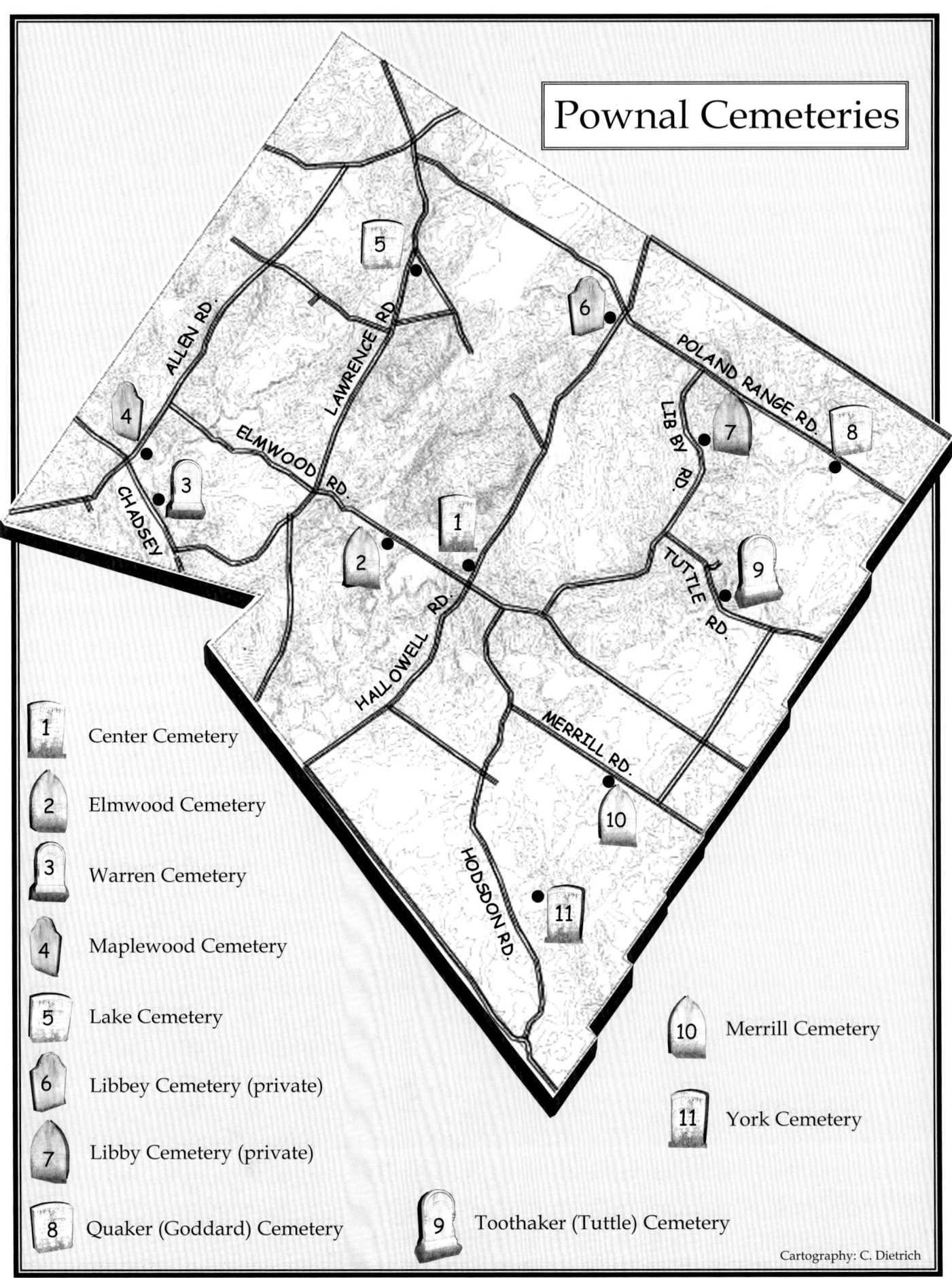

Chapter 8

Social Groups Contribute

Granite Grange No. 14 Officers standing in front of Mallett Hall c. December 1923. Front row l. to r.: Maude Tuttle (Flora), Helen Morris (Ceres), Sarah Hodsdon (Pomona). Middle row l. to r.: Abel Martin (Gate Keeper), Philip Tryon (Master), Nellie Pervier (Chaplain), Philip Pervier (possibly Overseer). Back row l. to r.: one of the Martin twins either Ada or Ida, unidentified woman, unidentified woman, unidentified man in doorway, Mellen Tryon (Treasurer), William Pervier.

Social and service organizations have always been a feature of American communities, and Pownal is no exception. Over the past one hundred years many diverse groups came into being for a variety of purposes, bringing together children, adults, seniors, neighborhoods, farm families, creative individuals, and people with a common social purpose. While structuring their activities around the needs and interests of their members, all of these groups also undertook to benefit the larger community in some way.

As times changed or as key individuals came and went, the numbers and nature of Pownal's organizations changed. Many once-active groups withered and disappeared because of an aging membership, changes in social attitudes, or competing activities beyond Pownal's borders. The United Order of the Golden Cross once even had its own large building in North Pownal but is now virtually forgotten. The Order of Pocahontas, a ladies' adjunct to the Improved Order of Red Men, and the Firemen's Auxiliary, a support organization of women, went the way of earlier conceptions of female roles. Other groups managed to transform themselves into something new, as they changed with the times. Meanwhile, new groups appeared to fill new needs. This chapter is not a comprehensive study of Pownal's social organizations, but highlights several which are currently active or which have only recently disappeared, providing a brief look at their purposes and activities.

Granite Grange No. 14 of Pownal, Maine

The national Grange organization came into being in 1867 as the Order of Patrons of Husbandry, aiming to improve the economic and social status of the nation's farm population. From the start, the Grange encouraged its members to modernize their farms, breed better livestock and improve their depleted soil. To achieve these goals it worked closely with Land Grant universities and state boards of agriculture.

In April of 1874, Pownal's Granite Grange was formed, only the fourteenth chapter in the state. A few weeks later, the Maine State Grange established itself, and proceeded to bring a new sense of activism to Maine's farmers through its support of local Grange chapters. At that time, Pownal was a farm community of 1,053, and its granite industry was at peak production, so it took the name Granite Grange. Nathaniel Dyer, first master, was also elected to the executive committee of the state Grange.

It wasn't long before more Grange chapters and buildings appeared across Maine, even in isolated rural areas. Farmers found this new support for their efforts and lives extremely helpful, and Grange membership grew. Meetings featured programs, lectures, and discussions, all aimed at improving farming methods and economics. Soon, farmers began extending the organizing powers of the Grange to lobby for such things as free rural postal delivery, improved rural roads, homeowners insurance, and price supports. In many Grange halls an annual meeting addressed public policy and legislation concerns.

But the appeal and popularity of Grange meetings was not due solely to issues of farming and economics. In an era when entertainment and social interactions were largely confined to the local community, Grange meetings often included "fun" and social activities that appealed to both young and old. And this continued into recent times. Looking back in 1988, Josephine Pervier Allen wrote, "The Grange was one of our favorite activities...the social side... [S]quare dancing provided one of the best ways to talk to that special fellow... [A]lso the dramas that we put on...literary events...and we would tour other grange halls."

Grange Past Masters c. 1977, seated in from of stage with curtains opened and early scrim lowered. Seated l. to r.: Laurence Snow, Noyes Mitchell, Percy Wentworth, Philip Tryon, Joseph Pervier. Standing l. to r.: Thomas Vosmus, James Sanders, Edward Menchen, Edward Mitchell, Ralph Carter, Lewis Martin or Paul Hamilton, Earle Blake, Michael Menchen.

Over 134 years, Granite Grange served the community in many ways. Its most ambitious effort was the construction of the center fire station (see Chapters 1 and 5). Members maintained the second floor room of Mallett Hall (often referred to as the Grange room), by painting, providing drapes, refinishing floors, etc. They often helped with the upkeep of other areas of the building. They supported Freeport Community Services, education programs at Pownal's schools, children with AIDS, and cemetery maintenance and signage. Always involved in town events, the Grange donated generously to the Veterans' Memorial Project.

On June 30, 2007, after 134 years of service to the farmers of Pownal and to the community at large, members of Granite Grange No. 14 reached a difficult and sad decision, voting to close the Pownal chapter. Doris Blackstone stated, "The few active members could no longer support the work of the chapter, and many members were unable to be active due to ill health. The recent deaths of five members were a severe loss to the chapter, and the inability to attract younger members resulted in a declining membership." Before they disbanded, members voted to bequeath $3,700 to the town, to be used in establishing a park along the northeast side of Mallett Hall. The impact and influence of Granite Grange on the Pownal community is hard to overstate. Such a park will help assure that it is not forgotten.

Lois Vosmus Sanders (left) and Doris Carter Blackstone shepherded Granite Grange through its last days. Lois, a third generation Granger, was active for sixty-eight years, attaining Golden Sheaf status. Doris, a fourth generation Granger, was active for forty-nine years and in 1979 became the first woman Master.

Granite Grange Officers 2007. Seated at stations l. to r.: Theona Penley Blackstone (Flora), Lois Vosmus Sanders (Ceres and Treasurer), Edna Snow Menchen (Pomona and Chaplain). Standing l. to r.: Doris Carter Blackstone (Secretary), Thomas H. Vosmus (Master), Dorothy Hayward (Lady Assistant Steward), William Hayward (Assistant Steward), Sheila Menchen Merritt (member).

Pownal 4-H

The Bradbury Mountain Girls 4-H Club, under the leadership of Clara Keith Snow, at a field day held in 1940. Front row l. to r.: Arleen Tryon, Assistant Leader; Margaret Whitcher, unknown, Greta Keith. Middle: Unknown, Dorothy Tryon, Phyllis Tryon, Donna Tuttle. Back: Unknown, Unknown.

The earliest reliable evidence of a 4-H club in Pownal comes from an interview with Edna Snow Menchen. She recalled that she joined a girls' club around 1927. "I might have been ten and we went down to Mrs. Mary Sweetser's house. [Our first year project] was sewing. We made a bag first thing. It had a drawstring top."

Four-H had its origins in 1902 in Ohio. Boys' and girls' clubs were formed to spread hands-on learning and make public school education more connected to rural life. The movement gained national standing in 1914 when Congress created the Agricultural Extension Service under the Agriculture Department and authorized it to support boys' and girls' clubs involved with agriculture, home economics, and related subjects. By 1924 these clubs were organized as "4-H" clubs, and the clover emblem was adopted. Thus Edna Menchen's girls club would have been one of the earliest, if not the earliest of such youth organizations in town. From then on, 4-H clubs flourished under many names, led by various adults. In the 1930s Thomas Vosmus tended a garden and raised a heifer for his projects. Interviewed in 2006, he recalled that the leader of this club was a Mrs. Smith. In the 1940s Clara Keith Snow and Arleen Tryon formed the Bradbury Mountain Girls, while for the boys there was the Ambitious Club, led by Ferne Wood and Daniel Whitcher. Joseph Pervier oversaw several of the boys' pig raising projects.

When World War II erupted, Pownal's 4-H club members responded to the call to contribute to the war effort. Virginia Pike (Vosmus), Louise Weed, and Frances Morrill made 210 stockings for the soldiers. Virginia Pike and Ella Duncan collected six pounds of fat. The Bradbury Mountain Girls helped to can 612 pints of vegetables. Just after the war, more 4-H clubs were formed, with names like Mohawks, Vikings, and Up and Doing Girls. Their leaders included J. A. Golden, Pearl Flint, and Edith Best. The Spread Sunshine Club, led by Gertrude Kimball York in the 1950s, took up a variety of activities. There were boys' clubs as well, for dairy cows, chickens, and gardening, although their names are now forgotten. Terry Snow, one of the participants, recalled, "I raised sheep. I raised cows. And I had the chickens. And we would show things at the Cumberland Fair." For their outstanding achievements, Albert Blackstone Jr. and Elizabeth Hawkins were selected to attend the national 4-H congress in Chicago in 1960.

By the 1960s, with the decline of farming, 4-H activity dropped off. The Girls' and Boys' of Pownal, or GABOP, formed in 1968, was the sole local group during that decade. It continued into the 1970s under the leadership of Sandra Randall, Wilma Ryder, and Doris Blackstone. In 1988 the Collars and Leashes dog obedience club was formed, lasting until 1991. Currently there is just "4-Paws-4-H," which teaches dog agility. Now in its fifteenth year, this club is led by Sherry Dietrich, Joan Rolfe, and Kelly Welch.

In recent years, some Pownal boys and girls have joined county-level clubs to pursue interests in sheep, poultry, rabbits, or independent projects. However, as Pownal grows ever more suburban, it becomes increasingly difficult to attract young people to 4-H programs.

Right: Albert Blackstone Jr. and Elizabeth Hawkins were rewarded with a trip to the National 4-H Congress in Chicago for their outstanding 4-H achievements in 1960.

Below: Pownal 4-H members win Best in Class rosette ribbons at the Cumberland County 4-H Style Review in May 1977. L.to r.: Heidi Dobson (skirt class), Linda Payson (formal dress), Barbara Payson (shirt and vest class). Photo: Don Hinkley Brunswick Times Record May 6, 1977.

4 Paws 4-H Dog Agility Club Leaders l. to r.: Sherry Dietrich with "Danny," Joan Rolfe, Kelly Welch with "Guster."

Improved Order of Redmen

The Red Men trace their beginnings to the Sons of Liberty founded in 1765 to help establish freedom and liberty in the early colonies. They concealed their identities and worked in secret. The most memorable event in their history was the Boston Tea Party, when on December 16, 1773 they disguised themselves as Indians and dumped 342 chests of English tea into Boston Harbor to protest the tax on tea. By 1888, the Red Men had organized in Maine under the name Great Council of Maine. Pownal's Westcustogo Tribe 37 of the Improved Order of Red Men was formed in 1896.

As of 2008, Pownal men will have supported the Red Men organization for 112 years, meeting every Saturday night in Mallett Hall to socialize and uphold the duties set forth in their charter. These duties include: love and respect for the American flag, preserving and defending our nation's free government, preserving the democratic way of life, helping those in need through organized charitable organizations, and keeping alive the customs, ceremonies and philosophy of the Great Iroquois Indian Nation on whose principles they are patterned.

The Red Men's service projects in town have included: care of monuments and grounds at the Center cemetery, support of charitable organizations, participation in Pownal Pride Day, and assistance to members in need. However, according to Sachem Kenneth Vosmus, "The future of the Red Men is uncertain, as so many members have died recently and young men are not interested in joining."

Red Man Harold "Bill" Snow. This photo was on the cover of The Shopping Notes *for July 7, 1982, taken by an unknown photographer at the Yarmouth Clam Festival parade on July 4.*

Officers for 2007-2008. Seated: Kenneth Vosmus (Sachem). Standing l. to r.: Donald Vosmus (Brave), Nate Allen (First Snnap), Craig Vosmus (Prophet and Collector of Wampum), Russell Allen (Keeper of Wampum), Arnold Blackstone (Chief of Records), Mark Carter (Sagamore), Luther Snow (Sagamore). Not pictured: Wedgewood Wheeler (Second Snnap).

North Pownal Community Club

Bernard Small (100 years old) and his sister Blanche Small Cook (106 years old) were honored for their service to the North Pownal community at their centennial birthday celebration, September 16, 2007.

On October 3, 1941, a group of North Pownal residents signed articles of association, forming the North Pownal Community Club. Bernard Small, his wife Maude, Seth Sawyer, Clifton Burns, Velma Bornheimer, and Alvin Tryon thus started a community social organization that continues to this day. One of their first challenges was to find the means to pay for the meeting hall they had purchased. For $350 and payment of 1941 taxes, Owen Farwell sold them the building at 857 Lawrence Road, a former general store with a history going back nearly 175 years.

In addition to meeting their own expenses, the club reached out to help the local community. They organized weekly whist parties, food sales, bean suppers, and rummage sales as sources of income. By the 1950s North Pownal Community Club had become a fixture in town, offering a meeting place for 4-H, teen activities, parties, and club events. They contributed both financially and in kind to the Methodist Church and the local one-room school.

Just as the original members were beginning to tire after more than thirty years of service to the club, Alan and Susan Bradstreet moved in across the road and joined. Alan was elected president in 1975 and would hold that office for the next seventeen years. Sue was elected trustee and treasurer and carried out these duties for nineteen years. Alice Hanson served as club secretary for seventeen years.

Over time, these individuals and others created renewed interest in the club, and membership increased. Attention was paid to much-needed structural repairs of the building, and the interior was renovated to make it more attractive and useful. Use of the building increased, with the Boy Scouts, the Pownal Scenic and Historical Society, and the Methodist Church routinely holding meetings and events there. The Pownal Food Coop began using it as their distribution site. Also during this period, the club began holding open-invitation potlucks that continue today as activities.

Currently, the club continues to function. Much of its attention is focused on restoring and repairing the building, resources for this coming mainly from an annual yard sale and from volunteer labor. Various groups use the building, and a recently instituted "Meet Your Neighbor" annual potluck dinner contributes to a sense of community. Officers for 2008 are: Robert McMahon, president; Janet Roberts, Vice President; Patricia Hodgdon, Secretary; and Craig Dietrich, Treasurer. Trustees are: Suzanne Crowell, Carol Cyr, Louis Hanson, Nancy Malone, and Jeremy Willis.

North Pownal Community Club officers l. to r.: Pat Hodgdon, Secretary; Bob McMahon, President; Jan Roberts Vice-President; Craig Dietrich, Treasurer.

Boy Scouts

As Pownal was entering its second century, the Scouting Movement was rapidly spreading in Europe and in America. Founded in 1910, the Boy Scouts of America became the largest youth organization in the United States.

Over the years, there have been a number of Boy Scout troops and Cub Scout packs active in Pownal. However, the records of their existence and activities are difficult to find. In the 1970s and 1980s, George Anderson Sr., himself an Eagle Scout, was master of Troop 107. In 1986 George Anderson Jr. also achieved this rank. This troop made headlines in 1983 for an act of heroism, as reported on December 1 in a Brunswick Times Record article, "Three Pownal Boy Scouts Honored for Warning Train." Reporter and Pownal resident Elsie Whidden wrote that the boys had been riding their bikes near the Canadian National Railroad track on the Allen Road overpass, when they noted that the track was twenty-four inches out of alignment. They waved the freight train to a stop, thus averting a serious accident.

Troop 107 continued to exist into the twenty-first century. From 1997 to 2001 Dennis Dyer was Scout Master. In 2003, under the leadership of Dennis Wheeler it merged with Freeport Troop 45, under Scout Master Tim Reed.

Boy Scouts honored for warning train. George Anderson, Boy Scout Master of Troop 107, presents Merit Certificates to l. to r.: Todd Richards, Troy Richards, and Perry Wiers. Photo: Don Hinkley, Brunswick Times Record, *December 1, 1983*

Ben Wheeler, son of Dennis and Joann Wheeler and member of Freeport Scout Troop 45, earned the rank of Eagle Scout at a Court of Honor Ceremony held at the First Parish Congregational Church on August 27, 2006. Ben's project, showing service and leadership to benefit the community, was to rebuild the handicapped ramp and deck at the church.

Girl Scouts

A scant two years after formation of the Boy Scouts of America, the Girl Scouts of the United States of America was established. The Brownies came into being in the 1920s, to allow younger girls to participate in scouting.

In Pownal, as with the boys, several Brownie and Girl Scout troops have flourished over the years, but unfortunately few having left records of their activities. Pamela DeMerchant and Judy Hilten led a Cadet Girl Scout troop in the early 1970s.

From 1987 to 1992 Lin White led Girl Scout Troop 188 through several busy and enjoyable years. As of 2008, Girl Scout Brownie Troop 222 is the only scouting group for girls active in Pownal. The troop leader is Leslie Searfoss, and co-leaders are Shannon Spaulding, Jesse Libby, and Elizabeth Munsen.

Girl Scout Brownie Troop 222 has an active group of ten girls. L. to r.: Kelcie McGonagle, Carlotta Ziervogel, Jasmen Libby, Anna Tryon, Amelia Searfoss, Natalie Bourassa, Shiloh Munsen, Halley Price, Brianna Spaulding, Sarah Metcalf.

Members of the Girl Scout Troop 188 present a map of Pownal Scenic and Historical Society's hearse house rose garden to the garden's planner June Tucci on April 9, 1991. Front row l. to r.: Martha Kucharik, Lisa Mitchell, Jill Barschdorf, Rebecca White, Back l. to r.: Leader Lin White and Pownal Scenic and Historical Society member, June Tucci.

Bradbury Mountain Owls

Members tour to Mt. Pocono, Pennsylvania on a Maine Line bus in 1993. L. to r.: Winnie and Lawrence Carter, Lois and Jim Sanders, Edna Menchen, Arlene Smith, Althea Blake, Theona Blackstone, Theona's friend, Jo Vosmus, Tom Vosmus and Ginny Hall.

The Bradbury Mountain Owls was organized in 1975, "to provide and maintain a cultural and recreational program for citizens of Pownal fifty-five years of age and over." Meetings are scheduled monthly at the First Parish Congregational Church and have included potluck luncheons followed by programs, lunch at favorite restaurants and at the local elementary school, special holiday celebrations, mystery trips for lunch and sightseeing on the school bus driven by Linwood Randall, and participation in Maine Line Tours outings to distant places. Over the years, the Owls have supported the Mallett Hall Building Fund, the Girl Scouts, and the Cancer Society. They have contributed to the Freeport-Pownal Christmas Project (later Freeport Community Services), and they continue to support members who are ill or otherwise need assistance.

Records are incomplete, but several members have served as officers for long periods of time. Notable are: presidents Alice Morrill (1985-90), Emmy Hogue (1990-93), and Joe Johnson (1994-2005), and secretary Althea Blake (1985-2000). According to current acting president Arlene Smith, "The future of the Owls is uncertain as membership has declined, perhaps because potential members today seem less interested in joining a formal seniors' organization."

Joe Johnson, club president for eleven years, leaves nothing but the shell behind as the Owls dine at Holbrooks' Lobster Shack in 2001.

Bradbury Mountain Arts

Reflecting the changing nature of Pownal society, Bradbury Mountain Arts (BMA) was founded in 1999 by a small group of local artists to provide a nurturing and collaborative environment in which to create and exhibit their work. The membership has since expanded to a seventeen-member guild that includes artists from surrounding communities. Although they work in a variety of mediums and come from diverse backgrounds, they all bring to their work a love and appreciation of living in an inspirational setting.

Monthly meetings of BMA usually take the form of a potluck supper followed by a guest speaker, a slide show, or a hands-on activity. A seasonal showcase is the annual Holiday Show held in early December at Mallett Hall. The 2008 show will mark the tenth anniversary of this popular event, where members exhibit and sell their creations. Many of the artists also routinely show and sell their work in galleries up and down the coast of Maine and beyond. In addition, BMA hosts Pownal Arts Night, a public event that features the arts, music, and talents of Pownal community members in a cabaret setting.

Members of BMA have held workshops and classes open to the community. The group sponsors a Community Arts Scholarship. This award has been used to send students to Fiddlehead Center for the Arts. It also has supplemented art and craft classes for residents and at Pownal Elementary School.

Members of Bradbury Mountain Arts 2007. Front row l. to r.: Evelyn Snow (evergreen wreath & garland maker), Nancy Greenleaf (weaver), Andrea van Voorst van Beest (painter & print maker), Liza Nichols (sailcloth totes), Kathy Hogue (jewelry), John Bowdren (painter). Back row l. to r.: Luther Snow (evergreen wreath & garland maker), Jeff Raymond (wood turner), John Bourassa (potter), Alan Bradstreet (wood artist), Lois Strickland Pervier (painter), Jan Pieter van Voorst van Beest (photographer). Not pictured: Erin Hogue (jewelry), Helen Warren (painter), Peter Asselyn (wood turner), Deb Cluchey (fiber artist), Sharon Townshend (ceramic artist & sculptor). Photo: Jan Pieter van Voorst van Beest

Pownal Land Trust

Land Trust officers for 2007 seated l. to r.: Co-Vice President Alix Hopkins, President Sam Merrill, Secretary-Treasurer Alan "Bo" Chesney, Co-Vice President Rosemary Whitney. Board of Directors, standing, l. to r.: Matt Bolinder, Suzanne Crowell, Chris Ayres, Tom Godfrey, and Mark Sheldon. Not pictured: Fred Fauver.

"Since 1989, the Pownal Land Trust has worked to preserve for future generations Pownal's fields and forest as we know them – to nurture the wildlife habitat and to share our land for the enjoyment of a variety of users. Using a combination of state funding through Land For Maine's Future Board, conservation easements and private donations of both land and money, we hope to preserve Pownal's character for future generations of hikers, snowmobilers, cross country skiers, equestrians, snowshoers, hunters, birders and other nature lovers wherever possible." So wrote Alix Hopkins and Rosemary Whitney, co-presidents of the Pownal Land Trust, in a letter to neighbors dated November 7, 2005.

The first project for the Land Trust involved the preservation of land surrounding the Knight Farm, land that became available following the death of Wilma Knight. Through Land Trust efforts, the Land For Maine's Future (LMF) Board agreed on August 7, 1990 to purchase 100 acres of Knight woodland adjoining the southern boundary of Bradbury Mountain State Park. They also purchased and added to the park another 132 acres known as the Spiegel property.

The Land Trust efforts were led by William Ginn who reported that purchase of these lands was "critical to forming 'a necklace' of trails, and to protect the view from Bradbury's 485-foot peak." The land was sold for $400,000, with the

Land Trust funding $225,000, Maine Parks & Recreation funding $150,000, and the Town and Land Trust funding $25,000. The Knight farmhouse and surrounding fields remain under private ownership, with a conservation easement to protect the surrounding fields from development.

In 2000, the Land Trust under the leadership of William Ginn, Jo D. Saffeir, Christopher Ayres, Alix Hopkins and Rosemary Whitney applied for a $840,000 grant from the LMF Board to

Alix Hopkins, 2004 Co-President and Chair of the Tryon celebration, visits with luncheon guests. Photo: Christopher Ayres.

purchase 500 acres of open space between Bradbury Mountain State Park and the public lands at Pineland. This purchase was to be a step toward linking the trails of the Park with those at Pineland to enhance public recreation. The grant was awarded on January 3, 2001, and members of the Land Trust partnered with members of the Bradbury-Pineland Corridor Project to begin developing the project. Additional grants from the Maine Outdoor Heritage Fund and the Casco Bay Estuary Project Habitat Protection Fund were key to moving ahead.

One of the key parcels in the 500 acres was owned by the Tryon family, and on October 24, 2004 a town-wide celebration was held honoring that family for the arrangement whereby 185 acres of family land became, as Alix Hopkins stated, "the key piece to the corridor, because of the mountain, its long-held family land and its beauty."

The Land Trust continues to direct its efforts toward land acquisition and easements for the corridor. They also maintain fields and trailheads as they strive to protect and enhance public recreation opportunities. At a September 2007 town meeting, voters approved accepting a $700 gift from the Trust to fund a needs assessment consultation for GIS mapping, a geographical aid the Trust feels will be of great help to the town in the future.

Rosemary Whitney (left) 2004 Co-President and Jack Rand (1924-2007), cartographer and geologist, explain land layout at the Tryon celebration. Photo: Christopher Ayres.

Pownal Scenic and Historical Society

Responding to a national call to "clean up and save" triggered by Senator Edmund Muskie's 1970 Earth Day event, Marjorie Mason led local efforts, as she said, "to improve the town's appearance and to preserve its historical heritage." She wrote in the *Shopping Notes* in April that, "Mother Nature gave our town an abundance of natural beauty… Let's all meet at the elementary school and see how we can help keep it beautiful."

Armed with literature from the state titled *If You Don't, Who Will*, Marjorie moved fast on two fronts: a town clean up and history preservation. Six people attended that initial meeting. Later that year, ten founding members established the Pownal Scenic and Historical Society, whose name aptly expressed Marjorie's two concerns. By the end of the summer, membership had grown to twenty-four, and they were fo on scenic efforts and fund raising to su their many plans. Initial efforts inc cleanup of Mallett Hall's first floor and gro installation of a bulletin board for postir nouncements (rather than nailing them o door), placement of street signs around planting crown vetch to prevent soil erosion of banks in town center, encouraging property owners to collect roadside litter around their homes, and a major effort, working with the National Guard, to remove junked cars from properties in town.

Marjorie's initial success at historical preservation was to locate Pownal's 1878 hearse and bring it back home. It was then housed in a town storage building that was in need of much repair. The town deeded this building to the so-

Founder of PSHS Marjorie Mason is pictured here in 1981 attending the museum open house and exhibit of "Mining in Pownal". A grant from the Maine Council for the Humanities and Public Policy funded the exhibit.

Marjorie Alward Mason (1913-1982), wife of Carl Mason and mother of George and Kathryne, founded the Pownal Scenic and Historical Society in 1970. Marjorie served as president for five years and was one of the authors of Pownal, A Rural Maine History, *published in 1977. She was a member of the First Parish Congregational Church, the Granite Grange, the Bradbury Mountain Owls, and the Conservation Commission. For many years, Marjorie operated a nursery school for local children to prepare them for elementary school. She worked tirelessly on fundraising for the move from one-room schools to the new SAD 62 facility.*

Authors of Pownal, A Rural Maine History *are pictured here in 1977 reviewing the recently published edition. L. to r.: Mary Goodwin, Sherry Dietrich, Marjorie Mason, Kathryne Moore, Donna Boyles.*

The 1997 Pumpkinfest served to showcase the restoration of Pownal's 1878 horse-drawn hearse. Reproduction oil lanterns and whip were purchased to complete the project. A generous gift from Carl Mason, in honor of his late wife Marjorie, made the restoration possible. Pictured are those who labored on the project. Seated l. to r.: Arthur Stackhouse, Donna Boyles, Mary Pat Bowen, Janice Roberts. Standing l. to r.: Jim Boyles, Tom Bowen, Judy Adcock. Not pictured: Craig Dietrich. Photo by James Saunders.

ciety, and its restoration began in 1972. The hearse now had a home, but required extensive restoration itself. Not until 1996 was the society able to hire a conservator and begin bringing it back to its original condition. Much of this work, including the acquisition of replacement lanterns, was financially supported by Marjorie's husband Carl in her memory.

Marjorie's next big project was to have the society publish a town history. This project took time to realize, as the society had no archives. So the call went out: "Do you have any pictures of Pownal's past that we could copy?" Town, state and national records were researched, residents were interviewed and their life stories transcribed, town cemeteries were indexed, architectural and deed research was begun, and the society proceeded to write and publish *Pownal, A Rural Maine History*. Along the way, the Hodsdon school site was deeded to the society and a marker was installed, and the Jacob Randall homestead was placed in the National Register of Historic Places. Book committee members Donna Boyles, Sherry Dietrich, Mary Goodwin, Marjorie Mason, and Kathryne Moore labored for two years prior to publication in 1977. The original copies sold out in 2006. Recently a second printing, with an updated Veterans list, has become available.

In 1980, the town gave the society use of the first floor kitchen room in Mallett Hall to use as a museum and town record center. After restoration, it was opened in July 1981 with a major display of Pownal's granite industry, funded in part by the Maine Humanities Council. Following Marjorie's death in 1982, the museum was

Society Cemetery Committee members Sherry Dietrich (left) and Janice West record epitaphs at the York Cemetery during the summer of 2007. Not pictured: Carrie Kivela.

The heritage plant sale held on Saturday May 16, 2006 was the society's most successful fundraiser to date. Workers were, front row l. to r.: Joan Stackhouse, Andrea van Voorst van Beest, Alix Hopkins, Carol Cyr, Donna Boyles. Middle: Arthur Stackhouse, Cathy Spencer, Johnna White, Lilyan Forbes, Jane Mittel. Back row l. to r.: Lin White, Joe Raymond, Judy Adcock (barely visible), Linda McMahon, Luther Snow. Not pictured: Jen Kaplan, Joe Johnson, Jim Boyles.

2008 Officers of the Pownal Scenic and Historical Society. Seated l. to r.: Jen Blackstone Kaplan, secretary; Donna Fulton Boyles, president; Jane Mittel, vice president. Standing: James Boyles, treasurer.

named in her honor. In recognition of her commitment to education, each year at the eighth grade graduation ceremony, a monetary award named for her is given to the student who excelled in social studies and history.

The society's support and membership has continued to grow, as it closely follows its original stated purposes. The archive of photographs, documents, interviews, news clippings, and diaries, has increasingly provided resources for research, program development, and publications. The collection is managed by Donna Boyles and Sherry Dietrich. The museum houses objects of historical interest, displays, and some of the society's records. Care of the hearse house and hearse, which date to 1834 and 1878 respectively, and which are located beside the Center cemetery, is overseen by committee co-chairs, Jim Boyles and Arthur Stackhouse. Three gardens planted with heritage roses and perennials are maintained by the society: the Hodsdon one-room school site tended by Bill and Thelma DeWitt, the Hearse house rose garden tended by Donna Boyles and Jane Mittel, and the Mallett Hall garden tended by Jane Mittel, Sherry Dietrich, Carol and Sarah Cyr, Andrea van Voorst van Beest, Carrie Kivela and Donna Boyles. The Cemetery Committee of Sherry Dietrich, Janice West and Carrie Kivela, has re-inventoried and recorded epitaphs on ten of Pownal's eleven cemeteries. Currently, they are working on Pownal's largest and most active burial site, the Elmwood cemetery. The society, having been instrumental in placing Mallett Hall in the National Register of Historic Places, has been involved in restoration plans for the building and has contributed financially to both the addition and original building.

The major source of funding for society activities has come from its very successful heritage plant sales, begun in 1990. These events are held biennially at Mallett Hall on the third Saturday of May and have become very popular with area residents. Jane Mittel and Donna Boyles co-chair the effort, with over forty members contributing plant materials and help. Undoubtedly, the most ambitious project recently undertaken by the society was the writing and publication in 2008 of the town history titled *On Pownal Time – One Hundred Years In A Rural Maine Town – 1908 to 2008*, the book you are now holding.

Appendix I: Elected Town Officers 1908-2008

NOTE
For the year-ranges given (except where otherwise stated), service begins in March of the first year given and ends in March of the last year given.

Board of Selectmen, Assessors, and Overseers of the Poor

1907-1908	Harlan B. True, Mellen Tryon, William A Brown
1908-1909	Harlan B. True, William A. Brown, Frank Lobdell
1909-1910	Mellen Tryon, William A. Brown, Oscar L. Jordon
1910-1912	Harlan B. True, William A. Brown, Oscar L. Jordon
1912-1913	Dr. S. Addison Vosmus, William A. Brown, Oscar L. Jordon
1913-1914	Dr. S. Addison Vosmus, Mellen Tryon, H. W. Loring
1914-1915	Dr. S. Addison Vosmus, Conrad S. Snow, Fred W. Allen
1915-1918	Dr. S. Addison Vosmus, Charles P. Heywood, C. L. Fickett
1918-1919	Charles P. Heywood, C. L. Fickett, Eben Nevins
1919-1920	Charles P. Heywood, Eben Nevins, Claude L. Snow
1920-1921	Eben Nevins, William A. Brown, Oscar L. Jordon
1921-1922	William A. Brown, Oscar L. Jordon, William J. Pervier
1922-1923	Oscar L. Jordon, William J. Pervier, Stephen W. Libby
1923-1925	Oscar L. Jordon, William J. Pervier, Claude L. Snow
1925-1926	William J. Pervier, Claude L. Snow, Henry T. Sweetser
1926-1927	Claude L. Snow, Henry T. Sweetser, S. W. Libby
1927-1928	S. W. Libby, Joseph H. Periver, Francis C. Handy
1928-1930	Joseph H. Pervier, S. W. Libby, Philip R. Tryon
1930-1931	Joseph H. Pervier, S. W. Libby, M. J. Whitcher
1931-1932	Joseph H. Pervier, M. J. Whitcher, P. O. Decoster
1932-1933	J. W. Ramsdell, S. W. Libby, V. S. Litchfield
1933-1934	J. W. Ramsdell, H. S. Allen, V. S. Litchfield
1934-1935	Robert A. Smith, Philip R. Tryon, V. S. Litchfield
1935-1936	Philip R. Tryon, V. S. Litchfield, Merton S. Larrabee
1936-1938	Lauren H. Tuttle, Merton S. Larrabee, Leon R. Carleton
1938-1939	Lauren H. Tuttle, Philip R. Tryon, Algernon D. Whitcher
1939-1940	Lauren H. Tuttle, Philip R. Tryon, Robert H. Hodsdon
1940-1942	Lauren H. Tuttle, Philip R. Tryon, Josiah K. Perry
1942-1943	Lauren H. Tuttle, Philip R. Tryon, Albert H. Blackstone, Sr.
1943-1944	Laurence W. Snow, Donald Keith, J. Noyes Mitchell
1944-1945	Donald Keith, J. Noyes Mitchell, Lauren H. Tuttle
1945-1946	J. Noyes Mitchell, Lauren H. Tuttle, Laurence W. Snow
1946-1948	Lauren H. Tuttle, Virgil E. Best, Stephen W. Libby
1948-1949	Virgil E. Best, Earl R. Babbidge, Walter E. Slocum
1949-1951	Lauren H. Tuttle, Laurence W. Snow, Walter E. Slocum
1951-1952	Lauren H. Tuttle, Edward D. Menchen, Walter E. Slocum (resigned), George D. Daniels (appointed)
1952-1953	Lauren H. Tuttle, George D. Daniels, Edward D. Menchen
1953-1954	George D. Daniels, Edward D. Menchen, Lawrence E. Carter
1954-1955	George D. Daniels, Lauren H. Tuttle, Virgil E. Best
1955-1956	Edward D. Menchen, Lawrence E. Carter, Laurence W. Snow
1956-1957	Lauren H. Tuttle, Laurence W. Snow, Philip R. Tryon
1957-1958	Philip R. Tryon, Elbert K. Babbidge, Lauren H. Tuttle
1958-1960	Philip R. Tryon, Elbert K. Babbidge, Everett J. Petto
1960-1961	Philip R. Tryon, Everett J. Petto, Laurence W. Snow
1961-1966	Edward D. Menchen, Lawrence E. Carter, Robert E. Slocum
1966-1970	Edward D. Menchen, James A. Sanders, Edward L. Mitchell
1970-1971	Edward D. Menchen, James A. Sanders, Frederick W. Stasinowsky
1971-1972	Edward D. Menchen, James A. Sanders, Frederick W. Stasinowsky, Joseph R. Mitchell
1972-1973	Frederick W. Stasinowsky, Joseph R. Mitchell, Edward D. Menchen
1973-1974	Edward D. Menchen, Joseph R. Mitchell, Frederick W. Stasinowsky
1974-1977	Joseph R. Mitchell, Frederick W. Stasinowsky, Gerald H. Rolfe

1977-1989	Gerald H. Rolfe, Frederick W. Stasinowsky, Craig A. Vosmus
1989-1993	Gerald H. Rolfe, Frederick W. Stasinowsky, Lauren H. Tuttle, Jr.
1993-1994	Lauren H. Tuttle, Jr., Frederick W. Stasinowsky, Arnold F. Blackstone
1994-1995	Lauren H. Tuttle, Jr., Arnold F. Blackstone, Susan C. Mack
1995-1996	Arnold F. Blackstone, Susan C. Mack, Lauren H. Tuttle, Jr.
1996-1999	Susan C. Mack, Lauren H. Tuttle, Jr., Robert C. Greenlaw
1999-2003	Susan C. Mack, Lauren H. Tuttle, Jr., James H. Briggs
2003-2004	James H. Briggs, Philip M. Wentworth, Robert C. McMahon
2004-2005	James H. Briggs, Philip M. Wentworth, Sean O'Donnell Bennett
2005-2007	Philip M. Wentworth, William E. Crain, James H. Briggs
2007-2008	William E. Crain, Matthew Allen, Timothy Giddinge
2008-	Timothy Giddinge, Matthew Allen, Alfred Fauver

Clerk *(appointed after 2007)*

1883-1915	True Warren
1915-1930	Mellen Tryon
1930-1971	Claude L. Snow
1971-1975	Barbara Cain
1975-2002	Edna S. Menchen
2002-2007	Kelly M. Wentworth
2007-2008	Kathleen Malloy

Tax Collector *(appointed after 2009)*

1884-1933	Alroy Noyes
1933-1941	Alvin L. Tryon
1941-1964	Joseph Pervier
1964-1965	Maxine Gowen
1965-1967	Alice B. Smith
1967-1969	Anna C. Slocum
1969-1970	Robert E. Slocum
1970-1973	Ann P. Blaisdell
1973-1978	James E. Salisbury
1978-1990	Edward D. Menchen
1990-2001	Edna S. Menchen
2001-2008	Kelly M. Wentworth

Treasurer *(appointed after 2008)*

1884-1933	Alroy Noyes
1933-1941	Alvin L. Tryon
1941-1964	Joseph Pervier
1964-1967	Alice B. Smith
1967-1969	Anna C. Slocum
1969-1970	Robert E. Slocum
1970-1973	Ann P. Blaisdell
1973-1974	James E. Salisbury
1974-1990	Edward D. Menchen
1990-1995	Edna S. Menchen
1995-2002	Gerald H. Rolfe
2002-2008	Kelly M. Wentworth

Road Commissioner *(appointed after 1987)*

1907-1917	Ernest Tuttle
1917-1918	William A. Brown
1918-1919	Henry T. Sweetser
1919-1920	C. L. Fickett
1920-1931	Ernest Tuttle
1931-1932	C. L. Fickett
1932-1933	Ernest Tuttle
1933-1935	Earl C. Libby
1935-1936	Daniel W. Newcomb
1936-1943	C. L. Fickett
1943-1947	Everett A. Cates
1947-1948	Isaac Bowen
1948-1951	Thomas J. Vosmus
1951-1952	Earl C. Libby
1952-1953	Ernest Fickett
1953-1954	Thomas J. Vosmus
1954-1959	Roy C. Tufts
1959-1960	Thomas J. Vosmus
1960-1961	Fred St. Pierre
1961-1964	Thomas J. Vosmus
1964-1987	Carl I. Knight
1987-2003	Darrel Thurber
2003-2008	Shawn M. Bennett

Moderator *(Dates here refer to Town Meeting date)*

1907 thru 1911	Harlan B. True
1912 thru 1914	Oliver Stover
1915 thru 1919	Henry W. Loring
1920	Dr. S. Addison Vosmus
1921 thru 1922	Henry W. Loring
1923 thru 1924	Charles P. Heywood
1925 thru 1928	Joseph H. Pervier
1929	Charles P. Heywood
1930	Francis C. Handy
1931 thru 1934	Oliver O. Stover
1935 thru 1941	Joseph H. Pervier
1942 thru 1944	Laurence W. Snow
1945	Philip R. Tryon
1946 thru 1950	Joseph H. Pervier
1951	Philip R. Tryon
1952 thru 1955	Joseph H. Pervier
1956 thru 1962	Philip R. Tryon
1963 thru 1970	Robert E. Slocum
1971 thru 1972	Philip R. Tryon
1973	Edward L. Mitchell
1974	Joseph R. Mitchell
1975	Edward L. Mitchell
1976 thru 1977	Laurence W. Snow
1978 thru 1982	Edward D. Menchen
1983 thru 1990	James A. Sanders
1991	Laurence W. Snow
1992 thru 2008	James G. Boyles

Fire Ward/Fire Chief

1914-1915	Ernest Tuttle	1923-1926	Leigh W. Loring
1915-1916	Daniel W. Newcomb	1926-1959	Joseph H. Pervier
1916-1920	Thomas F. Noyes	1959-1982	Earle A. Blake
1920-1923	Levi S. Berry	1982-2003	Lester A. Blake
		2003-2007	David Malone
		2007-2008	Scott Pollock

Cemetery Commissioner

1926-1931	Charles P. Heywood, George P. Cushman, C. L. Fickett
1931-1933	Charles P. Heywood, C. L. Fickett, Oscar L. Jordan
1933-1938	Charles P. Heywood, Oscar L. Jordan, George P. Mitchell
1938-1940	Oscar L. Jordan, Joseph H. Pervier, Harry Sawyer
1940-1943	Oscar L. Jordan, Joseph H. Pervier, J. Noyes Mitchell
1943-1949	Joseph H. Pervier, J. Noyes Mitchell, Alvin L. Tryon
1949-1950	Joseph H. Pervier, J. Noyes Mitchell, William Mitchell
1950-1952	Joseph H. Pervier, William Mitchell, Thomas J. Vosmus
1952-1956	Joseph H. Pervier, Thomas J. Vosmus, Stephen W. Libby
1956-1959	Joseph H. Pervier, Thomas J. Vosmus, Roy C. Tufts
1959-1964	Joseph H. Pervier, Thomas J. Vosmus, Edward D. Menchen
1964-1969	Joseph H. Pervier, Thomas J. Vosmus, Ralph A. Vosmus
1969-1976	Joseph H. Pervier, Ralph A. Vosmus, Michael C. Menchen
1976-1981	Joseph H. Pervier, Ralph A. Vosmus, Donald C. Cain
1981-1983	Ralph A. Vosmus, Donald C. Cain, Paul W. Hamilton
1983-1984	Ralph A. Vosmus, Donald C. Cain, Paul W. Hamilton
1984-1993	Ralph A. Vosmus, Paul W. Hamilton, Kevin L. Thurber
1993-1999	Craig A. Vosmus, Paul W. Hamilton, Kirk T. Vosmus
1999-2000	Craig A. Vosmus, Kirk T. Vosmus, Lorraine Merrill
2000-2003	Craig A. Vosmus, Lorraine Merrill, Scott D. Kaplan
2003-2005	Craig A. Vosmus, Lorraine Merrill, Susan C. Mack
2005-2008	Craig A. Vosmus, Lorraine Merrill, Duane Snow

Superintending School Committee *(until 1969)*, Directors of SAD 62 *(after 1969)*

1907-1908	Merton E. Flood, Arthur Noyes, George B. Hodsdon
1908-1909	Arthur Noyes, George B. Hodsdon, Merton E. Flood
1909-1910	George B. Hodsdon, Merton E. Flood, Allan P. Corey
1910-1911	Merton E. Flood, Allan P. Corey, Rev. Daniel A. Tuttle
1911-1912	Charles P. Heywood, Rev. Daniel A. Tuttle, Dr. S. Addison Vosmus
1912-1913	Rev. Daniel A. Tuttle, Dr. S. Addison Vosmus, William A. Brown
1913-1914	Dr. S. Addison Vosmus, William A. Brown, Rev. Daniel A. Tuttle
1914-1915	William A. Brown, Rev. Daniel A. Tuttle, C. Roy Marston
1915-1916	Rev. Daniel A. Tuttle, Eben Nevins
1916-1917	Merton E. Flood, Eben Nevins, C. L. Dow
1917-1918	Eben Nevins, S. W. Libby, C. L. Dow
1918-1919	George B. Hodsdon, Rev. Daniel A. Tuttle, S. W. Libby
1919-1920	S. W. Libby, Rev. Daniel A. Tuttle, George B. Hodsdon
1920-1921	Rev. Daniel A. Tuttle, George B. Hodsdon, Oscar L. Jordon
1921-1922	George B. Hodsdon, Oscar L. Jordon, Sadie L. Menchen
1922-1923	Oscar L. Jordon, Sadie L. Menchen, Maurice E. Merrill
1923-1924	Sadie L. Menchen, Maurice E. Merrill, Dr. S. Addison Vosmus
1924-1925	Maurice E. Merrill. S. Addison Vosmus, Emma L. Pervier
1925-1926	Dr. S. Addison Vosmus, Emma L. Pervier, William A. Brown
1926-1927	Emma L. Pervier, William A. Brown, Dr. S. Addison Vosmus
1927-1928	William A. Brown, Dr. S. Addison Vosmus, Villa M. Snow, William J. Pervier
1928-1929	William J. Pervier, Villa M. Snow, Philip R. Tryon
1929-1930	Villa M. Snow, Philip R. Tryon, William J. Pervier
1930-1931	Philip R. Tryon, William J. Pervier, Vina M. Vosmus

1931-1932	William J. Pervier, Vina M. Vosmus, H. K. Newcomb
1932-1933	Vina M. Vosmus, H. K. Newcomb, George B. Hodsdon
1933-1934	H. K. Newcomb, George B. Hodsdon, Lena Cotterall
1934-1935	George B. Hodsdon, Lena Cotterall, Rev. Alfred T. Ware
1935-1936	Lena Cotterall, Rev. Alfred T. Ware, Oscar L. Jordon
1936-1937	Rev. Alfred T. Ware, Oscar L. Jordon, Josiah K. Perry, Emma L. Pervier
1937-1938	Oscar L. Jordan, Josiah K. Perry, Emma L. Pervier
1938-1939	Josiah K. Perry, Emma L. Pervier, Stephen W. Libby
1939-1940	Emma L. Pervier, Stephen W. Libby, Josiah K. Perry
1940-1941	Stephen W. Libby, Josiah K. Perry, Alverna Newcomb
1941-1942	Josiah K. Perry, Alverna Newcomb, Fred Phillips
1942-1943	Alverna Newcomb, Fred Phillips, Harry Morrill
1943-1944	Fred Phillips, Harry Morrill, Emma Hall
1944-1945	Fred Phillips, Edward D. Menchen, Robert Hodsdon, Lewis Martin
1945-1946	Edward D. Menchen, Robert Hodsdon, Pearl Flint
1946-1947	Robert Hodsdon, Pearl Flint, Josephine Snow (resigned), Edward D. Menchen (appointed)
1947-1948	Pearl Flint, Percy Wentworth, Carl Libby
1948-1949	Pearl Flint, Percy Wentworth, Carl Libby
1949-1950	Carl Libby, Percy Wentworth, Pearl Flint
1950-1951	Percy Wentworth, Pearl Flint, Robert E. Slocum
1951-1952	Percy Wentworth, Robert E. Slocum, Earle A. Blake
1952-1953	Earle A. Blake, Percy Wentworth, Ruth B. Keith
1953-1954	Earle A. Blake, Ruth B. Keith, Percy Wentworth
1954-1955	Ruth B. Keith, Percy Wentworth, Earle A. Blake
1955-1956	Percy Wentworth, Earle A. Blake, Evangeline T. Lee
1956-1957	Earle A. Blake, Evangeline T. Lee, Richard Haskell
1957-1958	Evangeline T. Lee, Dorothy Emmertz, Earle A. Blake
1958-1959	Dorothy Emmertz, Earle A. Blake, Robert E. Slocum
1959-1960	Earle A. Blake, Robert E. Slocum, Bruce Carroll
1960-1961	Robert E. Slocum, Bruce Carroll, Earle A. Blake
1961-1962	Bruce Carroll, Earle A. Blake, Robert E. Slocum
1962-1963	Earle A. Blake, Robert E. Slocum, Bruce Carroll
1963-1964	Robert E. Slocum, Bruce Carroll, James A. Sanders
1964-1965	Bruce Carroll, James A. Sanders, Evangeline T. Lee
1965-1966	James A. Sanders, Evangeline T. Lee, Edward L. Mitchell
1966-1967	Edward L. Mitchell, Evangeline T. Lee, Laurence W. Snow
1967-1968	Robert E. Slocum, Evangeline T. Lee, Edward L. Mitchell, Lawrence E. Carter, Laurence W. Snow
1968-1969	Edward L. Mitchell, Lawrence E. Carter, Laurence W. Snow, Faye E. Hilton, Evelyn Tryon
1969-1970	Edward L. Mitchell, Lawrence E. Carter, Laurence W. Snow, Faye E. Hilton, Evelyn Tryon
1970-1971	Edward L. Mitchell, Faye E. Hilton, Evelyn Tryon, Jarrett J. Staton, Paul Hamilton
1971-1972	Edward L. Mitchell, Jarrett J. Staton, Evelyn Tryon, Paul Hamilton, James A. Sanders
1972-1973	Jarrett J. Staton, Paul Hamilton, Donelle V. Nielsen, William B. Cordell, Dennis D. Pinkham
1973-1974	Jarrett J. Staton, Donelle V. Nielsen, William B. Cordell, Dennis D. Pinkham, Patricia A. Adams
1974-1975	William B. Cordell, Barbara Perrine, Jarrett J. Staton, James A. Sanders, Patricia A. Adams, James G. Boyles
1975-1976	James G. Boyles, Patricia A. Adams, Lauren H. Tuttle, Brewster Staples, Jane H. Mittel
1976-1977	James G. Boyles, Lauren H. Tuttle, Brewster Staples, Jane H. Mittel, James A. Sanders, Arnold F. Blackstone
1977-1978	Arnold F. Blackstone, Jane H. Mittel, Brewster Staples, Joseph A. Raymond, Stephen V. Litchfield
1978-1979	Arnold F. Blackstone, Jane H. Mittel, Joseph A. Raymond, Stephen V. Litchfield, George F. Bookataub
1979-1980	Arnold F. Blackstone, Jane H. Mittel, Joseph A. Raymond, Stephen V. Litchfield, George F. Bookataub
1980-1981	Jane H. Mittel, Arnold F. Blackstone, Stephen V. Litchfield, George F. Bookataub, James H. Graham
1981-1982	Jane H. Mittel, Arnold F. Blackstone, James H. Graham, George F. Bookataub, Everett F. Johnson Jr.
1982-1983	Arnold F. Blackstone, James H. Graham, George F. Bookataub, Everett F. Johnson, Jr., Robert F. Thurrell
1983-1984	Arnold F. Blackstone, Everett F. Johnson, Jr., George F. Bookataub, Robert F. Thurrell, James H. Graham
1984-1985	Arnold F. Blackstone, Robert F. Thurrell, Everett F. Johnson, Jr., James H. Graham, Luther T. Estabrook
1985-1986	Everett F. Johnson, Jr., James H. Graham, Luther T. Estabrook, Sandra D. Randall, Joan B. Mueller
1986-1987	Luther T. Estabrook, Joan B. Mueller, Lawrence T. Lonegan, Linda A. Rowbottom, Joseph A. Raymond
1987-1988	Luther T. Estabrook, Joan B. Mueller, Lawrence T. Lonegan, Linda A. Rowbottom, Eleanor L. Ginn
1988-1989	Luther T. Estabrook, Allen H. Greenleaf, Joan B. Mueller, Eleanor L. Ginn, Nancy A. Bennis
1989-1990	Luther T. Estabrook, Allen H. Greenleaf, Joan B. Mueller, Eleanor L. Ginn, Nancy A. Bennis
1990-1991	Joan B. Mueller, Nancy A. Bennis, Caroline C. Hyde, Allen H. Greenleaf, Ronald R. Hodsdon
1991-1992	Nancy A. Bennis, Caroline C. Hyde, James H. Briggs, Thomas E. Harlow, Jill Hutchins Lea

1992-1993	Nancy A. Bennis, Caroline C. Hyde, James H. Briggs, Thomas E. Harlow, Jill Hutchins Lea
1993-1994	Nancy A. Bennis, Thomas E. Harlow, James H. Briggs, Mildred D. Blanchard, Christopher J. White
1994-1995	Nancy A. Bennis, Christopher J. White, Mildred D. Blanchard, Robert C. McMahon, Susan N. Thompson
1995-1996	Christopher J. White, Mildred D. Blanchard, Robert H. Farrington, Robert C. McMahon, Susan N. Thompson
1996-1997	Robert C. McMahon, Susan N. Thompson, Robert H. Farrington, James H. Briggs, Phyllis J. Jones
1997-1998	Robert C. McMahon, Phyllis J. Jones, James H. Briggs, Robert H. Farrington, Mari M. Loeschner
1998-1999	Robert C. McMahon, James H. Briggs, Phyllis J. Jones, Paul D. Schumann, Brian Tuttle
1999-2000	Paul D. Schumann, Robert C. McMahon, Brian Tuttle, Susan Jordan, C. Marsha Martino
2000-2001	Paul D. Schumann, Robert C. McMahon, Brian Tuttle, Susan Jordan, C. Marsha Martino
2001-2002	Paul D. Schumann, Susan Jordan, C. Marsha Martino, Robert C. McMahon, Brian Tuttle
2002-2003	Paul D. Schumann, C. Marsha Martino, Robert C. McMahon, Johnathan Morris, Brian Tuttle
2003-2004	Paul D. Schumann, C. Marsha Martino, Johnathan Morris, Brian Tuttle, Karen L. Badger
2004-2005	Paul D. Schumann, C. Marsha Martino, Johnathan Morris, Karen L. Badger, Amy M. Curry
2005-2006	Paul D. Schumann, C. Marsha Martino, Karen L. Badger, Amy M. Curry, Jennifer Blackstone Kaplan
2006-2007	Paul D. Schumann, Jennifer Blackstone Kaplan, Karen L. Badger, Amy M. Curry, Carol Cyr
2007-2008	Paul D. Schumann, Jennifer Blackstone Kaplan, Karen L. Badger, Amy M. Curry (resigned), Carol Cyr
2008-2009	Paul D. Schumann, Jennifer Blackstone Kaplan, Karen L. Badger, Carol Cyr,

Superintendent of Schools *(Not elected - dates here refer to school year)*

1908 thru 1909	Oliver O. Stover
1910 thru 1911	Conrad S. Snow
1912 thru 1914	Lauren H. Tuttle Sr.
1915 thru 1918	Dr. S. Addison Vosmus
1919 thru 1925	Frank H. Byram
1926 thru 1945	Ralph G. Oakes
1946 thru 1952	Howard D. Fowlie
1953 thru 1957	Hamilton B. Grant
1958 thru 1966	James B. Morrison Jr.
1967 thru 1968	Frank H. Harrison
1969	Gary C. Cairns
1970 thru 1980	Robert E. Cartmill
1981 thru 1985	Frances H. Hale
1986 thru 1992	Jon Gale
1993 thru 1996	Frank H. Harrison
1997 thru 1998	Michael Wood
1999 thru 2008	Joseph Feeney

Appendix II: Military Veterans

World War I

Allen, Frank
Bradbury, George Sr.
Burnham, Clarence
Cotton, Barrett
Derrington, William
Flood, Elmer
Hanscome, John
Hawkes, William
Johnson, James W. C.
Kimball, Clarence
Kimball, Harold
Knight, Kenneth
Lachance, Napoleon
Leonard, Horace
Libby, Earl
Lowell, Mary E.
Marsh, Phillip M.
Oba, Willie
Peterson, Carl
Pike, George
Sawyer, Harry
Smith, R. A.
Stubbs, Clyde
True, William
Tryon, Carl
Tryon, George
Tuttle, Charles
West, Arthur

World War II

Allen, Edward
Anderson, Oscar L.
Ayer, Vernon Earl
Best, Martin W. Jr.
Best, Virgil E.
Blackstone, Chester F.
Blackstone, George
Blake, Earle A.
Bradbury, Helen
Britt, Harry
Britt, John
Britt, Robert W.
Britt, Roy
Carter, John A.
Cass, Colin Creath
Cass, Delroy D.
Clark, Carol W.
Clark, Claude
Cotton, Austin
Cox, Richard M.
Currier, Irving
Currier, Owen
Cyr, Leo Alton
Darkis, George Henry
Darkis, Harold A.
Darkis, John Hiram
Davis, Harold
DeCoster, Robert
Edwards, Hall
Edwards, Walter H.
Emery, Leland Alvan
Emery, Merrill W. Jr.
Farrington, Herman
Fickett, Nathan
Field, Arthur Jr.
Flint, Milford M.
Frank, Melvin A.
Gallison, George R.
George, Lawrence
George, Lloyd
George, Philip
Giggey, Horton
Gilliam, Vernard
Glidden, Russel W.
Golding, James
Grant, Kenneth J.
Hall, Donald Irason
Hartwell, Calvin
Horne, Carlyle M.
Hustus, Walter Lewis
Jordan, Charles
Jordan, Malcom
Keith, Leon Earl
Keith, Scott
Kent, Willis E.
King, Harold B.
Lee, John Ellis
Leighton, Robert
Libby, Hiram
Libby, Kenneth J.
Libby, Scott
Litchfield, Donald R.
Malier, Esric S.
Menchen, Edward D.
Mitchell, Robert G.
Penley, Bertrand
Penley, Channing
Peterson, Donald E.
Pike, Harvey
Pollock, Earl
Quint, Franklin E.
Rand, John
Richards, Irvin
Ringrose, Walter
Ryder, Lawrence P.
Sanders, Crandall Jr.
Sanders, James A.
Schmidt, Walter
Small, Orland H.
Smith, Donald
Smith, Grace L.
Snow, Carleton E.
Snow, Raymond L.
Sommers, Burton E.
Spaulding, Dwight H.
Stanton, William
Stetson, Charles
Stimpson, Archie L.
Stone, George L. Jr.
Stone, Milton Starling
Stover, John
Sweetser, Austin
Sweetser, Elsie W.
Sylvester, Everett
Thurber, Arthur
Thurber, George
Thurber, Kenneth E.
Thurber, Marvin L.
Thurber, Shirley*
Trimm, Maurice C.
Turcotte, Maurice C.
Vosmus, Kenneth
Vosmus, Ralph Alan
Vosmus, Thomas H.
Vosmus, Vina
Wallace, James E. Jr.
Ward, Donald
Watson, Clyde Elroy
Wentworth, Paul
Whitcher, Daniel
Whitcher, William
Whitcomb, Janice
York, Calvin
York, George Jr.
York, Hartwell
York, Linwood
York, Stanley K.

* Certificate of Honorable War Service from FBI.

Korean War and Cold War Era

Alcott, Reginald
Allen, Ronald
Bieske, John F.
Blake, David
Bowie, Roger L.
Bradbury, George L. Jr.
Britt, Bernard
Britt, Donald
Britt, Robert
Capen, James I.
Cavanaugh, Richard V.
Colby, Caroline J.
DeWitt, William S.
Edwards, George W. Jr.
Foss, Ronald E. Jr.
Gilliam, Earle S.
Goss, Roland
Hibbard, Harold Jr.
Hicks, Jack E.
Hinkley, Harold G.
Irish, Vincent M.
Leighton, Harvey S.
Maltby, Miles H.
Mitchell, Harry W.
Mitchell, John N. Jr.
Mitchell, Joseph R.
Nolen, James H.
Pavasars, Viesturs
Raymond, Joseph
Ringrose, Harold F.
Rogers, Frank R.
Ryder, Kenneth A.
Sampson, David O.
Slocum, Gordon L.
Snow, Luther
Stackhouse, Arthur
Taylor, Otis O.
Tryon, Richard M.
Tufts, Roy C. Jr.
Tuttle, Lauren H. Jr.
Upton, Elaine R.
Weed, Percival E.
Wyman, Jack P.

Vietnam War Era

- Beard, Barry
- Best, Jerome M.
- Blackstone, Albert Jr.
- Blackstone, Arnold F.
- Bowman, Thomas E.
- Carey, Joseph L.
- Cheney, John
- Currier, David B.
- Daniels, James
- Darling, Paul E.
- Davis, Robert N.
- Davis, Theodore R.
- Dobson, Allen D.
- Foss, Donald E. Jr.
- Frost, Robert W.
- Golding, William
- Gordon, Ralph A. Jr.
- Goss, Peter W.
- Harlow, Garry H.
- Harlow, Peter F.
- Hawkins, David A.
- Heavel, Donna M.
- Hicks, Roger E.
- Hilton, Bruce E.
- Jackson, Brian
- Jewett, Terrance A.
- Jordan, Deane L.
- Jordan, William C.
- Keith, Stephen P.
- Lee, Michael
- Lewis, Carleton A.
- Lewis, Corliss
- Litchfield, Steven V.
- Lowell, Kenneth R.
- MacLean, Angus J.
- Malone, Allen F. Jr.
- Mason, George L.
- McCarthy, Bruce G.
- Menchen, Michael D.
- Menchen, Wendy C.
- Merrill, Larry A.
- Moore, Gerald M.
- Newell, Ronald E.
- Packard, Donald E.
- Packard, Ralph M.
- Purinton, Robert D.
- Russell, Francis E.
- Sanders, Roger B.
- Slocum, Robert H.
- Snow, Terry N.
- Spinney, Gary T.
- St. Pierre, Jack B.
- Staton, Frank M.
- Vosmus, Craig A.
- Weatherbee, Robert D.
- Wentworth, Douglas L.
- White, Christopher
- White, Ingram Jr.
- White, John C.
- White, Sherry M.
- Williams, Michael L.
- Williamson, Fred T.
- Wilson, Steven S.
- Yakimchuk, Charles J.

- Carter, Terry
- Goodwin, Stephen

Appendix III: SAD 62 Faculty & Staff 2007-2008

Administrative Services

Boucher, Diane: Accountant
Callnan, Kim: Special Ed. Secretary
Feeney, Joseph R.: Supintendent/Principal
Hartzell, Lynda: School Nurse
Nielson, Donelle: Administrative Secretary
Russell, Melissa: Office/Lunch Program Assistant

Teachers & Educational Technicians

Carkin, Joye: Pre K-K Teacher
Carter, Christine: Guidance/Spec. Services Grades 6-8
Crosman, Kari: Technology Coordinator
Donoghue, Jim: Physical Ed. & Health
Dupont, Erika: Middle School Teacher
Higgison, Chake: Art Teacher
Lambert, Karen: Speech/Language Teacher
McCullough, Andrew: Middle School Teacher
Moore, Elaine: Grade 5 Teacher
Mosher, Diana: Music, Band, Chorus, Mindstretch
Moulton, Beth: Middle School Teacher
Neill, Stephen: Grade 4 Teacher
Ordway, Kim: Educational Technician
Page, Cheryl: Educational Technician
Passmore, Diana: Special Ed. Grades Pre-5.
Pierce, Ann: Librarian
Shannon, Sara: Foreign Language Teacher
Slattery, Ann: Grade 2 Teacher
Welch, Tamia: Grade 1 Teacher
Wentworth, Barbara: Educational Technician
Woodard, Linda: Grade 3 Teacher

Non-instructional Staff

Borden, Tracy: Bus Driver
Coro, Deanna: Food Services
Duford, Armon: Custodian
Raymond, Breanne: Bus Driver/Custodian
Sylvain, Karen: Bus Driver

SOURCES

Abbreviations:
>*BTR*, Brunswick (Maine) Times Record
>*MST*, Maine Sunday Telegram
>*PPH*, Portland (Maine) Press Herald
>PSHS, Pownal Scenic and Historical Society – used to denote presence in archives

GENERAL

Archives of the Pownal Scenic and Historical Society. Pownal, Maine. PSHS.
Baier, Ursula, editor. *North Yarmouth 1680 – 1980*. 2nd Ed. Falmouth, Maine: Grace Press, 1991. PSHS.
Barringer, Richard, editor. *Changing Maine 1960 – 2010*. Gardiner, Maine: Tilbury House, 2004. PSHS.
Boyles, Donna F., Sherilyn Dietrich, Mary Goodwin, Marjorie Mason, and Kathryne Moore. *Pownal, A Rural Maine History*. Falmouth, Maine: Grace Press, 1977. PSHS.
Clark, Charles E., James S. Leamon, and Karen Bowden. *Maine in the Early Republic*. Hanover and London: Univ. Press of New England, 1988. PSHS.
Collection. *Archival Books*. Pownal, ME: PSHS. Vols. I to XXX.
Hubka, Thomas C. *Big House, Little House, Back House, Barn*. Hanover, New Hampshire: University Press of New England, 1984. PSHS.
Judd, Richard W., Edwin A. Churchill, and Joel W. Eastman. *Maine the Pine Tree State From Prehistory to the Present*. Orono, Maine: Univ. of Maine Press, 1995. PSHS.
Kimball, Richard S. *Pineland's Past – The First One Hundred Years*. Portsmouth, New Hampshire: Peter E. Randall Publisher, 2001. PSHS.
Latham, Ettie J. *History of the Town of Pownal*. Lewiston, Maine: Lewiston Journal Company, 1908. PSHS.
Linton, Calvin D., editor. *The Bicentennial Almanac 200 Years of America*. Nashville, Tennessee: Thomas Nelson Inc., 1975. PSHS.
Maine. *Maine Register State Year-Book and Legislative Manual #51*. Portland, Maine: Portland Directory Company, 1920. PSHS.
Maine. *Maine Register State Year-Book and Legislative Manual #67*. Portland, Maine: Fred L. Tower Companies, 1936. PSHS.
Merrill, Lincoln J. Jr., and Holly K. Hurd. *Images of America Around North Yarmouth*. Portsmouth, New Hampshire: Arcadia Publishing, 2006. PSHS.
Miller, James, and John Thompson. *Almanac of American History*. Washington, D.C.: National Geographic, 2005. PSHS.
Murphy, John K., executive editor. "1632 – 1982 Greater Portland Celebration 350 Special Edition." *Portland Evening Express*, May 29 1982. PSHS.
Pownal. *Annual Town Reports*. Pownal, Maine: Self-published, 1900 to 2007.
Pownal. *Land Use Codes*. Pownal, Maine: Self-published, June 19, 2000.
Pownal. *Personal Property Tax Records*. Pownal, Maine: Self-published, 1900 to 1970.
Pownal. *Town Clerks Records*. Pownal, Maine: Self-published, 1908 to 2007.
Wiley, Sarah, editor. *The Freeport Bicentennial Commemorative Journal*. Freeport, Maine: Village Press, 1989. PSHS.

CHAPTER 1 — A New Century

Anonymous. "Big Celebration At Pownal Today." *Lewiston Journal*, September 2, 1908. PSHS.
Anonymous. "Hand Crank Telephones Bow Out in Pownal." *N. E. Telephone & Telegraph Bulletin*, July 1948. PSHS.
Anonymous. "Oldest Tin Pedlar in America." Unknown Newspaper, July 25, 1939. PSHS.
Anonymous. "Pownal Centennial Celebration of the Town." *Daily Eastern Argus*, September 3, 1908. PSHS.
Anonymous. "Three Lives Sacrificed." *Daily Eastern Argus*, September 20, 1902. PSHS.
Bateman, L. C. "Reminiscenses of Pownal Oldtimers." *Lewiston Journal*, July 1907. PSHS.
Blackstone, Christina. "Living in Pownal Center 1930s – 1970s." Interview with Donna Boyles and Sherilyn Dietrich. October 13, 1975. PSHS.
Estes, Calvin E. "God's Country."*Pownal Annual Town Report*, 1995. PSHS.
Greene, Priscilla DeCoster. Private communication with Donna Boyles regarding the depression years. January 11, 2006.
Holt, Jeff. *The Grand Trunk in New England*. Toronto, Canada: Railfare Enterprises Limited, 1986.
Orent, Wendy. "Under the Strain – A Deadly Tandem." *MST*, April 24, 2005. PSHS.
Pervier, Joseph. "Remembering the 1920s – 1970s." Interview with Sherilyn Dietrich. February 18, 1976. PSHS.
Pratt, Louisa Merrill. "Greetings From California." Poem, 1908. PSHS.
Snow, Villa. "Memories of Living in Pownal 1920 – 1970." Interview with Sherilyn Dietrich. March 24, 1976. PSHS.
Vosmus, Thomas H. and Lois Vosmus Sanders. "Remembering 1920s – 2006." Interview with Sherilyn Dietrich and Jennifer Kaplan. January 19, 2006. PSHS.

CHAPTER 1 — War and Its Aftermath

Anonymous. "Maine's Hurricane Edna 1954." *Gannett Publishing Co. Pictorial Review*, 1954. PSHS.
Anonymous. "Pownal Celebrates Its 150th Anniversary." *MST*, August 31, 1958. PSHS.
Blackstone, Theona, and Katie Genovese. Private communication with Donna Boyles regarding family scrapbook of WWII. February 6, 2006.
Boyles, Donna. "Remembering Pownal in the 1950s." Script of presentation given March 17, 2005. PSHS.
Colby, Charlotte Edwards. Private communication with Donna Boyles regarding the Edwards family and hurricane Edna of 1954. March 18, 2006.
Daniels, James D. "Vietnam War Recollections." Interview with Craig Dietrich. December 11, 2006. PSHS.
Forbes, Lilyan. "Moving to Pownal in 1948." Interview with Sherilyn Dietrich. April 19, 2006. PSHS.
Goad, Meridith. "Relics Tell POW's Grueling Story." *PPH*, November 11, 2000. PSHS.
Goss, Josephine Whitcher. Private communication with Donna Boyles regarding Daniel Whitcher in WWII. February 2, 2006.
Litchfield, Stephen V. "It Was Interesting – Vietnam War." Interview with Craig Dietrich. November 14, 2006. PSHS.
Malone, Allan (Pat). "Vietnam War Experiences." Interview with Craig Dietrich. March 18, 2006. PSHS.
Reed, Marion Knight. Private communication with Donna Boyles regarding the Edwards family tragedy in 1954. 2003. PSHS.
Sanders, Lois Vosmus. Private communication with Donna Boyles regarding the Sanders family during WWII. January 30, 2006.
St. Pierre, Jack. "Vietnam War Experiences." Interview with Craig Dietrich. March 7, 2006. PSHS.
Stackhouse, Arthur. Private communication with Donna Boyles regarding Civil defense during WWII. August 12, 2006.
Stone, George Jr. "WWII Experiences." Interview with Craig Dietrich. July 3, 2006. PSHS.
Verrill, Shirley Thurber. Private communication with Donna Boyles regarding remembrances of WWII. February 23, 2006.
Verrill, Shirley, George Stone Jr., and Thelma Stone Chamberlain. "Pownal in the 1930s and 1940s." Interview with Donna Boyles and Sherilyn Dietrich. July 1, 2006. PSHS.
Vosmus, Craig. "Vietnam War Experiences." Interview with Craig Dietrich. March 28, 2006. PSHS.

CHAPTER 1 — Toward a Third Century

Boyles, James. "Severe Cut Back at Pownal School." *BTR*, July 31, 1975. PSHS.
Cox, Peter W. "Native and Newcomer." *Maine Times*, April 22, 1983. PSHS.
Geraghty, Gail. "Retirement Leaves Town Unequipped." *Portland Evening Express*, February 10, 1987. PSHS.
Pinkham, Alison. "School Board Makes Cuts." *BTR*, July 25, 1975. PSHS.
Richert, Evan. "Land Use in Maine – From Production to Consumption." In *Changing Maine 1960 – 2010*, edited by Richard Barringer. Gardiner, Maine: Tilbury House, 2004.
Saunders, James Jr. "Pownal Residents Join Pipeline Protest." *The Forecaster*, November 27, 1997. PSHS.

CHAPTER 2 — Farming

Albert, Ginger, and Michael Albert. Private communication with Donna Boyles regarding Venture Farm. July 12, 2007.
Alexander, Betsey. "Diary – Sept. 25, 1856 to Jan. 17, 1858." Transcribed and self-published by Arlene Litchfield Bradbury. 1970. PSHS.
Allen, Josephine Pervier. Private communication with Donna Boyles regarding Pervier family farming. December 8, 2006.
Allen, Josephine Pervier. *The Remarkable Couple*. Pownal, ME: Self-published, 1997. PSHS.
Best, Kim Rossbach. Private communication with Donna Boyles regarding the Rossbach dairy farm. August 18, 2007.
Blackstone, Albert Jr. "Farming." Interview with Jennifer Kaplan. March 16, 2006. PSHS.
Bradbury, Arlene Litchfield. Private communication with Donna Boyles regarding farming and the Litchfield family. December 26, 2006.
Carter, Nicole. Private communication with Donna Boyles regarding Upper Farm Alpacas. September 4, 2007.
Condon, Richard H. "Living in Two Worlds: Rural Maine in 1930." *Maine Historical Society Quarterly*, Fall 1985. PSHS.
Cotton, Austin. "Farming." Interview with Sherilyn Dietrich and Marjorie Sweetser. February 18, 1975. PSHS.
Davis, Virginia Cates. "Farming." Interview with Donna Boyles and Sherilyn Dietrich. July 5, 2006. PSHS.
Day, Clarence Albert. *Farming in Maine 1860-1940*. Orono, ME: Univ. of Maine Press, 1963.
Frederic, Paul. *Canning Gold, Northern New England Sweet Corn Industry*. Lanham, Maryland: Univ. of America Press, 2002.
Goss, Josephine. Private communication with Donna Boyles regarding the Whitcher family farm. 2006.
Harlow, Kathleen. Private communication with Donna Boyles regarding farming, haying, and horses. May 26, 2007.
Hawkins, Arthur. "Laurence Snows Make Family Farming Fun and Profitable." *MST*, September 14, 1958. PSHS.
Israel, Fred, editor. *1897 Sears Roebuck Catalogue*. Philadelphia, Pennsylvania: Chelsea House, 1993.
Kivela, Carrie, and Richard Kivela. Private communication with Donna Boyles regarding raising Llamas. May 26, 2007.
Litchfield, Arlene Davis. Private communication with Donna Boyles regarding the Alexander/Litchfield genealogy. July 25, 2007.

Merrill, Lincoln J. Jr. and Holly K. Hurd. *Around North Yarmouth, Images of America*. Portsmouth, New Hampshire: Arcadia Publishing Co., 2006. PSHS.

Morrison, Holly, and Susan Mack. Private communication with Donna Boyles regarding Scottish cattle. August 16, 2007.

Palmer, Elizabeth M. "Diary – February 11, 1929." PSHS.

Randall, Linwood, Paul Randall, and Sandie Randall. "Farming." Interview with Sherilyn Dietrich. June 17, 2005. PSHS.

Randall, Sandie. Private communication with Donna Boyles regarding the Randall farm. August 20, 2007.

Rolfe, Joan. Private communication with Donna Boyles regarding sheep farming. Feb. 26, 2007 & August 6, 2007.

Sanborn, Virginia Libby. Private communication with Donna Boyles regarding the Elmer Libby farm. February 12, 2007.

Sanders, Lois Vosmus. Private communication with Donna Boyles regarding blueberry farming. 2005.

Snow, Clara Keith, Terry Snow, and Duane Snow. "Laurence Snow Farm Family." Interview with Donna Boyles and Sherilyn Dietrich. March 18, 2007. PSHS.

Snow, Duane. Private communication with Donna Boyles regarding Snowfields Farm. July 8, 2007.

Snow, Luther, and Evelyn Lowell Snow. Private communication with Donna Boyles regarding the Allen-Snow farm. February 18, 2007.

Tryon, Mellen. "Diary – May 8, 1897 to Oct. 14, 1900." Transcribed by Barbara Tryon Clement. 2006. PSHS.

Tryon, Samuel Augustus. "Diary – Oct. 17, 1913 to April 9, 1914 & March 25, 1922 to Jan. 21, 1923." Transcribed by Sherilyn Dietrich. 2007. PSHS.

Tuttle, Maude. "Farming." Interview with Donna Boyles and Marjorie Sweetser. November 4, 1974. PSHS.

Verrill, Shirley Thurber. Private communication with Donna Boyles regarding ice harvesting. July 2006.

Victory, Melissa. Private communication with Donna Boyles regarding horse farming. August 21, 2007.

Whitcher, Hazel Libby. "Cyrus Libby Farm." Interview with Sherilyn Dietrich. April 25, 1973 & April 20, 1976. PSHS.

CHAPTER 2 — Bradbury Mountain State Park

Anonymous. "Story of Bradbury Mountain State Park Told in Benjamin H. Britt's Book." *News Clipping*, c. 1945. PSHS.

Britt, Benjamin. *Ranger's History of Bradbury Mountain State Park*. Pownal, Maine: n.p., c. 1940. PSHS.

Britt, Bernard (Mickey). Private communication with Craig Dietrich regarding Bradbury Mt. State Park. 2006.

Corliss, Augustus W. *Old Times of North Yarmouth, Maine*. Somersworth, New Hampshire: New Hampshire Publishing Co. 1881.

Cummings, Bob. "44 Parcels Nominated for State Preservation." *MST*, April 9, 1989. PSHS.

Dietrich, Sherilyn. "New Trail Dedicated." *Shopping Notes*, August 31, 1993. PSHS.

Earl, William. "A Maine Original." *PPH Community Leader*, July 2005. PSHS.

Elden, Alfred. "Bradbury Mountain Latest of State Parks." *MST*, October 5, 1941. PSHS.

Fleming, Deirdre. "Bradbury Welcomes Mountain Bikers, So they Help the Park." *PPH*, July 23, 2006. PSHS.

Heinz, Lauren. "Spiegel Family Donates 150 Acres to Bradbury Mountain State Park." *BTR*, December 30, 1996. PSHS.

Hopkins, Alix. Private communication with Craig Dietrich regarding Park land. 2006.

Kalish, Bob. "150K Given for Common & Trail Purchases." *BTR*, January 30, 2001. PSHS.

Latham, Ettie J. *History of the Town of Pownal*. Lewiston, Maine: Lewiston Journal Co., 1908. PSHS.

Monigaine, Bernice. "Bradbury Mountain Park to Grow by 100 Acres." *BTR*, August 7, 1990. PSHS.

Nacelewicz, Tess. "For Pownal's Tryon Family." *MST*, November 7, 2004. PSHS.

Pownal. *Conservation Board Minutes*. Pownal, Maine: n.p., 1967.

Pownal. *Planning Board Minutes*. Pownal, Maine: n.p., 1964-1969.

Rand, John R. *Cartography*. Pownal, Maine: n.p., 2005. PSHS.

Richardson, John. "Board Identifies Parcels to Save." *PPH*, January 31, 2001. PSHS.

Rogers, Michael (Mick). Private Communications with Craig Dietrich regarding the Park. 2006-2007.

Snow, Luther. Private communication with Craig Dietrich regarding Park history. October 30, 2006.

State of Maine Department of Conservation, Bureau of parks and Lands. *Acquisition History Data Sheet, Parks I.D. NO. 016.* n.d.

Talmadge, Leslie. "Saving Land, Saving Heritage." *BTR*, January 10, 2005. PSHS.

Whidden, Elsie. "Beauty and History Found at Bradbury Mountain." *BTR*, July 13, 1978. PSHS.

CHAPTER 2 — Utility Corridor

Allen, Josephine Pervier. *The Remarkable Couple*. Pownal, Maine: Self-published, 1977. PSHS.

Cummings, Bob. "CMP Takes Line of Least Resistance." *MST*, June 21, 1987. PSHS.

Houppert, Karen. "CMP Plans Draw 50 in Pownal." *Portland Evening Express*, January 19, 1988. PSHS.

Richert, Evan. "Land Use in Maine – From Production to Consumption." In *Changing Maine 1960 – 2010*, edited by Richard Barringer. Gardiner, Maine: Tilbury House, 2004.

Saunders, James Jr. "Pownal Residents Join Pipeline Protest." *The Forecaster*, November 27, 1997. PSHS.

CHAPTER II — Forest Products

Anonymous. "All Things Woods – Forests For Maine's Future 2006." *BTR*, October 6, 2006. PSHS.
Anonymous. "Brown tail Moth Health Alert." *Freeport Town Bulletin*, Spring 2005. PSHS.
Anonymous. "Frank Knight '25 Reminisces." *North Yarmouth Academy Chronicle*, 1995. PSHS.
Austin, Eric. "Gazette Profile: Marion Reed." *The N. Y. Gazette*, May 2004. PSHS.
Barry, William David. "Red Oaks to the Rescue." *Down East Magazine*, November 2000. PSHS.
Canfield, Ken (District Forester). Private communications with Donna Boyles regarding data from the Maine Forest Service. March 21 & March 28, 2007.
Hogue, Richard. Private communication with Donna Boyles regarding shingle making. May 15, 2007.
Knight, Frank A. Jr. "Living in Pownal 1908-1933." Interviews with Donna Boyles and Sherilyn Dietrich. March 2, 2006 and August 24, 2007. PSHS.
Lord, Gregory (Maine Forest Service). Private communication with Donna Boyles regarding Pownal wood harvests, March 28, 2007.
Merrill, Lincoln. "Frank Addison Knight '25 Celebrates His 80th Reunion." *North Yarmouth Academy Chronicle*, 2005. PSHS.
Reed, Marion Knight. Private communication with Donna Boyles regarding the Philip Knight saw mill. February 6, 2006.

CHAPTER 2 — Minerals

Alport, Susan. *Sermons In Stone*. New York: W. W. Norton Co., 1990.
Blackstone, Albert, Jr. "Sand and Gravel Business in Pownal." Interview with Jennifer Kaplan. March 20, 2006. PSHS.
Blaisdell, Ann. "Pownal Man Remembers Building with Granite." *BTR*, October 2, 1977. PSHS.
Boyles, Donna, and James Boyles. "The Transition in the Use of Mineral Resources in Pownal." Script of presentation given May 1981. PSHS.
Boyles, Donna. Cattle Pound Nomination to National Register of Historic Places. July 24, 2004. PSHS.
Clukey, Sue. "North Yarmouth Rocks, An Overview of the Quarrying Industry." *North Yarmouth Historical Society Gazette*, July 2006.
Clukey, Sue. "POW, ZAP, BAM! The Creation of North Yarmouth in 90 Seconds." *North Yarmouth Historical Society Gazette*, October 2005.
Ganong, Rachel. "Differing Views on How to Repair Cribstone Bridge." *BTR*, October 25, 2005. PSHS.
Hoey, Dennis. "Harpswell Uneasy Over Bridge Rapair Talk." *PPH*, August 18, 2003. PSHS.
Knight, Carl. "Sand and Gravel Business in Pownal." Interview with Jennifer Kaplan. March 4, 2006. PSHS.
Knight, Philip. "Remembering the Pownal Granite Industry." Interview with Donna Boyles and Marjorie Mason. February 9, 1974. PSHS.
Latty, Mark. Private communication with Donna Boyles regarding the Basil Latty quarry. March 5, 2007.
Lepage, Carolyn, Michael Foley, and Woodrow Thompson. "Mining in Maine: Past, Present, and Future." *Dept. of Conservation, Maine Geological Survey*, October 6, 2005.
Matave, Mary Ellen. "Cribstone Bridge is Honored." *BTR*, 1984. PSHS.
Moore, Darcie. "Cribstone Bridge Showing Its Age." *BTR*, August 27, 2003. PSHS.
Morris, Gerald. *The Maine Bicentennial Atlas – An Historical Survey*. Maine Historical Society, 1976.
Powers, Helen. "Yarmouth Church Restoration Involved Heart, Hands of Many." *MST*, August 7, 1977. PSHS.
Reed, Marion Knight. Private communications with Donna Boyles regarding Knight family history. 1970 to 2006.
Rocksmith Inc. Landscape Design and Construction. <http://www.rocksmith.net> (2 January 2008).
Rogers, Louise. "Puts Up Half-Mile of Stone Wall." *News clipping*, 1938. PSHS.
Small, Josephine Hodsdon. "Where Some of the Stone Has Gone From Pownal Quarries." Script from presentation given in 1908. PSHS.
Smith, Jordan. Private communication with Donna Boyles regarding Rocksmith Inc. January 2, 2008.
Strong, Mary Mitchell. "Memories of Grandfather Mitchell Working in Pownal Quarry." Private remembrance written in 2003. PSHS.

CHAPTER 3 – Businesses Change with the Times

Blaisdell, Ann. "Pownal Campground Opens." *BTR*, July 21, 1976. PSHS.
Crichlow, Beth. "The House That Charlie Built." *Down East,* September 1990. PSHS.
DeWitt, William. Private communication with Donna Boyles regarding Realtor business. June 6, 2007.
Edwards, Rose. Private communication with Donna Boyles regarding Short Stop business. June 14, 2007.
Farrell, Charles. Private communication with Donna Boyles regarding Farrell and Company. July 12, 2007.
Forbes, Lilyan. Private communication with Donna Boyles regarding Post Master Robert Forbes. June 17, 2007.
Greer, Dolores Worden. "Fred Worden's General Store and Diner." Interview with Donna Boyles and Sherilyn Dietrich. October 24, 2006. PSHS.

Hooper, William, and Donna Hooper. Private communication with Donna Boyles regarding Blueberry Pond Campground. June 17, 2007.
Johnson, John. "Pownal Woodworker Says He's the 'McDonalds' of Craftsmen." *BTR*, October 5, 1995. PSHS.
Keith, Scott. Private communication with Donna Boyles regarding Keith's Garage. May 16, 2007.
LeMay, Charles. "Farrell and Company – Building On tradition." *Maine Builder/Architect*, Fall 1993. PSHS.
Little, Carl. "June LaCombe: Artist, Educator, Sculptor's Friend." *Maine Boats and Harbors*, Autumn, 2006. PSHS.
Mack & Rodel. *A Journeyman's Journal.* Catalogue, 1998. PSHS.
Obituary. "Harold Hibbard." *BTR*, August 25, 1984. PSHS.
Peaslee, Dennis, Jr. *Garden Spot Farm 2005 Spring Catalog.* PSHS.
Rodel, Kevin , and Jonathan Binzen. *Arts and Crafts Furniture from Classic to Contemporary.* Newton, Connecticut: Taunton Press, 2003. PSHS.
Rodel, Kevin. Private communication with Donna Boyles regarding his Furniture and Design Studio. May 24, 2007.
Rousseau, John. Private communication with Jen Kaplan regarding Rousseau Builders. July 11, 2007.
Searfoss, Thurston. Private communication with Donna Boyles regarding Blueberry Pond Observatory. July 8, 2007.
Smith, Aaron. "Wood Wizard Is Making Its (book) Mark." *BTR*, October 13, 1999. PSHS.
Snow, Terry, Duane Snow, and Clara Snow. "The Laurence Snow Family." Interview with Donna Boyles and Sherilyn Dietrich. March 18, 2007. PSHS.
Starling, Henrietta. "Life in Pownal, 1920s to 1970s." Interview with Donna Boyles. February 24, 1975. PSHS.
Sutherland, Amy. "On a Mission." *PPH*, November 15, 1999. PSHS.
Talmadge, Leslie. "Marriage of Sculpture and Nature." *BTR*, March 25-27, 2005. PSHS.
Vosmus, Craig. Private communication with Donna Boyles regarding Vosmus Builders. July 10, 2007.
West, Janice. Private communication with Donna Boyles regarding W. A. Machine Co. July 9, 2007.
Whidden, Elsie. "Pownal Pilot Makes Old Planes Soar Again." *BTR*, October 24, 1983. PSHS.
Whidden, Elsie. "Who's Minding the General Store?" *BTR*, August 23, 1978. PSHS.
Wing, Carl. "F. C. Handy – West Pownal Store." Interview with Donna Boyles and Sherilyn Dietrich. July 8, 2006. PSHS.
Yost, Greg. Private communication with Donna Boyles regarding Hanley and Yost Builders. August 24, 2007.

CHAPTER 4 – Enduring Form, Increasing Complexity

Boyles, Donna. "Remembering Pownal in the 1950s." Script of presentation given March 17, 2005. PSHS.
Boyles, Donna. "Report on Compensation of Town Officials." *Pownal Budget Committee Minutes*, January 26, 1998. PSHS.
Pownal Web Site. http://pownalmaine.org (December 2007).
Pownal. *Annual Town Reports*. Pownal, Maine: Self-published, 1900 to 2007. PSHS.

CHAPTER 5 – Provided Services are Essential

Anonymous. *A History of Maine Roads*. Maine: State Highway Commission, 1970.
Anonymous. "Pownal Road Crew Resigns Over Benefits." *PPH*, March 3, 2003. PSHS.
Bennett, Shawn. *Pownal Highway Department, Your Tax Dollars at Work*. Pownal, ME: Self-published, March 9, 2006. PSHS.
Bennett, Shawn. Private communication with Donna Boyles regarding the Pownal public works department. February 8, 2008.
Boyles, Donna. "Comparative Study, 1999-2002, of Highways and Bridges Account." *Pownal Budget Committee Minutes*, June 24, 2002. PSHS.
Boyles, Donna. "Report on Compensation of Road Commissioner and Crew." *Pownal Budget Committee Minutes*, January 9, 2001. PSHS.
Boyles, James, Donna Boyles, and Sherilyn Dietrich. *Pownal Volunteer Fire Department 1948-1998, Celebrating Fifty Years of Service*. Pownal, ME: Self-published, 1998. PSHS.
Dietrich, Sherilyn. "Pownal Fire Department – Historical Notes." *Shopping Notes*, January 6 to December 8, 1998. PSHS.
Pollock, Scott. Private communication with Donna Boyles regarding the Pownal volunteer fire and rescue department. February 8, 2008.
Pownal. *Annual Town Reports*. Pownal, Maine: Self-published, 1900 to 2007. PSHS.
Vosmus, Kenneth, and Lois Vosmus Sanders. "Roads, 1949-1964." Interview with Donna Boyles and Sherilyn Dietrich. February 1, 2008. PSHS.

CHAPTER 6 – Schools and Schooling

Allen, Josephine Pervier. "Teaching Memories." *Univ. of Southern Maine Writing Project*, 1967-68. PSHS.
Allen, Josephine Pervier. Private communication with Donna Boyles regarding moving Merrill school. 2005.
Blackstone, Arnold. "Secondary School Options with Freeport H. S. and S.A.D. #51." *Report to Pownal Voters*, April 5, 1979. PSHS.

Blake, Earl, Bruce Carroll, and Robert Slocum. "A Future for Our Schools." *Report to Town of Pownal*, October 1962. PSHS.
Boyles, Donna, and Sherilyn Dietrich. "200 Years of Education in Pownal." Script of presentations given March 20, June 19, and November 20, 2003. PSHS.
Dietrich, Sherilyn. "Going It Alone – Part Two of S.A.D. #62 History." *Pownal School Newsletter*, 1993. PSHS.
Graham, David. "A Legislator's First Term." *The Nation*, January 10, 1966. PSHS.
Maine Department of Education. *Maine School Statistics*. January 1962. PSHS.
Maine Department of Education. *School Administrative District Organization and Educational Aid*. September 16, 1961. PSHS.
Merritt, Sheila Menchen. *Memories of the One-Room Schools*. Pownal, Maine: Self-published, 2005. PSHS.
Norton, Gwendolyn, and Margaret Frazier. "Pownal Shunned by Neighbors." *MST*, September 20, 1964. PSHS.
Noyes, Ruth. "Pownal's Dream Is Reality At Last." *PPH*, March, 1968. PSHS.
Randall, Donna. "Pownal Party Line." *The Post*, November 1, 1973. PSHS.
S.A.D 62. *Annual School Budgets*. Pownal, Maine: Self-published, 1967 to 2007.
S.A.D. 62. *Class Yearbooks*. Pownal, Maine: Self-published, class of 1980-81 and class of 1983-84. PSHS.
Sanders, James, Evangeline Lee, and Edward Mitchell. *A Proposal for the Formation of a School Administrative District Pownal Freeport*. Pownal, Maine: Self-published, 1966. PSHS.
Scanlan, Susan. "Alternative School [Collins Brook]Plans Expansion Merger." *BTR*, April 3, 1975. PSHS.
Westerberg, Karen. "Pownal Officials Seek to Expand School." *Portland Evening Express*, November 27, 1981. PSHS.
Whidden, Elsie. "New Pownal Principal Pioneered in Special Ed Field." *BTR*, July 25, 1980. PSHS.
Whidden, Elsie. "Renovations, Gym Additions New Completion." *BTR*, December 9, 1983. PSHS.

CHAPTER 7 – One Town, Two Churches

Allen, Josephine Pervier. *History of the Pownal Congregational Church*. Self-published, May, 1967. PSHS.
Allen, Josephine Pervier. *The Miracle of the Eighties*. Self-published, 1990. PSHS.
Anonymous. "150th Anniversary First Parish Congregational Church, Pownal, Maine." *Church Bulletin*, August 12, 1961. PSHS.
Anonymous. "175th Anniversary Service, First Parish Congregational Church." *Church Bulletin*, September 7, 1986. PSHS.
Anonymous. "Big Celebration at Pownal Today." *Lewiston Evening Journal*, September 2, 1908. PSHS.
Anonymous. "Congregational Church at Pownal Center Was Erected in 1811." *Portland Evening Express and Advertiser*, September 20, 1924. PSHS.
Anonymous. "First Parish Congregational Church at Pownal Holds Service of Rededication."Newspaper Clipping, August 12, 1961. PSHS.
Anonymous. "Program of Rededication, First Parish Congregational Church." *Church Bulletin*, July 20, 1975. PSHS.
Blackstone, Doris Carter. Private communication with Donna Boyles regarding the First Parish Congregational Church. September 28, 2007.
Clark, Charles E., James S. Leamon, and Karen Bowden. *Maine in the Early Republic*. Hanover and London: Univ. Press of New England, 1988.
Clukey, Sue. "Social Control of Pownal's First Parish Congregational Church, 1811-1911." Self Published, May 4, 1993. PSHS.
Malone, Nancy Mitchell. Private communications with Donna Boyles regarding the North Pownal United Methodist Church. September 25, 2007 and October 15, 2007.
McDine, Lucretia. "Baked Beans Help Balance Many Church Budgets." *BTR*, November 10, 1980. PSHS.
Menchen, Patricia. *150 Year History of the First Parish Congregational Church in Pownal*. Self-published, 1961. PSHS.
North Pownal United Methodist Church. *Church Directory*. Olan Mills, 1995-2005.
North Pownal United Methodist Church. *Church Records*. Self-published, 1943-1976.
Reid, Pam. "Cemetery Art and Symbolism." n.d., < http://angelfire.com/ky2/cemetery/reid.html> (September 20, 2007).
Sanders, Lois Vosmus. Private communication with Jen Kaplan regarding the First Parish Congregational Church. 2007.
Sheesley, Rev. C. Richard. Private communication with Donna Boyles regarding the North Pownal United Methodist Church. October 2, 2007.
Small, Lemuel. "Scrapbook Collection of Newspaper Clippings c. 1900." PSHS.
Smith, Ethel G. *A Mini-History of the North Pownal United Methodist Church*. Self-published, June, 1994. PSHS.

CHAPTER 8 – Social Groups Contribute

4-H USA Web Site. <http://4husa.org> (October 2007).
Blackstone, Doris. Private communication with Donna Boyles regarding Granite Grange. November 1, 2007.
Blaisdell, Ann. "Several win at dress revue." *BTR*, May 6, 1977. PSHS.
Bradbury Mountain Owls. *By-Laws*. Pownal, Maine: Self-published, 1975. PSHS.
Bradbury Mountain Owls. *Secretary Reports*. Pownal, Maine: Self-published, 1985-2000.
Cousins, Christopher. "Maine Outdoor Heritage Fund assists in purchase of key parcels." *BTR*, July 9, 2003. PSHS.
Cummings, Bob. "Land Board approves park expansion." *PPH*, August 7, 1990. PSHS.

Galle, Janet. "Remembering those old-time Saturday nights." *BTR*, March 21, 1988. PSHS.

Golden, James A. *Cooperative Extension Work in Agriculture and Home Economics: Annual Report of the County Club Agent in Cumberland County.* Orono, Maine: College of Agriculture of the University of Maine, U.S. Department of Agriculture, and the Cumberland County Farm Bureau, 1950-1951.

Hogue, Kathy. Private communication with Donna Boyles regarding Bradbury Mountain Arts. October 31, 2007.

Hopkins, Alix, and Rosemary Whitney. "Dear Pownal Neighbor." *Pownal Newsletter*, November 7, 2005. PSHS.

Johnson, Joe. Private communication with Donna Boyles regarding Bradbury Mountain Owls. October 25, 2007.

Kalish, Bob. "Pownal Land Trust gets $840,000 to buy more than 500 Acres." *BTR*, June 30, 2001. PSHS.

Leonard, Herbert. *Cooperative Extension Work in Agriculture and Home Economics: Annual Report of the County Club Agent in Cumberland County.* Orono, Maine: College of Agriculture of the University of Maine, U.S. Department of Agriculture, and the Cumberland County Farm Bureau, 1940-1941.

Menchen, Edna S. "Farming and 4-H." Interview with Sherilyn Dietrich. May 5, 2005. PSHS.

Merrill, Lincoln, Jr. *Nathaniel Dyer*. North Yarmouth, Maine: Self-published, February 11, 1998. PSHS.

Monegain, Bernie. "Bradbury Mountain Park to grow by 100 acres." *BTR*, July 31, 1990. PSHS.

Nacelewicz, Tess. "For Pownal's Tryon family, selling land was the best way to preserve it." *MST*, November 7, 2004. PSHS.

National Grange Web Site. <http://nationalgrange.org> (October 2007).

North Pownal Community Club. *Secretary's Reports*. Pownal, Maine: Self-published, 1940-2007.

Pike, Lillian. 4-H Log. 1943-1944. Personal files of Sherilyn Dietrich.

Sanders, Lois V., and Thomas Vosmus. "Farming in Pownal." Interviews with Jennifer Kaplan and Sherilyn Dietrich. January 19, 2006 and January 26, 2006. PSHS.

Searfoss, Leslie. Private communication with Donna Boyles regarding Girl Scout Troop #222. November 4, 2007.

Smith, Arlene Golding. Private communication with Donna Boyles regarding Bradbury Mountain Owls. October 12, 2007.

Snow, Clara K., Terry Snow, and Duane Snow. "Farming in Pownal." Interview with Donna Boyles and Sherilyn Dietrich. March 18, 2007. PSHS.

Snow, Luther. Private communication with Donna Boyles regarding the Improved Order of Red Men. November 5, 2007.

The Improved Order of Redmen Web Site. <http://redmen.org> (October 2007).

Vosmus, Kenneth. Private communication with Donna Boyles regarding the Improved Order of Red Men. November 7, 2007.

Wessel, Thomas R. and Marilyn Wessel. *4-H, an American Idea, 1900-1908: a History of 4-H.* Chevy Chase, Maryland: National 4-H Council, 1982.

Wheeler, Dennis. Private communication with Donna Boyles regarding Ben Wheeler, Eagle Scout. August 13, 2006.

Whidden, Elsie. "Three Pownal Boy Scouts Honored for Warning Train." *TR*, December 1, 1983. PSHS.

White, Lin. *Girl Scout Troop #188*. Pownal, Maine: Self-published, 2006. PSHS.

Index

4-H Club 20, 28, 53, 78, 84, 94, 95, **290**, **291**, 293
    -4 Paws Dog Agility 291
    -Ambitious Club 290
    -Bradbury Mountain Girls **290**, 291
    -Collars and Leashes 142, 291
    -*Earth Connections News* 142
    -Girls and Boys of Pownal (GABOP) 291
    -Mohawks 291
    -Sheep 108
    -Spread Sunshine Club 291
    -Up and Doing Girls 291
    -Vikings 291
"200 Years of Giving" 97
Adams, Andrew 285
    -Patricia, Dr. 174, **179**
Adcock, Judy Sweetser 7, **250**, **301**, 302
Aircraft Warning Service and Observation 22
Albert, Michael **87**
    -Virginia "Ginger" **87**
Alexander, Betsey Merriman 104, 105
    -Catherine C., see Litchfield
    -Eli 105
    -Thomas 104
    -William 104
Alice Andrews Library **254**
Allen, E. Leonard "Lennie" 80, **103**, 135
    -Edward L. Sr. **31**, 73, 103, 131
    -Fred 180
    -Greenfield T. 83, 100
    -Henry **78**, 83, 100
    -Job Jr. 78, 100
    -Josephine Pervier 71, 75, 77, 79, 82, 103, 123, 131, 156, 170, 224, 244, 245, 252, 253, **258-260**, **271**, 272, 288
    -Lillian, see Tryon
    -Linda 274
    -Malvina Snow 100
    -Marion 103
    -Matthew **197**, **262**
    -Nate **292**
    -Raymond **250**
    -Ronald E. **38**, 103
    -Russell **204**, **292**
    -Sarah Strickland 100
    -Snow homestead **100**, 101, 130
American Champion, road machine **211**
American Public Works Association 218, 219
Ancient North Yarmouth v.
Anderson, George Jr. **294**
    -George Sr. **294**
    -Janice **250**, **282**
    -Rebecca **260**
Androscoggin Power and Light 13
Arnold, Don **203**, 233, **234**
Arris, Christine **250**
    -Gerald **250**
    -Granville **250**
    -Leland **134**

Asselyn, Peter 297
Atkins, Arthur **113**, **134**
    -Beverly **113**
    -Edith Britt **113**
    -Elsie **113**
Atlantic and St. Lawrence Railroad 10
Atomic bomb 32
Austin, Susan M. W. **199**
Ayres, Christopher iv., 57, 61, 65, 96, 97, 229, 266, **298**, 299
Babb, Marguerite 253
Babbidge, Earle 34, 165
    -Elbert K. 188
Babbin, Ralph **134**
Bacon, Josephine, see Snow
Badger, Karen L. Wentworth **264**
    -Philip **263**, **282**
Baert, John 165
Bailey Island Bridge 140, **145**, **148**, **150**, **151**, 155
Baker, Angeline "Angie", see Penley
Baldacci, John, Gov. 261
Barba Associates 60
    -Nancy 200
Barker, Elizabeth **21**
Barry, William David 137
Barschdorf, Gayle **263**, **282**
    -Jayme **282**
    -Jennifer **282**
    -Jill **295**
    -Walter 278, 281
Bath Iron Works 22
Beard, Barry **283**
    -Caron 281, **283**
Beasley, William 278
Beau, Ray **250**
Beckford, Wald **136**
Bedell, Abby, see Tryon
Bennett, Sean O. 198, **202**, 203
    -Shawn 135, 194, 195, 206, **218**, 219, 220
Bennis, James 273, 285
    -Sarah **262**
Bernstein, Lisa Marie Hodsdon 147
Bessey, Paul 163
Best, Alvirdo H. **7**, 77
    -Arlene 169
    -Donna Tuttle **290**
    -Edith **291**
    -Jason 218
    -Jeremy **51**
    -Marion **250**
    -Vernon **7**
    -Virgil **7**, 34, 169, 249
Bicentennial celebration 63, 196
Bicentennial Executive Committee, 2008 **207**
Bieske, John **250**
    -Paul **250**
Bigelow, Arnie **250**
    -Mary Lee **250**
    -Rusty **250**

Blackstone, Albert H. Jr. **32**, **43**, 78, 79, 135, **158**, 159, **160**, 163, **250**, **291**; Brown Road gravel pit **157-159**; Elmwood Road gravel pit 159; Excavating 49, **160**
    -Albert H. Sr. 15, 19, **32**, 34, 73, 78, **80**, 159, 160, **163**; Homestead 33, **80**; General Store 14, **15**, 19, 34, 37, 80, **163**
    -Alice, see Smith
    -Arnold F. **43**, **173**, **200**, 257, **292**; Excavation 173
    -Asa 242
    -Bonnie Edwards 37
    -Chester **23**, 24
    -Christina Bradley 14, **19**, **21**, **32**, 163
    -homestead 33
    -Claudia **250**
    -Doris Carter 53, 207, **289**, 291
    -Harriet **55**
    -Heather 142
    -Jennifer, see Kaplan
    -Katie, see Genovese
    -Linda Edwards 37
    -Mabel, see Hodsdon
    -Moses 152
    -Sharon Copp 163
    -Theona Penley **21**, **23**, **24**, **55**, **243**, **289**, **296**
Blagdon, Nettie **239**
Blair, Irene **75**
    -Winnie **237**
Blaisdell, Ann **254**
    -Dennis 80
Blake, Althea **199**, **225**, **227**, **296**
    -David **250**
    -Earle A. 48, **51**, 188, 224, **225**, **227**, 228, 233, 247, **288**
    -Jared **199**, 227
    -Jessica, see Brown
    -Karen, see Sylvain
    -Lester **51**, 225, **226**, 227, 228, 229, 232
Blueberry Pond Campground 174
Blueberry Pond Observatory 174
Blueberry Ridge Farm **107**
Board of Appeals, 2008 **205**
Bolduc, Roger 165
Bolinder, Matthew **298**
Borden, Tracy 263
Bornheimer, Velma 293
Boston Tea Party 292
Boston Globe 3, 4
Boucher, Diane 263
Bourassa, John **203**, **297**
    -Natalie **295**
Bowden, Janet **91**
    -Joyce **91**
    -Mertie Libby **90**, 91
Bowdoinham Methodist Circuit 276
Bowdren, John **204**, **297**
Bowen, Mary Pat 284, **301**
    -Tom 196, **201**, 284, **301**

Bowie, Abel 12
   -Addie 12
   -Lucille 253
   -Rebecca 12
Bowman, Peter, Dr. 256
Boy Scouts 53, 55, 293, 294
Boyden, Paul **250**
Boyles, Donna Fulton iv., **vi.**, 53, 196, 201, 207, **254**, 284, **301**, **302**, **303**
   -Dorothy MacAllister 270, **271**, 285
   -James G. **vi.**, **57**, 193, 195, 196, **198**, **199**, 200, **201**, **206**, **207**, 254, 284, **301**, 302, **303**
   -Kristen **255**
Bradbury, Arlene L. Litchfield 105, **254**
   -George L. Jr. **38**
   -George L. Sr. **47**; homestead 15, **47**
   -Jane, see Carr
   -Minnie, 47; homestead 15, **47**
   -Samuel 110
Bradbury Mountain Arts 107, 221, **297**
Bradbury Mountain Garage **48**, **49**
Bradbury Mountain Owls 53, **296**, 300
Bradbury Mountain State Park 8, 15, 20, 29, 33, 41, 65, **110**- **117**, 118, 149, 157, 216, **264**, 298, 299
   -feldspar mine 156
   -Raptor Migration Project 116
Bradbury Pineland Protection Corridor **65**, 73, 97, 299
Bradstreet, Alan **177**, **202**, **205**, 212, 293, **297**
   -Susan **177**, 293
Branch Brook Farm 79
Briggs, James H. 193, **196**, **198**, **203**
Britt, Benjamin H. 39, 110, 111, 112, **113**
   -Bernard "Micky" **39**, 112, **113**
   -Donald L. **39**, 112, **113**
   -Edith, see Atkins
   -Emma **113**
   -Harry **39**, **113**
   -John Jr. **76**
   -Laura 244
   -Nellie Wilson **39**, **113**
   -Robert Wilson **39**, **113**
   -Roy **39**, **113**
   -Winona **113**
Britton, Melissa Wentworth 233, 234, **260**
Brooks, Edward Jr. **270**
   -Marjorie Cushman **247**, 280
Brower, Geraldine 226
   -Vernon C. **51**, 171, **226**, **230**
Browercraft Wood Products 171
Brown, Anna **263**
   -Dan **229**, 233, 234, 254
   -Jessica Blake 227, **229**, 233, 234
   -Mae "Mary" Augusta, see Knight
   -Morgan **263**
   -Myra, see Tryon
   -Pamela 29
   -William A. 184, **185**
   -William Jr. 242
Brumm, Virginia **21**
Brunswick United Methodist Church 278
Bucklin, Louise **250**
Budget Committee, 2008 **202**
Bull, Thomas **199**
Burnham, Stanwood 139
   -and Morrill Canning Company 72

Burns, Clifton 293
Burtt, Cecil **165**
Bush, George 262
Butler, Gail 249, 253, **255**, **258**, **259**
Buttrick, Norman 118, 119, 121
Byram, Frank 241
Callnan, Kim 263
Camp Stalag 17-B 29
Canadian National Railway 11
Canfield, Ken 138
Capital Projects Planning Committee, 2008 **206**
Capon, Eugene **250**
Card, Joyce Elaine **250**
Carkin, Joye 236, **259**, **263**
Carr, Jane Bradbury 47
Carroll, Bruce 247
Carson, Rachel 52
Carter, Christine **263**
   -Doris, see Blackstone
   -Gregory **89**, 139
   -John Jr. **250**
   -Lawrence E. **34**, **191**, 252, 272, **296**
   -Linda **250**
   -Mark **292**
   -Nicole Bowman **89**
   -Ralph **34**, **250**, **288**
   -Rebecca **262**
   -Wendy 204
   -Winnie Vosmus 106, **271**, 273, **275**, **296**
Cartmill, Robert 255
Casco Bay Estuary Project 299
Casco Shipbuilding Company **133**, 137
Cates, Everett A. 20, **92**, **213**; farm 92
   -Minnie 78, **92**, **93**; farm 92
   -Virginia, see Davis
Cattle Pound 111, 118, **149**, 152
Cavanaugh, Richard **250**
Centennial celebration 3, 4, 13, 34, 70, 71, 128
Central Maine Power 13, **59**, 60, 122, 123, 124
Chandler Brook 83, 90, 128, 129
Chapin, Rev. Perez 4
   -homestead 80
Charolais, cattle 28, 79, 98, **99**
Cheney, Deborah Whitcher 79, 98, **99**
Chesney, Alan "Bo" 196, **208**, **298**
Chibroski, Gordon 279
Church of God in Christ 267
Civil War, veterans **16**, 17
Clark, Cornelius, Dr. **270**
   -Jennifer **282**
Clark's Cove Fertilizers 76
Clayton Copp and Sons Building Movers 272
Cleaves, Edmund 190
   -Ryan 262
Cleveland Tractor Company 210
Cluchey, Deb 297
Clukey, Sue Hartford 56, 118, **120**, **259**
Coffin, Constance Sanders 25
   -David G. 269
   -David W. 139
Colby, Carolyn **250**
   -Charlotte Edwards 37
   -Janet **250**
Cold War 32, 33, 35

   -veterans **38**, **39**
Collins, Hayden **263**
Collins Brook School 256
Comprehensive Plan Committee, 2004-2006 **204**
Condon, Bev **250**
   -William **250**
Conservation Commission, 2008 **206**
"Conservin' Energy" 221
Cook, Blanche Small **293**
   -Carol Edwards 37
   -Jane, see Tryon
   -Mercy, see Tryon
   -Norman 37
Cordell, Ann 254
Corliss, Lucinda, see Tryon
Cotton, Austin 71, 72, **237**; homestead 111
   -Thomas 149
Coulombe, Roger 218, 219
   -Roland **255**
Crain, William E. 193, **197**, 198
Crosman, Kari 263
Crossroads Pizzeria 169
Crowell, Suzanne 293, **298**
Cuban Missile Crisis 38
Cumberland County Farm Bureau 79
Cumberland County Power and Light 13
Cunningham, Paul 58
Curry, Alan 139
Cushman, Eva 242
   -Howard 79, 80
   -Marjorie, see Brooks
   -Thomas 135, 138, **139**, **206**
Cutler, Eva, Rev. **278**, 280
Cyr, Carol **264**, 293, **302**, 303
   -Sarah 303
D-Day 24, 30
Daily Eastern Argus 3, 4, 277
Danforth, D. F. 165
Daniels, George D. **161**
   -James **44**, **45**, 165
   -Nancy 45
Darkis, Henry 112, **113**
Davis, Arlene, see Edwards
   -Arlene, see Litchfield
   -Marion, see Irish
   -Virginia Cates 78, **92**, 213
DeCoster, Priscilla, see Greene
DeMerchant, Pamela 295
   -Rhonda, see O'Shea
Dennison, Herbert 21
Deslauriers, Emile 128
Desrosiers, Yvonne **259**
"Devil's Seat" **110**, 111
DeWeaver, Mildred **243**
DeWitt, Jeffrey W. 173
   -Thelma 303
   -William S. 50, **57**, 135, **173**, **200**, **201**, **202**, 303; Real Estate Agency 173; room, Mallett Hall 63, 200
Diary of Betsey Alexander, The 104
Dietrich, Craig **vi.**, **viii.**, **201**, 284, **293**, 301
   -Diana **255**
   -Sherilyn iv., **vii.**, 53, 135, 142, 195, 196, 200, 202, **204**, **207**, **208**, 211, 229, **254**, 259, 261, 284, 285, **291**, **301**, **302**, 303
District No. 2, one-room school 3

Doble, Nancy **202**
Dobson, Heidi **255**, **291**
   -John 216
Donelon, Jane **259**
Donnell, Alvah 278
Donoghue, Jim **263**
Doughty, Cory **263**
Dow, Alice 180
   -Charles 8, 167, 180
   -General Store **167**, 180
Down East Magazine 32, 137, 176
Dresser, Albion K. P. 16, 76
Drew, Kim 281, 283
   -Rebecca, see Edwards
Drinkwater, Alice **21**
Drouin, Kenneth **260**
Dube, Eric 204
Duffy, Josephine E. Litchfield 104
   -Martin 104
Duford, Armon **263**
Dugas, Scott 159
Duncan, Ella 290
Dunn, Charles 75
DuPont, Erika **263**
Durham Methodist Circuit 276
Dutch Elm disease 35, 134, 141
Dyer, Clara L. 118
   -Dennis 173, 294
   -Nathaniel 288
Dyment, Natasha **263**
Earth Day 52, 300
Eklund, Elizabeth 270
   -John, Rev. 270
Edward Little High School 237, 238
Edwards, Annie, see Spaulding
   -Arlene Davis **37**
   -Barry **37**
   -Bertha, see Libby
   -Betty **37**
   -Bonnie, see Blackstone
   -Carol, see Cook
   -Charlotte, see Colby
   -Clayton **37**
   -David 281
   -Debbie **37**
   -George Jr. **37**
   -George Sr. **37**
   -Leroy Jr. **37**
   -Leroy Sr. **37**
   -Letha 72
   -Linda, see Blackstone
   -Llewelon N. 150
   -Louise **37**
   -Marcia **37**
   -Mary, see Hanlon
   -Rebecca Drew **37**
   -Rose 169, **177**
   -Walter **37**
   -Winona **37**, **250**
Eighteenth Amendment 14
Eisenhower, Gen. Dwight D. 27
   -Pres. Dwight D. 40
Elfin, Roxanne 61
Elizabeth Stift, diocese 28
Elmwood Cemetery 208, **285**, 286, 303
Emmertz, Dorothy 188
Enos, Connie, see Tryon
Estes, Calvin E. 4, 5, 13
   -Pinky **243**

Everett, Sherry
Farley, Melva 169
Farm Bureau News 93
Farmer's Wife 78
Farrell, Charles **176**
   -Mary Ellen 176, 274
Farrington, Christopher Z. **64**
   -Robert 205
Farwell, Owen 165, 166, 293
Fassett, Francis 3
Fauver, Fred 298
Federal Bureau of Investigation 27
Federal Emergency Relief Administration 15
Federal Energy Regulatory Commission 60
Feeney, Joseph R. **263**, 264
Fickett, Clarence "Cad" 212
   -Hathaway J. 8, **170**, 210
   -Nathan **243**
   -Thelma **243**
   -Verna, see Libby
Fiddlehead Center for the Arts 153, 297
Fire Department 34, 35, 36, 53, 95, 107, 115, 190, 214, 222-228, **229**, 230-233, **234**
   -Ladies Auxiliary 53, 214, 226, 227, 287
   -Muster Team **51**, 225
First Parish Congregational Church 3, **4**, 6, 13, **15**, 16, **33**, 35, 49, 53, **55**, **57**, **62**, 67, 80, 106, 225, 249, **250**, **265**, 266, **267**, **268**, **269**, 270, 271, **272**, **273**, 274, 275, 284, 294, 296, 300
   -Ladies Aid Society 16, 20, 35, 96, 268, 269, 273, 274, 275; Bean Suppers 270, 274, 275
   -parsonage **16**
First Responders Medical Team 107, 115, 227, 228, 232, **234**
Flanders, Phoebe 242
Flint, Pearl 291
Fogg, Richard Willis 18
   -Villa, see Snow
Fogstone Games 174
Forbes, Lilyan Petkus 200, 201, 207, **259**, **302**
   -Robert **180**
   -Tamia, see Welch
Forest Paper Company 140
Foster, Ben 150
   -Jesse, see Tuttle
Fowler, Mary Lee 195, 199, **202**, 205
Freeman, Dudley 144
   -quarry 155
Freeport Community Services 289, 296
Freeport High School 238, 247, 253, 255, 260
Freeport Lions Club 285
Freeport Press, The 216
Freeport Shoe Company 106
French, George 20, 32, 33, 41
Frost, Luella, see Libby
Fuller, Belle 75
Gagnon, Dorothy, see Mitchell
Gale, John 257
Gallion Road Grader **215**
Ganong, Rachel 151
Garden Spot Farm 153, **172**

Gendron, Susan 261
Genovese, Katie Blackstone **24**
Geological Survey Report, 2005 156
Gerrish, Jackie York 273, **275**
   -Wayne 273
Giddinge, Erica 207, 274
   -Timothy **197**, 261
Gilliam, Marcia **259**
Ginn, June, see LaCombe
   -William 85, 135, 260, 298, 299
Girl Scouts 53, 55, 295, 296
Gobeil, Joanne **260**
Goddard Cemetery, see Quaker Cemetery
Godfrey, Thomas 194, 195, **202**, **206**, **298**
Golden, J. A. **291**
Golden Acres Country Store **47**
Golden Cross Hall 8, 13, 36, 96, **212**, 277, 287
Goldfine, Michaela **117**
Golding, Arlene, see Smith
   -Evelyn **250**
   -Janice, see Litchfield
   -Wilma **250**
Good Road Machinery Company 185, 209, 211
Goodwin, Mary 53, **301**
   -Sasha **260**
Gordon, William R., Rev. 270
Goss, Josephine Whitcher 28, 98
   -Peter W. **43**
   -Roland B. **38**
Gowen, Charles **51**
   -Steve **51**
Graham, David L. 247, **251**
   -James **260**
Grand Trunk Railroad 8, 10, 11, 12, 13, 36, 161
   -Depot **10**, **13**, 36, 82, 90, 156, **161**
   -overpass, West Pownal **12**, **63**
Granholm, Ed **259**
   -Ruth 254
Granite Grange 20, 25, 28, 34, 35, 53, 55, 82, 94, 95, 96, 147, 155, 190, 225, **287-289**, 300
Grant, Andrea **263**
   -Martha 237
Great Depression 14, 20, 72, 103, 111, 237, 238, 269
Great Northern Paper Company 140
Greene, Fred, quarry 146
   -Pearl, see Whitcher
   -Priscilla DeCoster 15
Greenlaw, Byron **250**
   -Michael **250**
   -Robert **250**
   -Sam **250**
Greenleaf, Alan **201**
   -Nancy **297**
Greer, Delores Worden 168
Greely High School 255, 260
Greely Institute 238
Gross, Jeremiah **234**
Guile, Craig **234**
H. L. Forhan Canning Company 75
Hale, Frances H. **255**, 256, 257, **259**, 262
   -Jim 124
Hall, Donald 244
   -Ginny **296**
"Hamburg Parties" 79

Hamilton, Paul   254, **288**
Handy, Francis C.   14, 36, **167**, 168, 180
Haney, Frank   77
Hanley, Dennis   175
Hanley and Yost Builders   175
Hanlon, John   37
    -Mary Edwards   37
Hannah's Restaurant   169
Hannan, Ruth   135, **206**, 207
Hanscom, Leon   **134**
    -Leslie   165
    -Samantha   165
Hanson, Alice   293
    -Louis   293
    -Robert   135
Harbor School   256
Harlow, Beverly   **259**
    -Chelsea   **109**
    -Dorothy   47
    -Gary   254
    -Kathleen   80, **109**, 226
    -Katie   **109**
    -Kenneth   47
    -Golden Acres Country Store and homestead   47
    -Larry   **259**
    -Peter   250
    -Ryan   262
    -Tim   109
    -Tom   **282**
Harmon, Clarence   73, **75**; Company   106; Corn Shop   73, **75**
Harness shop, North Pownal   **8**
Harris, June   **21**
    -Rufus   128
Harrison, Frank   262
    -Gabriel   272
Hart, April   262
    -James W.   **64**
Hartzell, Lynda   **263**
"Harvest Time"   **78**
Harvey, Carlene   **202**
    -John   **203**, **206**
Haskell, Harriet, see Snow
    -Louis   213, 214, 236
    -Reuben, sawmill   **127**, **128**
    -Richard   165
Hathaway, Theodore   165
Hawk Ridge Farm   **85**, 178
Hawkins, Arthur   94
    -Elizabeth   **250**, **291**
    -Genevieve   252
Hayes, Sarah   **260**
Hearse   **55**, **284**, 300, **301**, 303
Hendee, Scott   233, 234
"Herbie", elm tree   **141**
Hewett, Allison   142
    -Nancy   **259**
Hayward, Dorothy   **289**
    -William   **289**
Heywood, Andrew   243
    -Charles P.   16, 83, **187**
Hibbard, Harold E. Jr.   **171**, **250**
    -James   **250**
    -Jody   273
    -Patty   **250**
Higgison, Chake   **263**
Highway Revenue Act   214
Hildreth, Gov. Horace   26

Hilton, Bruce E.   **43**
    -Judy   295
Hinkley, Don   171, 291, 294
History of the Town of Pownal, 1908   iv., 4, 53, 70, 110, 119, 144
Hodgkins, Maude, see Small
Hodgdon, Arleen, see Tryon
    -Patricia   **293**
    -Ronald   202
Hodsdon, Andrew   68, 69, **146**
    -homestead   **68**, **69**, 147
    -Charles Hinkley   16, 140, **146**, 147; quarry   144
    -Edith   **146**
    -Eliza Mitchell   16, 140, **146**
    -Elizabeth   **146**, 147
    -Ella   **146**
    -Florence   **146**, 147
    -George   68, 69, 140, **146**, 147, 159, 213, 242
    -Harold   69, 242, 243
    -Joe   **69**
    -Josephine, see Small
    -Josephine H.   4, 16, **17**, **146**, 147
    -Kate Coolidge, see Knight
    -Lisa Marie, see Bernstein
    -Mabel Blackstone   69, 147, **271**
    -Mary Ann Bailey   69, **147**, 196, **197**, **207**, **208**, **260**
    -Rachel (younger)   **146**, 147
    -Rachel York   68, 69, **146**
    -Robert (elder)   **69**, 147, 243
    -Robert   **147**
    -Robin, see Morin
    -Ronald "Hutch"   69, **147**, **204**, 233, **234**, **250**
    -Samuel   **147**
    -Sarah Johnson   68, 69, 147, **287**
    -homestead   68, **69**
    -Susie   **21**
Hodsdon School   237, 238, **239**, 241, 247, 249, 258, 301, 303
Hogue, Emmy   296
    -Erin   107, 297
    -Jon   107, **116**
    -Kathleen A.   56, **107**, 193, 195, 196, **197**, **201**, **207**, 297
    -Richard "Dick"   **107**, **138**, 195, **205**, 232, 233, **234**
Holway, Marjorie   **21**
Hood Dairy   98
Hooper, Donna   **174**
    -Shannon   **174**, **263**
    -William "Bill"   **174**
Hoover, J. Edgar   27
Hopkins, Alix   **298**, **299**, **302**
Horace Mann Club   244
Housing Committee, 2008   **203**
Howe, Dale   **250**
    -Marla   **250**
Hoyt, Anna   261
Huard, Glennis   **250**
Humphrey, Robert   202
Hunter, George   83
Hurricane Carol   37, 40
Hurricane Edna   37, 40, 214
Hustus, Barbara   29
    -Walter   29, 83, 190; homestead   **33**
Hutchinson, Ashley   262

    -Karen   **282**, 283
    -Ralph   281, **282**
Hyde, Stephen   135
Ice Storm, 1998   **58**, **59**
If You Don't, Who Will   300
Ingerson, Heidi   **260**
    -Mark   **64**
Ingles, Arthur D.   216
Iraq Wars   62
    -veterans   **64**
Irish, Don   **250**
    -Marion Davis   169
    -Vincent   **250**
    -Woodrow   **250**
Ives, A. Christopher, Rev.   278
J. B.'s Restaurant   169
Jewett, Darrell   **255**
    -Kelly   **260**
Johnson, Esther "Ettie", see Latham
    -Joe   **296**, 302
    -Oscar   **134**
    -Sarah, see Hodsdon
    -Pres. Lyndon B.   26
Jones, Cyrus   118
Jones' Inn   **118**, 119-121, 259
Jordan, Anna   **255**
    -Delia   237
    -Norman   136
    -Oscar   136
    -Tina   **260**
    -William   **204**
Kalleberg, Bryan   115, 233, 234
Kaplan, Able   **158**, 160
    -Jennifer Blackstone   **vii**, 194, **260**, 261, **264**, 302, **303**
    -Scott   202
Keith, Aaron   **260**
    -Clara, see Snow
    -Donald L., garage   169, 211
    -Floyd   244
    -Greta   **290**
    -Marilyn   **250**
    -Randa   **250**
    -Robert   **250**
    -Scott   169
    -Thelma   **250**
Kennedy, Matthew   **205**
    -Timothy   **260**
Kenny, Kate   270, 271
Kevin Rodel Furniture and Design Studio   178
Key Bank Building, Yarmouth   152
Kimball, Alice, see Morrill
    -G. Harold   **237**
    -Gertrude, see York
    -Helen   **237**
    -Howard   130
    -Lisa   **263**
King, Gov. Angus   57
Kivela, Carrie N.   **86**, 195, **197**, 285, 302, 303
    -Owen   **86**
    -Richard   **86**
Knapp, Minnie   **21**
Knight, Carl (elder)   145, 154
    -Carl I.   48, 54, 159, 213, 216, **217**
    -Charles "Bill" H. Jr.   46, 155, 159, 169; Big Sky gravel pit   159; homestead   **46**, 77

-Charles H. Sr. 6, 34, **69**, 128, 136, 140, 145, **154**, 155, 159; gravel pit 159; sawmill **127**, 140; quarry **143**, **144**, 148
-Clinton 154
-Donald 154
-Edward 154
-Elsie 154
-Eva Crockett **9**, 69, **75**, 136
-Frank A. Jr. 73, **140**, **141**
-Frank A. Sr. 6, 128, 140; granite quarry 140; sawmill **127**, 140
-Helen 154, 243
-Irene 136
-Jeremiah 155
-Kate Coolidge Hodsdon 140, **146**
-Kenneth **237**
-Levi Jr., homestead 90
-Mae "Mary" Augusta Brown 154, 242
-Marion, see Reed
-Mary Jane Soule 135, 154
-Philip E. **69**, **134**, **136**, 137, 140, **144**, 145, 148, 154; Lumber Company 134, 136, 137; sawmill 94, 97
-Wilma F. 46, 114, **298**; homestead **46**
-Zona Soule 155
Knights of Pythias 155
Knowlton, Donald 190
Knox, Mildred **250**
Koenig, Heinz 77
Korean War 33
-veterans **38**, **39**
Kucharik, Martha **295**
LD 1 62
LaCombe, June 85, **178**, 236, 260
Ladies Aid Society 16, 20, 35, 96, 268, 269, 273, 274, 275
-Bean Suppers 270, 274, 275
LaFreniere, Andrew 190
-Cheryl **250**
Lake, Eleazer 284
Lake Cemetery **284**, 286
Land For Maine's Future 46, 113, 114, **298**, 299
Larrabee, C. J. 281
-Everett 111
Merton **19**, 165, **166**, 212; General Store 91, **166**, 212
Lary, Gladys **239**
-Grace **239**
Latham, Eliab 77; homestead 70
-Esther "Ettie" Johnson iv., 4, 5, 53, 70, 110, 119, 144; homestead **70**
Latty, Basil 152
-Denise 152
-Elvin "Jack" 152
-Francis 152
-Mark 152
Lausier, Conrad 233, **234**
-Marie 233, **234**
Lawrence, James 16
-John T. 130
-homestead **70**
LeClair, Scott **262**
Lee, Evangeline Tuttle 188, 247, 252
Leighton, Dot St. Pierre **250**
-Kenneth **255**

-Laurice **239**
Leonard, Nate **263**
Levesque, Paul **250**
Lewis, Alice **250**
-Carole **250**
Lewis-Wadhams School 256
Lewiston Evening Journal 3, 4, 268
Libbey Cemetery 286
Libby, Ada **72**
-Alberta **72**
-Alice **72**
-Almeada **72**
-Alzada **72**
-Amy **72**
-Annie **243**
-Bertha Edwards 90, **91**, **166**; homestead 90
-Blanche 242
-Cyrus, homestead **47**, **66**
-Elmer F. **72**, **90**, **91**, **131**; homestead **90**
-Elvina, see Vosmus
-Gary 272
-Hazel, see Whitcher
-Jasmen **295**
-Jesse **295**
-Johanna **260**
-Josiah **72**; homestead **72**
-Kenneth "Chub" **90**, **91**, **131**, **134**, 136, **137**, **166**, **213**, **228**, **243**
-Leroy **72**
-Luella, see Merryman
-Luella Frost **72**; homestead **72**
-Mertie, see Bowden
-Mildred 242
-Steve **209**
-Verna Fickett **247**, 248
-Virginia, see Sanborn
-Walter 8, 167; General Store **167**, 180
Libby Cemetery 286
Liberty Bonds 22
Liberty Ships 22, 24
Libra Foundation 113, 230
Lichtenstein Engineering Company 151
Life Magazine 37
Lipman Poultry 77
Litchfield, Arlene Davis **275**
-Arlene L., see Bradbury
-Catherine C. Alexander **104**, 105 ; homestead 105
-Donald Robert **31**
-Edith **104**
-Iona Osgood **105**
-Janice Golding 44, 45, **105**, 273
-John 272
-Josephine E., see Duffy
-Josephine O., see Marr
-Nancy, see Daniels
-Samuel 104
-Stephen 44, **45**, 80, **105**, 205, 270, 273; farm 80, 105
-Thomas A. **104**
-Veazie B. **104**, 105; homestead 105
-Victor Scott Jr. 80, 83, **105**
-Victor Scott Sr. 83, **104**, **105**, **213**, 245
-Vina Vosmus **27**, **105**, 106, **275**
Locklin, Bob **134**
Loeschner, Lester 201

Lord, Gregory 138
Loring, Cornelia Plummer, homestead **71**
-Emma, see Pervier
-Fred Perley 102
-George Frederick "Fred" 77, 102; homestead 77
-Henry Warren 71, **186;** homestead **71**, 76
-Leigh 102, **222**, 223, 224
-Olive Marston 102; homestead 77
-Richard **75**
-Roy 102
Lovitch, Derek 117, 135, 205, 206
-Jeanette 117
Lowell, Evelyn, see Snow
Lyon, Lydia "Nellie", see Snow
Mack, Susan C. **57**, 58, 60, 88, 124, **125**, 178, **196**, **201**
Mack and Rodel Cabinetmakers 178
Maine Beef Producers Association 80
Maine Big Tree Register 142
Maine Board of Agriculture 76
Maine Botanical Gardens 176, 178
Maine Council for the Humanities 300
Maine Custom Firewood 139
Maine Custom Woodlands 138
Maine Department of Agriculture 111
Maine Department of Conservation 142
Maine Department of Economic Development **40**, 41
Maine Department of Education 262
Maine Department of Transportation 145, 151
Maine Farm Bureau Federation 76
Maine Forest Service 127, 132, 135, 138
Maine Historical Preservation Commission iv., 61
-Honor Award 61
Maine Historical Society iv., 29
Maine Humanities Council 301
Maine Humanities Millennium Grant 118
Maine Insane Hospital 186
Maine Maritime Museum 176
Maine Outdoor Heritage Fund 299
Maine Parks and Recreation 298
Maine Register, 1920 76, 77
-*1936* 77
Maine School for Feeble-Minded 8, 78, 168
Maine Sheep Breeders Association 108
Maine State Archives iv., 20, 32, 33, 41
Maine State Grange 288
Maine State Park Commission 111
Maine Yankee Nuclear Plant 122
"Maine's Year of the Donkey" 251
Mains, Niki 135
Mallet, Edmund B. Jr. 3, 146
Mallett, Brad 233, **234**
Mallett Hall 3, 6, 13, 16, 34, 40, 48, **49**, 53, **54**, **55**, **57**, **60**, **61**, 63, **79**, 124, **181**, 182, **183**, **184**, 185, 187, **188**, 191, **193**, 195, **200**, **201**, 205, 216, 218, 219, 223, **244**, 249, 254, **265**, 266, **287**, **288**, 289, 292, 296, 297, 300, 301, 303
Mallett Hall Building/Grounds Committee, 2008 **207**
Malloy, Kathleen **197**
Malone, Allen "Pat" Jr. **42**, **280**, **282**
-David 194, 195, 228, **229**, **232**, 233,

234
    -Nancy Mitchell 207, **280**, 281, **282**, 283, 293
Maltby, Barbara **255**
Maplewood Cemetery 286
Marion's Market 48, **169**
Maritimes and Northeast Pipeline L.L.C. 60, 124, 125
Marr, Josephine O. Litchfield **104**
Marriner, Prof. Ernest C. 16
Marshall, Ethel H. 16
Marston, Etta, see Starling
    -Maude, see Tuttle
    -Mrs. Fred 13
    -Olive, see Loring
Martin, Abel **287**
    -Ada **287**
    -Ida **287**
    -Lewis **288**
Martino, Marsha **202**
Mason, Carl 284, 300, 301
    -Ernest **21**
    -George **42**, 300
    -Kathryne 300
    -Marjorie Alward **53**, 135, 254, **300**, **301**, 303
Masonic Hall, Yarmouth 147
McCann, Marie Mason 253, **258**, **259**
McCarthy, Ruth 285
McCullough, Andrew **263**
McGonagle, Kelcie **295**
McGorman, Katheryne 237
McIntosh, Ed **259**
McKay, Danica **262**
McLaughlin, Clara **21**
McMahon, Linda 207, 233, **234**, **302**
    -Robert 135, 195, **206**, 228, 233, **234**, 293
    -Tim **255**
McManus, Carolyn **255**
McSpadden, Bruce, Rev. 278
Mechuwana, Camp 278, 281
Menchen, Edna Snow 18, 22, 94, **197**, **199**, 248, 273, **275**, **289**, 290, **296**; farm 82
    -Edward Dresser 48, **52**, **134**, **192**, **243**, 248, 270, 272, **288**; farm 82
    -John **134**
    -Michael **42**, **190**, 238, 239, 272, **288**
    -Patricia 249, **250**, 270
    -Sheila, see Merritt
Merrill, Caleb **263**
    -Greg **260**
    -Herbert 128, 129, 130
    -Horace P. **16**, 159
    -Lorraine S. 195, **197**, 208
    -Sam **298**
    -Sydney 248
    -Thelma **250**
    -Travis 219
Merrill Cemetery 286
Merrill School 237, 238, **239**, 244, **245**, **250**
Merritt, Sheila Menchen **248**, **249**, **250**, **289**
Merryman, Luella Libby 72
Metcalf, Cora, see Tryon
    -Dr. 269
    -Sarah **295**
Methodist Church 8, **35**, 53, 95, 96, 236, **267**, 269, 272, **276**, 277, 278, **279**, **281**, 282, 283, 293

    -B Naturals 55
    -Bean Suppers **283**
    -Brooks Room 236, 276, **279**, 280
    -Get-A-Ways 281
    -Ladies Benevolent Society 277
    -Snow Room **279**, 280, 283
    -Women's Service Club 277, 281
Methodist Meeting House, Durham 276
"Miracle of the Eighties" 272
Mitchell, Benjamin **102**; homestead **102**
    -Dorothy Gagnon **277**, 280
    -Edward L. 190, **192**, 252, **277**, 278, 280, **288**
    -Eliza, see Hodsdon
    -Ellen 242
    -George P. 148
    -Goldie Noyes 148
    -Joe (younger) **255**
    -Joseph R. 48, **194**
    -Leigh **21**
    -Letty **239**
    -Lisa **295**
    -Mary, see Strong
    -Nancy, see Malone
    - J. Noyes 83, **190**, **288**; homestead 34
Mittel, Amy **260**
    -Jane 53, **207**, 255, **302**, **303**
Mitton, Phyllis 253
Monmouth Canning Company 73
Monroe, George 152
Mooney, D. J. **263**
Moore, Elaine **263**
    -Kathryne 53, **301**
Morgan, Doris 281
Morgan's Diner 169
Morin, Edward 165
    -Joyce 165, 226; General Store **165**, 226
    -Robin Hodsdon 147, **260**
    -Roland 165, 226; General Store **165**, 226
    -Malia Hodsdon 147
Morrill, Alice **21**, **75**, 296
    -Frances 290
    -Harriett **250**
Morris, Helen **287**
Morrison, Conrad **51**
    -Holly **88**
Morton, Willis **243**
Mosher, Diana **263**
Mothers Club 20, 40
Moulton, Beth **263**
Mueller, Joan **204**
Munsen, Elizabeth **295**
    -Shiloh **295**
Muskie, Sen. Edmund **52**, 251, 300
Nadeau, Melissa **260**
Napier, Faye, see Vosmus
    -Norman 163
Napier's General Store **49**, 163
National Park Service 149
National Register of Historic Places 129, 149, 150, 152, 301, 303
Neill, Stephen **263**
New Deal 15, 111
New England Shipbuilding Corporation 22
New England Telephone and Telegraph Company 6, **7**
New Gloucester Cornet Band 4
Newcomb, Harold **239**
    -Janet 244
    -John **239**
    -Lula **239**
Newell, Hosea 162
    -Ronald **160**
Newman, Mike 234
Nichols, Elizabeth 195, **204**, **297**
    -Henry 278, **279**
    -Justin **205**
Nickerson, Kathy 281
Nielsen, Donelle **263**
    -Erik 232, 233, **234**
Niese, Cecily **117**
    -Kirk **117**, **205**
Nineteenth Amendment 14
"No Child Left Behind" 262
"No New Corridors" 60, **125**
North Pownal, Community Club 20, 35, 166, 293
    -fire house 36, 214, 225, 226, 227, **228**, **229**, **230**, **233**
    -general stores 6, 8, **19**, **34**, 35, **63**, 91, **164**-**166**, 212, 214, 226
    -Golden Cross Hall **8**, 13, 36, 96, **212**, 277, 287
    -Methodist Church 8, **35**, 53, 95, 96, 236, **267**, 269, 272, **276**, 277, 278, **279**, 280, **281**, 282, 283, 293; B Naturals 55; Bean Suppers **283**; Brooks Room 236, 276, **279**, 280; Ladies Benevolent Society 277; Snow Room **279**, 280, 283; Women's Service Club 277
    -sawmill 8, 36, 128, **129**
    -School 8, 36, **235**, 236, 237, 238, **243**, **247**, **249**, 258, **276**, 277, 278, 280, 293
North Yarmouth Academy 237, 238, 243
North Yarmouth Historical Society 76
Northern Forecaster, The 125
Norton, Robert H. 190
Noyes, Alroy 77, 184, **186**
    -Fred, homestead 16, **33**
    -Goldie, see Mitchell
    -John 6
Oakes, R. G. 244
Oakhurst Farm 83
O'Brien, David 85, 86
    -Patsy 85, 86
O'Shea, Rhonda 261, **264**
Old Home Days 56, 254
Old Homestead Farm **92**
Old Tavern Farm 82, 83, 101
Old Times of North Yarmouth, Maine 110
Orchard Crest Farm 77
Order of Patrons of Husbandry 288
Order of Pocahontas 20, 287
Ordinance Review Committee, 2008 **203**
Ordway, Kim **263**
Osgood, Iona, see Litchfield
"Our Farmhouse Kitchen" **93**
Overlock, Alden 253
Page, Cheryl 263
Paine School 237, 238, **239**, 241
Palmer, Elizabeth 83
Parent Teacher Club 40, 238, 253, 254, 260, 262
Paris Green 76

323

Parker, A. H. 130
-Annie **243**
-Daisy **243**
-Emery W. 76
-Raymond **243**
Pascarella, Nicholas **262**
Passmore, Diana 196, **207**, **263**
Patton, Gen. George 24, 30
Payson, Barbara **291**
-Linda **291**
-Philip, estate stone wall **155**
Peaco, Leslie 281, **282**
-Mavis 207, **282**, 283
Pearl Harbor 21, 24
Peaslee, Dennis C. Jr. **153**, **172**
-Dennis C. Sr. 172
-Neil **260**
-Patricia Vosmus 172
Penley, Angeline "Angie" Baker **277**
-B. W. 165
-Bertrand **243**
-Channing **129**, **243**
-Theona, see Blackstone
Perkins, DeForest 16
-Lillian **253**
Perrine, Kim **255**
Pervier, Abbie, see Vosmus
-Bessie **250**
`-Emma Loring **75**, 82, 102, 103, 140, **224**, **237**, **241**, 242, 258
-Felton 103, 170, 252
-Joseph H. 14, **17**, 74, 82, 83, 102, **103**, 123, 131, 156, 170, 188, **189**, 190, **209**, 212, **222**, 223, **224**, 228, 245, **288**, 290; fire truck **223**, 224
-Josephine, see Allen
-Lewis 102, 103, 123, **170**, 224; fire truck **223**, 224; Garage 123, **170**, **209**, 211, 224, **245**
-Lois Strickland **203**, 204, **205**, **297**
-Nellie Webster 22, **102**, 103, 132, **287**
-Philip 102, **103**, **287**
-Sally **250**
-William J. 82, **102**, 103, 132, **187**, **287**
Peterson, Hilda 243
Pettengill, Jason **260**
Phelps, Aaron **229**
-Christine **200**
Phillips, Celia **21**
Pierce, Ann **263**
Pike, Virginia Vosmus 290
Pineland Farms 114, 168, 230, 299
-State Hospital 78, 113, 179
Pinkham, Alison **259**
-Dennis 253, 255
-Martin **255**
Planning Board, 2008 **204**
Plummer, Cornelia, see Loring
-Moses 71
-Paul 233, 234
Pocock, Mike 203
Poland Spring Resort 132
Polley, Wallace 130
Pollock, Nicole **263**
-Scott 204, **206**, **229**, 232, **233**, **234**
Poor, John 10
Porter, Benjamin **218**
Portland Evening Express 216, **255**, 269
Portland Press Herald **23**, 78, 81, 93, 98

Portland Sunday Telegram **40**, 94
Post Office 8, **14**, 36, 94, 162, 164, **180**
Postal Studio Post Card Series **15**
Pownal 1900, baseball team 3
Pownal, A Rural Maine History, 1977 iv., vi., **53**, 65, 96, 118, 300, 301
Pownal Arts Evening 221, 297
Pownal Center, Cemetery **284**, 286, 292, 303
-fire house 34, 35, 190, 225, 226, 227, 228, **230**, **231**, 232, 288
-First Parish Congregational Church 3, **4**, 6, 13, **15**, 16, **33**, 35, 49, 53, **55**, **57**, **62**, 67, 80, 106, 225, 249, **250**, **265**, 266, **267**, **268**, **269**, 270, 271, **272**, **273**, 274, 275, 284, 294, 296, 300; Ladies Aid Society 16, 20, 35, 96, 268, 269, 273, 274, 275; Bean Suppers 270, 274, 275; parsonage 16
-garages 48, **49**
-hearse house **284**
-Mallett Hall **3**, 6, 13, 16, 34, 40, 48, **49**, 53, **54**, **55**, **57**, **60**, **61**, 63, **79**, 124, **181**, 182, **183**, **184**, 185, 187, **188**, 191, **193**, 195, **200**, **201**, 205, 216, 218, 219, 223, **244**, 249, 254, **265**, 266, **287**, **288**, 289, 292, 296, 297, 300, 301, 303
-sawmill 6, 35, **127**, **128**, 140
-Schools 6, 34, 35, 49, **184**, **188**, 190, **237**, 238, **239**, 241, 244, **248**, **250**
-stores **5**, 6, 14, **15**, **16**, 19, 34, 37, **48**, **49**, 62, 80, 160, **162**, **163**, 169, 177
Pownal Centers, baseball team 3
"Pownal Day" 57
Pownal Education Foundation 118, 260
Pownal Elementary School, see SAD 62
Pownal Food Coop 293
Pownal Land Trust 46, 65, 97, 113, 114, 298, 299
"Pownal Pride Day" 135, 205, 292
Pownal Scenic and Historical Society iv., 53, 54, 55, 60, 118, 129, 149, 155, 195, 225, 227, 228, 239, 259, 284, 293, 295, 300-303
Pratt, Louisa Merrill 4, 13
Price, Halley **295**
Prohibition 14
Pumpkinfest 57, 193, 229, 301
-brochure **56**
Quaker Cemetery 286
Quint, Carleton 244
Quirnon, Lionel **117**
R. E. A. Associated 261
Rackliffe, Arleen **97**
-Caleb **97**
-Elisha **97**
-Isaac **97**
-Greg **97**
-Jeanne Tryon **97**
-Joseph **97**
-Mary **97**
-Melinda **97**
-Millard **97**
-Seth **97**
Rand, John R. "Jack" viii., **299**
Randall, Benjamin 166; General Store 166, 276
-Brian **64**
-Donald **218**

-Elmer 166
-Harold **18**
-Jacob, homestead **129**, 301; sawmill 128, **129**
-Linwood 79, 83, **87**, **134**, **257**, **259**, 296
-Mabelle **21**
-Paul 79, **81**, **87**
-Raymond **250**
-Rebecca **260**
-Sandie 79, 87
-Sandra Ryder **250**, 291
-Stephen **81**
-Wayne **255**
Randall McAllister Company 18
Ranger's History of Bradbury Mountain 110
Raymond, Breanne **263**
-Jeff 135, **206**, 207, **297**
-Joseph A. iv., **vii.**, **38**, **205**, 207, **208**, **302**
Redmen, Improved Order of 20, 53, 55, 96, 287, **292**
Reed, Josiah 152
-Marion Knight 9, 75, 136, 137, 154
-quarry 152
-Tim 294
Regional School Units (RSUs) 261
Remarkable Couple, The 71, 75, 77, 103, 123
Reynolds, Harold Jr. 255
Richards, Andrea **255**
-Rodney 218
-Todd 218, **260**, **294**
-Troy **294**
Richardson, Howard F., Rev. 273, **274**
-Lynda McAllister 273, **274**
Richert, Evan 126
Roberts, Ernest, Rev. 278
-Janet 284, **293**, **301**
Rocksmith, Inc. 153
Rodel, Kevin P. **178**
Rogers, Cynthia **115**, 232
-Danica **115**
-Jamie **115**
-Krista **115**
-Louise 155
-Michael "Mick" **115**, 116, 195, 232
Rolfe, Christopher **84**, 108
-Gerald H. 84, **108**, **194**, **199**, 217; farm **108**
-Joan 84, **108**, **198**, **291**; farm **108**
-Jonathan **84**, 108
-Katherine **84**, 108
-Thomas **84**, 108
Roosevelt, Pres. Franklin D. 20, 21, 27
Ross, Helen **21**
Rossbach, Elise 85, 86
-Jill 85, 95
-Walter 83, **85**, 86, 95
Rousseau, John 176
Rousseau Builders 62, 163, 176
Royal, Fred **75**
Runaround Pond 83
Ruprecht, Cliff 261
Russell, Melissa **263**
-Sadie **263**
Ryan, Joseph 190
Ryder, Calvin Jr. **119**
-Calvin Sr. **250**
-Cathy **262**

-Heather **119**
-Lawrence 244
-Millie **250**
-Rita 142
-Sandra, see Randall
-Wilma 291
SAD 62   52, 53, 63, 118, 193, 194, **198**, **235**, 236, 247, **251**, **252**, 253, **254**, 255, 256, 257, 258, 259, 260, **261**, 262, 263, **264**, 297, 300
SLB Enterprises, Inc.   139
Sacred Heart Church, Yarmouth   **145**, 148, 155
Saffeir, Jesse   **142**
-Jo D.   299
-Lindley   **142**
Salisbury, James   165
Sanborn, Virginia Libby   90
Sanders, Constance, see Coffin
-Dale   25
-James A.   **25**, 247, **270**, **271**, **288**, **296**
-Lois Vosmus   22, **25**, 106, 213, 244, 270, **271**, 273, **275**, **289**, **296**
-Roger   25, **250**
Sargent, Paul D.   209
Saunders, James   125, **195**, 301
Sawmill, Hodsdon Road   6, 35
-Lawrence Road   8, 36
Sawyer, Christopher C.   77
-Elsie   242
-Janet   **250**
-Lemuel F.   166; General Store   **166**
-Raymond   243
-Seth   293
-William J.   6, 8, 164; General Store **164**
Schmidt, Walter   **201**
-William   **203**
School bus, first   **245**
"School Days"   248
School Improvement League   238, 244, 246
Schumann, Paul D.   194, **201**, 261, **264**
Scioto, The   **104**
Scott, Bonnie   85
Scribner, Elizabeth   **237**
Seabury, Ruth   21
Searfoss, Amelia   **295**
-Donald   174
-Leslie   295
-Patricia, see Adams, Dr.
-Thurston   **174**
Sears Roebuck Catalogue, 1897   **74**
Seely, Jean   180
-Joshua   **262**
Selective Service Act   25
Seminick, Linda   54
Sesquicentennial celebration   33, 34, 35, **40**, 41
Shannon, Sara   **263**
Shaw, Enoch   128
-J. B.   **278**
Sheesley, C. Richard, Rev.   280, **281**, **282**
-Ruth   280, **281**, **282**
Sheldon, Mark   **298**
Shettleworth, Earle Jr.   60
Shopping Notes, The   93, 211, 224, 229, 292, 300
Short Stop Convenience Store   62, 177
Sibley, Mary, see Sweetser

Silent Spring   52
Silvernail, David   262
Sinclair Act   189, 246, 261
Six Towns Times   **137**
Skillin, Rufus   210
Slattery, Ann   236, **263**
Slocum, Anna   165
-Robert   **191**, **247**, 252
Small, Bernard   **293**
-Blanche, see Cook
-Charles   136
-Clara   **75**
-Frederick C.   17
-Harold   278, **279**
-Joseph N., Capt.   164, 277; homestead   **6**, **63**
-Josephine   147
-Lemuel   6, 277
-Maude Hodgkins   243, **293**
-Robert   242
-Vina   **243**
-Walter A.   **9**
Smith, Alice Blackstone   253, **258**, **259**
-Arlene Golding   **275**, **296**
-Donald H.   **31**
-Ethel Stebbins   269, **278**, 280
-Gary Haven   178
-George   **250**
-Jordan A.   153
-Larry   **250**
-Lawrence   190
-Mari-Melinda   227, 228, **232**
-Michael   285
-Nancy   **250**
-Robert A.   77, 111, 156
-Ronald W., Rev.   269, **270**, 278
-Theresa   260
Snow, Carleton   94
-Charles S.   **64**
-Clara Keith   85, 94, **95**, 290
-Claude L.   18, 94, 134, 136, 188, **189**
-Conrad S.   **100**, **240**, 241
-David   139
-Duane   94, 180, **197**, **208**
-Edna, see Menchen
-Evelyn Lowell   78, 83, **101**, 139, 243, **297**; homestead **101**
-Gordon   73, **101**, **250**
-Harold "Bill"   72, 78, 83, **100**, **101**, **130**, 241, **292**; farm **82**, **100**
-Harriet Haskell   100
-Jean, see Worden
-Jonathan A.   18, **94**, 210; farm **94**
-Josephine Bacon   72, **81**, **100**, 101, **241**; farm **82**, **100**
-Karen   **255**
-Keith E.   94, **95**
-Laurence W.   **50**, 83, 85, 94, **95**, 134, 136, **180**, 190, **192**, 252, 278, **279**, **288**
-Luther   73, 78, **81**, 83, 100, **101**, 112, **138**, 139, **207**, **208**, **250**, **292**, **297**, **302**; homestead **101**
-Lydia "Nellie" Lyon   **94**; farm **94**
-Malvina, see Allen
-Maurice   **239**
-Terry N.   **43**, 94, **250**, 291
-Verne   100, **130**
-Villa Fogg   18, 19, 94, **180**, 210
Snowfields Dairy Farm   85, 86, 94, 95

Soil Conservation Service   111
Solid Waste Reduction and Recycling Committee, 2008   52, **205**
Sons of Liberty   292
Soule, Benjamin   66
-Mary Jane, see Knight
-Zona, see Knight
Spaulding, Annie Edwards   **37**
-Brianna   **295**
-Conrad Jr.   **51**
-Della   **250**
-Norma   **250**
-Ricky   **260**
-Roland   **250**
-Savannah   **263**
-Shannon   295
-Stanley   **250**
Spencer, Cathy   **302**
-Raymond   190
Spiegel, Anne   114
-Jack   114
Spinney, Rich   **250**
St. Pierre, Dot, see Leighton
-Jack B.   **42**, 233, **234**, **250**
-Portia   **250**
Stackhouse, Arthur P.   23, **38**, **55**, **121**, 284, **301**, **302**, 303
-Joan   **302**
Starling, Henrietta Marston   71, 78, 162
Stasinowsky, Frederick W.   48, **191**, 217
Staton, Frank   230
Steeves, Addison   **243**
-Earle, Rev.   166
-Elizabeth Vosmus   166, **243**
-Fredrick   **243**
-Priscilla   **243**
-Raymond   **243**
Stewart, David   273
Stilkey, Christopher   284, 285
Stone, George L Jr.   **30**, 244
-Milton S.   **30**
-Samuel J.   267
Stover, John   240
-Oliver   184, 185, **240**, 244
Stover Airport   240
Strait, Melanie   260
Strickland, Lois, see Pervier
-Sarah, see Allen
"Strike It Rich"   37
Strong, Mary Mitchell   148, **257**
-Neal   255
Strout, Betty   270, **272**
-M. Lester, Rev.   270, **272**
Stull, Jenna   **262**
Sturtevant, Kathryne   159
Surowiec substation   122, **124**
Sweetser, Elsie   **27**, **110**, **237**
-Harry   140
-Helen   110
-Henry T.   6, 7, 157, **211**
-Judy, see Adcock
-Katherine   **7**, 211
-Marjorie   **7**, **110**, 211, **237**, 285
-Mary Sibley   6, **7**, **110**, 211, 222, 290
-William   **110**
Sweetser Road Bridge Project   **219**
Sylvain, Karen   227, 263
Sylvester, Delmar   128, 129
-Everett   244

325

Tavani, Rebecca **142**
Taylor, Otis **250**
　-S. W., Rev. 278
　-Virginia **250**
Tenney, Harold **250**
Teriault, Shawn **285**
Tewksbury Cemetery, see Tuttle Cemetery
Thoits Brook 113
Thurber, Arthur **26**
　-Carl V. **26**, 169
　-Darrel 54, 217
　-George L. **26**
　-Gladys C. **26**, **75**
　-Kenneth E. **26**
　-Marvin **26**
　-Shirley, see Verrill
Thurlow, Hollis 109
Tibbetts, Arthur **250**
　-James **250**
　-Kathleen **250**
Times Record, The 58, 151, 171, 256, 261, 291, 294
Tin pedlar 9
Tompson, Frederick 3
Toothaker Bridge, see Tuttle Bridge
Town Seal 54
Townsend, Ernest **250**
Townshend, Sharon **203**, 297
Tripp, George, Rev. 278
True, Harlan B. 152, 184, 185
Truman, Pres. Harry S. 27, 29
Tryon, Abby Bedell, homestead **73**
　-Alvin L. **187**, 293
　-Andrew **97**, 281
　-Andrew Jackson 96
　-Anna **97**, **295**
　-Arleen Hodgdon **97**, 248, **249**, 253, **290**
　-Carl 73, 77, 78, 79, **97**, 210, **243**
　-Connie Enos **97**, 114, 281
　-Cora Metcalf 73
　-Dorothy **290**
　-Earl Augustus 73, **239**, **243**
　-Earl Haven 73, 114
　-George 73, **239**, **243**
　-Haven **97**
　-Jane Cook 96
　-Jeanne, see Rackliffe
　-Kenneth **81**, **97**
　-land **65**, 114, 299
　-Lillian Allen **96**, 97
　-Llacey **97**
　-Lucinda Corliss 96
　-Melissa **97**
　-Mellen 76, **96**, 97, 159, 184, **185**, **287**
　-Mercy Cook 96
　-monument **97**
　-Myra Brown 244, **246**
　-Philip R. (elder) 91, **96**, **97**, **130**, 188, **189**, 190, **287**, **288**
　-Philip **97**
　-Phyllis Arleen **97**, **290**
　-Samuel Augustus 73, 77
　-Samuel L., homestead **73**
　-Sarah **97**
　-Simeon **96**, 97; homestead **96**
　-Tammylee **97**
Tryon Mountain 110, 114, 156
　-feldspar mine **156**

Tucci, June **221**, 284, **295**
　-Tony **134**
Tufts, Dorothy 214
　-Roy C. 83, 165, 188, 189, **213**, **214**, 233
Turcotte, Minnie, see Cates
　-Paul **250**
　-Ronald **250**
　-Virginia **21**
Tuttle, Brandon **263**
　-Daniel A., Rev. 4, 16, 35, **67**, 242, 268, **269**
　-Donna, see Best
　-Ernest 70, 130, 185, **210**, 223; homestead **70**
　-Evangeline, see Lee
　-Jesse Foster 276; homestead **74**
　-Lauren H. Jr. **196**, 200
　-Lauren H. Sr. 15, **187**, 188, 238, **241**, 242, **270**; homestead **74**
　-Maude Marston 67, 72, **210**, **287**; homestead **70**
Tuttle Bridge 152
Tuttle Cemetery **285**, 286
Twenty-sixth Amendment, 1884 14
Twomey, Jeanne **255**
Tyler, John 149
Tyler School 237, 238, 246
University of Maine Agricultural College 222
Upper Farm Alpacas and Wool Products 89
Upper Farm Wood Products 139
Upton, Fred (father) **75**, **134**
　-Fred (son) **250**
U.S. Naval Air Station, Brunswick 22
U.S. Office of Price Administration 22
V-E Day 27
V-J Day 27
Van Voorst Van Beest, Andrea 183, **297**, **302**, 303
　-Jan Pieter **206**, **207**, **297**
Venture Farm 87
Verrill, Shirley Thurber 26, **27**, 77, 83, 130
Veterans Memorial **196**, **208**, 289
Veterans Memorial Sub-Committee, 2008 **208**
Victory, Brynne **89**
　-Drew **89**
　-Freyja **89**
　-Katyja **89**
　-Melissa **89**
Victory Garden 22
Vietnam War 33, 246
　-veterans **42-45**, 50
Volstead Act 14
Vosmus, Abbie Pervier 79, 102, **106**, 270, **271**; farm 106
　-Al 175
　-Cheryl **207**, **208**, 273, 274
　-Craig A. **42**, **175**, **195**, **197**, 200, **201**, 207, **208**, 217, 270, 272, 273, **292**
　-Donald 175, 272, **292**
　-Elizabeth, see Steeves
　-Elvina Libby 240
　-Evelyn, see Wheeler
　-Faye Napier 163
　-Josephine **296**
　-Kenneth L. **31**, 106, 175, 190, 212,
213, 214, 272, **292**
　-Lois, see Sanders
　-Patricia, see Peaslee
　-Ralph A. **31**, **34**, 106, 190, **225**
　-S. Addison, Dr. 8, **179**, 186, **240**
　-Thomas Henry Sr. 14, 15, 23, **31**, **106**, 175, 272, **289**, 290, **296**
　-Thomas J. **22**, 73, 79, **106**, 188, **190**, 214, **215**, **243**, **288**; farm 106
　-Vina, see Litchfield
　-Vina, Mrs. 16
　-Virginia, see Pike
　-Winnie, see Carter
Vosmus Builders 175
W. A. Machine Company **172**
Walnut Hill Station, North Yarmouth 82, 102
Walsh, Theodore J. 196, **207**, **253**, 255, **259**
War Manpower Commission 25
Ward, Andrew 233, 234
　-Michael **260**
Warren, George **285**
　-Helen 297
　-True 5, 6, **162**; General Store **162**, 244
Warren Cemetery **285**, 286
Watson, Dick **256**
　-Sharon 256
Webster, David **199**, 260
　-Nellie, see Pervier
Weed, Louise **290**
Weirs, Nicole **262**
　-Perry **294**
Welch, Jamie **205**
　-Kelly 204, **291**
　-Matt 135, **206**
　-Tamia Forbes **263**
Wendt, Marie **207**
Wentworth, Barbara **263**, 278, **280**, 281, **282**
　-Douglas **250**
　-Eric Sr. 139, 218
　-Jim 151
　-Karen L., see Badger
　-Kelly M. 196, **197**, 202, **207**
　-Kermit **138**, 139, **199**, **250**
　-Lucille 281, **282**, 283
　-Melissa, see Britton
　-Patty **250**
　-Percy 78, **270**, **288**
　-Philip M. 193, **198**, **218**, 278, 281
　-Robert **250**
Westcustogo Lodge 155
Westcustogo Tribe 37, see Redmen
Wesley, S. S. 267
West, Janice **172**, 284, 285, **302**, 303
　-Robert **172**
　-Thomas **260**
West Pownal, general store 14, 36, **167**, 180
　-post office 8, **14**, 36, 94, **167**, 180
　-railroad depot **10**, **13**, 36, 82, 90, 156, **161**; overpass **12**, **63**
　-School 36, 237, **238**, 247, 249, 280
Wheeler, Ben **294**
　-Dennis **294**
　-Evelyn Vosmus **275**
　-Joann **294**
　-Wedgewood 272, 273, **292**

326

Whidden, Elsie 294
Whitaker, Allison 195, 197
Whitcher, Algernon D. 28, 79, **98**, **99**, 130, 131, 133
 -Barbara 98
 -Daniel Albert **28**, **98**, 244, 290
 -Deborah, see Cheney
 -Hazel Libby 28, 66, 72, 98, **99**, 222
 -Josephine, see Goss
 -Margaret 79, 98, **290**
 -Milton 98, 130, 131, **133**
 -Pearl Greene **133**
 -William (elder) 79
 -William "Bill" **28**, 79, 98, **99**; Branch Brook Farm 79, 98; Branch Brook Mystic 98, **99**
White, Christopher J. **42**, **229**
 -Clyde 273
 -Johnna **302**
 -Lin **204**, **295**, **302**
 -Ralph D. 271
 -Rebecca **295**
White Pine Blister Rust 132, 138
Whitehouse, Charles **40**, 41
Whitmore, Sandy **259**
Whitney, Rosemary **116**, 203, **208**, **298**, **299**
Willis, Jeremy 293
Willow Farm 94

Willowbrook Museum, Newfield 79
Wilson, Evans, Rev. 278
 -Nellie, see Britt
 -Stanley 243
Wing, Carl 167
Winn, O. H. 165
Winslow, Florence 21
"Women On the Farm" **93**
Women's Motor Defense Corps **21**, 22
Women's Service Club 35
Wood, Ferne 290
 -Michael 262
Wood Wizard, The 177, 212
Woodard, Linda **263**
Woodside, Mattie **263**
Worden, Delores, see Greer
 -Fred 36, **168**; General Store **168**
 -Freddie 242
 -Jean Snow 36, **168**
 -Laura 168
Works Progress Administration 15, 111, 112, 213
World War I 13, 16, 74, 79, 237, 238, 277
World War II 20, 21, 77, 79, 98, 105, 112, 136, 214, 238, 246, 277, 290
 -veterans **24 – 31**, **39**
Wright, Pierce, and Whitmore Architects 252

Wyman, Jean **250**
 -Joyce **250**
 -Michael **255**
 -Walter 122
Yarmouth Clam Festival 292
Yarmouth High School 237
Yarmouth Water Works, building 152
Yates, Lawrence **134**
York, Capt. Joseph 146
 -Dewitt Builders 173
 -Frederick 50, 173
 -George **134**
 -Gertrude Kimball **75**, 291
 -Gladys, Rev. 277
 -Jackie, see Gerrish
 -Linwood **134**
 -Rachel, see Hodsdon
York Cemetery **284**, 286, **302**
Yost, Greg 175
Ziervogel, Carlotta **295**

The clock, featured prominently in this book, has its own interesting history. Made by the Sessions Clock Company in Connecticut, c. 1903, this clock spent its early years as the timepiece in the North Pownal one-room school house. Both Theona Penley Blackstone (see page 243) and Blanche Small Cook (see page 293) remember it hanging in the school house when they were students there. By 1957 it had become a permanent fixture in the North Pownal Community Club building, where it resided until 1996. At that time, the Scenic and Historical Society urged the Community Club to allow the clock to be professionally restored. The Balzer Family Clock Company, which did the work, donated much of the cost, and the town funded the balance. The clock is now on permanent loan from the Community Club and hangs in the main town office in Mallett Hall, where it continues to faithfully record Pownal time, as it has for over a century.